A COMPLETE GUIDE

THE SARASOTA, SANIBEL ISLAND & NAPLES BOOK

A COMPLETE GUIDE

4TH EDITION

The Sarasota, Sanibel Island & Naples Book

Chelle Koster Walton

The Countryman Press
Woodstock, Vermont

We welcome your comments and suggestions. Please contact Great Destinations Guide Editor, The Countryman Press, P.O. Box 748, Woodstock, VT 05091, or e-mail countrymanpress@wwnorton.com.

Fourth Edition

ISBN 978-1-58157-038-0
ISSN 1931-9630

Front cover photo © Karen T. Bartlett
Interior photos by the author unless otherwise specified
Book design by Bodenweber Design
Composition by PerfecType, Nashville, TN
Maps by Mapping Specialists Ltd., Madison, WI © The Countryman Press

Published by The Countryman Press, P.O. Box 748, Woodstock, Vermont 05091

Distributed by W. W. Norton & Company, Inc., 500 Fifth Avenue, New York, NY 10110

Manufactured in the United States of America

10 9 8 7 6 5 4 3 2 1

GREAT DESTINATIONS TRAVEL GUIDEBOOK SERIES

Recommended by *National Geographic Traveler* and *Travel + Leisure* magazines.

[A] CRISP AND CRITICAL APPROACH, FOR TRAVELERS WHO WANT TO LIVE LIKE LOCALS.
— *USA Today*

Great Destinations™ guidebooks are known for their comprehensive, critical coverage of regions of extraordinary cultural interest and natural beauty. The authors in this series are professional travel writers who have lived for many years in the regions they describe. Each title in this series is continuously updated with each printing to insure accurate and timely information. All the books contain more than one hundred photographs and maps.

Current titles available:
THE ADIRONDACK BOOK
ATLANTA
AUSTIN, SAN ANTONIO & THE TEXAS HILL COUNTRY
THE BERKSHIRE BOOK
BIG SUR, MONTEREY BAY & GOLD COAST WINE COUNTRY
CAPE CANAVERAL, COCOA BEACH & FLORIDA'S SPACE COAST
THE CHARLESTON, SAVANNAH & COASTAL ISLANDS BOOK
THE CHESAPEAKE BAY BOOK
THE COAST OF MAINE BOOK
COLORADO'S CLASSIC MOUNTAIN TOWNS: GREAT DESTINATIONS
THE FINGER LAKES BOOK
GALVESTON, SOUTH PADRE ISLAND & THE TEXAS GULF COAST
THE HAMPTONS BOOK
HONOLULU & OAHU: GREAT DESTINATIONS HAWAII
THE HUDSON VALLEY BOOK
LOS CABOS & BAJA CALIFORNIA SUR: GREAT DESTINATIONS MEXICO
THE NANTUCKET BOOK
THE NAPA & SONOMA BOOK
PALM BEACH, MIAMI & THE FLORIDA KEYS
PHOENIX, SCOTTSDALE, SEDONA & CENTRAL ARIZONA
PLAYA DEL CARMEN, TULUM & THE RIVIERA MAYA: GREAT DESTINATIONS MEXICO
SALT LAKE CITY, PARK CITY, PROVO & UTAH'S HIGH COUNTRY RESORTS
SAN DIEGO & TIJUANA
SAN JUAN, VIEQUES & CULEBRA: GREAT DESTINATIONS PUERTO RICO
THE SEATTLE & VANCOUVER BOOK: INCLUDES THE OLYMPIC PENINSULA, VICTORIA & MORE
THE SANTA FE & TAOS BOOK
THE SARASOTA, SANIBEL ISLAND & NAPLES BOOK
THE SHENANDOAH VALLEY BOOK
TOURING EAST COAST WINE COUNTRY

If you are traveling to, moving to, residing in, or just interested in any (or all!) of these enchanting regions, a Great Destinations guidebook is a superior companion. Honest and painstakingly critical, full of information only a local can provide, Great Destinations guidebooks give you all the practical knowledge you need to enjoy the best of each region. Why not own them all?

To Gene Koster,
who first instilled in me
a love for the road

Contents

Acknowledgments

I can't list all the people on whose patience and understanding I counted to see me through this project. First dibs on my gratitude must go to my husband, Rob, for not divorcing me, and my son, Aaron, who helped particularly with my beach and "kids' stuff" research. Thanks to Ron and Mindy Koster, who visited during my most intense stretch of writing-under-deadline and helped out in many ways.

Special thanks to Prudy Taylor Board, who checked up on my historical facts and who will no doubt cringe at the pirate legends I couldn't bring myself to omit. Thanks to Amy Ligon, who spent hours on the phone doing the nitty-gritty final fact-checking.

Nancy Hamilton at the Lee County Visitor & Convention Bureau, Rebecca Allen with Charlotte Harbor & the Gulf Island Visitor's Bureau, Jonell Modys representing Collier County, and Erin Duggan at the Sarasota Convention & Visitors Bureau have been particularly helpful.

INTRODUCTION

Morning dawns like a boater's dream. The sky is clear except for a trace of last night's moon: wispy, like a wadded-up cloud. The water stretches like cellophane pulled taut between Sanibel and Pine Islands. It is a morning to wonder why one ever does anything else on days off but return to the sea. On cue, a family of three dolphins pierces the surface with their fins and their smiles. The show has begun.

In the course of our leisurely, two-hour cruise between Sanibel Island and Boca Grande, we are entertained by leaping stingrays, a school of mackerel, and the usual dive-bombing squadron of brown pelicans.

At lights-out call—after lunch in a marina-side fish house, beach time on an unbridged island, and a duck-the-afternoon-rains cocktail at a historic island inn—nature's revue reaches its spectacular finale. In the moonless dark, the wake behind our boat sparkles like a watery fireworks display. The gulf has thrown an electric breaker switch. Liquid lightning strikes all around us as our 21-foot Mako powerboat parts the seas. Whitecaps puff like nuclear popcorn.

Scientists call the phenomena dinoflagellates. Lay folks call the glowing organisms phosphorescence. Jamaicans call them sea-blinkies. The Ancient Mariner called them death-fires. I call their unpredictable visits to our summer waters magic, imparting a topsy-turvy, ethereal feeling that someone—without warning—has transformed the sea into a starry sky.

Such a perfect day isn't required to fully appreciate this inimitable slice of Gulf Coast Florida, but such days do help to remind me why I moved here from long-johns land 20-some years ago. Like so many who constitute our hodgepodge population, I escaped, I loved, I dug in. I stayed for the exotic, warm quality of tropical nature. I remain because of the miracles I discover—and watch my young son discover—every day.

—Chelle Koster Walton, Sanibel Island, Florida

THE WAY THIS BOOK WORKS

Organization

The area bounded on the north by the Braden River and on the south by Ten Thousand
Islands is often lumped under the heading Southwest Florida. Sometimes the Bradenton-
Sarasota area is omitted from the region this heading defines and otherwise grouped with
Tampa as Central West Florida. For the purpose of this guide, the Bradenton-Sarasota area
is included in the coverage. The book often refers to the region covered as Gulf Coast
Florida or West Coast Florida, although, of course, it does not cover the entire coast. It
does cover in depth the cities, towns, and communities from Bradenton-Sarasota in the
north to Naples–Marco Island and the Everglades in the south.

I have sliced this delectable pie into four regional chapters, north to south: Sarasota Bay
Coast, Charlotte Harbor Coast, Island Coast, and South Coast. Within these chapters I scan
under separate headings each region's lodging, dining, culture, recreation, and shopping.

Other chapters deal with the coastline's history as a whole, transportation, and nitty-
gritty information.

A series of indexes at the back of the book provide easy access to information. The first,
a standard index, lists entries and subjects in alphabetical order. Next, hotels, inns, and
resorts are categorized by price. Restaurants are organized in two separate indexes: one by
price, one by type of cuisine.

List of Maps

The Gulf Coast of Florida
Gulf Coast Access Maps
Sarasota Bay Coast
Charlotte Harbor Coast
Island Coast
South Coast

High Fives

In the *Information* chapter, I have rated listings within a number of fun—and sometimes
quirky—categories, from Splurge Accommodations and Martini Meccas to Kid Cool and
Paddle Happy. They begin under the Chelle's High Fives heading on page 334.

Within the chapters, listings that have earned a High Five get a star ✪ next to their
names.

Prices

Rather than give specific prices, this guide rates dining and lodging options within a
range.

Lodging prices are normally based on per person/double occupancy for hotel rooms
and per unit for efficiencies, apartments, cottages, suites, and villas. Price ranges reflect
the difference in the off season and high season (usually Christmas through Easter).

Generally, the colder the weather up north, the higher the cost of accommodations here.
Rates can double during the course of a year. Many resorts offer off-season packages at

special rates. Pricing does not include the 6 percent Florida sales tax. Furthermore, many large resorts add gratuities or housekeeping charges, and most counties also impose a tourist tax, proceeds from which are applied to beach and environmental maintenance.

If rates seem high for rooms on the Gulf Coast, it's partially because many resorts cater to families by providing kitchen facilities. Take into consideration what this could save you on dining bills. A star after the pricing designation indicates that accommodations include at least continental breakfast with the cost of lodging; a few offer the American Plan, serving all meals, which is then explained within the description copy.

Dining cost categories are based on the range of dinner entrée prices or, if dinner is not served, on lunch entrées. Restaurants at some large resorts add gratuities to the tab. This is also customary for large parties at most restaurants, so check your bill carefully before leaving a tip. Satisfied diners are expected to tip between 15 and 20 percent.

Heavy state taxes on liquor served in-house can mount up a drinking tab quickly. Paying as you drink is a wise measure to prevent sticker shock.

Price Codes

	Lodging	*Dining*
Inexpensive	Up to $75	Up to $15
Moderate	$75 to $150	$15 to $25
Expensive	$150 to $200	$25 to $35
Very Expensive	$200 and up	$35 or more

(An asterisk after the pricing designation indicates that the rate includes at least a continental breakfast in the cost of lodging and possibly more extensive meal service as noted in the listing.)

The following abbreviations are used for credit card information:

AE: American Express   MC: MasterCard
D: Discover Card   V: Visa
DC: Diners Club

Area Code

The 941 area code applies to the Sarasota Bay coast and Charlotte Harbor coast; the Island coast and South coast regions use 239.

Numbers prefixed with 800, 888, 866, and 877 are toll free.

Tourist Information

Local visitors bureaus, tourism development councils, and chambers of commerce are adept at the dissemination of materials and information about their area. These are listed in chapter seven, *Information*.

For information on the entire region and other parts of Florida, contact Visit Florida, 661 E. Jefferson St., Suite 300, Tallahassee, FL 32301; 888-7FLA-USA; www.flausa.com.

1

History

Mangroves, Man, and Magnates

The essence of Gulf Coast Florida seems to be a balance of polar extremes: the ultimate in both natural wilderness and social civility. To understand the region and the richness of its heritage, culture, and environment, one must understand its roots, learn the names, and revel in the legends of its past—a past steeped in romance, adventure, and power.

The story begins with a single mangrove tree and evolves around humanity's need to conquer that tree's primeval world. Enter the characters: Ambition, Wealth, and Social Grace. How does the story end? Happily, we can hope, with the modern rediscovery of the coast's unique natural and historical heritage.

Natural History

From Grains of Sand

Each wave helps build a ridge of accumulating sand and shell that runs roughly parallel to the beach. Over a period of hundreds or thousands of years, a ridge may become a barrier island.
—Lynn Stone, Voyageurs Series, Sanibel Island, 1991

On the floor is a straw mat. Under the mat is a layer of sand that has been tracked into the cottage and has sifted through the straw. I have thought some of taking the mat up and sweeping the sand into a pile and removing it, but have decided against it. This is the way keys form, apparently, and I have no particular reason to interfere.
—E. B. White, "On a Florida Key," 1941

Billions of years ago, the Florida peninsula existed only as a scattering of volcanic keys, akin to the Caribbean islands. The passing years, silt, and the sea's power eventually buried all evidence of these volcanic origins. What is now Florida remained submerged until some 20 million years ago, when matter buildup brought land to the surface in the form of new islands.

Ice Age sea fluctuations molded Florida into solid land, and islands continued to grow along its fringes. From a single grain of sand or a lone mangrove sprout they stabilized into masses of sand and forests composed of leggy roots and finger shoots. As shells and marine encrustations accumulated, islands fell into formation along the Gulf Coast,

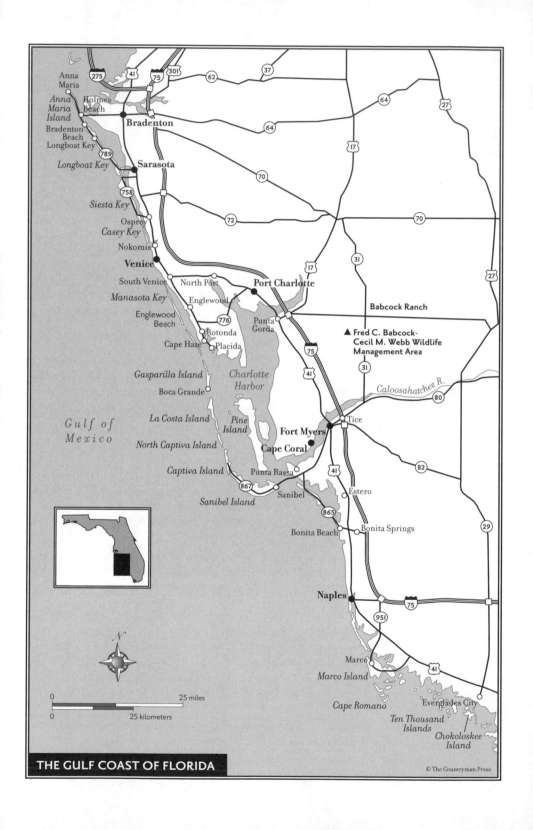

THE GULF COAST OF FLORIDA

protecting it from the battering of a storm-driven sea. In the gaps between the islands, the gulf's waters scoured the shore to forge inlets, estuaries, bayous, creeks, and rivers. The sea chiseled a mottled, labyrinthine shoreline that kept the southern Gulf Coast a secret while the rest of the state was being tamed.

During its infancy, the region hosted a slow parade of ever-changing creatures. In pre-historic graveyards modern archaeologists have found mummified remains of rhinoceroses, crocodiles, llamas, camels, pygmy horses, saber-toothed tigers, mastodons, and great woolly mammoths—Florida's first winter visitors at the advent of the Ice Age. Another era brought giant armadillos, tapirs, and other South American creatures. Fauna and flora from these ancient eras survive today: cabbage palms (the state tree), saw palmettos, garfish, seahorses, horseshoe crabs, alligators, manatees, armadillos, and loggerhead sea turtles.

An Early Picture

In the bay of Juan Ponce De León, in the west side of the land, we meet with innumerable small islands, and several fresh streams: the land in general is drowned mangrove swamp. . . . From this place Cape Romano, latitude 25:43 to latitude 26:30 are many inconsiderable inlets, all carefully laid down in the chart, here is Carlos Bay, and the Coloosa Hatchee, or Coloosa river, with the island San Ybell, where we find the southern entrance of Charlotte harbour. . . .

—Bernard Romans, 1775

One of the earliest recorders of Florida native life and topography, Bernard Romans is credited with naming Charlotte Harbor after the queen of his adopted homeland, England, and Cape Romano after himself. Native Americans and earlier Spanish explorers are responsible for other regional place names.

The harbor was already the center of west-coast life when the first explorers discovered it.

The Miracle of the Mangrove

The mangrove forest is both a fertile incubator and a marine graveyard, the home of an island construction crew and a vegetative ballet troupe. It is a self-sustaining world marked by vivid contrasts. The Mangrove Coast (as one local historian terms it) is riddled with red, black, and white species of the tree. Red mangroves strut along mainland coastlines, canals, and the leeward sides of islands on graceful prop roots—or at least they look graceful until low tide reveals the oysters, barnacles, and tiny marine metropolises that weigh them down and keep them connected to the sea.

Farther inland, black-and-white mangroves create thick, impenetrable forests that buffer waves, filter pollutants, send out shoots, and always busily build. Encrustations of shellfish grab algae, silt, and sand, creating rich soil out of decaying material. Fish, crabs, and mollusks skitter among the roots, nibbling dinner, depositing eggs, and tending to their young. Birds rest and nest in the mangroves' scraggly branches, ready to dive for the fish on which they feed. Mother trees send their tubular offspring bobbing upon sea currents to find a foothold elsewhere and perhaps begin a new island.

The cycle is ancient and ongoing, threatened only by the chainsaws of developers. A few decades ago these natural builders, the mangroves, were leveled in favor of cement seawalls. Today, strict regulations prohibit mangrove destruction. The crucial role of the mangrove in the survival of Florida's sea life finally has been realized—and cherished.

Its deep waters and barrier-island protection created a pocket of unusually mild climate, attracting early aborigines and their descendants.

Romans and his contemporaries found the Gulf Coast alive with wild turkeys, black bears, deer, golden panthers, bobcats, possums, raccoons, alligators, river otters, lizards, and snakes. Wild boars and scrub cattle roamed freely, descendants of stock brought by Spanish missionaries. Land birds and waterfowl of all varieties—some permanent, some migratory—filled the skies and back bays. Majestic ospreys and bald eagles swooped; kites soared effortlessly; sandhill cranes dotted the countryside; wood storks nested; pelicans came in colors of brown and white; gulls, terns, and sandpipers patrolled seashores; cormorants, ducks, anhingas, ibises, egrets, roseate spoonbills, and herons fed among the mangroves.

Marine life flourished. Manatees cleared waterways, dolphins frolicked in the waves, and mullet burst from bay waters like cannon shot. Tarpon, rays, snapper, snook, flounder, ladyfish, and mackerel churned the otherwise calm backwaters. Grouper, tripletail, tuna, and shark lurked in deep waters offshore.

On land, a wide variety of indigenous vegetation abounded. Sea grapes, mahoes, sea oats, nickerbeans, and railroad vines anchored sandy coasts. Thick, impenetrable jungles clogged inland areas. Cabbage palms and gumbo-limbo trees stood tall. Papayas flourished along with flowering shrubs. In mixed-wood forests pines climbed skyward, and live oaks fluttered their eerie veils of Spanish moss. Cedars fringed islands along the Sarasota Bay coast. Ferns and grasses carpeted the marshes. Swamplands were home to great cypress trees with bony knees and branches full of parasitic mistletoe and epiphytic orchids and bromeliads.

Primeval and teeming, Florida held an exotic and mysterious aura. The swamp and the estuary nurtured all of life, from the Everglades upward along the lowlands of the Gulf Coast. It was a perfect ecosystem, designed by nature to withstand all forces—except humankind.

Face-Lifts and Implants

With the arrival of the first settlers, the natural balance that existed along the Gulf Coast began to tilt. The Spanish brought citrus seedlings and livestock. Naturalists and growers introduced specimens from the north and south: mangoes, avocados, bougainvillea, hibiscus, frangipani, coconut palms, pineapples, sapodillas, tomatoes, and legumes. For the most part these exotics proved harmless to the fragile environment.

Three nonnative plants brought to the area in the past century, however, have harmed the ecosystem and changed the profile of the land. The prolific melaleuca tree (or cajeput), casuarina (Australian pine), and Brazilian pepper choke out the native vegetation that wildlife feeds on and harm both man and property. Many communities are attempting to eradicate these noxious plants, particularly the pepper tree.

The complexion of the west coast was changed further by dredging and plowing. In times when swampland was equated with slimy monsters and slick realtors, developers and governments thought nothing of filling it in to create more buildable land. This, too, threw the ecosystem off balance. Fortunately, such mistakes were recognized before their effects became irreversible. Today government strives to preserve, even restore, the delicate balance of the wetlands, most notably through the massive, $8 billion, 30-year Everglades restoration project.

SOCIAL HISTORY

Time line: Gulf Coast Florida

The modern settlement of Florida's southwest coast can be traced like a time line that begins on the shores of Sarasota Bay in 1841 and ends at Naples in 1887. At first glance this time frame makes the region look young, without the gracious patina of age and the wrinkles of an interesting past. Common is the belief, in fact, that the Gulf Coast has no history because it lacks Williamsburg's colonial homes or Philadelphia's monuments.

True, the Gulf Coast's early pioneers left no standing architecture. Termites, flimsy building styles, erosion, and tropical storms saw to that. But earlier settlers did leave other proof of their existence—artifacts that date as far back as 10,000 years. If that isn't history, what is?

Calusa Kingdom

Archaeologists of this century have discovered remnants of early architecture and lifeways in the shell mounds of the Calusa and Timucua tribes, who settled the coastlines more than 2,500 years ago. The Timucua inhabited the Sarasota Bay coast for many years and then migrated northward and to the east; the Calusa later moved into the Sarasota area and were centered around Charlotte Harbor.

Evidence of still earlier civilizations has been found, placing Florida's first immigrants, possibly from Asia, in the upper coast regions around 8200 BC. Little is known about these early arrivals except that they used pointed spears.

Archaeological excavations and the writings of Spanish explorers give us a more complete picture of the Calusa and other tribes, who built shell mounds to bury their dead and debris. Learned consensus brings the Calusa and the Timucua to southern Florida from Caribbean islands—evidence of similar lifestyles and sustained contact suggests a connection to the peaceful Arawak Indians of the West Indies. Similarities have also been found between the Calusa and South American tribes, and, given indications of the Florida's tribes' great engineering skills, some historians consider them wayward relatives of the Mayans or Aztecs. (Others say they are connected to the Mayans and Aztecs by trade rather than origin.)

The name Calusa, or Caloosa, was used first by Spanish conquerors, who understood the name of the tribe's chief to be Calos. They were said to be tall people with hip-length hair that men wore in a topknot. When clothed, men dressed in breeches of deerskin or woven palmetto fiber, and women fashioned garments out of Spanish moss. They cultivated corn, pumpkins, squash, and tobacco; fished for mullet and mackerel with harpoons and palmetto-fiber nets; hunted for turkey, deer, and bear with bow and arrow, deer-

A typical Timucua Indian village has been recreated at De Soto National Memorial Park in Bradenton.

Once an Indian trading post, Smallwood's Store today serves as a museum in the secluded Everglades outpost of Chokoloskee Island.

bone dirks, and Aztec-style weapons; and harvested wild sea grapes, fruit, yams, swamp cabbage (hearts of palm), and the coontie root, out of which they pounded flour for bread. Conch and whelk shells were crafted into tools for building and cooking. The natives spent their leisure time wrestling, celebrating the corn harvest, and worshiping the sun god. Great seafarers, the Calusa built canoes and traveled in them to Caribbean islands and the Yucatán. A different style of pirogue took them along rivers and bay waters to visit villages of their own tribe and those of other nations.

Much of our information about the Calusa comes from the son of a Spanish official stationed in Cartagena, in what is now Colombia. The youngster, Hernando de Escalante Fontaneda, was shipwrecked along Calusa shores en route to Spain. He lived among the tribe for 17 years, learned its language, and, upon returning to Spain in 1574, recorded its customs. In 1895 Frank Hamilton Cushing explored Charlotte Harbor's Amerindian heritage. He surmised that the Calusa's religious structures and palmetto-piling homes had perched on shell mounds along riverbanks and coastlines. Terraces and steps bit into the towering mounds where gardens and courts had been built. Manmade canals up to 30 feet wide connected neighboring villages. Pine Island, Mound Key, Manasota Key, and Marco Island were important religious and governmental centers for the Calusa.

Excavations along the Gulf Coast continually provide new information about the region's native inhabitants and their symbiotic relationship with nature. The University of Florida funds a research center on Pine Island for the sole purpose of excavating mounds to discover more truth about the vanished civilization.

Spanish Imposition

Greed and religious fervor eventually warped this idyllic picture, and the Calusa showed themselves to be vicious warriors in an attempt to preserve the life they knew. Juan Ponce de León first crashed the party in 1513. It's possible that early slavers from the Caribbean were responsible for the Calusa hostility he encountered, or perhaps the Amerindians' early hatred of the conquistadores was gained secondhand, from trading with island natives. Whatever the reason, Ponce was "blacklisted" by the Calusa shortly after he began his search, according to legend, for Bimini, a storied land of treasure and youth.

Ponce de León first landed on Florida's east coast at Eastertime without strife, and the conqueror named the land after the Spanish name for the holiday, *Pascua Florida*. However, on his second landing, days later, he was met by shell-tipped spears and bows and arrows. His three wounded sailors were the first Europeans known to shed blood in Florida. Ponce de León's ship continued to the west coast, where it stopped in the vicinity of Marco Island. Here one native astounded him by speaking to him in Spanish—learned, perhaps, from West Indies contacts. Impressed, Ponce de León allowed his party to be tricked by a marauding native army in canoes but escaped with the loss of only one man's life.

After several trips to Florida and the Gulf Coast, Ponce de León returned to Puerto Rico—still treasureless and now middle-aged—to plot a new scheme. In 1521 he set out to establish a Gulf Coast colony as a base for treasure explorations. This time the party he crashed had been forewarned, possibly by smoke signals. Calusa arrows pierced the heavy armor of the Spaniards, killing and wounding many, including the great seeker of youth himself. After returning to Havana for medical attention, Ponce de León died there at the age of 60.

Lust for gold overcame common sense as more explorers and invaders followed in Ponce de León's tragic footsteps. In 1539 Hernando de Soto sailed from Havana and headed up the Gulf Coast, seeking, it would seem, a way to confuse future historians. Three different crewmen described the expedition three different ways. The Smithsonian Institution has published a report some locals still dispute, which claims that de Soto landed first on Longboat Key and then, looking for fresh water, headed toward Tampa Bay. According to the Smithsonian, de Soto set up his first mainland camp at an abandoned native village at the mouth of the Manatee River, near modern-day Bradenton. Others are convinced that his first landfall was at Fort Myers Beach. Regardless of where the landing took place, we know that de Soto scoured the coast for gold, all the while torturing and killing Native Americans who would not, could not, lead him to it.

Sarasota and its environs embrace the Smithsonian study's findings. Some say the name of the town itself, initially written as "Sara Sota," comes from the conqueror. Others prefer a more romantic legend regarding his fictional daughter, Sara. Sarasota's first hotel, in any case, took its name from de Soto. Near Bradenton, a small national park marks the alleged spot of his first landing.

In Palmetto, visitors can climb to the top of an ancient Indian mound at Emerson Point Preserve.

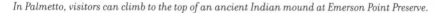

In 1565 Pedro Menéndez de Avilés came to the Gulf Coast, searching for a son lost to shipwreck and a group of Spaniards being held captive by the Calusa. With the aid of one of Chief Calos's Spanish captives, Menéndez befriended Calos with flattery and gifts, then built a fort and a mission at a spot called San Anton, believed to have been on Pine Island. But Menéndez insulted the great chieftain by rejecting his sister as a wife and allying himself with enemy tribes. Sensing Calos's anger, Menéndez tricked the leader into captivity and had him beheaded. When Menéndez later executed Calos's son and heir to the throne, along with 11 of his subchiefs, tribesmen burned their own villages, forcing the settlers to bail out in search of food.

The century that followed is considered the Golden Age of the Calusa. It was marked by freedom from European intrusion and great cultural advances, heightened by the contribution of Spanish captives who had refused to be saved by Menéndez's rescue party and by others who found Calusa ways preferable to "civilization."

Eventually, peaceful trading softened the hostility between Spanish settlers and the Calusa. Cuban immigrants began building a fishing industry around Charlotte Harbor. But although the Calusa had won the war against Spanish invaders, they were defenseless against the diseases the Europeans brought with them. By the turn of the 19th century, smallpox and other diseases had killed off most Calusa; the remainder were absorbed by intermarrying with the Cubans and newly arriving tribes. The most prominent of the latter were the Seminole—a name meaning "wanderer"—a mixture of Georgian Creek, African, and Spanish bloodlines.

The fountain from the old Hotel Charlotte Harbor now graces the grounds of Punta Gorda History Park.

The Varmint Era

"A haunt of the picaroons of all nations," wrote explorer James Grant Forbes in 1772, referring to Charlotte Harbor—layover, if not home, for every scoundrel who sailed its island-clotted waters. The Gulf Coast's maze of forbidding bayous and barely navigable waterways made it a favorite hideout for escaped criminals, bootleggers, government refugees, smugglers, and—that most popular of all local folk characters—buccaneers.

Pirate legends color the pages of regional history books in shades of blood red and doubloon gold. Besides willing to residents a certain cavalier spirit, these pirates have left—if one believes the tales—millions of dollars in buried treasure. "After researching the subject in 1950 . . . then State Attorney General Ralph E. Odum estimated that some $165 million is still buried beneath Florida's sands and waters," reported a 1978 issue of the *Miami Herald's Florida Almanac*, "$30 million of it originally the property of Jose Gaspar."

Besides the mostly mythical Gaspar, other picaresque names resound along the Gulf Coast: Jean Lafitte, of New Orleans fame; Bru Baker, Gaspar's Pine Island cohort; and a dark soul named Black Caesar. Henry Castor supposedly buried treasure on Egmont Key in the mid-1700s. Local legend places the notorious Calico Jack Rackham and his pirate lover, Anne Bonny, on the shores of Fort Myers Beach for a playful honeymoon. Black

---

Kingdom of Gasparilla

Of all the rum-chugging and throat-slashing visitors to have set foot upon southwest Florida's tolerant shores, José Gaspar (known by the more properly pirate-sounding name "Gasparilla") is the one remembered most fondly. Gaspar set up headquarters, it is said, on Gasparilla Island, where Boca Grande now sits. In his time it was called High Town. He built a palmetto palace there and furnished it with the finest booty. Low Town he placed on a separate island so as to distance himself from the crude lifestyles of his rowdy shipmates. Gasparilla's fort stood on Cayo Costa.

Legends say Gasparilla got his start as a pirate after some nasty business with the wife of a crown prince. He gave up his cushy position as admiral of the Spanish navy for the hardships of life at sea and in the jungles of late-18th-century Florida.

His address might have changed, but his love of beautiful women did not. He kidnapped the fairest and wealthiest of them from captured ships and whisked them off to another Gulf Coast island named for its inhabitants—Captiva—until ransom money arrived. Gasparilla took the most beautiful of his captives to High Town to woo them with fine wines, jewels, and Spanish poetry. One object of his affection, a Mexican princess named Joséfa, would have nothing to do with such a barbarian. Finally, driven to madness by her insults, Gasparilla beheaded his beloved. He carried her body to another key in his island fiefdom, where he buried her with remorse and sand. He named the island Joséfa, which, through the years and the twistings of rum-swollen tongues, has been perverted to Useppa. And so the exclusive island is called today.

Nearby Sanibel Island, according to one legend, got its name from the abandoned lover of Gaspar's gunner. However, variations of the story abound and improve with each telling. The legend began with the ramblings of old "Panther Key John" Gomez and was perpetuated by railroad press agents and optimistic treasure hunters.

Serious historians doubt the existence of a man named Gasparilla but concede that one of the many Gulf Coast pirates might have borrowed the island's name. Others hold tenaciously to the legend, plying coastal sands with shovels and dredges in search of his ill-gotten booty.

Augustus lived and died a hermit on Mound Key, to the south. On Panther Key, John Gomez, Gaspar's self-proclaimed cabin boy, lived to be 122 and sold maps purportedly leading to Gasparillan gold to many a gullible treasure hunter.

According to more reliable historical records, island pirate havens were replaced by or coexisted with crude Spanish fishing ranchos, which cropped up as early as the 1600s. The camps—which provided Cuban traders with salted mullet and roe to eat—consisted of thatched shacks, some built on pilings in shallow waters. Here families lived, according to customs inspector Henry B. Crews, "in a state of Savage Barbarism with no associate but the Seminole Indians and the lowest class of refugee Spaniards who from crime have most generally been compelled to abandon the haunts of civilized life."

Ice-making and railroads changed the direction of fish exportation from southern points to northern destinations. Punta Gorda, with the area's first railroad station, became the center for the transshipment of fresh fish. Major fish-shipping companies built stilt houses for the more than 200 men who harvested their mullet crops. These structures straddled shallows from Charlotte Harbor to Ten Thousand Islands, providing homes for the fishermen and their families until the late 1930s, when modern roads and the burning of Punta Gorda's Long Dock brought the era to a close. Fewer than a dozen of the historic fish shacks have survived hurricanes, erosion, and the state's determination to tear them down as a public nuisance. They strut along the shallows of Charlotte Harbor, in greatest concentration offshore of North Captiva Island.

"It is highly important that no person should be permitted to settle on the Islands forming 'Charlotte Harbor' . . . which are of no value for the purpose of agriculture, being in general formed of sand and shells," advised Assistant Adjutant General Captain Lorenzo Thomas in 1844. Nonetheless, out of this era of varmints sprouted a tradition of farming. Coconuts, citrus, tomatoes, and other crops were raised, despite hardship and heartbreak, as plucky pioneers trickled in to coax their livelihood from a hostile environment.

Years of Discontent

The bloody years of the Wars of Indian Removal began in 1821, when Andrew Jackson—then governor of the territory—decided to claim northern Florida from the Seminole tribes that were wreaking havoc on American settlers. By 1837 fighting had spread to the southern reaches of the peninsula, and two forts were built upriver from present-day Fort Myers. The following year the government reached an

The story of the Calusa and Seminole peoples, including Seminole Chief Billy Bowlegs, finds an audience along Venice's main thoroughfare.

agreement with the Seminoles, restricting them to mainland areas along the Charlotte Harbor coast, the Caloosahatchee River, and southward.

News of imminent peace prompted Josiah Gates to build a hotel on the banks of the Manatee River, near modern-day Bradenton, in anticipation of the influx of settlers from Fort Brooke (Tampa) that the treaty would bring. A modest community rose up around this precursor of southwest Florida resorts. Families of soldiers and wealthy Southern planters settled in the area. The latter brought their slaves and built sugarcane plantations on vast expanses of land that they bought for $1.25 an acre.

Sarasota got its first permanent settler in 1842 when William Whitaker, a fisherman, built his home on Yellow Bluff, overlooking Sarasota Bay. He and his new wife, daughter of one of the Manatee planters, had 10 children and later went into cattle ranching and farming.

The year after the peace treaty was signed, a tribe of Seminoles attacked a settlement across the river from their village, on the same site as present-day Fort Myers. The Harney Point Massacre rekindled the war. Fort Harvie was built near the site of the violent attack. Chief Billy Bowlegs led his people in evasive tactics through the wild and mysterious Everglades, but by 1842 the government had captured 230 of his people and shipped them west. Further pursuit was abandoned. Only Fort Harvie and one other fortification remained operational. A new agreement contained the Seminoles along the Caloosahatchee and barred them from the islands, to protect the fishermen and their families. The treaty made no mention of the swampland, probably because the government considered it useless; the Seminoles assumed the territory was theirs.

By 1848, three years after Florida's admission to the Union as the 27th state, there was a surge of interest in the wetlands. The government, envisioning drainage projects to create more land, offered the Seminoles $250 each to relocate in the West. When they refused, a systematic plan to conquer them went into effect. This plan included the repair of Fort Harvie, which was renamed Fort Myers after a U.S. colonel who had served for many years in Florida and was engaged to the commanding general's daughter. Manpower was increased there, and the fort was reinforced and enlarged. Scouting parties stalked the Seminoles but usually found only the remains of abandoned and burned villages when they arrived.

In December 1855, after soldiers destroyed Billy Bowlegs's prize banana patch, the Seminole chief and his people retaliated. Fort Myers became the center of war activity. The government placed a bounty on the head of any Seminole brought to the fort and offered $1,000 to each Seminole warrior ($100 to each woman and child) who agreed to leave the area. Finally, in 1858, after soldiers had captured his granddaughter and other women of the tribe, Billy Bowlegs capitulated, thus bringing an end to 37 years of killing and deception by the government and the military. Fort Myers was abandoned, and the remaining Seminole dispersed deep into the Everglades. Farmers, planters, fishermen, and cattlemen continued peacefully in their trades, although government vigilance against alliances with the Seminole forced some of the island fishing *ranchos* to close during the war's final years. Today the Seminole live on reservations, earning an income from tourism, fishing, and casinos.

In the late 1850s, Virginia planter Captain James Evans purchased Fort Myers on the auction block. He brought in his slaves to work the crops he envisioned—tropical fruits, coconut palms, coffee, and other exotic plants. The Civil War interrupted his venture, sending him back home. Florida joined the Confederacy in 1861. West coast inhabitants generally remained uninvolved until a federal blockade at Key West cut off supplies, at which point they turned to the profitable business of blockade running.

Cattle Kings, Carpetbaggers, and Crackers

Jacob Summerlin epitomized the Florida cattle king. He dressed in a floppy hat, leather boots, and trail dust. Having established a steady trade between Florida and ports south before the Civil War, Summerlin was in a good position to provide the Confederate Army with contraband beef. Working with his blockade-running partner, James McKay Sr., he drove his cattle from inland Florida to Punta Rassa, where the causeway from Sanibel Island makes landfall today. There he sold his scrub cattle, descendants of livestock left by the early Spaniards. The U.S. Navy eventually learned of these illegal dealings and stationed boats at Sanibel and Punta Rassa. In spite of attempts to thwart their trade, however, Summerlin and McKay sold 25,000 steers to the Confederates between 1861 and 1865.

Jake Summerlin lived by the seat of his pants, driving cattle to Punta Rassa and collecting big bags of Cuban gold—which he spent at the end of the line on drinking and gaming. In 1874 he built the Summerlin House at Punta Rassa, where he and his men could bunk and invest the profits of the business in frivolity.

The rough, free-and-easy lifestyle of the cow hunter attracted young post–Civil War drifters. In addition, Summerlin's success lured Civil War officers into the prosperous life of the cattle boss, including Captain F. A. Hendry, founder of an ongoing Fort Myers dynasty. Between 1870 and 1880 stockmen sold 165,000 head of cattle at Punta Rassa for more than $2 million. Into the 1900s, the cow hunters drove their herds through the streets of downtown Fort Myers, past the homes of investors, bankers, and other wealthy settlers, including Thomas Edison.

Reconstruction brought other settlers to Florida's west coast. One notable rebel refugee, Judah P. Benjamin—who had served as the Confederacy's secretary of state—ducked indictment as a war criminal by hiding out in Florida. His weeklong asylum at the old Gamble plantation near Bradenton ensured the landmark's preservation by the United Daughters of the Confederacy.

Stock left on Florida shores gave hoof to lucrative cattle-driving enterprises in the mid- to late 19th century.

The first postwar visitors to Fort Myers were the vultures who picked the fort clean of coveted building materials. Then came men who remembered the old fort in its heyday and hoped to settle with their families in this land of plenty. The first settler, Captain Manuel A. Gonzalez, had run a provisions boat from Tampa during the Seminole War. He and his family moved from Key West with another family named Vivas. Other war officers and refugees settled in and around the ruins of the old fort, planting gardens, opening stores, and living a blissful existence unknown elsewhere in the devastated South.

Captain James Evans returned to Fort Myers from Virginia to find his land comfortably occupied. After struggling in the courts to keep the land out of government hands, he split it with the squatters in exchange for a share of his legal fees. In 1872 the first school in Fort Myers was built. County government was centered 270 miles away, in Key West.

Some historians credit the cow hunters with contributing the name "Cracker" to early Florida settlers, which they say derives from the cracking of the long whips the cowmen used to drive their herds. Others say it originated with the Georgia settlers who cracked corn for their hush puppies, corn pone, and fritters. Georgians did, in fact, drift down to southwest Florida, most notably the Knight clan, which founded a settlement at Horse and Chaise, named by seamen to describe a landmark clump of trees. (The name was changed to Venice in 1888 by developer Frank Higel, who was reminded of the Italian city by the area's many bayous and creeks.)

The Homestead Act, passed in 1862, entitled each settler in Florida to 160 acres of land, provided they built a home and tended the land for five years. As had been intended, the act brought a flood of intrepid settlers into the area from all over the eastern seaboard and Deep South. Traveling by foot or boat, they built rough palmetto huts, burned cow chips to ward off mosquitoes that carried yellow fever, ate raccoon purloo and turtle steaks, and stubbornly endured the heat, hurricanes, and freezes that stymied a number of enterprises: sugar refining, fish-oil production, and pineapple and citrus farming.

Florida's cow hunters eventually proved detrimental to the agriculturally based ventures associated with the Crackers of the Sarasota Bay region. They allied themselves with greedy land speculators who, by 1883, underhandedly nullified the beneficial effects of the Homestead Act. These speculators had discovered a loophole in Florida's land development legislation, namely the Swamp Land Act, which allowed them to purchase flooded land at rock-bottom prices while overriding homestead claims. They succeeded in declaring arable property swampland and ultimately bought up a good 90 percent of present-day Manatee County, much of which had been worked for years by hardy pioneers. Together the speculators and the cattlemen fought farmers' protests against "free ranging," the practice of letting herds roam and feed without restriction. A Sara Sota Vigilance Committee formed in opposition, and by the time the fighting ended, two men lay dead.

As thatch homes gave way to wooden farmhouses—the tin-roofed vernacular style today termed Cracker—Gulf Coast settlements entered a new era, an era that made "riffraff" out of Crackers, rich men out of schemers, and exclusive getaways out of crude frontier towns.

At the Drop of a Name

When your first guests are Juan Ponce de León and Hernando de Soto, whom do you invite next? With such a standard set, it wouldn't do to host just anybody. So began west coast Florida's tradition of larger-than-life visitors with impressive names and pedigrees, all of whom just as impressively influenced the region's development. Thomas Edison, Henry Ford, Harvey Firestone, John and Charles Ringling, Charles Lindbergh, Teddy Roosevelt, Henry du Pont, Andrew Mellon, Rose Cleveland, and Shirley Temple were among the wide array of early southwest Florida winterers. Their fame and following quickly elevated the status of the lower Gulf Coast from crude and backward to avant-garde and exclusive, attracting the cutting-edge elite. They set national trends by declaring new hot spots—fresh, wild, unspoiled places about which no one else knew, especially the paparazzi. It was they who balanced the very wild coast with a very civilized clientele. The area's natural endowments of fish, fowl, and game attracted adventurers, fishermen, and hunters with the means to make the long, slow journey to it.

The first and most influential name in any Gulf Coast retrospective is Thomas Edison. Disappointed by the cold winters of St. Augustine, the ailing inventor embarked on a scouting cruise along the Gulf Coast in 1885, the same year Fort Myers was incorporated. As Edison sailed along the Caloosahatchee River, he sighted a stand of bamboo trees. Then and there he decided to move to Fort Myers. And he wanted that property!

The bamboo worked well as filament in Edison's lightbulb experiments, and the climate bolstered his failing health, helping to add another 46 years to his life. On the banks of the Caloosahatchee the inventor fashioned his ideal winter home, Seminole Lodge, complete with laboratory and tropical gardens. Holder of more than a thousand patents, the genius experimented with rare plants in his quest to produce inexpensive rubber for his friend, tire mogul Harvey Firestone. So enamored with Fort Myers was Edison that he persuaded Firestone to spend his winters there. He also set up fellow visionary Henry Ford on an estate next to his. A self-styled botanist, Edison planted the frequently photographed row of royal palms lining the street that eventually ran past his home, McGregor Boulevard, thereby earning the town its nickname: City of Palms.

Meanwhile, the Florida Mortgage and Investment Company—connected with such notables as the archbishop of Canterbury and estate owner Sir John Gillespie—lured a colony of politically disgruntled Scotsmen to Sara Sota, a paradise of genteel estates, bountiful orange groves, and cheap land. Or so the brochures promised. But instead of the Garden of Eden and ready-made manor houses about which they had read, the newcomers found shortages of food and building materials. Only through the kindness of the Whitakers and other pioneers did they survive their first month. Then the Gulf Coast's unpredictable winter weather dealt another cold blow, causing most of the colonists to return to their homeland. Those who stayed, however, brought life to the struggling village and sparked it with a determined spirit.

Old fish houses, like this one in Cortez, survive from the 1930s, when fishermen's families lived in and worked out of the stilted structures.

Most influential among the Scottish ranks was John Hamilton Gillespie, son of Sir John. He built the city's first hotel, the De Soto, and introduced the game of golf to Florida. Gillespie initially transplanted the sport from his homeland by building a two-hole links down Main Street, near his hotel; he later built the area's first real course and clubhouse nearby. When the town of Sarasota was incorporated on October 14, 1902, Gillespie became its first mayor.

It was an American woman, however, who firmly and definitively upgraded Sarasota's image. At the turn of the 20th century the name Mrs. (Bertha) Potter Palmer stood for social elitism—not only in her hometown, Chicago, but also in London and Paris, where she kept homes and hobnobbed with royalty. When the widowed socialite decided to visit Sarasota in 1910, hearts palpitated: She could make or break the new town. Enchanted by the area's beauty and the town's quaintness, Mrs. Palmer immediately bought 13 acres that eventually grew to 140,000. She built her home, The Oaks, and a cattle ranch in a community south of Sarasota called Osprey and from there proceeded to spread the word.

Mrs. Palmer's much-publicized love affair with the Gulf Coast drew the attention of John and Charles Ringling, the youngest of the illustrious circus family's seven sons. The two brothers, in a contest of one-upmanship, began buying property around town. They became active in civic affairs, built bridges to Sarasota's islands, and stoked the economy by making the town the winter home for the Ringling Circus. John Ringling, especially, and his wife, Mable, brought to Sarasota a new worldliness born of their extensive travels and love of European art.

The fate of the Charlotte Harbor coast lay mostly in the hands of one powerful man, Henry B. Plant. The west coast's counterpart to Henry Flagler—builder of the east coast's railroad and great hotels—Plant brought the railway to Tampa, where he built a fabulous resort of his own, always in competition with Flagler. At the same time, another railway company extended its tracks to an unknown, unsettled spot in the wilderness of Charlotte Harbor's shores and erected the Hotel Charlotte Harbor. It reigned briefly as the latest posh outpost for wealthy sportsmen and adventurers, counting Andrew Mellon and W. K. Vanderbilt among its patrons. But in 1897, after Plant had acquired the railway to Punta Gorda, he decided that the town's deepwater port and resort posed too much competition for his Tampa enterprises. So he choked the life out of a thriving commercial and resort town by severing the rails to Punta Gorda's Long Dock.

Deepwater ports, railroads, and fabulous hotels went hand in hand in those days: Developers had to provide transportation before they could attract visitors. At the end of the line, the visitors needed a place to stay. In Boca Grande, where a railroad had been built in 1906, the deep waters of Boca Grande Pass attracted Rockefellers, du Ponts, J. P. Morgan, and other industrialists who used the port for shipping phosphate from central Florida. To accommodate them, the graciously refined Gasparilla Inn was built in 1913.

Another man who was to influence the discovery and development of the Gulf Coast came to town in 1911. John M. Roach, Chicago streetcar magnate and owner of Useppa Island, introduced Barron Collier to the area. Collier eventually bought Useppa from his friend and there established the Useppa Inn and the Izaak Walton Club. Both attracted, according to local lore, tarpon-fishing enthusiasts such as Shirley Temple, Gloria Swanson, Mae West, Herbert Hoover, Zane Grey, and Mary Roberts Rinehart; the latter author then bought nearby Cabbage Key for her son and his bride.

Collier went on to infuse life into the southwest coast by underwriting the completion of the Tamiami Trail, stalled on its route from Tampa to Miami. He acquired land throughout

An exhibit at Manatee County Agricultural Museum in Palmetto illustrates the importance of commercial fishing to the region's economic development.

the county that today bears his name, after earlier attempts by Louisville publisher Walter Haldeman had failed to put Naples on the map.

Along the lower Gulf Coast of Florida, Collier bought more than one million acres, much of it under the infamous Swamp Act. Although he dreamed of development on the scale of Flagler and Plant, anticorporation outcry, hurricanes, the Depression, and war stymied his success. His sons inherited his kingdom, which they ruled with a heart for the unique environment their father so loved. Collier's influence increased awareness of the Gulf Coast as a refuge for crowd-weary stars and illuminati. Its islands still are popular with the rich and famous who seek anonymity.

But what about the ordinary people— Native Americans, fishermen, cattlemen, Crackers, pioneers, and common folk— who loved this land long before it became fashionable to do so? For the most part they lived side by side with this new brand of resident, called the "winterer" or "snowbird." (In Boca Grande they were termed "beachfronters" for their unusual-at-the-time idiosyncrasy of building dangerously close to the shore.) The locals became their fishing guides, cooks, and innkeepers. In some cases their heads were turned by brushes with great wealth. In other instances heightened standards pulled the curtain on cruder lifestyles, especially that of the cow hunter, whose boisterousness and preference for free-running stock hastened his extinction.

Sometimes the common folk protested big-bucks development and were classified as riffraff. The "Cracker" label today, despite the culture's enriching influence on architecture and cuisine, is considered an insult by some native Floridians.

Booms, Bursts, and Other Explosions

The Gulf Coast's resort reputation came of age at the turn of the 20th century. Sarasota's De Soto, the Hotel Charlotte Harbor, Boca Grande's Gasparilla Inn, the Useppa Inn, Fort Myers's Royal Palm Hotel, the Naples Hotel, and the Marco Inn pioneered in the hotel field, hosting visitors in styles ranging from bare bones to bend-over-backward. They sparked an era touched with Gatsby-type glamour, giddiness, and graciousness.

The Gulf Coast's halcyon days peaked in the early 1920s, as the state entered a decade known as the Great Florida Land Boom. Growth came quickly to the young communities of Bradenton, Sarasota, Fort Myers, and Naples. In fact, the good people of the Gulf Coast grew dizzy with the whirl of growth and success.

According to the 1910 census, Sarasota's population was 840; before the 1920s drew to a close, almost 8,400 people called it home. In the meantime the city shaped itself with sidewalks, streets, schools, a newspaper, a pier, an airfield, and the establishment of its own county, having split from Bradenton's Manatee County. A bridge to Siesta Key added a whole new element to the town's personality by plugging it into the gulf and attracting a seaside resort trade.

World War I briefly interfered. Prohibition brought to the coast yet another roguish character: the rumrunner. Homes and hotels popped up like toadstools after a summer rain shower. Increased lodging options opened the Gulf Coast to a wider range of vacationers. The average traveler could now afford Florida's Gulf Coast, no longer just a socialites' haven. A new class of winterer arrived in force, known as the tin-can tourist for the trailers and campers they pulled behind their vehicles. Tourist camps sprang up overnight, and southwest Florida became an Everyman's paradise. Real estate profits added to the lure of tourism, and many visitors decided to remain permanently.

The 1920s created Charlotte County along the Charlotte Harbor coast. A bridge was built across the Peace River, connecting the pioneer towns of Charlotte Harbor and Punta Gorda, spurring growth, and spawning subdivisions by the score.

Fort Myers became the seat of a new county named for Confederate General Robert E. Lee. Between 1920 and 1930, the population grew from 3,600 to 9,000, boosted by the completion of the Tamiami Trail in 1928. Fort Myers evolved from a raucous cattle town to a modern city with electricity (thanks to Edison), telephone lines, and a railroad. The Royal Palm Hotel treated guests to a regal departure from the cow trails that ran adjacent to the property. A country club put Fort Myers on the golfing map, and a bridge to Estero Island's beautiful beaches further boosted tourism. Real adventurers took the ferry to Sanibel Island, to be accommodated at Casa Ybel or the Palm Hotel.

South of Fort Myers, the farming community of Survey was renamed Bonita Springs. In 1923 Naples (previously a well-kept secret among buyers from such faraway places as Kentucky and Ohio and distinguished vacationers from the upper echelons) became a city, just in time to feel the effects of the tourism boom. The same year, Collier County seceded from Lee County. Everglades City became the first county seat; later, growing, thriving Naples took the honors. In 1927 the Naples Pier, which had served as a landing point for visitors and cargo since 1887, was replaced in importance by a railroad depot.

Gulf Coast skies had never been sunnier: Visitors spent lots of money. Residents prospered. Real estate prices soared. It seemed too good to be true. And indeed it was.

A 1926 hurricane hit Fort Myers, worsening a condition of already deepening debt. In Sarasota, John Ringling suffered severe financial losses from which he never recovered. On the southernmost coast, however, the national economy had little impact on the surge of interest sparked by the opening of the Tamiami Trail.

The Depression blunted the momentum with which the Gulf Coast had developed during the 1920s but in many ways affected the region less drastically than it did other parts of the country. Since it most tragically affected the middle class, wealthy Gulf Coast residents were largely spared. Works Progress Administration (WPA) recovery projects built Fort Myers its waterfront park, yacht basin, and the city's first hospital. The WPA also funded the building of Bayfront Park, a municipal auditorium, and the Lido Beach Casino along the Sarasota Bay coast. And despite serious financial problems, Ringling kept his promises to build bridges and an art museum.

By the beginning of World War II, southwest Florida had firmly joined the 20th century, with modern conveniences that made it popular among retirees. New golf courses accommodated active seniors, who often participated in the civic affairs of their adopted

Mina's Moonlight Garden at the Edison & Ford Winter Estates reflects the botanical fashion of the day, as commissioned by Edison's wife.

communities more vigorously than they had in those of their hometowns. Professional golf tournaments were introduced, first in Naples and then along the coast, making the area golf's winter home. Later, spring baseball camps brought another spectator sport to this land of year-round recreation.

Heat seekers turned their attention to the Gulf Coast's islands and beachfronts. Golfing communities and waterfront resorts swallowed up local farming and fishing industries. High-rise condominiums replaced Cracker houses, posh resorts toppled tourist fishing camps, and the Gulf Coast continued to grow—albeit not quite as loudly or erratically as in pre-Depression times.

Some areas learned to control their growth. Sanibel Island served as a model, taking grip of its fate after a causeway connected it to the mainland in 1963. It incorporated and introduced measures to protect wilderness areas and limit takeover by developers. The southward expansion of Interstate 75 during the 1970s and 1980s changed the Gulf Coast from a series of towns connected by two-lane roads to communities keeping pace with the world. Communication and transportation systems improved. Commercial development spread to the freeway corridor, leaving downtown areas to fade in bygone glory. Light industry and winter-weary entrepreneurs relocated. Postsecondary schools worked to pre-pare local youth for the changing marketplace. The construction and tourism industries continued to prosper.

The Gulf Coast remained seemingly untouched by the fluctuations of the American economy. Urban blight was a distant reality. Northerners fled to the Gulf Coast to escape overcrowding, smog, and crime. In previous decades this had caused unnatural develop-ment in some of the metropolitan areas. The delicate balance of infrastructure, human services, nature, heritage preservation, and the arts spun out of kilter. The coast lived very much in the present, deaf to the demands of residents, both human and otherwise.

Finally, though, the new trends of ecotourism and social responsibility amplified the voices of the few who had screamed over the decades for preservation of the environment against tourism and cultural sterility. While Sarasota and Naples served as cultural proto-types, Sanibel Island and Charlotte County provided environmental models. The 1990s brought an awareness of the frailty of the west coast's islands, wetlands, and shorelines. At the same time, interest in the area's history grew, and movements were launched to pre-serve architectural treasures that so far had been spared by the bulldozer. Eventually the dipping economic trends of the early 1990s affected the Gulf Coast. Construction slowed its racing pulse, and unemployment figures jumped as northerners continued to arrive, looking for jobs in this legendary land of treasure and youth.

All of these factors have contributed to the current perspective on the Gulf Coast. Economic fluctuations give city planners occasion to pause and rethink. Future growth is being mapped out with more care than ever before. Dying downtown neighborhoods and abandoned Cracker homes are being revitalized, now recognized as an important part of the area's heritage. Government is drawing into its blueprints the need for environmental preservation, cultural enrichment, and historic renovation. With the new millennium's economic boom came a more enlightened attitude that promises to return the sunshine to Gulf Coast skies, free of the recent past's dimming clouds.

However, in recent years, a new blight is having a profound effect on the pristine envi-ronment of Sanibel Island that once served as an environmental model. Nutrient runoff from sugar farming around Lake Okeechobee, in the center of the state, reaches the region's estuaries via the Caloosahatchee River. The resultant algae are killing sea grasses, thereby diminishing fish and bird populations in the sanctuary island and its environs. Grassroots movements struggle to remedy the situation and make plodding headway, hop-ing to reverse the damage before it's too late, hoping that the grain of sand and the man-grove pod from which this land was wrought will once again play a role in its future.

Coastal Culture

One of southwest Florida's great contradictions is that it lies more to the north than to the south on the cultural map. North of it or inland, you will find Deep South cookery, clog dancing, bluegrass music, and traditional Southern arts. In southwest Florida, however, Midwestern and Northeastern U.S. influences sway heavy. The only truly indigenous art forms have their origins in the Seminole Indian traditions of weaving, dancing, basket-making, and festivals. Other cultures have arrived through the centuries to create one of the nation's richest melting pots. African Americans, East Indians, Hispanics, Haitians, and Germans have most indelibly enriched the coastal makeup.

The arts have been heavily influenced through the years by the region's winter popula-tion. Many northern-based artists have relocated here, lured by the sea and tropical muses. Others bring with them their appetite for culture, sparking the finest in visual, performing, and culinary arts.

Southwest Florida Architecture

Years of simmering together Seminole, Cracker, "Yankee," and Caribbean traditions have yielded a unique southwest Florida style, particularly in architecture and cuisine. If one overall style could be said to represent local architecture, it would have to be Mediterranean—specifically, Italian and Spanish-mission forms.

Lumped together under the label "Mediterranean Revival," these southern European influences are found primarily in public and commercial buildings constructed during the boom years of the Roaring Twenties. They're revealed in stucco finish, mission arches, red barrel-tile roofing, bell towers, and rounded step façades. Re-revived Mediterranean Postmodern—updated Mediterranean Revival blended with elements of tropical styles adopted from the Cracker era—serves as a popular style for upscale housing developments and commercial enterprises.

Cracker vernacular runs a close architectural second. Pure Cracker style began as folk housing. From the single-pen home—a wood-frame one-room house featuring a shady veranda, a high tin roof, an elevated floor, and wood siding—grew more sophisticated interpretations of the style. With Gothic touches, Victorian embellishments, Palladian accents, and New England influences, the humble Cracker house evolved into a trendy, modern-day version termed "Old Florida." Boxy and built on stilts, its most distinctive characteristics include a tin roof and wide wraparound porch.

The latest influence on the Cracker house comes from the Caribbean and the Bahamas via the Keys. Since indigenous West Indian styles are greatly similar to Cracker, especially in their suitability to tropical weather, the convergence was inevitable. The result: sherbet colors and hand-carved fretwork—used as much for ventilation as for decoration—that add charm and whimsy to the basic unit.

Like the Cracker home, the Seminole Indians' chikee, or chickee (pronounced *chi-KEY*), hut conformed to the tropical climate with its high-peaked roof, wide overhangs, and open sides. Today the thatched roofing that is the chikee's most distinctive feature has become

A Seminole trademark, chickee huts have dotted the Everglades landscape since the Seminole Wars forced the Native Americans into the hostile swampland.

an art form. Still a popular style of housing for the Seminoles and Miccosukees of the Everglades, the chikee has evolved as a trademark of the Gulf Coast watering-hole tradition known as chikee, or tiki, bars.

With the mid-1920s influx of tin-can tourists, the mobile home replaced the Cracker house on the low end of the architectural totem pole. Mobile homes—homes that would "look a lot better as beer cans," according to an old Jimmy Buffett tune—still provide low-cost housing, mostly to part-time winter residents. The brutal winds of Hurricane Charley in 2004 went a long ways toward eliminating many of the structures. But despite their unsuitability, many mobile homes still remain.

The concrete-block ranch, a popular residential style of the 1970s, was built to withstand hurricanes. The flood regulations of the 1980s raised these up on pilings; lattice and fretwork added interest. Art Deco returned later in the decade, as Miami Beach's Art Deco District attracted attention.

Today's Gulf Coast towns are seasoned with period styles and spiced with contemporary looks that strive for compatibility with nature. Screened porches (often called lanais), windowed "Florida rooms," and lots of sliding doors let the outside in, taking full advantage of the unique, enviable climate and environment.

Coastal Cuisine

As for culinary *richesse*, southwest Florida has wowed hungry visitors since the first Europeans came ashore and discovered nature's abundantly stocked pantry. The seas were teeming with Neptune's bounty, and exotic fruits and vegetables flourished on land. In fact, one former Fort Myers newspaper columnist, Bob Morris, adheres to a theory that this was the original Paradise, and it was a sweet, luscious mango, not an apple, that caused Eve's downfall—hence the fruit's name: "Man! Go!"

Mangoes, though, are not actually native to southwest Florida but grow plentifully along with other naturalized tropical fruit: bananas, coconuts, pineapples, avocados, sapodillas, carambolas (star fruit), and lychees. Citrus fruit, particularly oranges, is of course the region's most visible and profitable crop. Key lime trees grow in profusion, as well. Practically year-round producers, they are a standard part of any good Florida cook's landscaping scheme. Here on the Gulf Coast, as in the Florida Keys, where the tree got its name and fame, key lime pie is a culinary paradigm, and each restaurant claims to make the best. In the finest restaurants with the most extravagant dessert menus, key lime pie inevitably outsells the rest. The classic recipe, created by Florida cooks before refrigeration, uses canned sweetened and condensed milk and is elegant in its simplicity. The most important factor is the freshness of the limes—sometimes a problem for restaurants since the fruit does not lend itself to commercial farming. One sure sign of an inauthentic version is the color green. Key limes turn yellow when ripe and, unless the cook adds food coloring, should impart a buttery hue to the pie.

Historically, crop farming has provided coastal residents with economic sustenance. Weather conditions bless farmers with two growing seasons for most ground crops. As land becomes too valuable to farm, agriculture has been pushed inland. Pine Island, known for its tropical fruits, is the region's final bastion of the agricultural tradition.

Seafood is most commonly associated with Gulf Coast cuisine, including some delicacies unique to Florida. Our prize catch, the stone crab (Florida author Marjorie Kinnan Rawlings once described the taste as being "almost as rare as nightingales' tongues"), was discovered as a food source in the Everglades. They are in season from October 15 through

Stone crab claws were "discovered" in the Everglades, and you don't find 'em any fresher than at local restaurants and fish markets.

May 15, and restaurants serve them hot with drawn butter or cold with tangy mustard sauce. Their aptly named shells are usually precracked to facilitate diners' enjoyment.

The gulf shrimp is an emblem of local cuisine. Its poorer cousin, the rock shrimp, gets less publicity because of its hard-to-peel shell. More economical and with a flavor and texture akin to lobster, the rock shrimp is certainly worth tasting. Restaurants change their menus—or at least their daily specials—according to what's in season. Grouper, the most versatile food fish in the area, traditionally has been available year-round, but environmental pressure is limiting its availability. A large and meaty fish, its taste is so mild that you hardly know it's fish. Winter months bring red and yellowtail snapper—my favorite—to diners' plates. Warmer weather means pompano, cobia, shark, and dolphinfish (also known as mahimahi). Tuna and flounder are caught year-round but sporadically. Some restaurants serve less well-known species, such as triggerfish and catfish, to offset spiraling costs caused by dwindling supplies of the more popular varieties. Fish farming also addresses these shortages. Catfish and a Brazilian fish called tilapia (which tastes similar to snapper) are cultivated most commonly. Fresh fish from around the world supplement local bounty.

The best Gulf Coast restaurants buy their seafood directly from the docks of local commercial fishermen to ensure the utmost freshness. The traditional style of cooking seafood in Florida is deep-frying. Although constituting a mortal sin in this age of gourmet standards and health awareness, it is a true art when properly executed. There's a vast difference between what you find in the frozen food department at the supermarket and what comes hand-breaded, crunchy, and flavor-sealed on your plate at the local fish house.

New Florida style, at the other extreme, has evolved from so-called California, new American, new world, and eclectic styles of cuisine. This type also depends on freshness—

of all its ingredients. For this reason it uses local produce, prepared in global culinary styles. Regional cookery—sometimes termed Gulfshore or Floribbean cuisine—prefers tropical foods and ingredients, inspired by the cuisines of New Orleans, Mexico, Cuba, Puerto Rico, Haiti, the Bahamas, Jamaica, and South America. Pacific Rim influences have become prominent in recent years. Depending on the cook, Deep South traditions take their place at the table, too. The outcome at its tamest merely twists the familiar; at its most adventurous, it can treat your taste buds to a veritable bungee jump.

Between the two extremes of old and new Florida styles, Continental cuisine survives in both classic and reinvented forms. Along with restaurants that serve the finest in French and Italian haute cuisine, you will find others that represent the Gulf Coast's melting pot, with authentic renditions or interpretations of a wide variety of cuisines: Native American, Thai, East Indian, Iranian, German, Irish, Greek, Cuban, Jamaican, Amish, Jewish, Mexican, and Puerto Rican.

In its cuisine and cultural makeup as well as its history, the map of Gulf Coast Florida resembles a patchwork quilt. It blankets its people in warmth, checkers its past with colorful and contrasting patterns, and layers its character with intriguing, international textures.

2

TRANSPORTATION

Blazing the Trail

The Gulf of Mexico and its great rivers and Intracoastal Waterway compose the region's oldest and lowest-maintenance transportation system. From the days when the Calusa paddled the streams and estuaries in dugout canoes, through the romantic steamboat era, and until 1927 when the railroad to Naples was completed, boat travel was the most popular means of getting around. Early homes lined the waterways, and historic houses face the water, not the roads that accommodate modern-day traffic. Even today the Caloosahatchee River, which empties into the sea along the Island Coast and connects to the east coast via Lake Okeechobee, constitutes part of a major intercoastal water route.

The railroad first came to Charlotte County's deepwater port in 1886 and created the town of Punta Gorda—much to the chagrin of Fort Myers's leaders, who had tried for years to persuade company officials to extend their Florida Southern Railroad to the Caloosahatchee River. Instead, an unpopulated location was selected and a fabulous hotel built there, according to the custom of Florida's great railroad builders of the day. Besides transporting wealthy winterers to the nation's southernmost railroad stop, the trains hauled fresh fish, cattle, and produce.

A train nicknamed "Slow and Wobbly" ran between Bradenton and Sarasota from 1892 to 1894. The Seaboard Railroad built a more reliable version to Bradenton in 1902. In 1911 it was extended beyond Venice, under the influence of Chicago socialite and major landholder Bertha Palmer. When Palmer named the railway terminus Venice, infuriated residents changed their town's name to Nokomis. Then the Charlotte Harbor and Northern Railway laid track in 1906 to ship phosphate from inland mines to the deep waters of Boca Grande Pass, off Gasparilla Island. Another refined resort came with it.

Fort Myers finally got its first railroad station in 1904. In 1922 the trestles reached Bonita Springs and were later extended to Naples and Marco Island. Famous passengers such as movie stars Hedy Lamarr, Greta Garbo, and Gary Cooper rode the rails to vacation at the posh Naples Beach Hotel & Golf Club, one of Florida's first resorts to boast golf greens on the property.

The concept of a Tamiami Trail made headway when, in 1923, a group called the Trail Blazers traveled the proposed route that would connect Tampa and Miami. Mules, oxen, and tractors were used to complete that first motorized crossing of the Everglades. Builders lived at the work site, and a whole body of legend grew up around the monumental task. Progress was slowed by dense jungles, forbidding swampland, devastating heat,

GULF COAST ACCESS

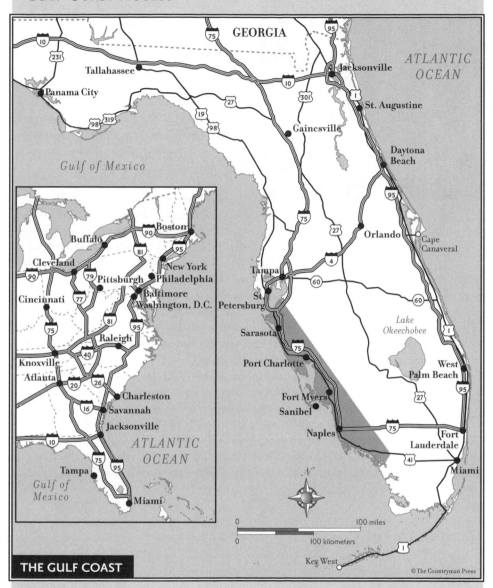

THE GULF COAST

© The Countryman Press

From Florida Cities

From	To Sarasota Bay	To Island Coast	To South Coast
Miami	212 mi./4.25 hr.	148 mi./2.5 hr.	110 mi./2 hr.
Orlando	132 mi./2.25 hr.	167 mi./3.5 hr.	187 mi./3.75 hr.
Daytona	185 mi./3.75 hr.	219 mi./4.25 hr.	241 mi./4.5 hr.
Jacksonville	239 mi./4.5 hr.	311 mi./6 hr.	325 mi./6.25 hr.

A growing museum gives new life to the old Naples Depot, where celebrities disembarked during the Roaring Twenties.

and mosquitoes so thick that they covered exposed skin like a buzzing body glove. The project was further hampered by war and depletion of funds. A special new dredge had to be invented to build the section across the Everglades. Before the trail was paved, it had a sand surface. Summer rains caused flooding. Old-timers remember getting out of the car to catch fish in the road while their parents worked to get their vehicle unstuck. Even after the rains subsided, jarring muck-crusted ruts made the trip less than comfortable.

As the trail's west coast leg inched toward its destination, it changed the communities it penetrated. Thirteen years in the building, the Tamiami Trail was met with euphoria when it was completed in 1928, opening communities to land travel, trade, and tourism. Today The Trail—also known as U.S. Highway 41—strings together the region's oldest towns and cities, and newer communities have grown up around it.

With the extension of parallel Interstate 75, the Tamiami Trail has lost its role as the sole intercoastal lifeline. Nonetheless, it remains the backbone of the lower west coast. Probing both metropolitan interiors and rural vistas, it provides glimpses of a cross-section of life—as it was and as it is—in southwest Florida.

Highway 41 runs through the middle of the area covered in this book. At the Gulf Coast's northern and southern extremes, the highway edges close to the shoreline. In midsections it reaches inland to communities built along harbors and rivers.

Interstate 75 draws the eastern boundary for this guide's coverage. The freeway glimpses, at top speed, Gulf Coast life as it zips into the 21st century. Although convenient and free of traffic lights, it misses the character that the more leisurely pace of the Tamiami Trail reveals. However, it does extend the boundaries of Highway 41's family of communities and create new ones.

GETTING TO THE COAST

By Car

Southwest Florida is plugged into Florida's more highly charged areas by both major conduits and small feeders. Tampa/St. Petersburg lies at the Sarasota Bay coast's back door, via U.S. Highway 41, Interstate 75, and Interstate 275. The Tamiami Trail ends here, but Highway 41 continues on. The interstate proceeds north and connects to Orlando and the east coast via Interstate 4. Highway 19 takes up the coastal route in St. Petersburg, heading toward Georgia. Highway 70 cuts across the state above Lake Okeechobee to connect the east coast to the Sarasota Bay coast at Bradenton, and at Sarasota and Punta Gorda via Routes 72 and 17 respectively. These roads meander into Native American reservation territory, Arcadia's cowboy country, and the expansive Myakka River State Park. The route runs jaggedly among the Island Coast, the big lake, and West Palm Beach, following a series of lazy two- and four-lane roads, including Routes 80, 27, 441, and 98.

Alligator Alley (Interstate 75) crosses the Everglades with a certain mystique. Once a two-lane toll road on which encounters with crossing gators and panthers were common (tragically, cars inevitably fared better in such encounters), today I-75 has been widened to four lanes, with underpasses for wildlife. At certain times of the year, it continues to earn its name, and a sharp eye can spot hundreds of gators sunning on water banks. But it's still a toll road and still less than user-friendly. Gas up before you approach: Fuel station/restaurant exit breaks are few and far between on the two-hour drive until it reaches the east coast at Fort Lauderdale. Highway 41 takes you into Miami and branches off into Highway 1 to the Florida Keys.

By Plane

Two major airports service the lower Gulf Coast: **Sarasota-Bradenton International Airport** (SRQ) and **Southwest Florida International** (RSW) in Fort Myers. The Sarasota-Bradenton facility gives a proper introduction to the region, with shark tanks and tropical orchids from local attractions, a two-story waterfall, and works from its prolific artist community. Southwest Florida recently expanded from 17 gates to 28. A new runway is in the planning.

Smaller airports and fields service shuttle, charter, and private planes. The Charlotte County airport caters mainly to private craft. North Captiva Island and Everglades City have their own landing strips for private planes, and seaplane service is available to some islands.

Sarasota-Bradenton International Airport (SRQ), 941-359-2770, 941-359-2777; www.srq-airport.com; 6000 Airport Circle, Sarasota 34243. AirTran, American Eagle, CanJet, Continental, Delta, JetBlue, Northwest/KLM, US Airways.

Charlotte County Airport (PGD), 888-700-2232 or 941-639-1101; www.charlottecounty airport.com; 28000 Airport Rd., Punta Gorda 33982.

Tamiami Trail bridges cross the wide Peace River from Punta Gorda to Port Charlotte.

Southwest Florida International Airport (RSW), 239-768-1000; www.flylcpa.com; 11000 Terminal Access Rd., Fort Myers 33913. Air Canada, Air Tran, American, Cape Air, Continental, Delta, Frontier, JetBlue, LTU International, Midwest Express, Northwest/KLM, Spirit Airlines, Sun Country, United, USA 3000, US Airways, WestJet.

Naples Municipal Airport (APF), 239-643-0733; www.flynaples.com; 160 Aviation Dr. N., Naples 34104. Delta Connection.

Marco Island Executive Airport (MKY), 239-394-3355; www.colliergov.net; Collier County Airport Authority, 2003 Mainsail Dr., Naples 34114.

By Bus
Greyhound Lines (www.greyhound.com) Depots are found along the west coast at Bradenton (941-747-2986; 3028 First St. W.), Sarasota (941-955-5735; 575 North Washington Blvd.), Port Charlotte (941-627-5836; 900 Kings Hwy.), Punta Gorda (941-875-2781; 26505 N. Jones Loop), Fort Myers (941-334-1011; 2250 Peck St.), and Naples (941-774-5660; 2669 Davis Blvd.).

GETTING AROUND THE GULF COAST

By Car
BEST ROUTES
The **Tamiami Trail** (Highway 41) forms the heart of the Gulf Coast's major metropolitan areas and provides north-south passage within and between them.

Early guests to Sanibel's historic Island Inn arrived by wagon, as portrayed in this circa-1910 photo. Island Inn

SARASOTA BAY COAST

In Bradenton and Sarasota, Highway 41 runs along bay shores and converges with Highway 301, another major trunk road. Principal through streets for east-west traffic in this area are generally those with exits off Interstate 75, north to south: Manatee Avenue (Route 64), Carter Road (Route 70), University Parkway (closest to the Ringling Museums), Fruitville Road (closest to downtown and the islands), Bee Ridge Road (closest to Siesta Key), Clark Road (Route 72), and Venice Avenue. Note that in 2002 Florida interstate exit numbers changed to correspond with actual mileage rather than numerical order. Old exit numbers are still noted on the exit signs, along with the new numbers.

Bradenton's 75th Street West (De Soto Memorial Highway) skims the town's western reaches close to the bay front. At exit 220 (old 42), Route 64 travels straight into downtown and out to Anna Maria Island. From the south, take exit 217 (old 41) and follow Route 70 to Highway 41. Head north on Highway 41, then turn west on Route 684 (Cortez Road/44th Avenue), which takes you across the south bridge. Both bridges lead to Gulf Drive (Route 789), the island's main road. Longboat Key lies to the south of Anna Maria Island, across a bridge, along Gulf of Mexico Drive. Lido Key is connected to Longboat Key by yet another bridge and also by bridge from the mainland in downtown Sarasota.

Streets hiccup through downtown Sarasota, starting and stopping without warning. Main Street runs east-west, crossed by Orange Avenue, one of the neighborhood's longest streets. Bayfront Drive arcs around the water and skirts a lot of the town's water-based recreation action. Bahia Vista intersects Orange at its southern extreme and constitutes a major route. To cross town from north to south between Highway 41 and Interstate 75, take Tuttle Avenue, Beneva Road, McIntosh Road, or Cattlemen Road.

To get to St. Armands Key and Lido Key from downtown Sarasota, follow the signs on Tamiami Trail to cross the Ringling Causeway, which recently replaced a drawbridge with a high span. To reach Siesta Key from I-75, take exit 205 (old 37/Clark Road) or 207 (old 38/Bee Ridge Road). From Bee Ridge Road, turn north on Highway 41 and west on Siesta Drive, which leads to the north bridge. Clark Road (Route 72) crosses the south bridge and becomes Stickney Point Road. On Siesta's north end, Higel Avenue and Ocean Boulevard are the main routes into the shopping district. Beach Road runs gulfside and intersects with Midnight Pass Road, which travels to the island's south end, intersecting Stickney Point Road.

Take Venice Avenue off Interstate 75 to get to Venice's beaches and old Mediterranean-influenced neighborhoods. Highway 41's business route splits from the Tamiami Trail at Venice and takes you to the older part of town. Harbor Drive travels north-south along the beaches. The Esplanade and Tarpon Center Road reach into waterfront communities.

CHARLOTTE HARBOR COAST

Highway 41 heads inland, running within miles of Interstate 75 at some points. In these parts getting to the gulf entails crossing several bodies of water. Most of the routes qualify as back roads and are listed under that heading. A toll bridge links Gasparilla Island (Boca Grande) to the mainland; it costs $4 for cars to cross, $1 for bicycles.

ISLAND COAST

Bonita Beach is touted as the closest sands to Interstate 75 in this area. Highway 41 again distances itself from its modern counterpart to take you into downtown business districts and past upscale golfing communities. Pine Island Road, Route 78, diverges from the major arteries and crosses North Fort Myers and Cape Coral to reach Pine Island. Del Prado Boulevard and Cape Coral Parkway, which intersect, are Cape Coral's main commercial routes; downtown Cape Coral, which city officials are intent on defining these days, runs along Cape Coral Parkway north of Del Prado. Stringfellow Road, which lies at the end of Pine Island Road, is Pine Island's principal north-south artery.

On the south side of the Caloosahatchee Bridge, Fort Myers's main east-west connectors are Martin Luther King Jr. Boulevard, Colonial Boulevard (which feeds into the Mid-Point Toll Bridge to Cape Coral), College Parkway (which also crosses the river between Fort Myers and Cape Coral at Cape Coral Parkway with a toll), and Daniels Parkway/Gladiolus Drive, which is also the airport exit. Traveling roughly from north to south, historic and royal-palm-lined McGregor Boulevard (Route 867) follows the river past the old homes that line it. Summerlin Road (Route 869) and Metro Parkway run parallel, to the east. The Tamiami Trail, also parallel and sandwiched between Summerlin Road and Metro Parkway, becomes Cleveland Avenue. Take McGregor or Summerlin west (they eventually merge) to get to Sanibel and Captiva Islands, land of no traffic lights. There's a $6 toll for crossing the bridge to Sanibel without a transponder gate-pass gizmo; stay in the right lanes unless you have one. The drawbridge was replaced by a high span in 2007. Periwinkle Way is Sanibel's main drag and connects to Sanibel-Captiva Road via Tarpon Bay Road. Policemen with white gloves direct traffic at the main intersections during high-traffic hours. Sanibel-Captiva Road turns into Captiva Drive at the pass between the two islands. San Carlos Boulevard off Summerlin Road takes you to Fort Myers Beach and the islands that lie to its south along Route 865 (Estero Boulevard in Fort Myers Beach, Hickory Boulevard in Bonita Beach). Alico Road exit 128 off of I-75 also has airport access and takes you to San Carlos Park; Corkscrew Road (Route 850) exit 123, to the south, goes to Estero.

SOUTH COAST

Here, Highway 41 (also known as Ninth Street) closes in on the sea once again as it travels through Naples. At Bonita Springs, Old Highway 41 branches off toward the town's business district. Bonita Beach Road (exit 116/old exit 18) crosses Highway 41 to travel to Bonita Beach. I-75 exit 111 (old 17) gets you to the Vanderbilt Beach/North Naples area via Route 846; exit 107 (old 16) dumps you into Pine Ridge Road, which leads to the north end of Naples. Interstate 75 then swings east, so that Route 951 at exit 101 (old exit 15) is closer to downtown Naples in a north-west direction but farther in an east-west direction. Depending on the time of year, you're sometimes better off taking exit 107 (old exit 16) to Highway 41 when approaching from the north, then heading south to get downtown. When coming from the south, take exit 101 and hook up with Highway 41. Plans are to widen Interstate 75 in these parts, but for now traffic slows to a crawl from Fort Myers through Naples at rush hour and in season.

Parallel to Highway 41 in Naples, major city dissectors include Goodlette-Frank Road (Route 851) and Airport-Pulling Road (Route 31). East-west trunks are, from north to south, the Naples-Immokalee Highway (Route 846) at the north edge of town; Pine Ridge Road (Route 896), Golden Gate Parkway (Route 886), Radio Road (Route 856), and Davis Boulevard (Route 84) in town; and Rattlesnake Hammock Road (Route 864) at the southern extreme.

To get to Marco Island from the north, take Route 951 (interstate exit 101), which will take you to the main high bridge at the island's north end. Route 951 becomes Collier

Boulevard and continues through the island's commercial section and along the gulf front. Bald Eagle Drive (Route 953) heads north-south to Olde Marco and mid-island. It connects to San Marco Drive (Route 92), which crosses the south bridge. The south-end bridge is a better access if you're approaching from the east along Highway 41. Turn southwest off Highway 41 onto Route 92 to cross the south bridge.

Route 29 takes you from Highway 41 to Everglades City. Take a right onto Camellia Street to get to School Drive along the river, lined with old fishing boats, stacks of crab traps, and fish houses. Copeland Avenue crosses the causeway to Choko-loskee Island.

Ed Frank (second from far right) invented the swamp buggy, an amphibious form of transportation engineered for travel in the Everglades. He poses here in 1947 with his brainchild and his hunting buddies. Collier County Historical Society, Inc.

ALTERNATE BACK ROADS AND SCENIC ROUTES

This section of Gulf Coast has many scenic back roads that bypass traffic and plunge the traveler into timeless scenes and unique neighborhoods. These routes are especially good to know when you tire of counting out-of-state license plates during rush hour in high season.

SARASOTA BAY COAST

Follow the twisty road through a string of barrier islands, from Anna Maria in the north to Bird Key at the end. Route 789 adopts a different name on each island: John Ringling Parkway, Gulf of Mexico Drive, and so on. To avoid Highway 41 traffic between downtown Sarasota and Siesta Key, turn west onto Orange Avenue, follow it through scenic neighborhoods along McClellan and Osprey Avenues to Siesta Drive, and then turn west again. Route 758, along Siesta Key, makes a short, beachy bypass between Siesta Drive and Stickney Point Road. The loop through lovely Casey Key begins between Sarasota and Venice at Blackburn Point Road, off Highway 41, then proceeds south through Nokomis Beach and back to the mainland.

CHARLOTTE HARBOR COAST

To reach Englewood from Venice, cross quiet, out-of-the-way Manasota Key along Route 776 through Englewood Beach. Then follow Routes 775 and 771 back to Route 776 for a scenic drive through the peninsula, separated from the mainland by Charlotte Harbor, or to get to Gasparilla Island. (It costs $4 to cross the causeway onto the island.) Park Avenue is the shopper's route in Boca; Gulf Boulevard takes you to the beaches. Staying on 776 takes you more directly to Highway 41. To skirt Highway 41's chain-outlet anonymity in the Port Charlotte area, take Collingswood Boulevard off 776 to Edgewater Drive and back to 41.

Between Charlotte County and the Island Coast, Route 765, or Burnt Store Road, was once the locals' secret bypass, but it is becoming clogged with developments and the trucks it takes to build them. This connects to Highway 78, which leads to Pine Island when taken west or to Highway 41 and I-75 when followed east. To enter Cape Coral the back way, follow Burnt Store Road through the Highway 78 intersection to Veterans' Parkway, then to Chiquita Boulevard, turn right and then left on Cape Coral Parkway.

ISLAND COAST
The back roads along the Island Coast's shores plunge you briefly into the frenzied activity of Fort Myers Beach along Routes 968 (San Carlos Boulevard) and 865 (Estero Boulevard), then carry you along at a more mellow pace as you cross into Lovers Key and Big and Little Hickory Islands, where 865 becomes Hickory Boulevard. Traffic creeps along this two-laner at high-season rush hours. The road returns you via Bonita Beach Road to Highway 41 at Bonita Springs.

SOUTH COAST
Gulfshore Boulevard, which stops and starts to make way for Naples's waterways, is the town's most scenic route, skirting beaches and beautiful homes.

South of Naples, Routes 951, 952, and 953 carry you to Isles of Capri, Marco Island, Goodland, and back to Highway 41 just before the Everglades.

CAR RENTALS
Rental agencies with airport offices or shuttle service are listed below:

Alamo: 800-462-5266; www.alamo.com (SRQ, 941-359-5540; RSW, 239-768-2424)

Avis: 800-331-1212; www.avis.com (SRQ, 941-359-5240; RSW, 239-768-2121; APF, 239-643-0900)

Sunset over the new Sanibel Island Causeway

Budget: 800-527-7000; www.budget.com (SRQ 941-359-5353; RSW, 239-768-1500)

Dollar: 800-800-4000; www.dollarcar.com (SRQ, 941-355-2996; APF, 239-793-2226)

Hertz: 800-654-3131; www.hertz.com (SRQ, 941-355-8848; RSW, 239-768-3100; APF, 239-643-1515)

National: 800-227-7368; www.nationalcar.com (SRQ, 941-355-7711; RSW, 239-768-2100)

Thrifty: 800-367-2277; www.thrifty.com (RSW, 239-768-2322)

Airport Taxis/Shuttles

Some hotels and resorts arrange pickup service to and from the airport. Taxi and limousine companies operate in most areas.

Taxi companies that provide transportation to and from the Bradenton-Sarasota airport include **Diplomat Taxi** (941-355-5155), **West Coast Executive Sedans** (941-355-9645, 941-359-8600), and **Longboat Limousine** (941-383-1235, 800-525-4661; www.longboat limousine.com). **Blue Sky Airport Limo Service** (941-484-9796, 800-637-6358 out-of-state; www.blueskylimo.net) serves passengers arriving at SRQ and RSW. For more companies that service the Bradenton-Sarasota airport, call 941-383-1235 or 800-525-4661.

Boca **Grande Limousine** (239-964-0455, 800-771-7433; www.bocagrandelimo.com) provides 24-hour connections to all Florida airports. For a more dramatic arrival or departure, call **Boca Grande Seaplane** (941-964-0234, 800-940-0234). **Charlotte Limousine Service** (800-208-6106 or 941-627-4494; www.charlottelimousine.com) will pick up from and deliver to all airports in the region. **Airport Limo & Car Service** (800-954-9404; www.airportlimoandcarservice.com) has a fleet that includes Lincolns and SUVs.

From Southwest Florida International Airport in Fort Myers, **Aaron Airport Transportation** (239-768-1898, 800-998-1898) makes pickups and deliveries throughout the region. Or call **AAA Airport Transportation** (800-872-2711). **Pine Island Taxi** (239-283-7777) provides 24-hour service anywhere with advance notice.

In the south coast area, call **Checker Cab** (239-455-5555), **Naples Taxi** (239-643-2148), or, on Marco Island, **A-Action** (239-394-4000).

By Bus

The Sarasota Bay coast boasts dependable public transportation, with discounts for schoolchildren and seniors. Buses run every day but Sunday, 6AM to 6PM. A downtown trolley runs around Sarasota and St. Armands Circle. For route information, call **Sarasota County Area Transit** (SCAT) (941-861-1234) or **Manatee County Transit** (MCAT) (941-749-7116; www.co.manatee.fl.us).

On the Island Coast, city buses follow routes around Fort Myers, Cape Coral, and south Fort Myers. Call **Lee Tran** (239-533-8726; www.leetran.com) for schedules and information about trolley rides to and around Fort Myers Beach's beach accesses, including Lovers Key.

The **Naples Trolley** (239-262-7300; www.naplestrolleytours.com) conducts sightseeing and shopping tours in the Naples area, with 23 scheduled stops. The **Marco Island Trolley** (239-394-1600) visits 13 different historical sites. **Collier Area Transit (CAT)** (239-596-7777; www.colliergov.net) travels throughout Naples and Marco Island.

By Carriage

Bogart Carriage (941-744-2340) does rides around St. Armands Circle in Sarasota.

The **Naples Horse and Carriage Company** (239-649-1210) provides evening tours of Old Naples, the beaches, and the fishing pier in season.

By Train

The **Seminole Gulf Railway** (239-275-8487, 800-SEM-GULF; www.semgulf .com), stationed at the corner of Colonial Boulevard and Metro Parkway in Fort Myers, does dinner trips, Murder Mystery Tours, and other excursions throughout the area.

Don't let winter-season traffic ruffle your feathers. Hit the scenic back roads.

By Water

Water no longer provides functional transportation routes on the Gulf Coast, except to the unbridged islands. Today boat travel is mostly recreational. The region boasts two trademark water vessels: the noisy, power-driven **airboat,** designed especially for the shallow waters of the Everglades, and the **swamp buggy,** an all-terrain vehicle built to carry 2 to 20 passengers and travel on fat tire treads. In addition, **pontoon boats** offer a more conventional way to explore the Everglades and coastal shallows.

Numerous sightseeing tours and charters originate daily at marinas and resorts. Some specialize in fishing, others in shelling or birding. Many include lunch at an exotic island restaurant, while a few serve meals on board. All cater to the sightseer. Most tour operators are knowledgeable about sights and history on local waterways. These are all listed in the "Recreation" section of each chapter.

3

Sarasota Bay Coast

Seashore Sophisticate

The cities of Bradenton and Sarasota dominate the Sarasota Bay coast, an expanse of metropolitan sprawl barricaded behind sybaritic, beach-centric islands. History and a heritage of high culture add dimension to this world of sand and city streets.

Bradenton draws much of its historical identity from the supposed landing of Hernando de Soto on local shores. Old Hernando—scoundrel and sadist though he turned out to be—gives the town a reason to celebrate its heritage each year when it reenacts his momentous arrival at a national park that honors the Indian-slaying conquistador.

Later in the history of Bradenton and the surrounding mainland communities, two pioneering influences dictated a low-key attitude and light development. The first, the wealthy plantation owners of the 1840s, ranked Manatee County as the largest area in the state for sugar and molasses production. Sugar's aristocratic families set the social standards of the town until the Civil War turned the sweetly lucrative industry sour. The second, 19th-century land speculators, exploited Florida's Swamp Act, which had a counterproductive, stunting effect on the area's development. By having homestead properties fraudulently declared wetlands, they prevented agricultural expansion and delayed its by-product, the building of railroads.

Sunrise at Sarasota's harbor

Wealthy social godparents guided Sarasota's early development. Mrs. Potter (Bertha Honore) Palmer, known as "queen of Chicago society," settled south of town in 1910, which eventually drew John Ringling and his circus to Sarasota. Though lesser known today, Mrs. Palmer exerted an influence equal to Ringling's in attracting attention to the area around Sarasota Bay. Sarasota continues to grow as a wealth-conscious town—not too big, not too small, just right. In past years, growth has been upward, as the downtown bayside

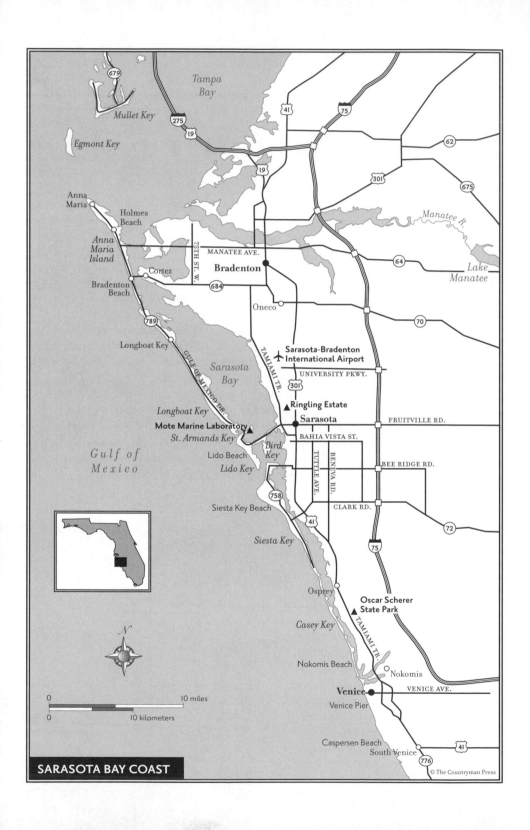

SARASOTA BAY COAST

skyline fills in with luxury condo and resort towers, the Ritz-Carlton and Renaissance among them. In 2006, the National Civic League included Sarasota County among its "All-American County" designations.

Most of **Bradenton's** modern growth has occurred since 1970, when tourism and shipping into deepwater Port Manatee became major income sources. Today, downtown waterfront restoration projects and a new artists' colony make Bradenton a vital city textured with an interesting past.

Across the Manatee River, preservation of the Gamble Plantation and original village structures, along with the development of long-sleepy, agriculturally driven **Palmetto**, extends Bradenton-area visitors' options to include more historic attractions and riverfront activity.

The village of **Cortez** lies southwest of Bradenton and several eras to the past. Fishing made this peninsular community, and fishing remains its livelihood. Along its southern waterfront, a working fishing operation and its toilers reside in a time-stilled setting.

Fishing, resorts, and heterogeneous neighborhoods mark the three incorporated towns of **Anna Maria Island**: **Anna Maria**, **Holmes Beach**, and **Bradenton Beach**. The first Anna Maria Island settlers of record, George Emerson Bean and his family, arrived around 1890. He developed the island in the early 1900s for tourists, who came by boat at the Anna Maria City pier. In 1921 the first bridge to the island was built from Cortez.

Longboat Key, to the south of Anna Maria Island, was mentioned often on the maps and journals of early Spanish explorers. It supposedly got its name from the longboats that Hernando de Soto's scouting party used to come ashore. Aside from one tucked-away village with a salty, local flavor, Longboat Key is known for its prim-and-properness. A series of seven historic markers relate Longboat Key's history as a 16th-century destination for Timucuan canoes and Spanish galleons, a World War II bombing target, and a major shipping port destroyed by the hurricane of 1921.

Remote **Siesta Key** resisted settlement until the turn of the 20th century, when a hotel launched the island's reputation as a restful place. A bridge built in 1917 finally brought

Old fishing traditions endure in the village of Cortez.

permanent residents to the island. Siesta Key has historically attracted creative types. One of its best-known citizens was prolific writer John D. Macdonald, most famous for his Travis McGee detective novels. It is believed that while living on Siesta Key he wrote more than 70 novels. Witty essayist E. B. White was a regular visitor around the 1940s. Pulitzer Prize–winning author MacKinlay Kantor and late abstractionist Syd Solomon also settled on the island, and Pulitzer Prize–winning cartoonist Mike Peters lived there for many years. Other cartoonists and artists have also found the area conducive to creativity. *Hagar the Horrible*'s Dik Browne made his home in the area until his death in 1989; now his son Chris has moved in. *Garfield*'s Jim Davis has wintered on Longboat Key. Surrealist Jimmy Ernst, son of Dada master Max Ernst, spent much time on Casey Key during his life. Artist Thornton Utz and jazz notable Jerry Jerome have also lived in the area.

The Webb family first arrived in the Sarasota area in 1867 to plant the seed for a town they named **Osprey** 17 years later. Here is where Bertha Honore Palmer headquartered when she arrived in 1910.

The original village of **Venice** sat where Nokomis does today. Venice moved south and seaward to its current location after the railroad bypassed it in 1922. Actually an island separated from the mainland by narrow waterways, the original Venice reflects the influence of John Ringling and visionary urban planner John Nolen, who was hired by the Brotherhood of Locomotive Engineers union after it purchased much of the town in the 1920s.

Casey Key was built on the principle that island real estate should be reserved for the well-to-do. This has kept it exclusive and lightly developed, particularly at its north end, where a narrow road snakes through a forest of mansions à la Palm Beach. Nokomis Beach, at the southern end, is a more casual, beachy, fishing-oriented resort area.

The Sarasota area has conveniently organized its environmental and historical attractions on a *Gulf Coast Heritage Trail* map, available at visitor information centers around town or by calling 941-359-5841.

Lodging

Most vacationers on the Sarasota Bay coast gravitate toward the barrier islands. On Siesta Key you won't find chain hotels; however, you will find accommodations large and small by the score. The other islands have their chains but more mom-and-pops, B&Bs, inns, destination resorts, and privately owned places. On the mainland, especially around the airport, business travelers find no-nonsense franchise and small motels. A couple of luxury options have opened in recent years: a Ritz-Carlton in 2001 and Hotel Indigo, the boutique branch of InterContinetal Hotels Group, in 2006. With downtown Sarasota's renewal, more and more vacationers are choosing mainland accommodations.

Privately owned second homes and condominiums provide another source of accommodations along the Sarasota Bay coast. Vacation brokers who match visitors with such properties are listed under "Home and Condo Rentals," at the end of this section.

I've listed here a well-rounded selection of Sarasota-area accommodations, including a few of the better chain hotels. Toll-free 800, 888, 866, or 877 reservation numbers, where available, are listed after local numbers.

Pricing codes are explained below. They are normally per person/double occupancy for hotel rooms and per unit for efficiencies, apartments, cottages, suites, and villas. The range spans low- and high-season rates. Many resorts offer off-season packages at special rates and free lodging for children. Pricing does not include the 6 percent Florida sales tax or Sarasota County's 4 percent tourist tax, which is allotted to beach revitalization, arts funding, and tourism promotion. Some large resorts add service gratuities or maid surcharges.

Rate Categories

Inexpensive	Up to $75
Moderate	$75 to $150
Expensive	$150 to $200
Very Expensive	$200 and up

(An asterisk after the pricing designation indicates that the rate includes at least a continental breakfast in the cost of lodging and possibly more extensive meal service as noted in the listing.)

The following abbreviations are used for credit card information:

AE: American Express
MC: MasterCard
D: Discover Card
V: Visa
DC: Diners Club

Note that under the Americans with Disabilities Act (ADA), accommodations built after January 26, 1993, and containing more than five rooms must be useable by persons with disabilities. I have indicated only those small places that do not make such allowances.

Accommodations

ANNA MARIA
ROD & REEL MOTEL
Office Manager: Janet Hoffmann
941-778-2780
www.rodandreelmotel.com
877 North Shore Dr., P.O. Box 1939, Anna Maria Island 34216
Price: Moderate to Expensive

Credit Cards: MC, V
Partial handicap access

This motel sits prettily on a narrow slab of bayside beach, with flowery landscaping, shuffleboard, picnic facilities, a sunning deck, and a tiki-roofed pavilion. Each of the 10 one-room efficiencies is fully furnished with a kitchenette (microwave, stovetop, and refrigerator), ironing board, couch, plastic dining room chairs, and spic-and-span housekeeping. The motel is next to the independently owned Rod & Reel Pier.

BRADENTON
✪ **HOLIDAY INN RIVERFRONT**
General Manager: Tom Jung
941-747-3727, 800-23-HOTEL
www.bradentonholidayinn.com
100 Riverfront Dr. W., Bradenton 34205
Price: Moderate to Expensive
Credit Cards: AE, D, DC, MC, V

Perched riverside, this is mainland Bradenton's loveliest property, pertly landscaped and designed to mesh with Bradenton's Spanish colonial heritage. Dark, heavy wood and wrought iron embellish the striking atrium lobby, off which lies a pleasant fountain courtyard dripping with hibiscus and oleander blossoms. Here you'll also find the pool and spa and the entrance to the hotel's restaurants and bars. A few steps away flows the Manatee River, edged by Bradenton Waterfront Park. Other amenities include a tiny fitness center and free wireless Internet access. All 153 dark-wood rooms and suites in the five-story hotel have narrow private balconies that overlook the river or courtyard and are stocked with coffeemakers and hair dryers; the suites have wet bars and refrigerators.

BRADENTON BEACH
BRIDGEWALK
Operations Manager: David Baldwin

941-779-2545, 866-779-2545
www.silverresorts.com
100 Bridge St., Bradenton Beach 34217
Price: Moderate to Very Expensive
Credit Cards: AE, D, MC, V
No handicap access

Key West–Caribbean in look, it colorfully
houses 28 studio suites, townhouses, and
mini apartments in three tin-roofed low
rises along the town's historic district.
Units are comfortably spacious with full or
minikitchens. Deluxe touches include
granite countertops, Jacuzzi tubs in some
units, and gulf views from one of the buildings. The resort also houses upscale shops,
eateries, and a day spa along the street. The
beach is a short walk across the street, and
a heated pool in the parking area cools off
guests on property.

SEASIDE INN & RESORT

Property Manager: Aaron C. Huffman
941-778-5254, 800-447-7124
www.seasideresort.com
2200 Gulf Dr. N., Bradenton Beach 34217
Price: Moderate to Very Expensive
Credit Cards: D, MC, V

Like the rest of Bradenton Beach, things
are constantly looking better here. Spotless and decorated with charm, the seven
efficiencies and three rooms have tiled
bathrooms and modern kitchen facilities:
toasters, refrigerators, and microwaves,
with stovetops in the efficiencies. Lovely
trompe l'oeil touches brighten white
walls. The penthouse (expensive to very
expensive) has a separate bedroom and
luxury appointments, and it can connect
to two other rooms for large family gatherings. Each room looks out on the gulf
with a patio or deck balcony, and the inn
has its own private walled beach, above
the public beach. Use of kayaks is
complimentary to guests. It's a good value
for beachside lodging with pleasant
amenities.

HOLMES BEACH
CEDAR COVE RESORT & COTTAGES

Innkeeper: Eric Carnes
941-778-1010, 800-206-6294
2710 Gulf Dr. N., Holmes Beach 34217
www.cedarcoveresort.com
Price: Moderate to Expensive
Credit Cards: MC, V

You have to love this place's casual, carefree
beachside attitude, but what I like most is
its sense of humor. As you walk up to the
office, a facsimile of a margarita teases you.
A sign offers the day's special—free margar-
itas—adding in small print, "yesterday."
The Nut House out back looks like a
Gilligan or Moondoggie kind of place to
hang out. Every one of the 22 one- and two-
bedroom suites comes with a kitchen, along
with surprises such as the scope and the
pinball machine in the two-bedroom villa.
Run by a Florida native, the resort has a feel
that is right on and conducive to the resort's
two rules: "zero stress, 100 percent relaxation."

✪ HARRINGTON HOUSE B&B

Innkeepers: JoAdele and Frank Davis and
Mark and Patti Davis
941-778-5444, 888-828-5566
5626 Gulf Dr., Holmes Beach 34217
www.harringtonhouse.com
Price: Expensive to Very Expensive (two-
night minimum weekends and holidays)
Credit Cards: MC, V

One of Florida's loveliest and best-
maintained bed-and-breakfasts,
Harrington adds to its homey, historic
allure with a beachfront. Built in 1925 of
local coquina rock and pecky cypress, with
Mediterranean flourishes, the Main House
was refurbished with casual elegance and
magical touches. Each of the seven rooms—
such as Renaissance, Birdsong, and
Sunset—is labeled with a needlepoint door
sign. Room sizes vary from spacious, with a
king-sized bed, to comfortably cozy. Each

guest room has its own bathroom, refrigerator, and TV. An eclectic collection of hand-picked antique furniture enhances guests' comfort. A dramatic cut-stone fireplace dominates the sitting room, where classical music recordings are interrupted only by an occasional piano solo and homemade chocolate chip cookies in the afternoon. Guests enjoy gourmet home-cooked breakfasts at individual tables amid Victorian pieces and filmy white curtains. Outdoor areas include sundecks, a pool, a wide beach, and charmingly colorful landscaping around picket fences and arched alcoves. Nine more suites, some with Jacuzzi-style tubs and fireplaces, occupy three beach houses down the beach. Bikes and kayaks are available for guests' use.

LIDO KEY

HISTORIC GULF BEACH RESORT MOTEL

General Manager: Sue Culpepper
941-388-2127, 800-232-2489
www.gulfbeachsarasota.com
930 Ben Franklin Dr., Sarasota 34236
Price: Moderate to Expensive
Credit Cards: D, MC, V

Just a couple of doors down from the towering Lido Beach Resort, Gulf Beach takes you to a circa-1950 era of Florida vacationing. All 49 rooms of this "condo-tel" are privately owned and therefore decorated with individual personality. They range from tiny motel rooms with minifridges, microwaves, and coffeemakers to roomy, two-bedroom, gulf-front apartments with all the comforts of home. Three one- and two-story cement-block buildings file between the main beach drag and the wide sands of Lido. There's a homey feel here. Owners have been coming for years, taking advantage of the welcoming pool, grilling area, shuffleboard, and sunset-perfect view. In 2003 Lido Key businesspeople saved this, Lido's first motel, from demise

and high-rise takeover by getting it designated a historic landmark.

LIDO BEACH RESORT

General Manager: Shannon Burdge
941-388-2161, 800-441-2113
www.lidobeachresort.com
700 Ben Franklin Dr., Sarasota 34236
Price: Moderate to Very Expensive
Credit Cards: AE, D, MC, V

Located next to Lido Key's public beach, the 222-unit resort, formerly a Radisson, provides attractive accommodations, furnished with sand and sea tones, and a full range of water sports in the thick of beach activity. Its newest tower, opened in 2003, holds 14 floors, a city-view restaurant named Christopher's, and business facilities. Between it and the original four-story hotel squirms a goldfish creek crossed by wooden walkways with tin-roofed gazebos. The two pools sit on the shell-scattered beach and have their own beach bar. Another café offers guests lunch and dinner in the lobby. Modern, nicely furnished rooms come with or without full kitchens. Some have a small refrigerator and microwave, instead; all have coffeemakers. The resort provides a complimentary shuttle to shopping at St. Armands Circle.

LONGBOAT KEY

✪ COLONY BEACH AND TENNIS RESORT

President and General Manager: Katherine Klauber Moulton
941-383-6464, 800-4COLONY
www.colonybeachresort.com
1620 Gulf of Mexico Dr., Longboat Key 34228
Price: Very Expensive
Credit Cards: AE, D, DC, MC, V

The Colony ranks among Florida's finest resorts, a place where you could hide indefinitely behind security gates without ever having to face the real world. Here, in fact, is where President George W. Bush was "hiding" when 9/11 happened. It stakes its reputation on top-notch tennis and dining: Ten of the 21 tennis courts have state-of-the-art soft surfaces. *Tennis* magazine has named it the top U.S. tennis resort for eight consecutive years. The Colony Dining Room, one of the property's two dining spots, also consistently wins awards. The other, ✪ **the Monkey Room**, features comical monkey murals and great martinis. The 18-acre oleander-trimmed resort occupies a stretch of broad private beach. Complimentary kids' recreational programs take young guests to the courts, beach, pool, and off-property attractions. The Colony's 234 privately owned units range from adult-only beachfront units to family-friendly one- or two-bedroom suites. All units contain modern kitchen facilities; designer lamps, art, and furnishings; and marble master baths. Guests have free use of tennis courts as well as a spa and a professionally staffed health club with a fitness studio. Golf is available at 10 local private and semiprivate clubs.

THE RESORT AT LONGBOAT KEY CLUB

General Managers: Rick Benninghove and Michael Welly
941-383-8821, 800-237-8821
www.longboatkeyclub.com
301 Gulf of Mexico Dr., Longboat Key 34228
Price: Expensive to Very Expensive
Credit Cards: AE, DC, MC, V

Serious golfers are most apt to appreciate this gated, 10-story beach resort in the midst of a private golf community. Besides the 45 holes of golf, 38 Har-Tru tennis courts, water sports, a spiffy fitness center, and a full-service spa satisfy the active vacationer. Dining is another huge plus. Open only to guests and members, the club's restaurants excel at flavor-bursting seafood dishes prepared with only the top ingredients and seasoned exotically. Rooms come in the one-bedroom or two-bedroom suite variety with complete kitchens, space to dance, and class-act appointments. Use of beach cabanas, umbrellas, and bikes is complimentary. Add-on extras include seasonal kids' programs, family portraits,

On Longboat Key, Rolling Waves provides guests with the ultimate beach-cottage vacation.

and water sports rentals. The resort has a no-cash policy; all charges go on a room tab.

✪ ROLLING WAVES COTTAGES

Owners: Theresa and Ed Woodland
941-383-1323
www.rollingwaves.com
6351 Gulf of Mexico Dr., Longboat Key
34228.
Price: Moderate to Very Expensive
Credit Cards: MC, V
No handicap access

What more could you ask of a beach vacation than a cute little 1940s cottage furnished modernly in bright colors, containing a remodeled full kitchen and bath, and complete with picnic table, grill, sea grapes, huge pink hibiscus blossoms, and a quiet beach outside the door? Rolling Waves's eight cottages are kept meticulous and are decorated with touches of character: clay-tile kitchen floors, rag rugs over wood floors in a couple of the cottages, full-sized futons in the living room, VCRs, and an exterior paint job that evokes the chattel houses of the Caribbean. Located in Longboat Key's old, historic section, it escapes the glitz and the throngs with classic class.

NOKOMIS BEACH
A BEACH RETREAT

General Managers: Natalie Lee and Greg Hendrix
941-485-8771, 866-232-2480
www.abeachretreat.com
105 Casey Key Rd., Nokomis 34275
Price: Moderate to Expensive
Credit Cards: MC, V

A Beach Retreat has efficiencies and apartments on both the beach and the bay. Fancied up with a jaunty yellow paint job and lattice trim, it also has a swimming pool on the bay side, where boat docks and 10 units accommodate guests and their vessels. The gulfside rooms, mostly ground level, are steps from a lovely, natural beach, but because of the wonderful tall sea oats, they have no view of the water. They cluster around a tropically vegetated courtyard and shuffleboard courts. The 27 units—from studios to three-bedroom suites (expensive to very expensive)—all have their own look and layout that is largely modern but with some imperfections that lend beach character. All but two have full kitchens.

SARASOTA
✪ THE CYPRESS

Innkeepers: Vicki Hadley and Robert and Nina Belott
941-955-4683
www.cypressbb.com
621 Gulfstream Ave. S., Sarasota 34236
Price: Expensive to Very Expensive*
Credit Cards: AE, D, MC, V

Details make a bed-and-breakfast inn, and The Cypress's attention to special touches, flourishes, and minutiae place it among the top in its genre. Notice the antique ice cream table with swivel-out stools in the sunny breakfast room, the fireplace, the vintage Edison phonograph and piano in the living room, the exquisite crown molding throughout, the fresh flowers in each of the five individually decorated rooms, the multicourse gourmet breakfasts, and the happy-hour cocktail and hors d'oeuvres at 6 PM. In short, the innkeepers spoil their guests. This trio of talent took over a 1940s home that the original owner's daughter refused to sell out to encroaching condos, making The Cypress—named for its sturdy building material a flower in the shadow of high-rises. Still, the location is quite enviable. From the front deck guests can watch the sun set over the masts of yachts in the marina across the way. Downtown's Palm Avenue district of galleries, sidewalk cafés, and specialty shops, meanwhile, is a short stroll away.

✪ HOTEL INDIGO

General Manager: Leslie Power
941-487-3800, 866-2-INDIGO
www.hotelindigo.com
1223 Boulevard of the Arts, Sarasota 34236
Price: Very Expensive
Credit Cards: AE, D, MC, V

From the people who bring you Holiday Inn and Crowne Plaza comes a fresh new concept, which made its Florida debut here in 2006. Hotel Indigo provides a stimulating environment in a boutique setting. Trademarks of the brand include lobby and room murals that change with the season. The lobby is even scented with seasonal aromas, such as cinnamon apple in fall. Oversized wooden Adirondack-style beach chairs decorate the lobby, where you'll also find Phi, a bright little café serving tapas, beer, and wine. The hotel's 95 rooms (12 of which are suites) are inviting and include hardwood floors, sleeper sofas, high-speed Internet access, and glassed-in shower stalls (no bathtubs). Two large whirlpools—one hot, one cold—are the centerpieces of an outdoor lunching and sunning deck. A coffee-pastry counter and fitness room complete the description of this so-called lifestyle hotel. Adjacent to the new Renaissance development, it is also close to Van Wezel Center, G.WIZ, and downtown attractions.

✪ THE RITZ-CARLTON SARASOTA

General Manager: Jim Veil
941-309-2000, 800-241-3333
www.ritzcarlton.com/hotels/sarasota
1111 Ritz-Carlton Dr., Sarasota 34236
Price: Expensive to Very Expensive
Credit Cards: AE, D, DC, MC, V

One of the first in the Ritz-Carlton line to offer living quarters, this hotel has 266 rooms and suites that deliver all the luxury you expect from the name. Perched on the edge of downtown, it's more of a city hotel than other Ritz-Carlton Florida properties, but it has its own off-site beach club. Some rooms have views of Sarasota Bay, others

Artistic and gracious, The Cypress B&B blends well with Sarasota's downtown personality.

overlook a neighboring marina. White marble bathrooms, oversized rooms, and wireless Internet and Ethernet hookups make it equally accommodating for leisure and business travelers. Available on the main campus are two spas and fitness centers, as well as a swimming pool, a fine American regional cuisine restaurant, and a sophisticated cigar bar called the ✪ **Cà d'Zan Lounge**. The main, full-service spa's fitness center requires a daily fee or membership. Small touches, such as a rubber turtle for the bathtub, Bulgari bath amenities, free shoeshine service, four different time-zone clocks set into the desk blotter, and over-the-top service define the inimitable Ritz experience. For the ultimate experience, book on the club floors and take advantage of the complimentary food and drink services. An hourly shuttle transports guests to shopping on St. Armands Key and the Beach Club on Lido Key, which includes a kids' club, pool, locker rooms, and West Indian–style restaurant. Guests enjoy golf privileges at a nearby course.

SIESTA KEY

Many of Siesta Key's accommodations require a minimum stay (usually one week) during season. The majority of beach accommodations are condos, villas, or homes.

SIESTA KEY BUNGALOWS

General Manager: Ted Matthews
941-349-9025, 888-5-SIESTA
www.siestakeybungalows.com
8212 Midnight Pass Rd., Siesta Key 34242
Price: Moderate to Very Expensive
Credit Cards: AE, D, DC, MC, V

Appealing to birders and seclusion-seekers, these 10 individually decorated one-bedroom bungalows on Heron Bay feature full kitchens (some with dishwashers), white wicker and rattan furnishings, and

double pillow-top mattresses. Hand-painted murals and accents match each bungalow's name, which include Hibiscus, Catamaran, and Dolphin. The living room areas contain sleeper sofas, making the bungalows convenient for families. Kayak and canoe use is complimentary, plus there's a swimming pool and a makeshift sand beach. Wireless Internet access is available free throughout the property.

TURTLE BEACH RESORT

Innkeepers: David and Gail Rubinfeld
941-349-4554
www.turtlebeachresort.com
9049 Midnight Pass Rd., Siesta Key 34242
Price: Very Expensive (minimum stay required in season; housekeeping is extra)
Credit Cards: D, MC, V

One of Sarasota's Small Superior Lodgings, this place is a real find at the southern, quiet end of the island, a three-minute walk from Turtle Beach. Ten cottages on the bay contain studio, one-bedroom, or two-bedroom accommodations, plus a private hot tub. Each cottage has its own personality, reflected in names such as Rain Forest, Montego Bay, and Southwestern. Modern designer furniture and lamps, objets d'art, and other decorative pieces carry out the themes. Ten new units across the street at the Inn at Turtle Beach, designed in a Tommy Bahama mode with private outdoor whirlpools, are ideal for couples. Most rooms at both properties have sleeper sofas; all come with complete kitchen facilities. Bathrobes, TVs, VCRs, free wireless Internet access, and sherry are provided in each of the cottages, which spread along a lushly landscaped strip. The well-planned property includes private nooks along waterside docks and two pools. Use of washers and dryers is free after 4 PM, and bicycles, canoes, kayaks, rowboats, and boat docks are available, complimentary for guests' enjoyment. Very romantic, the

A touch of the Old World at Banyan House, a venerable bed-and-breakfast in Venice

original resort is nonetheless conducive to families, and pets are permitted.

BANYAN HOUSE

Innkeepers: Chuck and Susan McCormick
941-484-1385
www.banyanhouse.com
519 S. Harbor Dr., Venice 34285
Price: Moderate to Expensive* (minimum two-night stay required)
Credit Cards: MC, V
No handicap access

In the mid-1920s architects designed Venice in accordance with its Italian name; homes and buildings are modeled after northern Mediterranean styles. The town's first community swimming pool was located in the backyard of one of the original homes, next to a fledgling banyan tree. Today that small pool, with its now-sprawling tree, resides at the same home, a red-tile-roofed B&B inn known as the Banyan House. Classic statuary, fountains, multi-hued blossoms, a courtyard, a sundeck, a billiard and fitness room, and a hot tub share the property. Five rooms, each with a private bath, exert their individual person-alities: The Palm Room has a fireplace. The Laurel Room features an outdoor balcony. The Tree House includes a sunny sitting room overlooking the pool. The Sun Deck has a separate entrance. The Palmetto Room offers hardwood floors and lavender hues. All units contain at least a small refrigera-tor; three are efficiencies. Two rooms and one apartment are also available in the car-riage house, rented by the month. Deluxe touches include bathrobes in the closet and wine in the fridge. Susan serves homemade gourmet breakfast in a solarium off the for-mal sitting room, the latter furnished with an antique Italian fireplace, a circa-1890 hoop-skirt bench, and other Victorian period pieces. Pecky cypress, wood-beam ceilings, terracotta slate tiling, and wrought-iron banisters are all original. Free use of bicycles allows guests to explore old Venice's nearby shopping mecca and beach. Smoking is not allowed in any of the rooms.

INN AT THE BEACH
General Manager: Tim Brown
941-484-8471, 800-255-8471
www.innatthebeach.com
725 W. Venice Ave., Venice 34285
Price: Moderate to Very Expensive*
Credit Cards: AE, D, DC, MC, V

This modern resort was built to include Mediterranean architectural overtones and contemporary Florida comfort and decor. Located across the street from the public access to Venice Beach, the hotel has 49 units; many of the second-floor ones overlook the gulf. Its well-maintained rooms have a clean white, light wood, understated floral motif. Plantation shutters and tile floors add designer touches. All contain at least a microwave, coffeemaker, and minifridge; efficiencies and one- and two-bedroom suites add full refrigerators, stovetops, dishwashers, dishware, and pans. Wireless Internet access is free. A small pool with spa and sundeck is tucked away behind the hotel in the parking lot—not high on atmosphere. I'd opt for the beach. Continental breakfast is included in the rate.

Home & Condo Rentals
Anna Maria Gulf Coast Rentals (941-778-3699 or 800-865-0800; www.amgcrentals.com; 5319 Gulf Dr., Holmes Beach 34217) Anna Maria Island is a hot market for home and condo rentals, from charming beach cottages to swank condos and multiroom homes.

A Paradise Rental Management (941-778-4800, 800-237-2252; www.aparadise rentals.com; 5201 Gulf Dr., Holmes Beach 34217) Rental condos and homes on Anna Maria Island for short and long term, starting under $1,000 for a week.

Resort Quest Southwest Florida (239-992-6620; www.resortquest.com; 26201 Hickory Blvd., Bonita Springs 34134) Rentals from Venice to Anna Maria Island.

Siesta Key Vacation Rentals (866-496-3200; www.stayonsiesta.com; 6604 Midnight Pass Rd., Siesta Key 34242) Condos, villas, and homes to rent on the island.

RV Resorts
Horseshoe Cove (941-758-5335, 800-291-3446; www.horseshoecove.net; 5100 60th St. E., Bradenton 34203) This 60-acre oak-grove riverfront site includes a 12-acre island with a pavilion and nature and biking trails. The resort has a heated pool and spa, a postal facility, hookup to phone and cable, lighted fishing docks on the Braden River, shuffleboard courts, and other recreational facilities. Musical jam sessions happen regularly.

Linger Lodge (941-755-2757; www.linger lodgeresort.com; 7205 Linger Lodge Rd., Bradenton 34202) By dint of its old-Florida-style character and slightly bizarre restaurant, this place has gained a reputation for funky. RV sites lie along or near the Braden River. Amenities include a boat ramp, fishing, and laundry.

Sarasota Bay Travel Trailer Park (941-794-1200, 800-247-8361; www.paradise bay-sarasotabayrvpark.com; 10777 44th Ave. W., Bradenton 34210, at Cortez Rd.) Located on the bay and having full hookups, a boat ramp and dock, fishing, horseshoes, exercise room, recreation hall, and entertainment, it caters mostly to permanent abodes, with some spots for transients. This is an exceptionally well-kept and scenic facility.

Venice Campground (941-488-0850; www.campvenice.com; 4085 E. Venice Ave., Venice 34292, at exit 191 off I-75) This campground has full hookups and waterfront sites, plus tent sites and cabin rentals. Amenities include security gates, a heated swimming pool, shuffleboard, horseshoe, a nature trail, fishing, boat and canoe rentals, a laundry room, and a supply store.

Dining

Bravo! Sarasota's individually owned restaurants have banded together to fight chain-restaurant homogeny and build their promotional muscle. Look for restaurants that display the "Fresh Originals" logo (www.freshoriginals.com).

For Sarasotans, eating out is as much a cultural event as attending the opera is. It is often an inextricable part of an evening at the theater or a gallery opening. Sarasotans take dining out quite seriously and keep restaurants full, even off season. Their enthusiasm for newness makes local kitchens more innovative than those of their neighbors to the south. (Out of 57 Golden Spoon winners awarded in 2006 by *Florida Trend* magazine, six—Beach Bistro, Euphemia Haye, Mattison's Steakhouse at the Plaza, Michael's on East, the Colony Dining Room, and Vernona at the Ritz-Carlton—are found in this region.) The town also counts one of the highest concentrations of Zagat-rated restaurants in Florida. Sarasota slides along the cutting edge of New World cuisine while maintaining classic favorites that range from rickety oyster bars to French cafés.

The following listings span the diversity of Sarasota Bay coast cuisine in these price categories:

Inexpensive	Up to $15
Moderate	$15 to $25
Expensive	$25 to $35
Very Expensive	$35 or more

Cost categories are based on the range of dinner entrée prices or, if dinner is not served, on lunch entrées. Those restaurants listed with "Healthy Selections" usually mark such on their menu.

The following abbreviations are used for credit card information and meals:

AE: American Express
D: Discover Card
DC: Diners Club
MC: MasterCard
V: Visa
B: Breakfast
L: Lunch
D: Dinner
SB: Sunday Brunch
Note: Florida law forbids smoking inside all restaurants and bars serving food. Smoking is permitted only in restaurants with outdoor seating.

Anna Maria
ROTTEN RALPH'S
941-778-3953
902 Bay Blvd. S., Anna Maria Island 34216
At the Anna Maria Yacht Basin
Price: Inexpensive to Moderate
Cuisine: Old Florida
Children's Menu: No (kid-suitable items on regular menu)
Liquor: Full
Serving: L, D
Credit Cards: D, MC, V
Handicap Access: Yes
Reservations: No
Special Features: Dock seating on the marina; early-dining menu

The atmosphere here is due entirely to the setting. It's a place that locals frequent and is full of character and characters. The laminated placemat menu describes several finger food selections (steamed shellfish, popcorn shrimp, oysters Rockefeller, onion rings, chicken wings, nachos), Old Florida fried seafood standards, fish and chips, sandwiches, and other, more gourmet, concessions such as shrimp linguine Alfredo, Danish baby-back ribs, and Cajun shrimp. I inevitably order the blackened grouper sandwich, which is totally fresh and well seasoned. We've always found the food fresh and tasty, but, truthfully, we enjoy the view more.

BRADENTON

✪ ALVAREZ MEXICAN FOOD

941-729-2232
1431 Eighth Ave. W., Palmetto 34221
Price: Inexpensive
Cuisine: Mexican
Children's Menu: Yes
Liquor: Beer and wine
Serving: B, L, D
Credit Cards: AE, D, MC, V
Handicap Access: Yes
Reservations: No
Special Features: Patio seating

Across the river from Bradenton, Palmetto is the seat of Manatee County's huge agricultural industry. That means a heritage of fresh produce and Hispanic cuisine. Alvarez has ruled the latter category since 1976. Farm workers mingle with white-collar tomato brokers for the real thing in Mexican. The dining room is small and worn, but the patio has more of a festive air and is the first choice when weather allows. The menu spans all the Tex-Mex favorites along with Alvarez specialties: *huevos rancheros* for breakfast, *camarones al Diablo* (spicy shrimp), *barbacoa* (Mexican barbecue), and rich *mole* with either pork or chicken. Daily lunch specials and "speedies" combinations offer bargains. Beware of the salsa: it appears simple but packs a wallop and tastes entirely of fresh tomatoes.

SNOOK RIVER GRILL

941-748-7694
2505 Manatee Ave. E., Bradenton 34208
Price: Inexpensive to Moderate
Cuisine: Southern
Children's Menu: Yes
Liquor: Full
Serving: L, D, SB
Credit Cards: AE, D, MC, V
Handicap Access: Yes
Reservations: No
Special Features: Patio seating

Alvarez Mexican Food serves the real thing and has since 1976.

With specialties the likes of Not Yo Mama's Meatloaf, Beer Can Chicken, Pecan-Crusted Tilapia, and Buck Naked Fish, this roadside eatery appeals to the fun-loving, down-home sort who appreciates food well prepared and atmosphere unstuffy. It's a cleaned-up version of Old Florida shanty restaurants, and the Southern-style food is as faultless as it is hardy. Take a booth inside or a table on the patio with a view of Bradenton's main thoroughfare. For lunch, I can personally vouch for the excellence of the chunky, fresh-tasting Chilled Gazpacho and the Stuck Pig pulled-pork sandwich, topped with a mess of yummy crispy onion strings—thinly sliced rings. Sunday brunch is a menu affair that includes one complimentary Bloody Mary (before noon) that you can spice up yourself at the condiment bar.

LEE'S CRAB TRAP II

941-729-7777
4815 17th St. E., P.O. Box 450, Ellenton 34222
Right off I-75 exit 224
Price: Moderate to Very Expensive
Cuisine: Seafood

Children's Menu: Yes
Liquor: Full
Serving: L, D
Credit Cards: D, MC, V
Handicap Access: Yes
Reservations: No
Special Features: View of the water

If you're visiting Gamble Mansion or happen to be passing by this interstate exit with a hunger on, this is a must stop and has been as long as I can remember. The notebook-sized menu is largely given over to, of course, crab. Try it steamed (stone or king), provençal, deviled, Norfolk style (baked in lemon juice and butter), or in a variety of other treatments. The grilled crab cakes—lightly bound chunks of prime meat—and three-crab soup with asparagus are excellent. All the soups have a distinct from-scratch, long-mulled flavor. The menu doesn't limit itself to seafood; it flexes wide to include fine Angus beef, frogs' legs, catfish, chicken, ostrich, kangaroo, wild boar, octopus, alligator, and pasta. The two large, wood-and-bamboo dining rooms have a comfortable, handsome feel with views of a pond out back. Expect a wait for lunch or dinner in season. The bar offers a more select, lighter version of the extensive menu.

Bradenton Beach
ISLAND CRÊPERIE
941-778-1011
127 Bridge St., Bradenton Beach 34217
Price: Inexpensive
Cuisine: French
Children's Menu: No
Liquor: Beer and wine
Serving: B, L, D (closed Sun. dinner)
Credit Cards: MC, V
Handicap Access: Yes
Reservations: Yes

Crêpes, of course, are the main draw at this tiny, seven-table eatery. Buckwheat crêpes, filled with such tasty combinations as ratatouille with egg and bacon, smoked salmon with artichoke and sour cream, or proscuitto with blue cheese and walnuts, are a specialty at lunchtime. At dinner, which is booked months in advance during the winter season, chef-owner Olivier Rose does a set of finely crafted French dishes such as beef bourguignon, fish à la provençale, or chicken à la Dijonnaise, served with a marvelous blue-cheese salad and potatoes au gratin for only $15.90. Twenty-two different dessert crêpes take their inspiration from Cape Cod (apple sauce with caramel), the Black Forest (red fruits with chocolate sauce), Jamaica (banana, cinnamon, flambé with white rum), and beyond.

SUN HOUSE RESTAURANT & BAR
941-782-1122
www.thesunhouserestaurant.com
111 Gulf Dr. S., Bradenton Beach 34217
At BridgeWalk resort
Price: Inexpensive to Moderate
Cuisine: American/Tropical
Children's Menu: Yes
Liquor: Full
Serving: L, D
Credit Cards: AE, D, MC, V
Handicap Access: Yes
Reservations: No; preferred seating
Special Features: Gulf views and outdoor dining

Hiked up on the second floor of the colorful BridgeWalk resort, it keeps in tropical theme with such creative inventions as tequila-marinated shrimp, grouper sautéed with baby shrimp and topped with key lime beurre blanc, and watermelon barbequed chicken. I usually order their Passionate Screw martini—a screwdriver spiked with passion fruit liqueur. Come for a sunset cocktail and munchies (the salsa has won awards and comes with a mélange of tropical chips) or stay for a full-blown meal; you won't be disappointed no matter what. But be sure to budget in a slice of the signature mango pie.

CASEY KEY
✪ CASEY KEY FISH HOUSE
941-966-1901
801 Blackburn Point Rd., Osprey 34229
Price: Inexpensive to Moderate
Cuisine: Florida
Children's Menu: Yes
Liquor: Full
Serving: L, D
Credit Cards: D, MC, V
Handicap Access: Yes
Reservations: No

It does not attempt to dazzle its boat- and drive-in customers with pretensions. Everyone's happy to find good food reasonably priced, a perennially cheerful staff, fresh seafood with little fuss but lots of freshness, and a view of the water and a great blue heron or two for atmosphere. Well, to be fair, there is an aquarium and a mounted dolphinfish as "decorator touches," but this place is about the seafood. The laminated menu warns that patience is a virtue if you wish food cooked to order. It then goes on to list standard Florida fish-house fare such as baskets of crab cakes, battered shrimp, fish and chips, and grouper sandwiches. Dinners dress it up a little with such choices as sea scallops provençal or fresh grilled salmon with cucumber-dill sauce. The blackboard lists the day's catches, which are served with toasted white bread, white rice, and steamed veggies on a plastic plate. Don't be fooled by these simplicities. My recent affair with a grouper special resulted in a wonderfully sautéed filet topped with black beans and corn off the cob in a limey butter sauce—a totally unexpected pleasure.

HOLMES BEACH
✪ BEACH BISTRO
941-778-6444
www.beachbistro.com

6600 Gulf Dr., Holmes Beach 34217
Price: Very Expensive
Cuisine: New American
Children's Menu: Yes, plus puzzles, fruit amusées, and more
Liquor: Full
Serving: D
Credit Cards: AE, D, DC, MC, V
Handicap Access: Limited; close quarters and no bathroom wheelchair access
Reservations: Yes
Special Features: Front room view of gulf

The talk of connoisseurs for many years, this little bit of gourmet heaven has fewer than 20 tables in its main dining area, a two-room cottage. (Most of them cluster around picture windows in a room with one of the best local-dining views of the sunset.) We came to understand all the hubbub as the meal progressed and our server attended us with skilled timing and pleasant surprises. Even before our appetizer came, we enjoyed herbed bread with a marvelous dip of tomatoes and basil, then two entwined shrimp with red pepper coulis. The exacting menu showcases the chefs' quirky talents, which are difficult to define but easy to enjoy. The "lobstercargots" appetizer, for instance, replaces those "chewy little slugs" with succulent morsels of Florida lobster in bubbling garlic butter and spinach. We had a hard time letting them cool before we ate them, they were that tantalizing. A signature "kicker" sauce keeps the jumbo shrimp from drying on the grill and adds a spark nicely complemented by its Grand Marnier ginger beurre blanc. Bouillabaisse with lobster, calamari, and fish is a signature, as is the "Food Heaven" marvel—lamb crowned with lobster and foie gras on brioche bread pudding. Each dish is executed to perfection. The vegetable accompaniments to our main courses were delicious enough to fight them for attention. And our wine by the glass was poured from the bottle, a touch I always appreciate. The recently expanded bar has initiated a casual bar menu for the less formally inclined, but the food there is every bit as tasty as in the main dining room. In short, if you hear critics and regular folks raving about Beach Bistro, it's all true.

LIDO KEY
✪ NEW PASS GRILL & BAIT SHOP
941-388-3050
www.newpassgrill.com
1498 Ken Thompson Pkwy. Sarasota 34236
On City Island, at New Pass Bridge
Price: Inexpensive
Cuisine: American
Children's Menu: Yes
Liquor: Beer, wine
Serving: B, L
Credit Cards: AE, D, V, MC

Seafood doesn't get any fresher or more affordable than at New Pass Grill.

Handicap Access: No
Reservations: No
Special Features: Old Florida waterfront location; boat docking

Here's a place to grab a quick lunch or breakfast if you're out boating or visiting Mote Marine Aquarium. Step up to the window; order your burger, hot dog, clam basket, fish and chips, or Boar's Head deli sandwich; then meander off to settle onto a jumbled selection of picnic tables and dock counter space along the water at New Pass. Watch the fleets of herons, egrets, pelicans, and boats while you wait for your name to be announced. The burgers are legendary, and the prices are unbeatable. Afterward, troll the bait-shop tanks and shelves for fishing supplies and leave with the satisfaction that places such as this still exist.

✪ OLD SALTY DOG
941-388-4311
www.theoldsaltydog.com
1601 Ken Thompson Pkwy., Sarasota 34236
On City Island
Price: Inexpensive
Cuisine: American/seafood
Children's Menu: No, but the menu offers child-appropriate selections.
Liquor: Beer, wine
Serving: L, D
Credit Cards: V, MC
Handicap Access: Yes
Reservations: No
Special Features: Outdoor waterfront seating

A spin-off of the Siesta Key original, this one has a more properly salty setting: a tin-roofed, red stucco building tucked into a marina in the shadow of the Longboat Key bridge. If you sit outside on the breezy patios, you'll be entertained by boaters, Waverunners, and water-skiers. The menu lists such fun casual eats as City Island wings with dill sauce, New England clam chowder, deep-fried clams on a bed of fries, peel-and-eat shrimp, burgers, fish and chips, and the trademark Salty Dog (beer-battered and deep-fried and not for the faint of heart). I ordered the grouper sandwich blackened and was pleased to have a choice of hot, medium, or mild. (Too many places assume palate sensitivity and water down the heat of a properly executed blackening.) I specified hot and got it just right—not so fiery as to overpower the full-flavored freshness of the fish. We like the wide selection of beer it offers, on tap as well as bottled. My son likes that we don't have to wait long for our food.

LONGBOAT KEY
EUPHEMIA HAYE
941-383-3633
www.euphemiahaye.com
5540 Gulf of Mexico Dr., Longboat Key 34228
Price: Moderate to Very Expensive
Cuisine: Continental
Children's Menu: No
Liquor: Full
Serving: D
Credit Cards: CB, DC, D, MC, V
Handicap Access: Yes, downstairs
Reservations: Yes
Special Features: Appetizer/dessert parlor; live entertainment

The name Euphemia Haye, odd and difficult to pronounce as it may seem, has come to define one of Sarasota's most coveted dining experiences. The appellation actually comes from the founder's grandmother. There's nothing grandmotherly about the concept and cuisine, although you will find elements of comfort food sprinkled among international and house specialties: a smoked salmon appetizer on crêpes from Russia, lamb shank from Greece, taglatelle alla carbonara from Italy, shrimp Taj Mahal from India, French calves' sweetbreads, and so on. The signature roast duckling is a fine example of the details that make a meal at Euphemia Haye

a blend of familiar and exotic. With bread stuffing and a seasonally changing fruit sauce (orange and green peppercorn last time I sampled it), it arrives with a simple parsley sprig garnish. Filet mignon Fritzie is another Euphemia specialty; it sits atop a potato pancake with caramelized shallots and bourbon demi-glace. To top off the experience, a trip upstairs to the Haye Loft for dessert is de rigueur. The selection is mind-boggling (not to mention diet-blowing, but let that thought go in this atmosphere). Besides sinful desserts, you can order coffee and after-dinner drinks. The peanut butter mousse with chocolate rum topping was much heavier than its name suggests, enough to go around a table of four; the coconut cream pie was extraordinary.

✪ MAR-VISTA DOCKSIDE RESAURANT & PUB
941-383-2391
www.groupersandwich.com
760 Broadway St., Longboat Key 34228
In the Village
Price: Inexpensive to Moderate
Cuisine: Seafood
Children's Menu: Yes
Liquor: Full
Serving: L, D
Credit Cards: AE, D, DC, MC, V
Handicap Access: Restaurant, yes; restrooms, no
Reservations: No; preferred seating
Special Features: Boat access

Locals refer to it as the Pub, a hangover from years gone by. Casual at its best, it has that lovely, lived-in, borderline ramshackle look on the outside, crowned by an appropriately rusting tin roof. Inside, tables don't match, mounted fish and sailors' dollar bills adorn the wall, boaters hoist beers at the bar, and a view of the harbor dominates the decorator's scheme. There's also seating on plastic chairs on the patio, which has heaters when it's cool (and where you may occasionally get an earful of cooks' disagreements in the kitchen). The seafood is fresh and prepared with signature twists: vegetable and conch fritters, a fresh-catch Rueben sandwich, garlic-fried shrimp, Longbeach bouillabaisse, sesame tuna, and Caribbean grilled chicken. Steamer pots in four sizes brim with shellfish and vegetables. We've enjoyed the cuisine and casual atmosphere here many times.

NOKOMIS

✪ CAPTAIN EDDIE'S SEAFOOD RESTAURANT
941-484-4623
107 Colonia Ln. E., Nokomis 34275
Price: Inexpensive to Moderate
Cuisine: Seafood/Florida
Children's Menu: Yes
Liquor: Beer and wine
Serving: L, D
Credit Cards: D, MC, V
Handicap Access: Restaurant, yes; restrooms, no
Reservations: No

Ask anyone around the Venice-Nokomis-Osprey area where to get fresh seafood, and 9 out of 10 will recommend, without pause, Captain Eddie's. The restaurant began as a fish market that took over a convenience store and set up a few picnic tables to fill the space. Those picnic tables came to be in such great demand that the market eventually grew into a restaurant where the locals know they can get their money's worth in fresh fish. The picnic tables remain; if you're a small party, you may be sharing with others. Or you can sit at the counter. This is a true Florida fish house—my favorite brand of dining. Don't expect tableware that won't get tossed at the end of the meal. Do expect a roll of paper towels for linen and neighborly service. The hostess calls most of the patrons by name. The menu carries a lot of fried-fish items such

as shrimp, catfish, and oysters (but fried right and in canola oil) as well as broiled options. After an appetizer of alligator bites, I tried a broiled grouper sandwich that was the best I've tasted since my husband came home from a deep-sea fishing trip. Broiled grouper can be bland, but this was tastefully prepared, served on a yummy hoagie in a plastic basket. The lone dessert, key lime pie, is the real thing, though with a discernible "off flavor" that sometimes comes from bottled lime juice. (But then I have my own lime tree and am something of a snob!)

ST. ARMANDS CIRCLE

✪ CAFÉ L'EUROPE
941-388-4415
www.cafeleurope.net
431 St. Armands Circle, Sarasota 34236
Price: Moderate to Very Expensive
Cuisine: French
Children's Menu: No
Liquor: Full
Serving: L, D (Closed for lunch off season.)
Credit Cards: AE, D, DC, MC, V
Handicap Access: Yes
Reservations: Yes, for both lunch and dinner

Café L'Europe remains a shining star that offers French classics with a New Age tweak. Dark woods and redbrick archways set an atmosphere that's warm in an inviting way, yet offer a cool, cellarlike break from Florida heat. When the weather allows, you can also sit outdoors on the patio to sip your French pinot blanc and sample such stunning selections as the roasted mushroom pecorino cheese with honeycomb and berries on garlic crustini appetizer, bourbon pecan salad, signature brandied duckling, pan-seared scallops with feta mashed potatoes, lobster-stuffed shrimp, potato-crusted grouper, or tableside porterhouse steak for two.

LYNCHES PUB & GRUB

941-388-5550
www.lynchespubandgrub.com
19B N. Blvd. of Presidents, Sarasota 34236
At St. Armands Circle
Price: Inexpensive to Moderate
Cuisine: Irish
Children's Menu: No
Liquor: Full
Serving: L, D
Credit Cards: AE, D, DC, MC, V
Handicap Access: Yes
Reservations: No

For something easygoing, affordable, and affable on the Circle, stop in for lunch or dinner and hoist a pint. Besides typical pub fare such as corned beef and cabbage, Irish stew, and cottage pie, the shamrock-decked long and narrow pub serves grouper sandwiches, hot dogs, omelets, and salads all day long. The Irish stew is authentic, made with lamb, though heavier on onions and celery than lamb. The vegetarian platter, piled with sautéed cabbage, fresh spinach, and whatever else the kitchen has in stock, makes a satisfying alternative. Save room for Irish coffee cake or rhubarb pie.

SARASOTA
BIJOU CAFÉ

941-366-8111
www.bijoucafe.net
1287 First St., Sarasota 34236
Price: Moderate to Expensive.
Cuisine: New American
Children's Menu: No
Liquor: Full
Serving: L, D (Closed Sun. in summer, Sat. and Sun. for lunch year-round.)
Credit Cards: AE, DC, MC, V
Handicap Access: Yes
Reservations: Yes, recommended
Special Features: Complimentary valet parking

Situated in the midst of the theater and arts district, the Bijou is the pick of the pre- and post-theater crowd and upper-echelon business community of Sarasota. Small and simply decorated, only lacy curtains, some heavily framed paintings, and a few stylish vases (here you'd pronounce that *vah-zes*) embellish. Linen and fresh flowers dress the tables, even at lunch, when the clientele is equally dressed up. The eclectic menu offers choices from Continental, New Orleans, and American cuisine, from fruit soup to duck. One of my favorite dishes, shrimp Piri-Piri, makes a classic example of how chef/owner Jean-Pierre Knaggs perfectly balances flavors to create entirely fresh taste sensations. It is mildly spicy with citrus tones and appears on both the lunch and dinner menus. Other dinner specialties include roast duckling, salmon crusted with grain mustard and dill, pan-seared pork chop with a prunes and cider tarragon sauce, and braised lamb shanks in Burgundy and rosemary. The pommes gratin Dauphinois with Gruyère is a signature side dish, available à la carte. Desserts, made in-house, have an excellent reputation. Lunch draws a brisk business crowd and can include dishes such as handmade spinach and ricotta ravioli, boursin-glazed shrimp, crab cakes remoulade, chicken panini with creamed feta and walnut pesto olivade, and the like.

CAFÉ BACI

941-921-4848
www.cafebaci.net
4001 S. Tamiami Trail, Sarasota 34231
Price: Moderate to Expensive
Cuisine: Northern Italian
Children's Menu: Yes
Liquor: Full
Serving: L, D (Closed for lunch Sat. and Sun., also all day Mon. during the summer.)
Credit Cards: AE, D, DC, MC, V

Handicap Access: Restaurant, yes; restrooms, no
Reservations: Yes, for dinner

I describe this place as "affordably dressy."
It has, after all, a porte cochere out front
and linens on the tables (even at lunch)
inside; the business clientele and older
crowd wear nice clothes; and the Tuscan-
Roman specialties dwell in the realm of
fine cuisine. Yet its location on the plebeian
South Tamiami Trail, away from Sarasota's
centers of chichi, allows for a reasonably
priced menu. Lunch is especially popular
with locals, who squeeze the parking lot full
to capacity. I enjoy lunch there, too; it
imparts a bit of affordable elegance in the
middle of a hectic day alongside a road-
rage street. Though Café Baci is unspectac-
ular in atmosphere, its food has kept it at
the head of growing Italian competition.
Many of the dinner entrées are available in
smaller portions and prices at lunchtime. I
have ordered, for example, the ravioli di
funghi (available at dinner as an appetizer),
an exquisite plate of homemade half-moon
pasta pockets filled with delicately creamed
wild mushrooms and topped with a buttery
tomato cream sauce. It is, with its rich
sauce, the most I could eat for lunch—in
part because of the accompanying bread
basket, which was filled with marvelous
tomato focaccia squares. The mussels-and-
linguine lunch is another winner when
offered (the menu changes every couple of
weeks); the tomato and basil broth so tasty
I requested a soupspoon. Both lunch and
dinner menus touch on the four major
Italian food groups: pasta, veal, chicken,
and seafood. These are tended with a creative hand. Here's a taste: tilapia Milanese
(parmesan and herb crusted with a spinach
and pancetta wine sauce), duck with raspberry balsamic demi-glaze, veal saltimbuca,
tortellini Stefano (with grilled chicken,
dried cranberries, spinach, mushrooms,
and goat cheese in sage butter cream

sauce), and Tuscan fisherman's stew. The
extensive wine list has received the Wine
Spectator Award of Excellence.

✪ CAPTAIN BRIAN'S SEAFOOD MARKET RESTAURANT
941-351-4492
8421 N. Tamiami Trail, Sarasota 34243
Price: Inexpensive to Moderate
Cuisine: Seafood
Children's Menu: Yes
Liquor: Beer and wine
Serving: L, D (closed Sun.)
Credit Cards: AE, D, DC, MC, V
Handicap Access: Yes
Reservations: No
Special features: Fresh-fish market

When fresh seafood is priority one and
affordability priority two, go see Captain
Brian. I'm not sure such a person actually
exists, but the T-shirted staff here can
quickly fix you up with the best seafood
available. The first thing you notice when
you enter the inconspicuous storefront is
that it looks like a seafood market, but it
doesn't smell like one. Clean as humanly
possible, it makes seafood relishing totally
appealing. The daily lunch and dinner
menus, besides including fried shrimp baskets, fish sandwiches, crab cakes, seafood
combo platters, and such, spell out a long
list of fresh catches that you can order fried,
grilled, or blackened. I asked for my favorite
fish—red snapper, grilled—and it was elegant in its simplicity: flapping fresh and
unadorned but for a side of black bean
salad. You can opt for the salad bar rather
than a starch side, and there you have yourself a meal that's not only inherently good
but also good for you. The decor is simple:
tables and booths, blue-checkered oilcloths,
and fish. Keep your eye peeled for this local
secret just north of the airport.

✪ DEREK'S CULINARY CASUAL
941-366-6565

www.dereks-sarasota.com
314 Central Ave., Sarasota 34236
In the Rosemary District
Price: Moderate to Expensive
Cuisine: New American
Children's Menu: No
Liquor: Beer and wine
Serving: L, D (Closed Sun. and Mon., also Sat. for lunch.)
Credit Cards: AE, DC, MC, V
Handicap Access: Yes
Reservations: Yes, recommended for dinner

Before you even think of ordering your opening courses, decide to save room for the poached pear dessert. Simmered with lavender and honey, then topped with goat cheese and minced mint in a pool of home-made black pepper caramel, it is totally original and amazing. It gives you an idea of the gutsy creativity that goes on in the on-display kitchen in this corner of spare urban urbanity. Servers, who are at the top of their game, served the soup of the day when I lunched there recently by present-ing a bowl with a dollop of yogurt on the bottom sprinkled with toasted almond. Atop it they poured a pureed blend of tomatillo and cucumber that was wonder-fully sweet, garlicky, and refreshing. My main course, the grouper cheeks, came with wedges of chorizo sausage and plump little corn fritters in a sweet-tangy sauce flavored with red peppers and parsley. Derek's is so fresh and cutting-edge, it has its own vocabulary, defined on the back of the menu. Whet your appetite on crispy rabbit sous vide (with powdered chorizo, poached egg, and ricotta salata vinaigrette), "Caesaresque" salad with grilled shrimp escabeche, foie gras with pomegranete gelee and pink peppercorn and grapefruit vinaigrette, a mole pulled pork sandwich on chorizo cornbread with fried pickle threads, duck two ways (seared breast and pecan-crusted leg confit with creamed

spaetzle, bacon braised greens, and burnt honey jus), gulf shrimp with tasso and pear ravioli, caramelized fennel and carrot mash, candied olives, and toasted paprika tea.

FRED'S

941-364-5811
www.epicureanlife.com
1917 S. Osprey Ave., Sarasota 34239
Price: Moderate to Very Expensive
Cuisine: New American
Children's Menu: No
Liquor: Full
Serving: L, D, SB
Credit Cards: AE, D, DC, MC, V
Handicap Access: Yes
Reservations: Accepted for lunch or dinner

Down in burgeoning Southside Village, the people at Morton's Market are sewing up food service along Osprey Avenue. Their Fred's is a warm and convivial spot for a polished lunch and dinner with flair. The Power Lunch costs $9 and includes soup, fries or salad, and a choice of interesting sandwiches or flatbread pizza. Other salads, soups, and small-portion entrées show the same creativity as those on the dinner menu: dilled shrimp salad wrap, bacon-wrapped meatloaf, and buffalo mozzarella flatbread. Dinner begins with a basket of Mexican-style corn muffins, breadsticks, and lavosh. Starters run the gamut from Southern-fried calamari to porcini mush-room herb-fried ravioli with vodka-mari-nara sauce or shrimp stuffed avocado with brandied remoulade sauce. Entrées, which change regularly, could include Jamaican-spiced salmon, black sesame seed–crusted grouper, braised beef short ribs with pancetta-scallion risotto, and pork chop with a ragout of Asian pears and scallions. A large selection of wines, featuring several by the glass, starts in the reasonable range and climbs to more than $500. Don't find the wine you want? Just ask your server, and he'll run to the neighboring wine store owned by the chain and get it for you, which was what happened when I asked for a certain type of chardonnay. For dessert, just try to pass up the Southern-style bread pudding, chocolate mousse tower, or trilogy of crème brûlées. It's not hard to understand why this place is a local favorite.

❂ MICHAEL'S ON EAST

941-366-0007
www.bestfood.com
1212 East Ave. S., Sarasota 34239
In Midtown Plaza at Bahia Vista St. and Tamiami Trail
Price: Moderate to Very Expensive
Cuisine: New American
Children's Menu: No, but will halve portions
Liquor: Full
Serving: L, D (Closed Sat. and Sun. lunch.)
Credit Cards: AE, DC, MC, V
Handicap Access: Yes
Reservations: Recommended for lunch or dinner
Special Features: Early-dining menu; piano bar with late-night menu

Michael Klauber is a well-respected name in Sarasota culinary circles. He learned successful restauraterering early in life as a member of Longboat Key's Colony Beach Resort family. He created an immediate sensation when he opened his own place back in 1987, and Michael's on East remains the pinnacle of cutting-edge cuisine and atmosphere. Oh so Art Deco, its wavy motif is completely devoid of square corners. You can dine around the circular bar or in two other rooms separated by scrims and etched glass (wavy, of course, and très chic). On the lunch menu, the best value is one of the $11.95 combinations, where you have your choice of any two of the following: duck spring rolls, Caesar salad, angel-hair onion rings, chef's soup, seasonal salad, calamari, and a half turkey wrap. If your idea of calamari has anything to do with rubber bands, try Michael's cornmeal-battered, hand-breaded version—tender to a T and complemented with a wonderful sauce and corn-pancetta relish. The lunch menu also features a lengthy selection of glorious salads, such as warm chicken on greens with dried cranberries, candied pecans, and goat cheese. Such are the touches that make Michael's a consistent winner. Specialties on the dinner menu include pan-seared Chilean sea bass with mushroom risotto, porcini-rubbed rack of lamb, Maine lobster fra diavolo on linguine, and pan-roasted crab cakes with truffle-roasted potatoes. For dessert, try the flash-fried hazelnut rice pudding or key lime tart. Michael's is also known for its extensive wine list, which features a generous selection of wines by the glass, including sparkling varieties.

PHILLIPPI CREEK VILLAGE OYSTER BAR

941-925-4444
www.creekseafood.com
5353 S. Tamiami Trail, Sarasota 34231
Price: Inexpensive to Expensive
Cuisine: Seafood/Old Florida
Children's Menu: Yes
Liquor: Full
Serving: L, D
Credit Cards: AE, MC, V
Handicap Access: Yes
Reservations: No
Special Features: Patio and creekside floating dock seating

In Sarasota they call their fish houses "oyster bars," and Phillippi Creek is one of the oldest. Combo pots for two are the specialty of the house and include pans full of steamed oysters, shrimp, corn on the cob, and a selection of specialty items (clams, crab, or scallops). The seafood is so fresh, it ought to be slapped. We've eaten here on several occasions; it's my husband's first choice for casual dining when we're in town. He loves the gooey-thick clam chowder and fried oyster sandwich. I typically pick the blackened grouper sandwich, which comes with a mustardy tartar sauce. You have your choice of settings here, either indoors, glassed-in with a boathouse motif, or out in the breeze on the dry dock. Either way you get a backwater view and the kind of service that puts you at ease.

✪ SELVA GRILL
941-362-4427
www.selvagrill.com
1345 Main St., Sarasota 34236
Price: Moderate to Very Expensive
Cuisine: Peruvian
Children's Menu: No
Liquor: Full
Serving: D
Credit Cards: AE, D, MC, V
Handicap Access: Yes
Reservations: Yes
Special Features: Live music, sidewalk seating

This new downtown sensation claims Peru as its country of culinary inspiration, but the good looks of its exotic dining rooms, clientele, and kitchen art bespeak much deeper dimensions. Of course, there is the ubiquitous selection of ceviches, a signature Peruvian creation. The Mixto Ceviche is true to the lime-marinated seafood tradition but with an interesting blend of corvine, shrimp, octopus, and mussels. Other starters include tuna tartare in tamarind vinaigrette and yucca in garlic sauce. Meat and seafood get equal time on the entrées menu. The menu describes *arroz con pato* as a gourmet version of a traditional duck-breast dish of northern Peru, and most of the dishes are likewise Peruvian dressed up for discriminating American palates. Purple potatoes, corn, fruit, and other trademark Peruvian products accompany roasted lamb rack with macadamia nut herb pesto, the excellent sweet-chili-glazed salmon with crab and

mango, the *arroz con pato* (cilantro- and beer-infused risotto with duck breast and salsa criollaç), and other exotic specialties.

THE TABLE
941-365-4558
www.thetablesarasota.com
1934 Hillview St., Sarasota 34239
Price: Moderate to Expensive
Cuisine: Atlantic Rim
Children's Menu: No
Liquor: Full
Serving: L, D
Credit Cards: AE, D, MC, V
Handicap Access: Yes
Reservations: Yes
Special Features: Late-night menu in the lounge

Move over "Floribbean." The Table has reinvented the genre, naming it "Atlantic Rim," to add a South American influence to the mix of Caribbean and Florida. The new "it" restaurant in Southside Village paints a pretty picture of design-forward ambience and cuisine. Enter into Mesa Lounge, where mojitos and caipirinhas are the specialty and come in flavors from kiwi to cucumber. The handsome bar with its oversized stuffed chairs also carries a mean import beer list, heavy on the Belgians. The dining room is large, but filmy veils, strategically placed, give the illusion of privacy. At lunchtime, salads take precedence. On my recent visit, I began with a shrimp and limon-rum ceviche stuffed into a small blue tortilla cone. It was packed with flavor and the right bite. Other flavors include yuzu chipotle tuna and salmon with ponzu lime vinaigrette. I waffled between the sangria-roasted chicken salad, the flank steak salad with watermelon and tomato ceviche, and the winner Valencia orange–glazed wild king salmon. And a winner it was, served artistically with Brazilian grilled hearts of palm and a subtly horseradish-flavored avocado vinaigrette. I will return for dinner, where entrées sweep the lower coastal latitudes with such temptations as Havana short-rib spring roll with guava pistachio spread, lobster gazpacho, annatto coriander–crusted lamb chops with vegetable–Yukon potato lasagna and fig demi-glaze, pan-seared diver scallops with a mash of Caribbean pumpkin and pancetta, and Venezuelan crab–crusted wild king salmon. Even the bread—sweet, round little rolls made from yucca flour and filled with mozzarella cheese—breaks the mold.

YODER'S

941-955-7771
www.yodersrestaurant.com
3434 Bahia Vista St., Sarasota 34239
Price: Inexpensive
Cuisine: Amish/Home-Style
Children's Menu: Yes
Liquor: No
Serving: B, L, D (closed Sun.)
Credit Cards: No
Handicap Access: Yes
Reservations: No

The Lobster Pot injects an element of Down East into Siesta Key Village.

A happy outgrowth of the Amish/Mennonite community in Sarasota, home-style restaurants throughout the area feature comfort-food goodness. These folks are principally farmers, so you can expect farmhouse-style freshness at their table. Yoder's sits squarely in the midst of the Pinecraft Amish community, and you know it's the real thing because many of the patrons are wearing long beards and suspenders or white bonnets and full-body aprons over their plain dresses. Amish photography, art, quilts, and other handiwork decorate the dining room, which is almost always full. Although you'll find typical sandwiches and hamburgers, Midwestern comfort food predominantly makes up the all-day menu and its daily specials: fried chicken, liver and onions, turkey and dressing, pulled smoked pork, meatloaf, and roast beef. There's no replacement for homemade goodness, and even my meatloaf sandwich benefited from red juicy tomatoes and home-baked bread. Pies are the claim to local fame here, and there's a window where fans come to pick up their whole cream or baked pies. I can vouch for only the rhubarb; tart and encased in a crumbly, sugar-glazed crust, it is the perfect ending to a meal like my mother would have made.

SIESTA KEY
THE LOBSTER POT

941-349-2323
www.sarasota-lobsterpot.com
5157 Ocean Blvd., Siesta Key 34242
Price: Inexpensive to Very Expensive
Cuisine: Seafood
Children's Menu: Yes
Liquor: Beer and wine
Serving: L, D
Credit Cards: AE, D, DC, MC, V
Handicap Access: Yes
Reservations: No

Get your Maine lobster fix here, where it even feels a little like Down East with the requisite fish netting and other nautical paraphernalia. The sliding glass door looking out on Siesta Key Village and local fish on the menu let you know you're in Florida. The generous menu starts you off with Portuguese soup (kale, kidney beans, and sausage), feta salad, raw oysters, kettle of mussels, and steamer pots. It then nods to meat-lovers with a couple of steaks and chops before getting down to the business of clams, shrimp, scallops, and, most importantly, lobster. Have it boiled, broiled, Newburg, thermidor, scampi, or ravioli. Expect to pay upward of $35 for a 1 1/4 pound lobster and closer to $40 for baked stuffed lobster duchess, the house specialty. I went for the lobster ravioli, served in a velvety, delicious tomato-basil cream sauce with a grilled lobster tail. "Deck Hand Lunches" include New England sea rolls (lobster, scallop, clam, or oyster), the signature crab-cake sandwich, quesadillas, a shrimp plate, and more.

VENICE
✪ THE CROW'S NEST
941-484-9551
www.crowsnest-venice.com
1968 Tarpon Center Dr., Venice 34285
Price: Inexpensive to Expensive
Cuisine: Seafood
Children's Menu: Yes
Liquor: Full
Serving: L, D
Credit Cards: AE, D, MC, V
Handicap Access: Yes, downstairs
Reservations: Yes
Special Features: Early-bird menu; live music weekends in the tavern

A seaworthy Venice institution, it serves the finer side of fresh seafood, including specialties such as roasted Bahamian lobster tail, walnut-crusted salmon, griddled crab cakes, and shrimp and scallops Alfredo. Meat-lovers can choose from ale-marinated ribeye, chicken picatta, and surf-and-turf selections. Service is sometimes a little off, but a lot can be forgiven when you're staring out at yachts bobbing in the harbor. The two-story, window-lined dining room has a stateroom-level nautical feel. Downstairs in the faintly lit tavern, you can order sandwiches and pub fare all day, plus there's a daily lunch menu of sandwiches and entrées such as a chipotle roast beef sandwich, sautéed pork tenderloin medallions, and fajita-seared tenderloin tips salad. As a fun alternative to key lime pie, try the ice cream drink called Key Lime Treat, bolstered with Stoli vanilla vodka. In season, be sure to make reservations well in advance, because this place has a great local following.

✪ SNOOK HAVEN
941-485-7221
www.snookhavenretreat.com
5000 E. Venice Ave., Venice 34292
Exit 191 off Interstate 75
Price: Inexpensive to Moderate
Cuisine: Old Florida/Seafood
Children's Menu: Yes
Liquor: Beer and wine
Serving: L, D
Credit Cards: MC, V
Handicap Access: Yes; restrooms not accessible
Reservations: No
Special Features: Live music nightly in season and Thursday through Monday during the summer; view of the Myakka River with canoeing available

For a poignant taste of rural Old Florida close to the interstate, visit Snook Haven at dinnertime for good, affordable eats and live country music. Hear the legend of the killer turtles (a leftover from the 1940s on-site filming of Tarzan's *Revenge of the Killer Turtles*). If you find you can't leave the peace, you may be able to rent one of the old, rustic cottages at the retreat. Or stop in for lunch and enjoy paper-basket dining—with burgers, barbecued ribs, grouper sandwich, crab cakes, and homemade ice cream—on the banks of the wild and scenic Myakka River. Choose the degree of casual seating: at the stretch tables and plastic chairs in the air-conditioned interior or the screened porch or at a picnic table on the riverside deck. Afterward, rent a canoe and paddle as slowly as time moves in these parts. It's truly a "y'all come" kind of place.

THE SODA FOUNTAIN
941-412-9860
349 W. Venice Ave., Venice 34285
Price: Inexpensive
Cuisine: American
Children's Menu: No, but all regular selections are suitable for children.
Liquor: None
Serving: L, D
Credit Cards: AE, D, DC, MC, V
Handicap Access: Yes
Reservations: No

Reward yourself with a downtown shopping break at this treat. Your inner and outer child(ren) will thank you. New, but decorated like an old-fashioned soda fountain, with black-and-white checked floors and chrome-edged swivel stools at the counter, it serves all-American sandwiches and burgers. These, however, are secondary to the main course: ice cream. Have it scooped up in a cone, slathered with syrup in a sundae, or whizzed in a canister as a shake or malted. They even sell phosphates and egg creams. Everything comes in umpteen flavors, including the hot dogs. The menu lists 18 varieties of the quarter-pound beef franks; some, such as the BLT dog and Hawaiian dog with pineapple, are quite unusual. We tried the day's lobster bisque, which was done surprisingly well, its sherry pronounced but well balanced. The Cuban sandwich and pulled-pork sandwich, the day's specials, were both tasty—but not as tasty as my chocolate—peanut butter shake.

FOOD PURVEYORS

Bakeries
Bakery d'Europa (941-795-1719; 6753 Manatee Ave. W., Bradenton 34209, at Northwest Promenade) A true bakery, with luscious cakes, cookies, desserts, pastries, muffins, bagels, and fragrant coffees.

The Broken Egg (941-346-2750; www.thebrokenegg.com; 210 Avenida Madera, Siesta Key 34242; also 941-388-6898; 6115 Exchange Way, Lakewood Ranch 34202) Yummy cinnamon swirls, muffins, coffee cakes, and pies.

C'est La Vie (941-906-9575; 1553 Main St., Sarasota 34236) This authentic French bakery holds showcases full of breads, pastries, tarts, cake, and other sweets. It also serves breakfast and lunch sidewalk side and in the café inside.

Gabby's Patisserie (941-966-CAKE; 106 Tamiami Trail N., Osprey) Croissants, muffins, éclairs, gourmet cakes, specialty coffees, frappes, smoothies, and breakfast and lunch specialties. Drive-through service available.

Pastry Art (941-955-7545; www.pastryartonmain.com; 1512 Main St., Sarasota 34236) Exquisite pastries, cakes in every flavor, tortes, cookies, cheesecakes, European-style fruit tarts, French-press coffees, and espressos.

Breakfast

Blue Dolphin Café (941-383-3787; 5370 Gulf of Mexico Dr., Longboat Key 34228, at the Centre Shops; also 941-388-3566; 470 John Ringling Blvd., Sarasota 34236, at St. Armands Circle) Stylish eatery serving breakfast all day; muffins, banana granola pancakes, Belgian waffles, omelets (try the spinach-feta). Also lunch.

✪ **The Broken Egg** (941-346-2750; www.thebrokenegg.com; 210 Avenida Madera, Siesta Key 34242; also 941-388-6898; 6115 Exchange Way, Lakewood Ranch 34202) Huge and yummy pancakes in a dozen varieties, seven types of benedicts, six omelets. Also bakery goods and lunch.

Café on the Beach (941-778-0784; 4000 Gulf Dr., Holmes Beach 34217, at Manatee County Park) Locals know this as one of the most affordable and scenic places to start the morning. Belgian waffles are a specialty, and the all-you-can-eat pancakes with sausage ($5.95) are a draw. Also lunch and dinner.

✪ **Gulf Drive Café** (941-778-1919; 900 Gulf Dr., Bradenton Beach 34207) A longtime, wildly popular spot for hotcakes, eggs, or Belgian waffles on the beach, all day long. Also lunch and dinner.

Candy & Ice Cream

Bently's Homemade Ice Cream (941-486-1816; 720 Albee Rd., Nokomis 34275) Hard and soft-serve ice cream, sorbet, Italian ices, gelato, and ice cream cakes.

Big Olaf Creamery (941-349-9392; 5208 Ocean Blvd., Siesta Key 34242) A vintage purveyor of fresh fudge, handmade waffle cones, homemade ice cream, skinny dips (low-fat frozen desserts), espresso, and cappuccino.

Joe's Eats & Sweets (941-778-0007; www.joeseatsandsweets.com; 219 Gulf Dr. S., Bradenton Beach 34217) Forty gourmet flavors of ice cream (pumpkin, cappuccino crunch, and pineapple coconut, among them) made on the premises, including sugar-free, lactose-free, and fat-free varieties, plus low-fat yogurt. Homemade fudge in dozens of unusual flavors, sodas, creative sundaes (chocolate-dipped cheesecake, latte crème, apple pickers, and wet walnut, for instance), shakes, espresso, and cappuccino.

Kilwin's Chocolates & Ice Cream (941-388-3200; 312 John Ringling Blvd., Sarasota 34236, at St. Armands Circle) Homemade ice cream, specialty sundaes, Mackinac Island fudge, and handmade chocolates.

Scoop Daddy's (941-388-1650; 373 St. Armands Circle) Combines the nostalgia of a soda fountain and retro '50s entertainment; features a jukebox and reproduction gifts.

Two Scoops (941-779-2422); 101 S. Bay Blvd. #A2, Anna Maria 34216) Near the city pier, this has become the talk of local sweet-tooth types. Offers scrumptious sundaes; a long line of ice cream flavors, such as birthday cake and trash can; an espresso bar; teas; plus muffins, bagels, and luncheon wrap sandwiches.

Coffee

Bella Coffee House (941-747-1687; 417 Old Main St., Bradenton 34205) Espresso, lattes, French-press coffee, frappes, teas, fruit smoothies, pastries, and desserts.

The B'Towne Coffee Co. (941-745-3100; 4400 12th St. W., Bradenton 34205) Joffrey's coffee and espresso, plus ice cream, bakery treats, and wireless Internet access.

If Teacups Could Talk (941-488-4400; 239 W. Miami Ave., Venice 34285) A Victorian-style coffee and tea room with a wide selection of teas, plus traditional tea service and other luncheon items.

Island Gourmet (941-484-3667; 201 Venice Ave. W., Venice 34285) Buy gourmet coffee by the bag or cup at the espresso bar. Also teas, wine, spices, and hard-to-find gourmet food items.

Local Coffee & Tea (941-870-2671; www.localcoffee.com; 5138 Ocean Blvd., Sarasota, in Siesta Key Village) Espresso, lattes, more than 20 loose-leaf teas, smoothies, and bakery goods. Free Wi-Fi access.

Deli & Specialty Foods

Geier's Sausage Kitchen (941-923-3004; 7447 Tamiami Trail, Sarasota 34231) European-style sausage and smoked meats, prime fresh meats, imported cheeses, beer, wine, pastries, and other gourmet items.

The Gourmet Market (941-953-9101, 888-953-9101; www.thegourmetmarket.com; 1469 Main St., Sarasota 34236) A delightful place full of good smells, cheeses, Godiva chocolates, pastas, oils, vinegars, coffees, wine, and hot sauces.

✪ **Morton's Market** (941-955-9856; www.epicureanlife.com; 1924 S. Osprey Ave., Sarasota 34239, at Southside Village) The ultimate gourmet's delight, it sells hot and cold prepared items for takeout, fresh produce, deli and fresh meats, seafood, coffees, shelves of gourmet products—you name it.

Productos Latinos (941-955-2071; 1145 S. Tamiami Trail, Sarasota 34239, at Bahia Vista St.) Fresh yucca and other produce, tortillas, hot pepper sauces, Mexican cheese, and other packaged Latin food products.

St. Armands Gifts & Winery (941-388-5330 or 800-591-5330; www.starmandswinery .com; 466 John Ringling Blvd., Sarasota 34236) Tropical fruit wines are the specialty here, but it also sells other tasty treats, such as rum cake and bottled sauces.

✪ **Sarasota Olive Oil Company** (941-366-2008; www.sarasotaoliveoil.com; 1419 Fifth St., Sarasota 34228) A very cool little "tongues-on" place in the Rosemary District. Taste a couple of dozen different kinds of salt from the salt bar, condiments such as artichoke sauce or cider confit with apples and calvados from one table, and multiple types of olive oil from around the world or flavored with garlic, jalapeno, basil, navel orange, and more.

Southside Deli (941-330-9302; 1825 Hillview St., Sarasota 34239) Popular spot for a take-out or eat-in lunch. Breakfast, luncheon sandwiches and salads, smoothies.

A Taste of the Columbia Restaurant (941-388-1026; www.columbiarestaurant.com; 411 St. Armands Circle, Sarasota 34236) Dressings, black-beans mix, sangria jelly, cookbooks, coffee, wine, cigars, and other items sold in the renowned Spanish restaurant.

Too Jay's (941-362-3692; www.toojays.com ; Westfield Southgate, 3501 S. Tamiami Trail, Sarasota 34239) This import from the Tampa area is the ultimate in deli food: sandwiches, hot comfort-food dishes, and the real thing in New York cheesecake.

Fruit & Vegetable Stands

Albritton Fruit (800-237-3682 or 941-923-2573; www.albrittonfruit.com; 5430 Proctor Rd., Sarasota 34233) With five locations throughout the area, Albritton is a well-known name in citrus.

Mixon Fruit Farms (941-748-5829, 800-608-2525; www.mixon.com; 2712 26th Ave. E., P.O. Box 25200, Bradenton 34206) A large, old, family-owned business specializing in citrus. Tram tours of the grove and processing plant, free samples, shipping, and a gift shop selling fruit, fudge, ice cream, and jellies. Open November through April.

Sarasota Farmers' Market (941-951-2656; Lemon Ave., between First St. and Main St., downtown Sarasota) Florida fruits, vegetables, flowers, plants, and honey. Every Saturday, 7 AM to noon.

Internet Cafés

Bella Luna Café (941-497-2504; 200 Miami Ave., Venice 34285) Coffee and pastries. Wireless access but no electric plug-ins.

Local Coffee & Tea (941-870-2671; www.localcoffee.com; 5138 Ocean Blvd., Sarasota, in Siesta Key Village) Free Wi-Fi; coffee drinks, teas, smoothies, and bakery goods.

Natural Foods

Good Earth Natural Foods (941-795-0478, 800-638-5201; www.goodearthfoods.com; 6717 Manatee Ave. W., Bradenton 34209) A full line of organic produce and healthy food products. Two other Bradenton locations where licensed nutritional counselors are on site.

The Granary Natural Foods Market (941-924-4754; 1930 Stickney Point Rd., Sarasota 34231, east of the Siesta Key bridge) A full-service mart with a juice bar, hot and cold deli, salad and burrito bar, and a large fresh produce and grains area.

Richard's Whole Foods (941-966-0596; www.richardswholefoods.com; 1092 Tamiami Trail S., Osprey 34229) One of several area locations, it carries a good stock of bulk natural foods and organic groceries.

Pizza & Takeout

Crusty's Pizza (941-366-3100; 3800 Tamiami Trail S. #29, Sarasota 34239, at Paradise Plaza) Stuffed, pan, or Chicago-style thin-crust pizza. Also wings, soups, salads, sandwiches, and pasta dishes to go.

Main Bar Sandwich Shop (941-955-8733; www.themainbar.com; 1944 Main St., Sarasota 34236) A long list of sandwiches, hot and cold, plus salads and desserts. Specialties include the Aztec sandwich with roast beef, provolone, and jalapeño dressing and the New Orleans Muffuletta and Veggiletta.

✪ **Morton's Market** (941-955-9856; www.epicureanlife.com; 1924 S. Osprey Ave., Sarasota 34239, at Southside Village; also 941-782-0916; 8140 Lakewood Main St., Lakewood Ranch 34202) Wildly popular (practically legendary), Morton's sells hot prepared items, pizza, deli sandwiches, salads, bakery goods, and homemade desserts for takeout, plus fresh produce, deli and fresh meats, seafood, coffees, and gourmet products.

Seafood

Captain Brian's Seafood Market (941-351-4492; 8421 N. Tamiami Trail, Sarasota 34243) Fresh local and imported seafood in a large, dine-in venue.

Captain Eddie's Retail Market (941-484-4623; 107 Colonia Ln. E., Nokomis 342750) "Stone crab headquarters," it proclaims. Fresh seafood of all varieties in a restaurant venue.

✪ **Star Fish Company** (941-794-1243; 12306 46th Ave. W., P.O. Box 1, Cortez 34215) To get any closer to the source, you'd have to get wet. This long-standing tradition is the anchor of Cortez village's working waterfront, where crusted old fishing boats pull up and murals and plaques deliver lessons on history and heritage. Buy fresh, fresh fish in the market to take home, or order it off the menu to enjoy on dockside picnic tables.

CULTURE

Culture arrived on the Sarasota Bay coast with the early settlers of wealth and means. Eager at first to escape metropolitan ways for the simplicity of life on the beach, they eventually craved access to theater and fine arts, and so ensured the existence of both.

Sarasota benefited most from the generous cultural endowment of the Ringling brothers. Not only did the Ringlings bring circus magic to a quiet frontier town, but they also exposed the pioneers to the wonders of Gilded Age European art and architecture. In their wake they left a spirit that is still palpable and entirely unique to the Gulf Coast. Art schools and theater groups in Sarasota breed a freshness, vitality, daring, and avant-garde attitude that is unusual for a town of this size. Siesta Key, especially, has an atmosphere that has attracted writers, artists, actors, and cartoonists since folks began settling there.

Sarasota's cultural heritage began with an influx of Scottish settlers at the turn of the century. Now widely varied, its population includes a colony of Amish/Mennonite residents in a district known as Pinecraft, around Bahia Vista Street and Beneva Road. Here you'll see long-bearded men driving tractors down the streets, a Mennonite church, simple homes, a neighborhood park, and an Amish restaurant or two. The historic African American district is known as Rosemary District and lies between Highways 41 and 301 and between 10th and Myrtle streets.

Architecture

In the **Bradenton** area, the Greek Revival–style plantation house has left its mark. The best example of this style survives grandly at ✪ **Gamble Plantation** (see "Historic Sites"). Pioneer styles are preserved at the **Manatee Historical Village**, which includes a Cracker Gothic farmhouse, a one-room schoolhouse, and an early brick store. In downtown Bradenton you'll find a Mediterranean influence in commercial buildings such as the South Florida Museum. Old Florida–Victorian style survives in the homes of neighborhoods around downtown.

On **Longboat Key,** resorts and mansions are modern and ostentatious. In the village once known as Longbeach, one finds a return to comfortable, older styles and a bit of New England charm.

Sarasota's downtown and bay areas hold a smorgasbord of old European styles, from the lavish, Italian-inspired ✪ **Cà d'Zan** at the Ringling Estate to the recently renovated

Robert Gamble's Greek Revival plantation home reflected his Virginia origins.

and expanded ✪ **Sarasota Opera House** downtown. Fine examples of old residential architecture are found on the fringes of the downtown area. In contrast, the Frank Lloyd Wright Foundation's ✪ **Van Wezel Performing Arts Hall** makes a big-purple-shell statement on the bay shoreline.

In the 1950s Sarasota revolutionized local architecture by developing a contemporary style suitable to the environment. Examples of the Sarasota School of Architecture are spread throughout the area. Often overlooked, **Venice** houses many architectural treasures created in the 1920s, when the Brotherhood of Locomotive Engineers selected it as a retirement center and subsequently built a model city in northern Italian style. Two shining examples of this style are the **Park Place Nursing Home**—originally the Hotel Venice— at Tampa Avenue and Nassau Street and the nearby **Venice Mall**, once the San Marco Hotel, later the Kentucky Military Institute. The length of **West Venice Avenue** reveals stunning shops and homes in the prevailing Mediterranean Revival style, as does the **Venezia Park** neighborhood along nearby Nassau Street. You'll find architectural treasures throughout the city, which strives to preserve its treasures.

Cinema
FILM
Sarasota is a hotbed for film, with its celebrated film festivals, alternative cinema, and ideal locations for filming.

Sarasota Film Society (941-364-8662, box office: 941-955-FILM; www.filmsociety.org; Burns Court Cinema, 506 Burns Ln., Sarasota 34236, downtown; P.O. Box 3378, Sarasota 34230) This group is devoted to screening quality international films, both first-run and classic, year-round. It sponsors the Cine-World Film Festival (see "Calendar of Events" at the end of this chapter).

MOVIES

AMC 12 Theatres at Westfield Sarasota Square (941-922-9609; westfield.com/Sarasota; 8201 S. Tamiami Trail, Sarasota 34238, at Beneva Rd.)

Burns Court Cinema (941-955-3456; www.filmsociety.org; 506 Burns Ln., Sarasota 34236) A bright pink movie theater, showing art and other out-of-the-mainstream films on three screens.

Regal Hollywood 20 (941-365-2000; www.regalcinemas.com; 1993 Main St. at Hwy. 301, Sarasota 34236, downtown) State-of-the-art theaters with stadium seating and surround-sound stereo.

Regal Oakmont 8 (941-795-4106; www.regalcinemas.com; 4801 Cortez Rd. W., Bradenton 34210)

Dance

American International Dance Centre (941-955-8363; 556 S. Pineapple Ave., Sarasota 34236) Ballroom dancing instruction and competition for adults and children.

Gotta Dance Studio (941-486-0326; 303 Tamiami Trail S., Nokomis 34275; www.gottadancestudio.net) Classes in tango, children's ballroom, and more for beginners and experienced dancers.

Sarasota Ballet (941-351-8000, 800-361-8388; www.sarasotaballet.org; 5555 N. Tamiami Trail, Sarasota 34243) Classic and interpretative dance performances are staged by professionals at the FSU Center for the Performing Arts, Sarasota Opera House, and Van Wezel Performing Arts Center, from October to April.

Gardens

HISTORIC SPANISH POINT

941-966-5214
www.historicspanishpoint.org
337 N. Tamiami Trail, P.O. Box 846, Osprey 34229
Open: 9–5, Mon.–Sat.; 12–5, Sun.
Admission: $9 adults, $8 Florida residents and seniors, $3 children ages 6–12. Docent tram tours $3 extra each.

Marie Selby Gardens shows off more than 5,000 orchids in its lush setting.

This multiera historic attraction (see "Historic Homes & Sites," below) features the ornamental and native gardens built by Sarasota matriarch Bertha Honore Palmer in the 1910s. The Duchene Lawn, the most dramatic, is lined with towering palms and holds a Greek-column portal that once framed a view of the sea. To create the lovely jungle walk, Mrs. Palmer built a miniature aqueduct system. A sunken garden and pergola, fern walk, and ornamental pond also provide oases of lush respite along the path at this 30-acre site.

MARIE SELBY BOTANICAL GARDENS

941-366-5731
www.selby.org
811 S. Palm Ave., Sarasota 34236
Open: Daily 10–5
Admission: $12 adults, $6 children ages 6–11, free for children ages 5 and under

This 1920s residence on Sarasota Bay occupies 15 acres of gardens that wow plant lovers with plots of palm, bamboo, hibiscus, tropical food plants, herbs, and other exotic flora. Selby is world renowned for its collection of more than 5,000 orchids in a lush rainforest setting of bromeliads and rare tropical plants. New, artsy interpretative signage tells the different plants' stories, and a secret children's garden with a maze and tree platform is forthcoming. Delightful shops and a café operated by Michael's on East (see "Dining") add to the natural pleasures.

RINGLING ESTATE ROSE GARDEN AND GROUNDS

941-355-5101
www.ringling.org
5401 Bay Shore Rd., Sarasota 34243
On the Ringling Estate
Open: Daily 10–5:30
Admission: Free with admission to the Ringling complex

Mammoth banyan trees (gifts from Thomas Edison, who had an estate in Fort Myers), a showy poinciana, statuesque royal palms, and a rose garden planted in 1913 are the center-pieces of the lovely bayfront Ringling Estate. Near Cà d'Zan, family graves are situated in the Secret Garden, rediscovered 25 years ago and recently rededicated. The Dwarf Garden lies between the art museum and the visitors center.

SARASOTA JUNGLE GARDENS

941-355-5305
www.sarasotajunglegardens.com
3701 Bayshore Rd., Sarasota 34234
Open: Daily 9–5
Admission: $12 adults, $11 seniors, $8 children ages 3–12

Although this is largely a kiddie attraction, plant lovers will enjoy the botanical gardens and cool, tropical jungle. Winding paved paths lead easily through the grounds' 16 acres, a hundred varieties of palms, and countless species of indigenous and exotic flora, all iden-tified. Private nooks, arbored benches, and bubbling brooks make this a lovely spot for quiet reflection, especially in the early morning before the throngs arrive. Exotic birds and other attractions are gravy for the connoisseur of nature. (See "Kids' Stuff" in this section.) Snack bar and gift shop.

Historic Homes & Sites
BRADEN CASTLE RUINS

27th St. E. and Rte. 64, Bradenton
Open: Daily sunrise to sunset
Admission: Free

At the juncture of the Manatee and Braden Rivers, antebellum memories crumble gracefully in a setting recognized by the National Register of Historic Sites. Just short of spectacular, the plantation house ruins are surrounded by chain-link fences and posted with KEEP OUT DANGER signs. They hide at the center of a retirement trailer community in a riverside park that's not easy to find. A marker tells the story of Dr. Joseph Addison Braden from Virginia and his ill-fated Braden Plantation.

CÀ D'ZAN

941-355-5101
www.ringling.org
5401 Bay Shore Rd., Sarasota 34243
On the Ringling Estate
Open: Daily 10–5:30
Admission: $15 adults, $13 seniors, $5 students and Florida teachers with ID, free for children under age 5; covers admission to all Ringling attractions

A new visitors center with gift shop, restored 18th-century European theater, and restaurant welcomes you to the Ringling complex, which also contains the centerpiece art museum, a circus museum and a new circus exhibit building, gardens, and John Ringling's fabulous *palazzo* Cà d'zan. Six years and a $15 million restoration, completed in April 2002, have brought this 32-room showpiece back to its Gilded Age glory. Visitors can take a self-guided tour of the first floor or sign up for a guided tour of the first two floors. The latter is really the best option, but try to get there early for the best tour and shortest wait. (Guides shorten the tours if a lot of people have signed up for the 22-person tours.) For an extra $20, you can get the private tour of upper floors and the tower. Using the Doges Palace in Venice as a model, circus king John Ringling spared no expense building this monument to success and overindulgence in the 1920s. He imported styles, materials, and pieces from Italy, France, and elsewhere around the world to embellish his eponymous (in Italian dialect) "House of John." Baroque, Gothic, and Renaissance elements, marble, colored tiles, and jesterlike, multicolor-tinted leaded windows contribute to a breathtaking, ornate Roaring Twenties opulence in the $1.5 million (nearly $17 million in today's currency) mansion on the bay at the John and Mable Ringling Museum of Art (see "Visual Arts Centers & Resources," below).

CORTEZ VILLAGE

Cortez Rd. and 123rd St., Bradenton
Remnants of an 1880s fishing village include old tin-roofed fish houses, boat works, and a waterfront store. Exhibits and painted murals throughout the salty district describe local culture and environmental practices.

✪ DE SOTO NATIONAL MEMORIAL

941-792-0458
www.nps.gov/deso
75th St. NW, P.O. Box 15390, Bradenton 34280
Open: Visitors center open daily 9–5; park open daily sunrise to sunset
Admission: Free

Somewhat off the beaten path, this is a place where you can imagine yourself back in the 16th century with conquistadores in heavy armor trying to survive among irate Native Americans, mosquitoes, and sweltering heat. Engraved plaques, a re-created Amerindian village, and a half-mile-long trail tell the story of Hernando de Soto's life and adventures here, where supposedly he first breached the shores of the Florida mainland to begin his heroic trek to the Mississippi River. A visitors center holds artifacts and shells, and a 22-minute video presentation is available. In the winter, rangers and volunteers dress up and play the parts of 16th-century inhabitants, demonstrating weaponry and methods of food preparation.

DOWNTOWN BRADENTON

Main St. and Manatee Ave. (Route 64)

Old Main Street and the city yacht basin are the historic downtown district's backbone. Because the area is compact, it's easy to walk and experience the old architecture, a fine museum, an intimate theater, park benches, sidewalk eateries, antique stores, and brick-paved crosswalks. Locals are trying hard to pump new life into a river town that died with the advent of the automobile. A walking plaza is in the works, and the future looks bright. In the meantime, visit the shops on Main Street and have lunch, then stroll around nearby Point Pleasant for a taste of Bradenton's oak-studded homeyness and heritage. Every Saturday, October through April, visit the farmers' market.

GAMBLE PLANTATION HISTORIC STATE PARK

941-723-4536

www.floridastateparks.org/gambleplantation

3708 Patten Ave., Ellenton 34222

Route 301 near I-75, exit 224

Open: Visitors center 8–4:30 (closed 11:45–12:45); tours depart at 9:30, 10:30, 1, 2, 3, and 4. Closed: Tues. and Wed.

Admission: Mansion tour, $5 adults, $3 children ages 6–12. Free admission to visitors center museum.

Major Robert Gamble, originally from Scotland, learned about sugar planting in Virginia and Tallahassee before he moved to the Manatee River. He eventually cleared 1,500 acres of jungle using slave labor and built a Greek Revival–style home. He constructed the mansion's crowning touch—18 Greek columns—with a mortar, known as tabby, made of crushed and burned seashells. The spacious (by the time's standards) palace was inhabited by bachelor Gamble alone but served as the area's social hub until the major was forced to sell it in 1856 because of hurricane and frost damage and market losses. In 1925 the United Daughters of the Confederacy rescued the mansion from decades of neglect. The site was declared a Confederate shrine for its role in sheltering Confederate secretary of state Judah P. Benjamin when he fled for his life after the Civil War. The United Daughters donated the monument to the state a couple of years later. Visitors can see the inside of the home only by a tour, which takes less than an hour. The two floors contain period furnishings and housewares, which the park ranger explains in lively, interesting dialogue. You'll learn, for example, how such expressions as "hush puppy," "sleep tight," and "pop goes the weasel" came to be and about the lives of 19th-century plantation owners and slaves. The museum in the visitors center tells the plantation's story through the eras. A picnic shelter accommodates lunchers.

✪ HISTORIC SPANISH POINT

941-966-5214
www.historicspanishpoint.org
337 N. Tamiami Trail, P.O. Box 846, Osprey 34229
Open: 9–5 Mon.–Sat., 12–5 Sun.
Admission: $9 adults, $8 Florida residents and seniors, $3 children ages 6–12. Docent tram tours $3 extra each.

This historic site spans multiple eras of the region's past—from 2150 BCE through 1918. Its importance lies not only in its historical aspects but also in its environmental and archae-ological significance. Assembled on the 30-acre Little Sarasota Bay estate, once owned by socialite Bertha Palmer, are prehistoric Indian burial grounds, a cutaway of a shell midden mound, the relocated homestead and family chapel of the pioneering Webb dynasty, Mrs. Palmer's restored gardens (see "Gardens" in this section), and a late Victorian pioneer home. Local actors give living-history performances on Saturdays and Sundays in the win-ter. Guided tours, tram rides, and boat tours are available; reserve ahead for the tram tours. Another tip: Bring mosquito repellent in warm weather.

MANATEE VILLAGE HISTORICAL PARK

941-741-4075
www.manateeclerk.com/ClerkServices/HisVill/village.htm
604 15th St. E., Bradenton 34208
At Manatee Ave.

The Stephens House represents pioneer home life at Manatee Village Historical Park.

Open: 9–4:30 weekdays, 1:30–4:30 Sun.
Admission: Free

Several buildings with local historical significance have been restored and moved to a pleasant, oak-shaded park strongly representative of Bradenton's old wooded and winding neighborhoods. The County Courthouse, completed in 1860, is the oldest. Others include a circa-1889 church (the oldest congregation south of Tampa), a Cracker farmhouse, a one-room schoolhouse, a smokehouse, and a brick general store from the early 19th century. A museum of artifacts, photographs, and hands-on exhibits for children is located in the general store. The Cracker-Gothic Stephens House is stocked with preserves, period kitchen items, furniture, and farm implements. Fogarty Boat Works reflects Bradenton's boat-building heritage. The staff sometimes wears historically accurate dress. Across the street lies the Manatee Burying Ground, which dates from 1850. All in all, the park is a romantic site, grossly underrated and lightly visited.

PALMETTO HISTORICAL PARK

941-723-4991
www.manateeclerk.com/ClerkServices/HisVill/village.htm
515 10th Ave. W., P.O. Box 1192, Palmetto 34221.
Open: 10 noon and 1–4 Tues.–Fri. and the first and third Sat. of the month
Admission: Free

Check in at the Carnegie Library to visit historic museum exhibits and to gain admission to some of the village's other buildings, including a circa-1880 post office, a wedding chapel that is a composite of three Palmetto historic churches, a one-room schoolhouse, and the Cypress House Museum, which is devoted to military artifacts. Within the park, the Manatee County Agricultural Museum is a staffed facility housed in a barnlike structure; it holds hands-on and other displays demonstrating the importance of farming to Manatee County past and present.

Kids' Stuff
BAYFRONT PARK

Downtown Sarasota
Admission: Free

Toddlers especially love the shallow pool, with its squirting fountains and sculptures of frogs, manatees, turtles, gators, and fish that they can climb. It's a good place for strolling, people-watching from a park bench, jogging, inline skating, and shopping for boat charters. There's a small, inexpensive restaurant and water-sports concession within. In 2001 the park began hosting a seasonal Bayfront Exhibition of street sculptures. The exhibitions have now become a year-round event and feature artists from around the world.

THE CHILDREN'S GARDEN

941-330-1711
www.sarasotachildrensgarden.com
1670 Tenth Way, Sarasota 34236
Open: 10–5 Tues.–Sun.
Admission: $10 adults, $5 children ages 3–12

This magical fantasy, an especially popular place for parties, uses recycled products and old-fashioned concepts to entertain children. Kids can dress up in their choice from a roomful of costumes; take the yellow brick road to play gardens where pirate ships, dragons, and an octopus lurk; find their way through the maze; visit the butterfly garden; run, climb, jump, and make believe.

✪ G.WIZ
941-309-4949
www.gwiz.org
1001 Boulevard of the Arts, Sarasota 34236
Selby Library Building
Open: 10–5 Mon.–Fri., 10–6, Sat., noon–6 Sun.
Admission: $9 adults, $8 seniors, $6 children ages 3–18

G.WIZ stands for Gulfcoast Wonder and Imagination Zone. But "G.WIZ" about sums it up, as does "wow!" All shiny and high-tech, it offers hours of enrichment and entertainment in an uncrowded, gallerylike, glass geodesic structure. The state-of-the-art outdoor playground is free and includes much more than mere swings and slides. Inside, on two levels, theme areas explore various scientific and artistic phenomena. Kids love to make timed dashes against one another and the jump measurer. The Kids' Zone is geared toward toddlers and includes a table for fossil digging, a bubble table, and fun-house mirrors. Upstairs, we like the animation workstations best. Here kids can pose and click action figures and other toys one frame at a time to create a short film. For constructive play, this is the best place around to take the kids. Sutton's Garden/Habitat Zone has butterflies on the loose and snakes and bees contained. A special camera lets you spy underwater at the fish pond. Don't forget to stop in the gift shop (as if the kids would let you) for educational playthings.

SARASOTA JUNGLE GARDENS
941-355-5305
www.sarasotajunglegardens.com
3701 Bayshore Rd., Sarasota 34234
Open: Daily 9–5
Admission: $12 adults, $11 seniors, $8 children ages 3–12

A birds-of-prey exhibit and show, reptile and rainforest-bird shows (starring *Ed Sullivan Show* star Frosty), a Meet the Keeper program, free-strolling flamingos you can handfeed, a playground with a jungle theme, a bird posing area, pony rides ($3 each, $8 with photo, daily, 11–2), monkeys, swans, wallabies, and other live animals and feathered friends make this one of the area's favorite children's attractions. Its peaceful, junglelike gardens appeal to others. (See "Gardens" in this section.)

SOUTH FLORIDA MUSEUM & BISHOP PLANETARIUM
941-746-4131
www.southfloridamuseum.org
201 10th St. W., Bradenton 32405
Open: 10–5 Mon.–Sat., 12–5 Sun., Jan.–Apr., July
Closed: Mon. during all other months and closed last two weeks of Aug.

Snooty, South Florida Museum's celebrity manatee, takes the stage.

Admission: $15.95 adults, $13.95 seniors, $11.95 children ages 5–12. Adults $7.95 after 5 PM on Thurs.; kids half price all day Thurs.

The newly renovated downtown museum has a designated Discovery Place for kids' hands-on enjoyment. In the regular museum, kids especially love the prehistoric skeleton casts, live manatees, and the drawer of shrunken heads in the "visible storage" area. Special Thursday-evening programs keep the museum open until 9 PM with manatee presentations, crafts, special tours, and planetarium shows.

VENICE LITTLE THEATRE FOR YOUNG PEOPLE

941-488-1115
www.venicestage.com
140 W. Tampa Ave., Venice 34285

One of the most successful nonprofit community theaters in the United States, the Little Theatre hosts off-season summer theatrical instruction (call 941-486-8679) and three musical performances for youngsters from October through May.

Museums

(For art museums, see "Visual Arts Centers & Resources.")

✪ ANNA MARIA ISLAND HISTORICAL MUSEUM

941-778-0492
402 Pine Ave., Anna Maria 34216
Open: Tues.–Sat. 10–4, Sept.–Apr.; Mon.–Fri. 10–1, May–Aug.
Closed: Sun. and Mon. in season; weekends in summer
Admission: Donations accepted

A homey little museum inside a 1920s icehouse holds a wealth of photos, maps, records, books, a shell collection, a loggerhead turtle display, and vintage movies on video. Next door sits the old jail, its humorous graffiti worth a chuckle. The newest adjunct to the museum, Belle Haven Cottage, is filled with antiques, and shares space with a natural garden.

FLORIDA GULF COAST MARITIME MUSEUM
941-708-4935
www.manateeclerk.com
4415 119th St. W., P.O. Box 100, Cortez 34215
Open: Tues.–Sat. 8–5

Newly completed in fall 2007 in the 1912 Cortez Schoolhouse, this ongoing project explores the state's maritime heritage from Cedar Keys to the Florida Keys, with special emphasis on Cortez. Displays include artwork, ship models, artifacts, and photographs from prehistoric times to present. The museum restores historic watercraft and builds models from historic plans. Visitors who call ahead are welcome to join in.

✪ RINGLING CIRCUS MUSEUM & TIBBALS LEARNING CENTER
941-355-5101
www.ringling.org
5401 Bay Shore Rd., Sarasota 34243
On the Ringling Estate
Open: Daily 10–5:30
Admission: $15 adults, $13 seniors, $5 students and Florida teachers with ID, free for children under age 5; covers admission to all Ringling attractions.

The circus museum was Florida's way of saying thank you to John Ringling back in 1948. Its re-creation of Big Top magic paid tribute to a man whom many believed invented the circus and who bequeathed to the city a legacy of exotica, sophistication, and art appreciation. The museum reflects Ringling's seemingly contradictory interests. Fine-arts displays counterbalance high-wire exhibits. Black-and-white photography is juxtaposed with gilded fantasy. Tasteful cloth mannequins model plumed and sequined costumes. The museum plays up Sarasota's role as winter headquarters for the circus and its part in the filming of the movie *The Greatest Show on Earth*. In 2006, Tibbals Learning Center opened next to the museum; the addition is a more modern tribute to the art and magic of the circus in a larger sense than Ringling and Sarasota. The experience begins with a short film of historic footage that deals with the logistics of the moving city known as a circus. The complexity of visiting 150 towns in one season with 100 railcars inspired Howard Tibbals to create a 3,800-square-foot miniature model of the circus—the largest in the world—that covers every aspect of the circus from its arrival into a town by train to behind the scenes and the Big Top main event. Upstairs, exhibits include another miniature circus, memorabilia, and a time line chronicling the circus from its ancient origins, through its Golden Age, and up to its modern incarnations. The museum and learning center are located on the grounds of the John and Mable Ringling Museum of Art (see "Visual Arts Centers & Resources," below).

✪ SARASOTA CLASSIC CAR MUSEUM
941-355-6228
www.sarasotacarmuseum.org

5500 N. Tamiami Trail, Sarasota 34239
Open: Daily 9–6
Admission: $8.50 adults, $7.65 seniors, $5.75 juniors ages 13–17, $4 children ages 6–12

More than 125 antique, classic, muscle, and celebrity cars park under one roof. See the DeLorean from *Back to the Future*; four of the Beatles' cars, including the psychedelic party car; John Ringling's Rolls Royces and Pierce Arrows; and vintage motorized vehicles dating from 1903. The kids will get a kick out of the vintage game arcade, where for as little as a nickel they can make Peppy the Musical Clown dance, get their fortune told by the Great Swami, and motor cross-country on the Drive Mobile. It's lots more fun than modern-day arcades.

SOUTH FLORIDA MUSEUM & BISHOP PLANETARIUM

941-746-4131
www.southfloridamuseum.org
201 10th St. W., Bradenton 32405
Open: 10–5 Mon.–Sat., 12–5 Sun., Jan.–Apr., July
Closed: Mon. during all other months and closed the last two weeks of Aug.
Admission: $15.95 adults, $13.95 seniors, $11.95 children ages 5–12

This two-story museum is undergoing a $5 million renovation that has installed shiny new, impressive displays and a planetarium so state-of-the-art there's only two more like it in the world. The museum's first floor focuses on ancient history and features prehistoric skeleton casts, realistic life-size Native American dioramas, and appropriate sound effects. One of the museum's most prized exhibits, the Tallant Collection, displays Amerindian artifacts excavated mostly from Manatee County. Upstairs is still undergoing a

The new Tibbals Learning Center at Ringling Estates recreates the magic of the Big Top.

makeover that, when completed in 2008, will simulate different local environments and include exhibits that virtually take you underwater in a mangrove forest and the gulf. The star of the museum is Snooty, the oldest known manatee born in captivity (since 1948) in the United States. You can watch him and his current playmate underwater through aquarium windows or from above at the Parker Aquarium, where interactive exhibits explain the plight of the endangered manatee and educational presentations take place throughout the day. The outdoor Spanish Plaza holds a 16th-century chapel, manor house, and typical village home. Bishop Planetarium shows include IMAX-like movies narrated by Tom Hanks and Harrison Ford.

VENICE ARCHIVES AND AREA HISTORICAL COLLECTION
941-486-2487
351 S. Nassau St., Venice 34285
www.venicegov.com/archives.htm
Open: Mon. and Wed. 10–4, June–Dec.; Mon., Tues., and Wed. 10–4, Jan.–May
Admission: Free or by donation

The most interesting relic here is the building that houses the facility. A 1927 Italianate structure with a triangular base and a Renaissance tower, it once was called the Triangle Inn. Stop for a peek at whatever exhibit is showing, a room full of local fossils, and another room honoring city father Dr. Fred Albee, whose operating table you'll find among the other memorabilia. A city park lies across the street.

Music & Nightlife
Sarasota dances with action throughout the week and especially on weekends. Local bands and up-and-coming stars appear in theaters, cabarets, and nightclubs. Cores of activity include downtown and posh St. Armands Circle. Every Friday check the *Sarasota Herald-Tribune*'s "Ticket" and *Bradenton Herald*'s "Weekend" to learn what's happening in area clubs.

BRADENTON
The Distillery (941-739-7845; www.thedistillery.com; 108 44th Ave. E., Bradenton 34203) Live Southern rock, '80s tunes, and more.

BRADENTON BEACH
Beachhouse (941-779-2222; www.groupersandwich.com; 200 Gulf Dr. N., Bradenton Beach 34217) Live reggae and island music most evenings.

ST. ARMANDS KEY
Cha Cha Coconuts (941-388-3300; 417 St. Armands Circle, Sarasota 34236) Contemporary music and dancing Thursday through Sunday and some Wednesdays.

SARASOTA
Concerts at Ringling (941-359-5700; www.ringling.org; John and Mable Ringling Museum of Art, 5401 Bay Shore Rd., Sarasota 34243) Local and international musicians perform seasonally in the courtyard and in the Rubens Galleries.

Five O'Clock Club (941-366-5555; www.5oclockclub.net; 1930 Hillview St., Sarasota, 34239) The hottest thing going away from downtown, it hosts live bands nightly. Happy hour here lasts from 11 AM to 8 PM!

Florida West Coast Symphony (941-953-3434; www.fwcs.org; 709 Tamiami Trail N., Sarasota 34236) Besides holding classical symphony concerts in Bradenton and Sarasota from September to May, this group sponsors June's Sarasota Music Festival, a chamber orchestra, and other special performances.

✪ **The Gator Club** (941-366-5969; www.thegatorclub.com; 1490 Main St., Sarasota 34236) One of the hottest places downtown, in historic digs with a pressed-tin ceiling and straw ceiling fans. Live music nightly.

Jazz Club of Sarasota (941-366-1552, hot line 941-316-9207; www.jazzclubsarasota.com; 330 S. Pineapple Ave., Suite 111, Sarasota 34236) This organization dedicates itself to the perpetuation and encouragement of jazz performance by presenting various monthly and annual events, Saturday jazz jams, members' concerts, special presentations, and youth programs. It also has a musical instrument lending library and sponsors the weeklong Sarasota Jazz Festival in March (see "Calendar of Events").

Sarasota Concert Band (941-364-2263; www.sarasotaconcertband.homestead.com; 1345 Main St., Sarasota 34236) This ensemble's 50-some members perform from October through May at Van Wezel Performing Arts Hall and other venues and at outdoor concerts throughout the area.

Sarasota Friends of Folk Music (941-377-9256; www.sarafolk.org; 3874 Wolverine St., Sarasota 34232) This group specializes in Florida folk music and performs free monthly concerts on City Island at the Sarasota Sailing Squadron.

SIESTA KEY

✪ **Beach Club** (941-349-6311; 5151 Ocean Blvd., Siesta Key 34242) Once a rowdy college bar, this pool hall–nightclub has been hosting local rock, jazz, and reggae groups nightly since 1947.

VENICE

Crow's Nest (941-484-9551; www.crowsnest-venice.com; 1968 Tarpon Center Dr., Venice 34285) Features live soloists and duets on a changing calendar, every night but Sunday.

Venice Symphony (941-488-1010; www.thevenicesymphony.org; P.O. Box 1561, Venice 34284) Classical and pops concerts December through April at Church of the Nazarene (1535 E. Venice Ave.) and a free outdoor pops concert in March.

Specialty Libraries

Family Heritage House (941-752-5319; www.familyheritagehouse.com; Manatee Community College, 5840 26th St. W., Bradenton 34207) Part of Florida's Black Heritage Trail, it contains children's books, videotapes, audiotapes, adult books, magazines, and other materials relevant to the Underground Railroad and to black heritage, arts, and culture.

John and Mable Ringling Museum of Art Research Library (941-359-5700, ext 2701; www.ringling.org; 5401 Bay Shore Rd., Sarasota 34243) One of the largest art libraries in the Southeast, it specializes in Italian and European Baroque art, Peter Paul Rubens, and decorative art. Open to the public Wednesday and Friday, 1 to 5 PM, or by appointment.

Manatee County Central Library (941-748-5555; www.co.manatee.fl.us/library/master
.html; 1301 Barcarrotta Blvd. W., Bradenton 34205) The Eaton Room contains a collection of
state and county historical photographs, newspapers, books, census records, and articles.

Selby Public Library (941-861-1100; www.suncat.co.sarasota.fl.us/Libraries/Selby.aspx;
1331 First St., Sarasota 34236) The city's central and most impressive-looking library, it
schedules cultural events throughout the year. Arranged in a circular design, the library
features an exciting youth wing that you enter through a glass aquarium arch.

Verman Kimbrough Memorial Library (941-359-7587; www.lib.rsad.edu; Ringling
College of Art and Design, 2700 N. Tamiami Trail, Sarasota 34234) Art history and instruction.

Theater

Anna Maria Island Players (941-778-5755; www.home.earthlink.net/~islandplayers;
10009 Gulf Dr. at Pine Ave., Anna Maria Island 34216) October through May. Community
theater in an Old Florida–style building.

✪ **Asolo Center for the Performing Arts/Florida State University Acting Conservatory**
(Box office: 941-351-8000, 800-361-8388; www.asolo.org; 5555 N. Tamiami Trail,
Sarasota 34243, across from the Ringling Estate) The original Asolo Theatre was built in
Italy in 1798 as part of a queen's castle. It ended up on the Ringling Estate in the 1940s,
where it was reconstructed and, in 1965, designated the State Theater of Florida. The
building has been restored and is part of the Ringling visitors center across the street from
the new Asolo center, which was built in the early 1980s. The new Asolo incorporated into
the interior of one of its venues a different dismantled, historic European theater: a circa
1900 Scottish opera house. Carved box fronts, friezes, and ornate cornice work from the
old theater decorate the new, lending the latter an aura of Old World heritage. Opened in
1989, the 500-seat Harold E. and Esther M. Mertz Theatre hosts the excellent, nearly 50-
year-old Asolo Repertory Theatre troupe from November through May. Free tours are
available Wednesday through Saturday at 10 and 11 AM, November through May. A separate,
more intimate, 161-seat theater, called the Jane B. Cook Theatre, is the home of Florida
State University's graduate actor training program. Its season runs concurrently with the
Mertz's.

Banyan Theater (941-358-5330; www.banyantheatercompany.com; P.O. Box 49483,
Sarasota 34230) Professional theater group that performs the classics during the summer
season at the Asolo and the Ringling Estate.

✪ **Circus Sarasota** (941-355-9335; www.circussarasota.org; P.O. Box 18638, Sarasota
34276; performances at Fruitville Rd. and Tuttle Rd.) This troupe resurrects Sarasota's
deeply entrenched Big Top tradition with a February schedule of performances. Conceived
by Sarasota native Dolly Jacobs (daughter of the late, great circus clown Lou Jacobs), it's a
not-for-profit, educational organization hosting clown-arts seminars and a kids' club.

Florida Studio Theatre and Cabaret Club (941-366-9000; www.fst2000.org; 1241 N.
Palm Ave., Sarasota 34236, downtown) A major testing ground for budding playwrights
and new works. Florida Studio Theatre's professional troupe performs in its Mainstage and
experimental Stage III theaters from October through June and hosts a summertime
Florida Playwrights Festival (see "Calendar of Events" at the end of this chapter). There are

Florida State University's drama branch is at home in Sarasota's Asolo Center for the Performing Arts, on the grounds of the Ringling Estates.

musical revues, improv, and other light entertainment, plus full-service dining, in the Parisian-style Cabaret Club.

Glenridge Performing Arts Center (941-552-5298, 888-999-4536; www.theglenridge .com; 7333 Scotland Way, Sarasota 34238) In addition to live theater, this 267 seat state of-the-art facility hosts films and concerts from chamber music to jazz.

Golden Apple Dinner Theatre (941-366-5454, 800-652-0920; www.thegoldenapple .com; 25 N. Pineapple Ave., Sarasota 34236, downtown) Year-round Broadway dinner entertainment since 1971.

Historic Ringling Asolo Theatre (941-355-5101; www.ringling.org; 5401 Bay Shore Rd., Sarasota 34243) Recently restored and merged into the Ringling Estate's new visitors center, it hosts a couple performances each season from the new Asolo Center's (see below) repertoire. Docents give tours of the theater five times daily, hourly beginning at 11:30 AM. The tour includes a 37-minute film, "The Life and Times of John and Mable Ringling." Tour cost is $5 per person.

Manatee Players Riverfront Theater (941-748-0111, box office: 748-5875; www.manatee players.com; 102 Old Main St., Bradenton 34205) Community theater in an intimate, historic setting. Also theatrical performances for children and families.

The Players of Sarasota (941-365-2494; www.theplayers.org; 838 N. Tamiami Trail, Sarasota 34236) Community theater group that stages Broadway musicals, plus live music and other programs, from September through April.

✪ **Sarasota Opera House** (941-366-8450, 888-673-7212; www.sarasotaopera.org; 61 N. Pineapple Ave., Sarasota 34236, downtown) Don't even try to park or dine downtown on opera opening nights during the January–March season. Southwest Florida's oldest opera company's opening galas are popular events that require ticket purchase months in advance. That may change for the better with the theater's 2007–2008 renovation and expansion. In operation for more than 40 years, the Sarasota Opera Association stages all the classics in its beautifully restored, 1926 Spanish-mission-style structure, located in the Theater and Arts District. You can tour the facility (and see the chandelier from the set of *Gone With the Wind*) for $7. Advance arrangements required.

✪ **Van Wezel Performing Arts Hall** (941-953-3368, 800-826-9303; www.vanwezel.org; 777 N. Tamiami Trail, Sarasota 34236) The Van Wezel, that purple eye-catcher radiating outward like a scallop shell from the shores of Sarasota Bay, was designed by the Frank Lloyd Wright Foundation and hosts name comedians, musicians, and dance groups; Broadway shows; major orchestras; ethnic music and dance groups; and chamber and choral music.

Venice Little Theatre (941-488-1115; www.venicestage.com; 140 W. Tampa Ave., Venice 34285, downtown) This community-theater company has outgrown its name as it has spread to two venues. In its Mediterranean Revival structure, the troupe performs six main-stage shows from October through May, four contemporary plays at Stage II from November through April, plus occasional cabarets and concerts. It conducts theater classes, workshops, and summer camp for adults and kids (call 941-486-8679).

Visual Arts Centers & Resources

The canvas of Sarasota Bay arts reveals a complex masterpiece, layered with the diverse patterns and local color of its many communities. With its backdrop of artistic types, dating back to avid collector John Ringling, Sarasota leads the region to avant-garde heights. The following entries introduce you to opportunities for experiencing art as either an appreciator or a practicing artist. A listing of commercial galleries is included under "Shopping," below.

The sculpture Applause greets visitors to the Van Wezel Performing Arts Center.

ArtCenter Manatee (941-746-2862; www.artcentermanatee.org; 209 Ninth St. W., Bradenton 34205) It hosts changing monthly exhibitions, an artists' market, classes, and workshops.

Art Center Sarasota (941-365-2032; www.artsarasota.org; 707 N. Tamiami Trail, Sarasota 34236) Exhibition and sales galleries feature the paintings, jewelry, sculpture, pottery, and enamelware of local and national artists. Art instruction and demonstrations are available. The gallery features an outdoor sculpture garden. Most activities take place November through May. Open Tuesday through Saturday, 10 to 4.

Art League of Manatee County (941-746-2862; www.almc.org; 209 Ninth St. W., Bradenton 34205) Classes and demonstrations in all media for all ages; sales gallery.

Bradenton's Village of the Arts brightened a drug-infested neighborhood with the studios and workshops of working artists.

The Fine Arts Society of Sarasota (941-330-0680, 371-7719; www.vanwezel.org/aboutUs/ guidedTours.cfm; Van Wezel Performing Arts Hall, 777 N. Tamiami Trail, Sarasota 34236,Box 1342, Sarasota 32230) Van Wezel houses a permanent collection of prominent Florida artists' works on loan from the Society, which conducts tours at 10 AM the first Tuesday of each month from October through May. Cost is $5 per person.

✪ **The John and Mable Ringling Museum of Art** (941-355-5101; www.ringling.org; 5401 Bay Shore Rd., Sarasota 34243) Sarasota's pride and joy, and designated the State Art Museum of Florida, this is not only an art museum but also the nucleus of tourism activity and the heart of the local art community. It shares its 66 acre bay front estate with Ringling's extravagant Cà d'Zan palace (see "Historic Homes"), a circus museum and new learning center (see "Museums"), a rose garden (see "Gardens"), and a new visitors center with gift shop, restaurant, and a restored historic Italian theater. The collection, much of which was purchased by Ringling, covers 500 years of European art and specializes in late-medieval and Renaissance Italian works. The Old Masters collection contains five original Rubens tapestries as well as Spanish Baroque, French, Dutch, and northern European works (mostly portraits of a religious nature). The museum continually augments its collection of American and contemporary works in its two originals wings and a new wing and Education Conservation Complex that opened in 2007 to house traveling exhibits. The lushly landscaped courtyards feature reproductions of classic statues and Italian decorative columns, which Ringling originally purchased for the hotel he hoped to build on Longboat Key. The museum is opens daily from 10 to 5:30; the grounds are open from 9:30 to 6. Admission covers all Ringling property attractions: $15 adults, $13 seniors, $5 students and Florida teachers with ID, free for children under age 5. Admission to the museum only is free every Monday.

Longboat Key Center for the Arts (941-383-2345; www.lbkca.org; 6860 Longboat Dr. S., Longboat Key 34228) Hidden from mainstream traffic, here is a find for the buyer and would-be artisan. Galleries sell works mostly by Florida artists. Changing and permanent exhibits feature local, emerging, and experimental artists. A crafts shop sells wares made at the center's surrounding workshops, where classes are taught in basketry, watercolor, jewelry making, metal craft, pottery, and more. In season, second Tuesdays bring jazz concerts to the center.

The Manatee Arts Council Gallery (941-746-2223; 926 12th St. W., Bradenton 34205; www.manateearts.org, in Village of the Arts) It hosts shows by local artists on a monthly rotating basis.

Selby Gallery (941-359-7563; www.ringling.edu/selbygallery; 2700 N. Tamiami Trail, Sarasota 34234; at the Ringling College of Art and Design) This intimate, modern space exhibits the works of contemporary students, faculty, and local, national, and international artists and designers. Free admission. Open 10–4 Mon.–Sat., 10–7 Tues.; May–Aug. Mon.–Fri. 10–4 only.

✪ **Towles Court Artist Colony** (www.towlescourt.com; 1943 Morrill St., Sarasota 34236) A delightful, blossomy village of restored and brightly painted tin-roofed bungalows turned art colony. Showings, studios, and galleries. Third Friday gallery walks, 6–10 PM.

Venice Art Center (941-485-7136; www.veniceartcenter.com ; 390 S. Nokomis Ave., Venice 34285) Local artists' exhibitions, gift shop, café, and art instruction.

✪ **Village of the Arts** (941-747-8056; www.villageofthearts.com; P.O. Box 729, Bradenton 34206, 18-block radius around 12th Street and 11th Avenue West, Bradenton) Officially welcomed in January 2001, this artist colony revitalized a former drug neighborhood, turning it into a work of pride for the community. Nearly 40 artists and artisans from all disciplines—visual arts, healing arts, culinary arts—have moved into the neighborhood to work and sell their art and services. Most are concentrated on 12th Street and open Friday and Saturday, from 11 AM to 4 PM; look for the Village of Arts signs in front of houses. A couple of my favorites include **The Baobab Tree Gallery** (941-447-3795; 1113 12th St. W.) and **Kaos** (941-747-0823, www.kaosgallery.com; 1122 12th St. W.). The village hosts a First Weekend Art Fest each month. In 2006, the Village mounted a gecko auction, and you can still see the colorfully decorated fiberglass creatures crawling the sides of buildings around town. Plans are to expand the Village and initiate trolley service between it and downtown's Riverwalk district.

RECREATION

Known both for its superlative white sand beaches and as the birthplace of Florida golfing, Sarasota and its environs draw outdoors lovers to their year-round playgrounds.

Beaches

The Sarasota area claims more than 35 miles of sandy seashore. Island beaches are, for the most part, highly developed, with lots of facilities and concessions. Recent years have seen a concession of another sort—to nature—as boardwalks and sea oat plantings restore the dunes. On the islands, erosion takes its toll, and beaches must be periodically renourished. This stretch of the Gulf Coast boasts some of the whitest beaches this side of the Florida Panhandle—and some of the darkest. Parking is free at all area beaches. Pets (except where noted) and glass containers are prohibited. So is walking across dune vegetation any way but on the boardwalk crossovers.

ANNA MARIA BAYFRONT PARK

Northeast end of Anna Maria Island
Facilities: Picnic areas, restrooms, showers, playground, recreational facilities, fishing pier

One of the region's more secluded beach parks, this one is narrower than the rest of the island's beaches. You get a magnificent view of St. Petersburg's Sunshine Skyway Bridge from the bay. A historical marker tells about the island's early settlers. Heed danger signs that mark where heavy tidal currents make swimming perilous.

BROHARD BEACH

941-316-1172
1600 S. Harbor Dr., Venice 34285
Facilities: Picnic areas, restrooms, showers, fitness trail, fishing pier, restaurant

This narrow, dark-flecked sand beach threads under the Venice Fishing Pier and around covered picnic tables. Folks come here to fish, hang out at the pier tiki bar, and hunt for sharks' teeth. A part of it to the south is a designated dogs-allowed beach.

CASPERSEN BEACH

941-316-1172
South end of Harbor Dr., Venice
Facilities: Picnic areas, restrooms, showers, nature trail, playground, bike path, bayside fishing pier, kayak launch

At the end of the road lies natural Caspersen Beach, where a series of boardwalks cross scrub-vegetated dunes onto diminishing dark sands. It's popular with shark-tooth hunters and young beachgoers. From here you can walk to Manasota Key Beach, to the south. On the bayside, the county has built a new bike path, fishing pier, and kayak launch along the Venetian Waterway.

✪ COQUINA BEACH

Southern end of Gulf Dr., Bradenton Beach, Anna Maria Island
Facilities: Picnic areas, restrooms, showers, lifeguard, café, volleyball, concessions, boat ramps

This large and popular park boasts plump, wide sands edged in Australian pines. Waters at the south end provide good snorkeling. The park continues on the bay, where swimming should be avoided because of currents and boat traffic. The Coquina BayWalk takes you to environmentally restored Leffis Key.

CORTEZ BEACH

North end of Gulf Dr., Bradenton Beach, Anna Maria Island
Facilities: Picnic tables, restrooms, showers, lifeguard

Here's a long stretch of revamped sands at the end of the Cortez Bridge. It meets up with Coquina, its more popular cousin. Surfers like it here. It's convenient for the heavily laden beachgoer because you park right along the sand's edge.

LIDO BEACH
941- 316-1172
400 Benjamin Franklin Dr., Lido Key 34236
Facilities: Picnic areas, restrooms, showers, lifeguards, historic swimming pool, snack
bar, swings, volleyball, beach wheelchairs
Admission: pool is $2 for adults, free for children

Heavily developed and popular, this is the main beach on Lido Key. Canvas cabanas and
stylish, umbrella-shaded lounge chairs may be rented along the stretch of sand carpeted
with small shells and shell hash. South of the pavilion at the Lido Beach Resort, you'll find
water-sports equipment rentals. In 2001, residents rallied to save the circa-1926 community pool on the beach, a throwback to the glamour days of John Ringling and friends.

LONGBOAT KEY
Public accesses at Broadway St. on the north end of island
Longboat Key has beautiful beaches, mostly enjoyed by resort guests and waterfront resi-
dents. Public accesses are marked subtly with blue signs at Atlas Street, Gulfside Road, and
Broadway Street. Parking is limited, and there are no facilities or lifeguards. The beach
stretches wide as well as long and has fluffy white sand and dramatic sunset views.

✪ MANATEE COUNTY PARK
941-778-0784
Gulf Dr. and 40th St., Holmes Beach
Facilities: Picnic area, restrooms, showers, lifeguard, playground, restaurant, ice cream,
shop, beach rentals, volleyball

The hot spot of Anna Maria Island beachgoing, this park appeals to families because of its
full complement of facilities. The beach is wide enough to accommodate rows and rows of
beach towels. Australian pines shade picnic areas.

Sea grapes and sea oats fringe Holmes Beach sands.

✪ NOKOMIS BEACH/NORTH JETTY
941-486-2311
South end of Casey Key Rd., Casey Key
Facilities: Picnic area and shelters, restrooms, showers, lifeguards, concessions, boat ramp, beach wheelchairs

Remote and exclusive Casey Key gives way to beachy abandon at its southern end. The town of Nokomis Beach is a fisherman's haven, and North Jetty, at its southernmost point, lures anglers. (South Jetty lies across the pass on Venice Beach.) A bait shop keeps fishermen supplied. The beach's wide sands, festooned with Australian pines and sea grape trees, are well loved by serious local beachgoers. When the waves kick up, the surfing crowd heads here.

NORTH LIDO BEACH
941-316-1172
North end of Ben Franklin Dr., Lido Key

The beach less traveled on Lido, this one extends from the main beach up to New Pass. A lack of facilities and limited parking keep the throngs away at this naturally maintained park. It is wide, with fine, spic-and-span sand, plus trails for hiking and running.

PALMA SOLA CAUSEWAY BEACH
Anna Maria Bridge, Route 64
Facilities: Picnic area, restrooms, restaurant, water-sports rentals

Fairly narrow sands edge the causeway between the mainland and Anna Maria Island. They gain some character from Australian pines and are popular with windsurfers and jet skiers.

POINT OF ROCKS BEACH
941-316-1172
South of Siesta Public Beach on Midnight Pass Rd. near Stickney Point Rd. intersection, Siesta Key

Part of Crescent Beach—named for its shape—this beach is popular with snorkelers and fishermen because of an accumulation of rocks that attracts marine life. Like the main public beach (see below), it boasts sands whiter than white but has neither the facilities nor the ease of parking.

SERVICE CLUB PARK
941-316-1172
S. Harbor Dr., Venice
Facilities: Picnic areas and shelters, restrooms, showers, tot play area, volleyball

An extensive system of boardwalks crosses scrub pinelands (watch for rare scrub jays and gopher tortoises) and provides picnic nooks off the beach. This is quieter than neighboring Brohard Park and its fishing pier but within walking distance of both.

✪ SIESTA KEY COUNTY BEACH

941-861-2150

Midnight Pass Rd. at Beach Way Dr., Siesta Key

Facilities: Picnic areas and shelters, restrooms, showers, lifeguard, snack bar, playground, volleyball, tennis, ball fields, soccer field, fitness trail, sundecks, beach wheelchairs

Siesta Key's Crescent Beach sand was once judged "the finest, whitest beach in the world" by the Woods Hole Oceanographic Institute. (Anna Maria Island's beach placed third.) In 2003 the Travel Channel named it the "Best Sand Beach in America." The blinding whiteness comes from its quartz (99 percent) origins; the sand's fineness comes from Mother Nature's efficient pulverizer, the sea. Unfortunately, these facts have not been kept secret. The park averages about 20,000 visitors a day. Arrive early to find a parking space. Condos and motels line the wide beach. Swimming is wonderful, because the beach has gradually sloping sands and usually clear waters. Public accesses along Beach Road to the north provide more seclusion, but parking is on the street and limited. On Sunday evenings, drummers and other musicians assemble to hail the sunset.

SOUTH BROHARD PARK

941-316-1172

S. Harbor Dr., Venice

South of Brohard Park, parking and boardwalks over mangrove wetlands provide access to the beach that is away from noise, fishing hooks, and crowds. The undeveloped natural beach appeals to escapists, who are nonetheless within walking distance of facilities at Brohard.

SOUTH JETTY

941-316-1172

End of Tarpon Center Dr., Venice.

Facilities: Restrooms, picnic tables, food concession

For a change, try making sand angels—in Siesta Key's heavenly white sand.

Also known as Humphris Park, the jetty at Casey's Pass—a favorite of fishing types—is shored with huge boulders. Past them stretches a span of condo-lined beach that's popular with surfers and sailboarders. Here, people while away time eating lunch and watching boat traffic through the pass. Across the pass lies Nokomis Beach's North Jetty.

SOUTH LIDO BEACH PARK
941-316-1172
2201 Benjamin Franklin Dr., Lido Key
Facilities: Picnic areas, restrooms, showers, playground, volleyball, ball fields, horseshoes, soccer field, fitness trail, nature trail, canoe trail, observation tower, sundecks

A wide beige beach wraps around the tip of Lido Key from the gulf to the bay, facing Siesta Key to the south. Picnic areas are overhung with Australian pines and carpeted by their needles. Park renovation is underway to remove the nonnative pines. Within its 100 acres several Florida ecosystems thrive on different waterfronts. Squirrels are the most evident wildlife throughout the park. Hiking trails lead you along the mangrove worlds of Little Grassy and Big Grassy lagoons. Brushy Bayou is a good place to canoe. Swift waters in the pass make swimming treacherous but fishing fine.

TURTLE BEACH
South end of Blind Pass Rd., Siesta Key
Facilities: Picnic areas, restrooms, showers, playground, volleyball, boat ramp, horseshoes; restaurants and bars across the street

The sands become coarser and more shell studded at Siesta's lower extremes as the high-rise buildings become scarcer. Along here and Midnight Pass Road the island's upper echelon resides behind iron gates. Less crowded than the other Siesta beaches, it's sports and family oriented but without lifeguards. If you walk southward, you'll reach ✪ **Palmer Point Beach** (otherwise only reachable by boat), where Midnight Pass between Siesta and Casey keys has filled in and sharks' teeth are easy to find.

✪ VENICE BEACH
941-316-1172
100 The Esplanade, Venice
Facilities: Picnic area, restrooms, showers, food concession, lifeguards, volleyball, beach wheelchairs

This beach feels cramped and more urban to me than Venice's spacious south-end beaches. Buildings border the sands, which spread wide here. Wooden benches provide places to gaze at the normally calm sea. This beach is especially popular with divers because a reef fronts the sands a quarter mile out.

Bicycling
Sarasota's best bikeways lie on barrier islands, in parks, and in rural areas to the east. Most biking elsewhere is on the sides of roads or sidewalks.

By state law, bicyclists must conduct themselves as pedestrians when using sidewalks. Where they share the road with other vehicles, they must follow all the rules of the road. Children under 16 must wear helmets.

BEST BIKING

The ✪ **Historical Manatee Riverwalk** takes in downtown Bradenton for strollers and cyclists. It zigzags through downtown and crosses the Green Bridge (Business 41) to Palmetto. Brochure maps are available through the local Chamber of Commerce. In Palmetto, **Emerson Point Preserve** offers a pleasant bike ride on an almost 3-mile, partially paved path that runs along waterfront vistas.

✪ **Longboat Key**'s 12 miles of bike path and lane parallel Gulf of Mexico Drive's vista of good taste and wealth on both sides of the road. Bike paths travel through parts of **Lido Key** and **Siesta Key**. When completed, the **Venetian Waterway Park** in Venice will run along both sides of the Intracoastal Waterway and stretch for nearly 10 miles. Currently, the eight miles of completed trail runs along the waterway's west side from Venice Avenue to Caspersen Beach. **Oscar Scherer State Park** provides a more natural backdrop for biking. In Sarasota, county buses are equipped with bike racks for pedal-and-ride passengers.

RENTAL SHOPS

Resorts and parks often rent bikes or provide free use of them.

Beach Bikes & Trikes (941-412-3821; 127 Tampa Ave. E. #10, Venice 34285) Rentals, repairs, and sales. Located near the Venetian Waterway Park.

Bicycle Center (941-377-4505; 4084 Bee Ridge Rd., Sarasota 34233) Offers pickup and delivery on mountain bike and beach cruiser rentals.

Island Scooter Rentals (941-726-3163; www.islandscooters.com; Silver Surf Resort, 1301 Gulf Dr. N., Bradenton Beach 34217) Rents bikes by the hour, day, and week to the public. Customer pickup and drop-off available.

Siesta Sports Rentals (941-346-1797; www.siestasportsrentals.com; 6551 Midnight Pass Rd., Southbridge Mall, Siesta Key 34242) Has beach cruisers, speed bikes, kid bikes, tandems, surreys, jogger strollers, and inline skates.

Boats & Boating
CANOEING AND KAYAKING

In addition to the outlets listed below, many resorts and parks rent canoes and kayaks. Best trails include those that run along the Myakka and Manatee rivers and in intracoastal waters.

Almost Heaven Kayak Adventures (941-504-6296; www.kayakfl.com; 7134 87th Ln. E., Palmetto 34221) Offers tours in and around the islands, bays, and rivers of Sarasota and Bradenton; lessons included. One 2-1/2-hour tour in Longboat Key waters stops for lunch at Mar-Vista Restaurant, where participants receive a 20 percent discount. Daily and weekly rentals and drop-off and pickup service.

Enticer Watersports (941-366-7245; 5 Bayfront Dr., Sarasota 34236, at Bayfront Park) Rents kayaks, sailboats, and Waverunners by the half hour or hour.

Native Rental (941-778-7757; 5416 Marina Dr., Holmes Beach 34217) Quality rentals and guided and self-guided tours through bay waters and bird islands.

✪ **Oscar Scherer State Park** (941-483-5956; www.floridastateparks.org/oscarscherer; 1843 S. Tamiami Trail, Osprey 34229) Canoe rentals and tidal creek canoeing along scrubby and pine flatwoods. River otters and alligators inhabit the waters; scrub jays, bobcats, and bald eagles inhabit the land.

Siesta Sports Rentals (941-346-1797; www.siestasportsrentals.com; 6551 Midnight Pass Rd., Southbridge Mall, Siesta Key 34242) Rents single and double kayaks, plus snorkels, boogie and skim boards, and other beach equipment.

Silent Sports (941-966-5477; www.adventuresinflorida.net/silentsportsoutfitters.htm; 2301 Tamiami Trail, Nokomis 34275) Rents kayaks and canoes and leads three-hour tours.

Snook Haven (941-485-7221; www.snookhavenretreat.com; 5000 E. Venice Ave., Venice 34292) Canoe rentals and tours on the Myakka River.

Tropical Kayak Rentals (941-346-7419; www.tropicalkayakrentals.com) Free delivery and pickup for rentals. Also offers sunset, fishing, birding, and Lido Key mangroves tours.

PERSONAL WATERCRAFT RENTAL/TOURS

Florida law now requires operators between ages 18 and 21 to have a boater safety card. Many rental agents can qualify you for the card.

Enticer Watersports (941-366-7245; 5 Bayfront Dr., Sarasota 34236, at Bayfront Park) Rents kayaks, paddleboats, sailboats, and Waverunners by the half hour, hour, day, or week.

Siesta Key Jet Ski (941-346-3000; 1249 Stickney Point Rd., Siesta Key 34242, at CB's Saltwater Outfitters) Rents by the hour.

POWERBOAT RENTALS

Bradenton Beach Marina (941-778-2288; www.bradentonbeachmarina.com; 402 Church Ave., Bradenton Beach 34217) Runabouts and pontoons.

Cannons Marina (941-383-1311; www.cannons.com; 6040 Gulf of Mexico Dr., Longboat Key 34228) Rentals by half day, day, and week; runabouts, deck boats, and open skiffs; also fishing tackle and water skis.

CB's Saltwater Outfitters (941-349-4400; www.cbsoutfitters.com; 1249 Stickney Point Rd., Siesta Key 34242) Runabouts, center console boats, pontoons, and deck boats; also rod and reel rentals, fishing licenses, tackle shop, and fishing guides.

Sarasota Boat Rental (941-951-0550; www.sarasotaboatrental.com; 2 Marina Plaza, Sarasota 34236, at Marina Jack) Center console fishing boats, deck boats, and pontoons by the half or full day. Also water skis, kneeboards, and fishing equipment.

Snook Haven (941-485-7221; www.snookhavenretreat.com; 5000 E. Venice Ave., Venice 34292) Rents mini pontoon boats and 12- to 14-foot motorboats for use on the Myakka River.

Ultimate Power Sports of Bradenton (941-761-7433; www.bradentonjetski.com; 12310 Manatee Ave. W., Bradenton 34209, on Anna Maria Island causeway) Jet ski and pontoon rentals.

PUBLIC BOAT RAMPS

City Island (Ken Thompson Pkwy.) Three ramps.

Coquina Beach Bayside Park (Gulf Blvd., Bradenton Beach) Picnic and recreational facilities; restrooms nearby.

Higel Park (Tarpon Center Dr., Venice Beach, Venice Inlet)

Kingfish Ramp (Hwy. 64 on causeway to Anna Maria Island) Picnic facilities.

Marina Boat Ramp Park (215 E. Venice Ave., Venice)

Nokomis Beach (Venice Inlet)

Palma Sola Causeway (Palma Sola Bay and Rte. 64) Restrooms and picnicking.

Palmetto (Riverside Dr., just west of the Green Bridge) On the Manatee River

Turtle Beach (Blind Pass Rd., Siesta Key) Two ramps.

SAILBOAT CHARTERS

The Enterprise Sailing Charters (941-951-1833, 888-232-7768; www.sarasotasailing
.com; 2 Marina Plaza, Sarasota 34236, in Bayfront Park) Morning, afternoon, and sunset sails, lasting two to four hours, on a tall-masted Morgan 41-footer.

Key Sailing (941-346-7245; www.siestakeysailing.com; 1219 Southport Dr., Sarasota 34242, at Marina Jack) Two-hour to full-day sail-away adventures aboard a 41-foot Morgan Classic.

Pirate Pete's Watersports (941-366-7245; 5 Bayfront Dr., Sarasota 34236, at Bayfront Park) Rents kayaks, sailboats, and Waverunners.

Sara-Bay Sailing (941-914-5132; www.sarabaysailing.com; City Island, Sarasota, at New Pass Grill & Bait Shop) Captained charters by the half day or full day, sailboat rentals, and American Sailing Association (ASA) certification courses.

Spice Sailing Charters (941-704-0773; http://charters2.tripod.com; 902 Bay Blvd. S., Anna Maria 34216, at the Galati Yacht Basin) Half-day and sunset sails to Egmont Key aboard a 30-foot vessel. Sailing lessons available.

Spindrift Yacht Services (941-383-7781; www.spindrift-yachts.com; 410 Gulf of Mexico Dr., Longboat Key 34228) Sailing ventures for up to 12.

SAILBOAT RENTALS & INSTRUCTION

Many resorts have concessions that rent Hobie Cats and other small sailboats. Instruction is often available with the rental. For something more sophisticated, try:

Coastal Watersport Rentals (941-778-4969; 1301 Gulf Dr., Bradenton Beach 34217) Free lessons with catamaran rentals; also rents Waverunners and kayaks.

Sara-Bay Sailing (941-914-5132; www.sarabaysailing.com; City Island, Sarasota, at New Pass Grill & Bait Shop) ASA-certification courses.

SIGHTSEEING & ENTERTAINMENT CRUISES

Look under "Wildlife Tours & Charters" for nature excursions.

Just Ducky (941-485-6366; 1011 S. Tamiami Trail, Nokomis, one block south of Captain Eddie's Seafood Restaurant) Go dry and wet on this wacky amphibious tour of the Venice area.

LeBarge Tropical Cruises (941-366-6116; www.lebargetropicalcruises.com, 2 Marine Plaza, Sarasota 34236, at Marina Jack in Bayfront Park) Island-style crooning, an aquarium bar, and live onboard coconut palms put the tropical in this excursion. Sightseeing, dolphin, nature, and sunset-party cruises depart daily. Light snacks and drinks available.

Terry's River Tours (941-255-0400; www.venice-fla.com/snookhaven; Snook Haven, 5000 E. Venice Ave., Venice 34292) One-hour narrated trips on the Myakka River, Wednesday through Sunday.

Fishing

Nonresidents 16 and older must obtain a license unless they are fishing from a vessel or pier that's covered by its own license. You can buy inexpensive, temporary, nonresident licenses at county tax collectors' offices and most Kmarts, hardware stores, marinas, and bait shops.

In the Intracoastal Waterway between Sarasota and Venice, snook are so plentiful, it's been dubbed "Snook Alley." The Bradenton area is known for its mammoth grouper. Other fine catches include mangrove snapper, sheepshead, and pompano in backwaters, and grouper, amberjack, and mackerel in deep seas. Check local regulations for season, size, and catch restrictions.

DEEP-SEA PARTY BOATS

Flying Fish Fleet (941-366-3373; www.flyingfishfleet.com; 627 Avenida del Norte, Sarasota 34242, at Marina Jack in Bayfront Park) Half-day, six-hour, and all-day deep-sea charters and party boat excursions.

FISHING CHARTERS/OUTFITTERS

To find fishing guides, check with major marinas such as Marina Jack's in downtown Sarasota. Capacity is smaller and prices higher than for party-boat excursions.

Big Catch (941-366-3373; www.flyingfishfleet.com/bigcatch.html; 627 Avenida del Norte, Sarasota 34242, at Marina Jack's in Bayfront Park) Four- to eight-hour charters.

CB's Saltwater Outfitters (941-349-4400; www.cbsoutfitters.com; 1249 Stickney Point Rd., Siesta Key 34242) Light-tackle sportfishing charters in Sarasota Bay, the gulf, Snook Alley, and Charlotte Harbor. Four to eight hours. Orvis endorsed.

Charter Boat Shark (941-365-2161; www.charterboatshark.com; 2 Marina Plaza, Sarasota 34236, at Marina Jack) Catch tuna, kingfish, mackerel, shark, and more offshore aboard an air-conditioned 41-foot boat.

Cortez Fishing Center (941-795-6969 or 888-844-4140; www.cortezkat.com; 12507 Cortez Rd. W., Cortez 34215) Here's your one-stop place for fishing licenses, bait, deep-sea fishing, backwater fishing, and sightseeing charters. Deep-sea fishing trips aboard the Cortez Kat party boat last four to 24 hours.

Lucky Dawg Charters (941-951-0819, 941-587-9852 (cell); www.sarasotafishingcharters .com; 2576 Hillview St., Sarasota 34239) Light-tackle sportfishing the flats, backcountry, and in shore for snook, trout, redfish, and tarpon. Half-day, six-hour, and full-day trips.

Spindrift Yacht Services (941-383-7781; www.spindrift-yachts.com; 410 Gulf of Mexico Dr., Longboat Key 34228) Half-day offshore and bay-fishing excursions.

Stray Dog Charter Boat (941-794-5615; www.straydogcharters.com; 12507 Cortez Rd. W., P.O. Box 131, Cortez 34215) One of several guide charters docked along "Charter Row" at Cortez Fishing Center (see above), it takes fishermen off shore on a 43-foot custom boat with private head.

FISHING PIERS

Anna Maria City Pier (Pine Ave., Anna Maria Island) It juts 678 feet into Anna Maria Sound at the south end of Bayshore Park.

Bradenton Beach City Pier (Bridge St., Bradenton Beach) Reaching into Intracoastal waters, the pier was originally part of the first bridge from the island to the mainland. Restaurant and bait concession. Restaurant to be completed in 2008.

Green Bridge Pier (Business Hwy. 41 over the Manatee River, downtown Bradenton)

Ken Thompson Pier (941-316-1172; 1700 Ken Thompson Pkwy., City Island) Three small piers into New Pass.

✪ **Nokomis Beach's North Jetty** (941-316-1172; south end Casey Key Rd., Nokomis Beach) Manmade rock projection into the gulf. Beach and picnic area.

Osprey Fishing Pier (west end of Main St., Osprey) A neighborhood pier in an off-the-beaten-path area; no parking.

Rod & Reel Pier (941-778-1885; www.rodandreelpier.com; 875 North Shore Dr., Anna Maria 34216) A privately owned fishermen's complex extending 350 feet into Tampa Bay. Includes a café and bait shop. Admission for fishing only.

The Flying Fish fleet meets every angler's needs.

Venice Fishing Pier stretches 740 feet long.

Tony Saprito Fishing Pier (Hart's Landing, Ringling Causeway Park en route to St. Armands Key) Bait store across the road. For 24-hour tide and fishing information, call the hotline at 941-366-TIDE.

✪ **Venice Fishing Pier** (1600 S. Harbor Dr., Venice 34285, at Brohard Park) It's 740 feet long, complete with restrooms, showers, bait shop, rod and reel rentals, and restaurant. Admission to the pier is now free.

Venice's South Jetty (941-316-1172; Tarpon Center Dr., Venice) A stretch of boulder buffer with a paved walkway at Venice's north end.

Golf

In 1902 Sarasota's founder and first mayor, a Scotsman, built a two-hole golf course in the middle of town. This is believed to have been Florida's first golf course. Through the years the sport has grown in Sarasota, and today there are more courses than you can swing a club at. The majority are private or semiprivate. Several large resorts have their own greens or arrange golf-around programs at local links. In winter season, rates are highest, and greens are the most crowded. Carts are often required. Make tee times well in advance.

GOLF CENTERS

David Leadbetter Golf Academy (941-752-2661; www.imgaacademies.com; IMG Academies, 5500 34th St. W., Bradenton 34210) A highly respected full-time boarding school that also offers summer and week-long lesson programs.

Evie's Golf Center (941-377-2399; 4735 Bee Ridge Rd., Sarasota 34233) Practice sand traps, chipping and putting greens, lessons with PGA pros, miniature golf.

Mark Reid Golf School (941-705-5566; www.teachingprofessional.com; The River Club, 6600 River Club Blvd., Bradenton 34202) One-hour to week-long programs for juniors and adults.

PUBLIC GOLF COURSES

Bobby Jones Golf Course (941-365-4653; www.bobbyjonesgolfclub.com; 1000 Circus Blvd., Sarasota 34232) Sarasota's only municipal course, it has 36 holes plus a 9-hole executive course, practice range, and chipping and putting greens. Restaurant and lounge. Named for one of the sport's late greats, who personally dedicated the course in 1927.

Manatee County Golf Course (941-792-6773; www.co.manatee.fl.us/golf.html; 6415 53rd Ave. W., Bradenton 34210) One of the county's most popular courses. Eighteen holes, par 72. Clubhouse and restaurant. Reasonable rates; twilight rate applies.

Sarasota Golf Club (941-371-2431; 7280 N. Leewynn Dr., Sarasota 34240) Public course with 18 holes, par 72, and driving range. Restaurant and bar. Reasonable rates, especially in summer.

Health & Fitness Clubs

Arlington Park & Aquatic Complex (941-316-1346; 2650 Waldemere St., Sarasota 34239) City-owned, county-operated facility with swimming pool, fitness center, tennis, racquetball, and basketball.

Evalyn Sadlier Jones YMCA (941-922-9622; www.sarasota-ymca.org; 8301 Potter Park, Sarasota 34238) With an Olympic-sized pool and kids' water park, this Y goes beyond fitness to fun. For workouts, there are classes, a weight room, an indoor track and pool, an

Boats bob in Sarasota Bay—a scenic, serene downtown backdrop.

outdoor 50-meter pool, diving boards, and a Jacuzzi area. At the water park families will enjoy the activity pool, slides, water cannons, fountains, and other cool stuff, plus there's an adjacent climbing tower. A childwatch program supervises the little ones while parents work out. Daily, weekly, and monthly memberships available and transferable to other Sarasota Ys.

Lifestyle Family Fitness (941-921-4400; 8383 S. Tamiami Trail, Sarasota 34238) Exercise equipment, sauna, whirlpool, lap pool.

Sarasota Family YMCA (941-366-6778; www.sarasota-ymca.org; 1991 Main St., Ste. 200, Sarasota 34236) Weight machines, sauna and steam room, classes. Daily, weekly, and monthly memberships available and transferable to other Sarasota Ys.

South County Family YMCA (941-492-9622; www.veniceymca.com; 701 Center Rd., Venice 34285) Wellness center with strength-building and extensive cardio equipment, plus two racquetball courts, massage therapy, babysitting, and a food court.

Hiking

Emerson Point Conservation Preserve (941-721-6885; 5801 17th St. W., Palmetto 34221) This lovely chin of land on Snead Island lays out trails up ancient Indian mounds, along the river and bay, and through thick woods. Bring your binoculars for some spectacular birding.

Myakka State Forest (941-460-1333; 2000 S. River Rd., Englewood 34223) With access off U.S. 41 south of North Port, it opens 14 miles of multiuse trails along the Myakka River from sunrise to sunset.

✪ **Oscar Scherer State Park** (941-483-5956; www.floridastateparks.org/oscarscherer; 1843 S. Tamiami Trail, Osprey 34229) More than 12 miles of six level-ground nature trails, including a half-mile barrier-free trail. An audio device introduces the scrub habitat of the marked, 5-mile Yellow Trail.

Sarasota Bay Walk (1550 Ken Thompson Pkwy., City Island, next to Mote Marine Aquarium) Self-guided nature hike.

South Lido Park (941-316-1172; south end of Benjamin Franklin Dr., Lido Key) Nature trails into the wetlands of Brushy Bayou.

Hunting

For information on hunting licenses, permits, and seasons, visit www.myfwc.com/hunting.

Knight Trail Park (941-486-2350; 3333 Rustic Road, Nokomis 34275, east of Interstate 75 at exit 195, Laurel Rd.) Public facility maintained by the Sarasota Parks and Recreation Department. Trap and skeet, pistol and rifle range, archery range, picnic areas.

Kids' Stuff

Holmes Beach Skateboard Park (5801 Marina Dr. Holmes Beach) Open to BMX bikers, skateboarders, and inline skaters.

Pirates Cove Fun Park (941-755-4608; www.piratescovefunpark.com; 5410 14th St. W., Bradenton 34207) Laser tag, go-carts for all ages, miniature golf, kiddie rides, game rooms, and a snack bar entertain families at this older but well-maintained indoor-outdoor facility. Admission is free; charges per activity.

Smuggler's Cove Adventure Golf (941-756-0043; www.smugglersgolf.com; 2000 Cortez Rd. W., Bradenton 34207; also 941-351-6620; 3815 Tamiami Tr., Sarasota 34234) "Adventure style" 18 holes of miniature golf and live gators, with a pirate's motif. Admission is per player per game.

Racquet Sports

Anna Maria Youth Center (Magnolia Ave., Anna Maria Island) Two lit tennis courts.

Bayfront Park (941-316-1980; www.longboatkey.org/departments/rec/rec.htm; Longboat Key)

City of Venice Public Tennis Courts (W. Venice Ave.) Six courts lit for night play.

Gillespie Park (941-316-1172; 710 N. Osprey Ave., Sarasota 34236) Three unlit tennis courts.

Glazier Gates Park (Manatee Ave. E., Bradenton) Two unlit, cement, public tennis courts.

G. T. Bray Recreation Center (941-742-5923; www.co.manatee.fl.us; 5502 33rd Ave. Dr. W., Bradenton 34209) Eight each of cement, clay, and racquetball courts. Also swimming pool, splash park, and skate park.

Hecksher Park (941-316-1172; 450 W. Venice Ave., Venice 34285) Six tennis courts with lights. Also shuffleboard.

Holmes Beach Courts (near City Hall, Holmes Beach) Three lit tennis courts.

Jessie P. Miller (9th Ave. and 43rd St. W., Bradenton) Four lit cement tennis courts and one handball court.

Nick Bollettieri Tennis at IMG Academies (941-755-1000, 800-872-6425; www.img academies.com; 5500 34th St. W., Bradenton 34210) Training camp for adults and juniors. Includes state-of-the-art tennis, 72 courts (6 of them indoors), swimming pools, a sports-therapy care center, and high-tech sports center. Andre Agassi, Venus and Serena Williams, Anna Kournikova, and other pros have trained here.

Siesta Key County Beach (941-861-2150; Midnight Pass Rd. at Beach Way Dr., Siesta Key) Four tennis courts with lights.

South County Family YMCA (941-492-9622; www.veniceymca.com; 701 Center Rd., Venice 34285) Two racquetball courts, plus workout and fitness rooms and classes.

Shelling

Though not comparable to the coast's southern beaches for shelling, the islands of Bradenton and Sarasota do yield some unusual finds. Venice Beach, for instance, is known for its sharks' teeth, which come in all sizes and various shades from black to rare white. Manasota Beach and the south end of Siesta Key also boast toothy waters, but Venice's beaches have the best pickings.

Sharks continually shed teeth and grow new ones. Most of what you find is prehistoric. The white ones are recent sheddings. Teeth range in size from one-eighth of an inch to a rare three inches. Some resorts provide "Florida snow shovels"—screen baskets fastened to broomsticks for sifting through the sand. You can also buy them in local hardware stores. Digging for specimens is taboo.

Spas

Body & Spirit (941-921-1388; www.bodyandspirit.net; 500 Southgate Plaza, Sarasota 34239) A luxury day spa with massage, body treatments, facials, salon services.

Hollywood Salon & Spa (941-364-3322; www.hollywoodsalonandspa.com; 1812 Hillview St., Sarasota 34239) A complete menu of facials, massages, scrubs, polishes, and body masks, as well as manicures, pedicures, waxing, air-brush tanning, and other salon services.

The Key Spa & Salon (941-349-9005; www.siestakeyspa.com; 5150 Ocean Blvd., Ste. A, Siesta Key 34242, at Tropical Breeze Resort) Complete massage, skin care, and beauty treatments, plus lunch packages, in a charming island setting.

Mandala Medi Spa & Yoga Sanctuary (941-927-2278, www.mandalamedispa.com, 1715 Stickney Point Rd.) Indonesian body treatments, massage, salon services, acupuncture, and medical aesthetics.

The Met (941-388-1772; www.themetsarasota.com; 35 S. Blvd. of Presidents, St. Armands Circle, Sarasota 34236) Up a sweeping staircase from a posh clothing store in an elegant setting, the Met offers full spa and beauty facilities and treatments, including wraps, massages, and facials. Also offers a spa lunch.

Plumeria Day Spa (941-782-1123; 110 Bridge St., Bradenton Beach 34217, at the BridgeWalk resort) Package and à la carte treatments cover all the beauty and body-care bases, including massage, facials, and wraps.

The Springs (941-426-1692; www.warmmineralsprings.com; 12200 San Servando Ave., North Port 34287; south of Venice near North Port) Water of a rare quality attracts health seekers to a 1.4-acre lake fed by 9 million gallons of salt water each day. If you know your spas, you will appreciate the springs' chemical analysis of 19,870 parts per million of fixed solid minerals, the third highest in the world. The lake, which maintains a year-round temperature of 87 degrees, has soothing and, some believe, healing powers that attract people from around the world. Folks bathe at a roped-off beach and children's area and sun on a grassy lawn. A thatched chikee pavilion provides shade, and a picnic area is provided. Opened in 1940 as Warm Mineral Springs, the facilities look a bit time-worn, but enjoy a strong international following. Archaeologists have discovered artifacts in the lake suggesting that Native Americans came here for a bit of mineral-washed R & R 10,000 years ago. Some claim this was the Fountain of Youth about which they told Ponce de León. Learn more at free history talks Sunday and Wednesday mornings. Massages, facials, body wraps, Reiki, acupuncture, spiritual counseling, and healing are now available at the springs' facility, along with an on-site cafeteria. Spa enthusiasts can stay at a motel down the street or buy an on-property condo. Admission is $20 per person, $14 for students, and $8 for children ages 12 and under. Ten-day passes are available, and you can rent beachwear, chairs, and towels. Bottled mineral spring water is for sale in the gift shop. Open daily 9 to 5.

Spectator Sports
GREYHOUND RACING
Sarasota Kennel Club (941-355-7744; www.sarasotakennel.com; 5400 Bradenton Rd., Sarasota 34234) Greyhound night and matinee racing from November to mid-April. Parimutuel betting, Texas Hold 'Em, matinee and evening shows year-round. Thoroughbred horse racing is simulcast from Miami and other tracks year-round. Admission. Closed Sunday. Must be 18 or older to enter.

POLO
Sarasota Polo Club (941-907-0000; www.sarasotapolo.com; 8201 Polo Club Ln., Sarasota 34240, 3-1/2 miles east of I-75 exit 213) Watch from the grandstands, or bring a tailgate picnic. Game time is 1 PM every Sunday, mid-December through Easter. Admission.

PRO BASEBALL
Ed Smith Stadium (941-954-4101; 2700 12th St., Sarasota 34237) Spring-training home (March and early April) of the Cincinnati Reds (941-954-4464; www.cincinnatireds.com) and off-season home of the Sarasota Reds (941-365-4460).

McKechnie Field (941-748-4610; Ninth St. and 17th Ave. W., Bradenton 34205) Site of the Pittsburgh Pirates' exhibition games during March and into April; a small but fun park.

Pirate City (941-747-3031; 1701 27th St. E., Bradenton 34208) Spring-practice field for the Pittsburgh Pirates' major and minor leagues. Catch the major leaguers during spring season working out from 10 AM to 1:30 PM. The minor leaguers train here in March and early April.

WATERSKIING
Sarasota Ski-A-Rees Show (941-388-1666; www.skiarees.com; P.O. Box 1493, Sarasota 34230, at Ken Thompson Park, adjacent to Mote Marine Aquarium) Free amateur water-skiing and wake-boarding performances in the bay Sundays from February through April (except Easter) at 2 PM. See Web site for off-season shows schedule.

Water Sports
PARASAILING & WATERSKIING
Adventure Parasail (941-926-1300; 1968 Tarpon Center Drive, Venice 34285, at the Crow's Nest Marina) Serving Casey Key, Nokomis, Manasota Key, Englewood, and Charlotte County.

Cortez Parasail (941-795-2700, 888-844-4140; www.cortezkat.com; 12507 Cortez Rd., Bradenton 34210, at the bridge) Rides up to 1,200 feet, with an option to free fall.

Fun & Sun Parasail (941-795-1000; www.funsunparasail.com; 135 Bridge St., Bradenton Beach 34217) Fly single, double, or triple over Anna Maria Island.

Siesta Key Parasailing (941-586-1972; 1265 Old Stickney Point Rd., Siesta Key 34242, at Dockside Marine) Single, double, and triple rides.

Water Sports
SAILBOARDING & SURFING
Sailboarders find fine conditions all along the coast.

The newest watersport to hit Florida seas, kiteboarding requires extensive training and lots of cash.

As far as Florida's West Coast surfing reputation goes—which isn't very far—Bradenton Beach is one of the prime spots for surfing, especially in winter when cold fronts approach or summer before and after tropical storms. Look in the "Beaches" section for other surfing and windsurfing venues.

Island Style Wind & Watersport (941-954-1009; 2433 N. Tamiami Trail, Sarasota 34234) Offers kiteboarding lessons.

Snorkeling & Scuba
Of all the southern Gulf Coast, this region generally boasts the best visibility for underwater exploration, especially in spring. Manmade reefs make up for the lack of natural reefs on Florida's west coast. At Venice Beach, a reef lays just a quarter mile from the beach, making shore dives possible. South of Crescent Beach, at the island's central zone, rocks, underwater caves, and coral formations make good submerged sightseeing at **Point of Rocks** beach.

At Bradenton Beach, the sunken sugar barge *Regina* houses various forms of marine life. Both snorkelers and divers look for sharks' teeth fossils.

Dolphin Dive Center (941-924-2785; www.floridakayak.com; 6018 S. Tamiami Trail, Sarasota 34231) Local charters, instruction, snorkel and scuba rentals.

Scuba Quest (941-366-1530; www.scubaquestusa.com; 1129 S. Tamiami Trail, Sarasota 34236, at Bahia Vista St.) With several locations in the Sarasota-Bradenton area, this company offers NAUI certification classes, charters, and equipment sales.

SeaTrek Divers (941-779-1506; www.seatrekdivers.com; 105 Seventh St. N., Bradenton Beach 34217) Located across the street from the barge wreck, this firm offers two-tank, near-shore dives and scuba certification courses.

Wilderness Camping
✪ **Oscar Scherer State Park** (941-483-5956; www.floridastateparks.org./oscarscherer; 1843 S. Tamiami Trail, Osprey 34229) Nearly 1,400 acres in size, this natural oasis provides 98 full-service campsites in a wooded, creek-side setting of palmettos, pines, and venerable moss-draped oaks. The threatened Florida scrub jay seeks refuge here, along with bald eagles, bobcats, river otters, gopher tortoises, and alligators. You can swim in a freshwater lake or enjoy a bird walk, nature and canoe trails, picnicking, and fishing. To reserve a campsite or cabin, call 800-326-3521, or go to www.reserveamerica.com.

Wildlife Spotting
BIRDS
The Sarasota coast is the least natural of the Gulf Coast's four regions. Determined bird spotters can find feathered friends at parks and refuges such as the Passage Key sanctuary, north of Anna Maria Island (bring binoculars—landing ashore is forbidden); Rookery

Holy Sea Cows!

Today we know them as Florida manatees: 1,300-pound blimps with skin like burlap and a face only a nature buff could love. They also go by the name sea cows, although they are more closely related to the elephant. In days of yore, many a sea-weary sailor mistook them for mermaids.

Well, Ariel they're not, but bewitching they can be. Gentle and herbivorous—consuming up to 100 pounds of aquatic plants daily—they make no enemies and have only one stumbling block to survival: human activity. Being mammals, manatees must surface for air, like whales and dolphins. Their girth makes them a prime target for boaters speeding through their habitat. Warning signs designate popular manatee areas. Instead of zipping through these waters and further threatening the seriously endangered manatee population, boaters can better benefit by slowing down and trying to spot the reclusive creatures as they take a breath. It requires a sharp eye, patience, and experience. Watch channels during low tides, when the manatees take to deeper water. Concentric circles, known as "manatee footprints," signal surfacing animals. The manatees usually travel in a line and appear as drifting coconuts or fronds.

A sculpture at Bradenton Pier pays homage to the county's namesake.

To report manatee deaths, injuries, harassment, or orphans, call 941-332-6972.

Islands, north of Siesta Key (also approachable by boat only); Venice Area Audubon Rookery (at the end of Annex Road in South Venice, 0.5 mile south of the junction of U.S. 41 and Route 776), and Oscar Scherer State Park in Osprey, home of the endangered Florida scrub jay. Look for feral peacocks roaming the streets of the village on Longboat Key.

DOLPHINS

Dolphins often follow in the wake of tour boats, but they're unpredictable. You can't plan on them; you can only be thrilled and charmed when they do appear. If you learn their feeding schedules, you have a better chance of catching their act.

MANATEES

Named after the lovable creatures, Bradenton's Manatee County has erected MANATEE WATCH signs at manatee-frequented areas: on the bridges and city pier of the Manatee River, on the Palma Sola Causeway, and on Anna Maria Island at Bayfront Park, Coquina Beach and Boat Ramp, and Kingfish Boat Ramp.

NATURE PRESERVES & ECO-ATTRACTIONS
✪ MOTE MARINE LABORATORY AQUARIUM

941-388-2451, 800-691-MOTE

www.mote.org

1600 Ken Thompson Pkwy., Sarasota 34236
On City Island, northeast of Lido Key
Open: Daily 10–5
Admission: $15 for adults, $10 for children ages 4–12

Mote Marine is known around the world for its research on sharks, marine mammals, and environmental pollutants. Its two visitors centers educate the public on projects and marine life. A 135,000-gallon shark tank centerpieces the original facility and is kept stocked with sharks and fish typical of the area: grouper, snook, pompano, and snapper. Dozens of smaller aquariums and a touch tank hold more than 200 varieties of common and unusual species. Colorful signs challenge kids to ponder and learn about aquarium denizens. The original visitors center has expanded its shark focus in the new millennium with a sensory Shark Attack cinema, a Sharktracker interactive exhibit, and the entirely cool new Immersion Cinema, where visitors use individual touch screens to make their way through an underwater adventure. A 1,500-gallon Remarkable Rays touch tank sits outside in a chikee hut, and a mollusk exhibit features a preserved 25-foot giant squid from 2,000 feet down off the coast of New Zealand. In the Marine Mammal Visitors' Center, the main attraction is a floor-to-ceiling glass tank that holds manatees Hugh and Buffett. The center also features a marine mammal rehabilitation tank and a sea turtle exhibit, which host some of the world's most fascinating sea creatures.

✪ OSCAR SCHERER STATE PARK
941-483-5956
www.floridastateparks.org/oscarscherer
1843 S. Tamiami Trail, Osprey 34229
Open: Sunrise to sunset.
Admission: $4 per car, $1 per pedestrian or cyclist

Mote Marine Laboratory Aquarium built its reputation on shark and other marine-creature research.

Home of the threatened Florida scrub jay, plus bald eagles, bobcats, river otters, gopher tortoises, and alligators. Experience wildlife in a canoe along a salt-water tidal creek or by hiking an extensive system of nature trails. Take heed: If you swim in the freshwater lake, you may become more closely acquainted with an alligator than you would care to be. Also, signs warn of amoeba threats in the warm summer months. The 1,384-acre park offers camping, swimming, canoeing, fishing, and picnicking.

QUICK POINT NATURE PRESERVE
www.longboatkey.org/parks/
quick_point.htm
100 Gulf of Mexico Dr.
South end of Longboat Key

Open: Daily
Admission: Free

The town of Longboat Key worked to restore the natural environment of this 34-acre plot, once covered over and nearly destroyed by sand dredged from New Pass. Park on the west side of the road and follow a boardwalk under the bridge to get to the trails through beach, uplands, mangrove, and lagoon habitats. It's a popular spot for ospreys, egrets, ibises, and shorebirds.

SARASOTA BAY WALK
1550 Ken Thompson Pkwy., Sarasota 34236
On City Island, next to Mote Marine Aquarium
Admission: Free

Take a quiet, self-guided walk along the bay, estuaries, lagoons, and uplands to learn more

The Town the Circus Built

The circus comes as close to being the world in microcosm as anything I know; in a way it puts all the rest of show business in the shade. Its magic is universal and complex.
—*E. B. White,* Ring of Times, *1956*

Legend has it that Bird Key and St. Armands Key, two of Sarasota's barrier islands, became John Ringling's possessions in a poker game. Tales of the circus master's influence on the area's development have grown to mythic proportions: elephants that built bridges, midgets who built fortunes, and an eccentric who built himself an Italian palace. However true the legends, during the 20 years after John Ringling came to Sarasota to house his circus here in winter, he demonstrated a three-ring influence over the city and its barrier islands.

After falling in love with the fledgling mainland village and purchasing real estate offshore, Ringling erected his lavish mansion, Cà d'Zan ("House of John" in Italian, modeled after a Venetian palazzo). He also began constructing a causeway to Lido Key by filling and dredging, and he dreamed of a city park and a shoppers' haven on St. Armands Key. For Longboat Key he envisioned a world-class hotel. With unbridled fervor he set out during his worldwide travels to acquire a fine collection of Baroque art for public display in a museum.

The dreams Ringling failed to realize before he died in 1936 were not abandoned. The causeway was completed and donated to the state. St. Armands Circle today is famed for its shops. The steel skeleton of what was to be the world's finest hotel sat rusting on Longboat Key for years until it was reborn as a modern resort. The John and Mable Ringling Museum of Art encompasses acres of bayside estate, and its collection and grounds include Baroque statuary, original Rubens masterpieces, a rose garden, the restored Venetian Gothic mansion Cà d'Zan, circus museums, and an antique Italian theater.

In addition to his concrete legacy to Sarasota, Ringling bequeathed it an undying commitment to beauty, fantasy, art, and showmanship. The circus remains an important industry in Sarasota—in fact, at the high school, circus is an extracurricular activity, like football. Theaters and galleries thrive thanks to Ringling's patronage of the arts. Without his influence, the entire coast might well have remained a cultural frontier for many more decades.

about coastland ecology. Boardwalk and shell paths lead you past mangroves, old fishing boats bobbing on the bay, egrets, and illustrated signs detailing nature's wonders.

Wildlife Tours & Charters

Sarasota Bay Explorers (941-388-4200; www.sarasotabayexplorers.com; Mote Marine Laboratory Aquarium, 1600 Ken Thompson Pkwy., Sarasota 34236, on City Island) A marine pontoon tour takes you into the Intracoastal waters between City Island and Siesta Key. Features include trawl-net tossing, binocular study of rookery islands, and a marine-biologist narration. Kids love the hands-on quality of this educational tour. It also offers custom and kayak tours. Packages with Mote Marine are available.

SHOPPING

In season you may well be tempted, like everyone else, to save shopping and sightseeing for rainy, cold, off-beach days. Don't. You'll lose your diligently attained good beach attitude by the time you've found your first parking spot. Go in the morning for best results and the most relaxing experience.

Sarasota's **St. Armands Circle** is known far and wide for its arena of posh shops, galleries, and restaurants. **Downtown Sarasota** is steadily improving its shopping outlook, especially for art and antiques lovers. Nearby **Southside Village**, at Hillview Street and Osprey Avenue, has grown into an intriguing little shopping and dining destination. On the islands you'll find fun shops and beach boutiques that blend with the sand and sun.

Shopping Centers & Malls

De Soto Square (941-747-5868; www.desoto-square.com; 303 Hwy. 301, Bradenton 34205) Some 700,000 feet of shop-till-you-drop opportunities in more than 100 stores, including Sears, Macy's, and Dillards, a high-end Florida department-store chain.

✪ **Downtown Sarasota** (941-366-7040; www.greatermainstreet.com) One of the Gulf Coast's most successful downtown restoration projects has returned Sarasota's vitality to Main Street and its environs. The area encompasses approximately 1.5 square miles and is centered at Five Points, where Main Street intersects with four other streets. Renovated old buildings house galleries, bookstores, clothing boutiques, antiques shops, restaurants, sidewalk cafés, clubs, and gift shops. The Palm Avenue Association hosts gallery walks, with music, refreshments, and gallery openings, the first Friday of each month, beginning at 6 PM (941-953-5790; www.palmavenue.net). At Historic Burns Square (Pineapple and Orange Avenues), a unique shopping enclave of historic bungalows and unusual finds hosts lively "first Friday" gallery strolls each month.

Lakewood Ranch Main Street (941-907-3750; www.mainstreetatlakewoodranch.com; Lakewood Ranch, east of I-75 via Route 70) The newest posh address, it is lined with one-of-a-kind or Sarasota-Bradenton shop clones, plus some nice eateries and a cinema complex.

Longboat Key You'll find a smattering of interesting shops and galleries at The Centre Shops (5370 Gulf of Mexico Dr.) and Avenue of Flowers (off Gulf of Mexico Dr.).

✪ **St. Armands Circle** (941-388-1554; www.starmandscircleassoc.com; 300 Madison Dr., Sarasota 34236, on St. Armands Key) On one of the Sarasota barrier islands that he owned,

John Ringling envisioned a world-class shopping center, complete with park-lined walkways and Baroque statuary. He would be gratified by St. Armands Circle. On a scale with Beverly Hills's Rodeo Drive and Palm Beach's Worth Avenue, it was named for developer Charles St. Amand (whose name was misspelled "Armand" in later land deeds—and it is this spelling that persists). Its spin-off formation is suited geographically to the pancake shape of the island. Four sections arc off the circular center drive. "The Circle," as it is known in local shorthand, encompasses shops of the most upscale nature, galleries, restaurants, clubs, and specialty boutiques. International style is well represented. The Circle is a hub of activity for the entire region. Horse-drawn carriages offer sunset rides. The Circus Ring of Fame honors distinguished Big Top entertainers. People dress in finery just to shop here, but don't feel obligated. On the fourth Friday of every month October through May, it hosts Smooth Jazz on St. Armands from 6 to 9 PM. Parking is free on the street and in a garage nearby.

Siesta Key (www.siestakeychamber.com/shopping.htm) Located in the village along Ocean Boulevard, Siesta Key's shopping district has a refreshingly barefoot atmosphere with a touch of beach bawdiness. Mixed in with the shops is a generous dose of casual eateries and daiquiri bars. You'll find a more refined collection of shops around Stickney Point Road.

Downtown Venice (941-484-6722; P.O. Box 602, Venice 34248, at Venice Ave. W. and adjacent streets) Down a Mediterranean-type, date-palm-lined boulevard, you'll find shops and restaurants to fit every budget. Wander a block to the south for antiques and secondhand collectibles. A Third Thursday Stroll takes place every month from 5:30 to 8 PM. Centennial Park runs along Venice Avenue across from its shops. Here musicians often entertain at the gazebo, and children splash in the interactive fountains. North of the park, Venice Mall holds history and more options for shoppers.

Westfield Sarasota Square (941-922-9609; www.westfield.com/sarasota; 8201 S. Tamiami Trail, Sarasota 34238, at Beneva Rd.) Your choice of four major department stores, movie theaters, and more than 140 specialty shops and eateries.

Westfield Southgate (941-955-0900; www.westfield.com; 3501 S. Tamiami Trail, Sarasota 34239; at Bee Ridge Rd.) Smaller than Sarasota Square, this one houses Macy's, Dillards, and Saks Fifth Avenue, plus an above-average food court.

Antiques & Collectibles

Antique shops are plentiful and easy to find in and around Sarasota. You'll find a row of them on Pineapple Street and another on Fruitville Avenue, both downtown. In Venice, look along Miami Avenue, parallel to the main shopping drag, Venice Avenue. Pick up a copy of the *Sarasota Antique Guide & Locator Map* from the Sarasota Visitors Center.

Antiques and Chatchkes Fine Antique Mall (941-906-1221; 1542 Fruitville Rd., Sarasota 34236) Mainly furniture and things for the home.

Jack Vinales Antiques (941-957-0002; 539 Pineapple Ave. S., Sarasota 34236) More contemporary than most of Sarasota's antique stock, this shop concentrates on nostalgia of the '40s and '50s, Art Deco, pottery, lamps, and Bakelite and Fiesta ware.

Lucia's Treasures (941-412-1939; 225 W. Miami Ave. #2A, Venice 34285) Fine estate wares; a little bit of everything, from furniture to crystal.

Old Feed Store Antique Mall (941-729-1379; 4407 Hwy. 301, Ellenton 34222) Around Gamble Plantation historic site you'll find a few interesting antique markets, including this one.

Sarasota Art & Antique Center (640 S. Washington Ave., Sarasota 34236) This huge pink building holds a number of fine antique galleries, including **Crissy Galleries** (941-957-1110; www.crissy.com), selling quality furniture, jewelry, and art; **Sarasota Rare Coin Gallery** (941-366-2191, 800-447-8778; www.sarasotacoin.com); **Yellow Bird Antiques** (941-388-1823), specializing in imported decorative items; and **Sarasota Estate & Jewelry** (941-364-5158), specializing in vintage diamond jewelry.

The Sea Hagg (941-795-5756; www.seahagg.com; 12304 Cortez Rd. W., Cortez 34215) It's tough to pigeonhole this into one shopping category, but it fits here with its stock of antique periscopes, sextants, rods and reels, and other nautical and fishing memorabilia. Browse its two shops and yards for everything from old crab traps to sea glass by the scoop and metal bird and fish sculptures. This is a place to buy a piece of Cortez maritime heritage.

Shadow Box (941-957-3896; 1522 Fruitville Rd., Sarasota 34236) Along Fruitville Road, which runs on the edge of downtown, you can find antique shops mixed among thrift and consignment outlets. These antique shops are generally more affordable than mainstream downtown's. This one carries a nice collection of 18th-century, Victorian, Art Deco, and modern home furnishings and decoratives.

Pretty palms and historic architecture make downtown Venice shopping painless.

Books

❂ **Charlie's Café, Books, and Hops** (941-779-2665; 5904 Marina Dr., Holmes Beach 34217) Sip a beer or espresso, slurp excellent homemade soup, or munch on gourmet salads, panini sandwiches, pizza, and seafood while you dig in to your newly purchased used book.

Circle Books (941-388-2850; www.circlebooks.net; 478 John Ringling Blvd., Sarasota 34236, at St. Armands Circle) Small but packed with books for all ages, plus puzzles and games for kids; features regular author signings.

❂ **Main Bookshop** (941-366-7653; www.mainbookshop.com; 1962 Main St., Sarasota 34236, downtown) A landmark store, with four floors full of new, discounted (30 to 90 percent off), and used books on all subjects.

❂ **Sarasota News & Books** (941-365-6332; www.sarasotanewsandbooks.com; 1341 Main St., Sarasota 34236, downtown) Specializes in art, architecture, and literature. Beyond books and lots of periodicals, Sarasota News sells cards, gifts, coffee, and lunch.

A sampling of colorful wares at Bradenton's Village of the Arts

Venice Newsstand (941-488-6969; 329 W. Venice Ave., Venice 34285) An old-fashioned newsstand, selling cigars, greeting cards, magazines, out-of-town newspapers, and paperbacks.

Clothing

AJ's on Main (941-907-8077; 8141 Lakewood Main St., Ste. 105, Lakewood Ranch 34202) Shop for Florida-style casual and fun fashions for men and women.

Captain's Landing (941-485-2329; 319 W. Venice Ave., Venice 34285) High-quality Hawaiian, golf, and sporty fashions for men.

Cuddlebugs Children's Boutique (941-388-1735; 319 John Ringling Blvd., Sarasota 34236, at St. Armands Circle) High-end baby and toddler clothing, plus toys.

Dream Weaver (941-388-1974; www.dreamweavercollection.com; 364 St. Armands Circle, Sarasota 34236) Fine woven wear—in silk, suede, and other extravagant materials—that crosses the line into fabric art.

Cortez's Sea Hagg takes shopping into a treasure-hunting dimension.

Ivory Coast (941-388-1999; 15 N. Blvd. of Presidents, Sarasota 34236, at St. Armands Circle) Outstanding imported women's fashions, jewelry, and decorative items inspired by Africa.

LaCheape Boutique (941-488-6388; 530 U.S. 41 Bypass S., Venice 34292) Liquidated stock from expensive boutiques sold at greatly reduced cost.

Little Bo-Tique (941-388-1737; 367-A St. Armands Circle, Sarasota 34236) Adorable and stylish children's wear for boys and girls.

The Met (941-388-1772; 35 S. Blvd. of Presidents, Sarasota 34236, at St. Armands Circle) Expensive dressy and casual designer fashions for men and women in a divine setting.

Nana's (941-488-4108; 223 W. Venice Ave., Venice 34285) Quality kids' clothes and toys.

Phasion Pashion (941-366-7100; 1540 Main St., Sarasota 34236) Casual clothing with high style for women and men.

SunBug (941-485-7946; www.venicemainstreet.com/sunbug; 141 W. Venice Ave., Venice 34285) The most fun in women's fashions, from dressy to casual. Great cotton styles, swimsuits, and unusual, comfortable dresses.

Venice Tropical Shop (941-483-4533; 213 W. Venice Ave., Venice 34285) Stand-out, tasteful women's fashions, flirty and sexy in style; handcrafted jewelry; evening wear.

Consignment/Thrift

In Sarasota buying secondhand is not the embarrassment that it is in some places. In fact, recycled apparel is the "in" thing among the young and artistic. Because of the wealth and transient nature of its residents, the area offers the possibility of great discoveries in its consignment shops. Fruitville Road is a good place to shop for recycled goods. Some of the stores benefit local charities.

Divine Consign (941-488-3219; 203 W. Miami Ave., Venice 34285) Benefits a local church. Furniture, housewares, ladies' clothing, and jewelry.

The Elephant's Trunk Thrift Shop (941-483-3056; 595 Tamiami Trail, Venice 34285, behind the Chamber of Commerce) Lots of furniture and other household goods, including discontinued merchandise. Operated by Healthcare Volunteers of Venice.

Encore & More (941-953-4222; www.thewomensresourcecenter.org; 1439 Main St., Sarasota 34236) It sells women's clothing and accessories, furniture, and art to benefit the Women's Resource Center.

Green Butterfly (941-485-6223; 211 W. Miami Ave., Venice 34285) Antique, old, and new home accessories and furniture to benefit a local charity.

Kiss & Co. (941-378-9002; 4214 Bee Ridge Rd., Sarasota 34233) Women's business, sports, and cocktail attire.

Woman's Exchange (941-955-7873; 539 S. Orange Ave., Sarasota 34236, downtown) Furniture, family clothing, antiques, housewares, and china. Profits support local arts.

Factory Outlet Centers

Prime Outlets (941-723-1150, 888-260-7608; www.primeoutlets.com; 5461 Factory Shops Blvd., Ellenton 34222, at Interstate 75 exit 224) As far as the factory outlet malls covered in this book go, this is the most comprehensive, with more than 130 shops, a nice food court, and a children's playground in a Caribbean setting. Besides the typical kitchen and clothing stores, it boasts some top designer names, such as Off 5th (outlet for Saks Fifth Avenue), Brooks Brothers, Liz Claiborne, Waterford/Wedgewood, and others.

Flea Markets & Bazaars

The Dome (941-493-6773; 5115 Rte. 775, Venice) A small indoor market open Saturday and Sunday, 9–4.

Downtown Farmers' Market (941-951-2656; Lemon Ave. and Main St., downtown Sarasota) Fresh fruits, vegetables, baked goods, plants, arts and crafts. Open 7–noon Saturday, year-round. In season, the market also opens on Wednesday.

Red Barn Flea Market (941-747-3794, 800-274-FLEA; www.redbarnfleamarket.com;

1707 First St. E., Bradenton 34208) More than 600 stores and booths selling everything from baseball cards to car parts. Fully open 8–4 Friday, Saturday, and Sunday (also Wednesday, from November through April); mall-area stores (about 40) are open Tuesday through Sunday 10–4.

Galleries

Art Uptown Gallery (941-955-5409; 1367 Main St., Sarasota) One of downtown's more affordable galleries, this nonprofit cooperative carries the various media of local artists. Lots of vibrancy.

Abbott Galleries (941-388-1818; www.abbottgalleries; 18 S. Blvd. of the Presidents, Sarasota 34236, at St. Armands Circle; also 941-388-1818; 1907 S. Osprey Ave., Sarasota 34239) A tantalizing blend of haute and pop works.

Everything But the Girl (941-954-8800; 430 Central, Sarasota 34236) Art and gifts by local artists and designers—from paintings to circus-inspired bead earrings and herbal food products.

Galleria Silecchia (941-365-7414; 888-366-7414; www.galleriasilecchia.com; 12 and 20 S. Palm Ave., Sarasota 34236) These two storefronts contain some of the most interesting art we've seen in all of Sarasota. The larger, corner gallery contains large bronze sculptures and other pieces. The smaller one showcases the exquisite glass lamp works of Ulla Darni, whimsical cut-metal wall sculptures, colorful painted sculptures, and a select collection of decorative art.

O Gallery (941-228-2627; 240 W. Tampa Ave., Venice 34285, at Venice Mall) Local artists create everything from local scenes to stunning abstracts.

Sarasota's International Art Gallery (941-365-4443; 53 S. Palm Ave., Sarasota 34236) A collection of small high-end galleries selling serious art, from African masks and jewelry to glass and paintings.

✪ **Towles Court Artist Colony** (www.towlescourt.com; 1938 Adams Ln., Sarasota 34236, off Hwy. 301) A charming district of restored and brightly painted bungalows has been turned into an art colony. It features the galleries and working art studios of artists in all media. The Towles Court Art Center contains several galleries and a café. It is the colony's headquarters, and other studio-galleries are scattered around it. The **Katharine Butler Galleries** (941955-4546; www.kbutlergallery.com; 1943 Morrill St. Sarasota 34236) carries the artist's diverse work, plus that of 17 other artists. Third Friday art walks, 6–10 PM, include live music.

Venice Gallery & Studio (941-486-0811, 888-999-9113; www.clydebutcher.com; 237 Warfield Ave., Venice 34285) Off the beaten path, search out this home to Clyde Butcher, Florida's unofficial photographer laureate. Here are his darkroom and workshops, plus a collection of his limited-edition and giclée black-and-white portraits of Florida and other scenic locations. He is known for his large-format photography and is often compared to Ansel Adams.

Gifts

Some of the best gifts and souvenirs are found in attraction gift shops, especially those at the Ringling museums, Sarasota Jungle Gardens, G.WIZ, and the South Florida Museum.

Artisans (941-388-0082; 301 John Ringling Blvd., Sarasota 34236, at St. Armands Circle) Inexpensive, flirty, and unusual handbags, jewelry, and home art.

Artisans' World Marketplace (941-365-5994; 128 S. Pineapple Ave., P.O. Box 5994, Sarasota 34277) This not-for-profit has made a commitment to selling the work of below-poverty-level artisans and features such items as ginger soap made in Chicago, telephone-wire baskets from Africa, metal-drum sculptures from Haiti, and wood carvings from Kenya. The resourcefulness reflected in the delightful scope of work is remarkable.

Elysian Fields (941-361-3006; www.elysianfieldsonline.com; 1273 Tamiami Trail S., Sarasota 34239, at Midtown Plaza) This shop's subtitle tells it succinctly enough: "books and gifts for conscious living." It's filled with wonderful New Age accoutrements, aromatherapy supplies, feng shui books and items, sushi and sake sets, cards, candles, and books.

European Focus: Past & Present (941-330-0877; www.europeanfocus.biz; 508 S. Pineapple Ave., Sarasota 34236) Jewelry, tableware, linens, woolen hats, and other imported gifts from Germany, Ireland, France, and Italy.

Exit Art Gallery (941-383-4099 or 800-833-0894; www.exit-art.com; 5380 Gulf of Mexico Dr., Longboat Key 34228, at the Centre Shops) Artistically designed home and office tools, pop art, colorful tableware, jewelry, and clothes.

Giving Tree Wood Gallery (941-388-1353; www.thegivingtreewoodgallery.com; 5 N. Boulevard of Presidents, Sarasota 34236, at St. Armands Circle) Beautiful inset and sculpted wood art, unique jewelry, glassware, and other fine and unusual gifts.

Hurricane Rita (941-346-7712; www.hurricaneritas.com; 5212 Ocean Blvd., Siesta Key Village, Siesta Key 34242). Island-style gifts and home decor items at affordable prices.

Toy Lab (941-363-0064; 1529 Main St., Sarasota 34236) Don't look for Playstation games here. This old-fashioned toy shop has educational toys and games, puppets, stuffed animals, and Brio and Playmobil sets.

Jewelry

Bari Jewelers (941-484-9197; 315 W. Miami Ave., Venice 34285) Buy your sharks' teeth necklaces and large fossil specimens here; also sea-motif charms, gold, diamonds, and other fine pieces.

Coffrin Jewelers (941-366-6871; 1829 S. Osprey Ave., Sarasota 34239, at Southside Village) Fine creations in gold, silver, and platinum; specializing in original designs. Also a vendor of hand-painted French Quimper tableware.

Jewelry by Cole (941-388-3323, 800-572-9375; 7 N. Blvd. of Presidents, Sarasota 34236, at St. Armands Circle) Lovely set gems; a wide variety of the usual to the unusual in sea-themed pieces; custom work.

✪ **Joan Michlin Galleries** (941-388-1199 or 800-630-7770; www.joanmichlin.com; 380 St. Armands Circle, Sarasota 34236) Named for the New York artist who designs the "wearable sculpture" she sells, this shop carries the most exquisite and smartly balanced gold and precious stone creations in town.

June Simmons Designs (941-388-4535; 68 S. Palm Ave., Sarasota 34236) Artistic, exclusive edition jewelry and custom work.

Michael & Co. Jewelers (941-349-5478; www.siestakeyjewelers.com; 5221 Ocean Blvd., Siesta Key 34242) Specializing in nautical pieces, diamonds, and creative jewel settings.

Tilden Ross Jewelers (9941-388-3338; www.tildenross.com; 410 St. Armands Circle, Sarasota 34236) All that glitters! Damiani, Patek Lombardi, and other top designers provide a showroom of exquisite sparkle, from pearls to gems to pale-blue beaded collars and unusual gold rings.

Kitchenware & Home Decor
Annabelle's Home & Kitchen (941-552-0339; www.epicureanlife.com; 1924 S. Osprey Ave., Sarasota 34239; also 941-782-0918; 8130 Lakewood Main St. #104, Lakewood Ranch 34202) Connected to Morton's Market (see "Deli & Specialty Foods"), it sells the finest in kitchen- and tableware.

Artisans (941-388-0082; 301 John Ringling Blvd., Sarasota 34236, at St. Armands Circle) Fun glassworks, jewelry, painted furniture, neon art, and more.

Basketville (941-493-0007; 4411 S. Tamiami Trail, Venice 34293) Region's widest selection of basketry, pottery, wicker furniture, silk flowers, and other household items.

Garden Argosy (941-388-6402; www.gardenargosy.com; 361 St. Armands Circle, Sarasota 34236) Gifts for the home and garden: an extensive selection of candles, frames, painted wood bowls, garden statues, fountains.

The Pineapple House Collection (941-373-6558; 1841 Main St., Ste. 104, Lakewood Ranch 34202) The items in this collection—everything from candles to select pieces of furniture—were obviously handpicked for the most discriminating home decorator.

Restoration Hardware (941-952-9666; Westfield Southgate, 3501 S. Tamiami Trail, Sarasota 34239) Those familiar with the chain need no introduction to its smooth and classy line of furnishings, home accessories, and, yes, hardware—that is, the fancy kind, such as drawer pulls and light fixtures.

Rolling Pin Kitchen Emporium (941-925-2434; www.myrollingpin.com; 8201 S. Tamiami Trail, Sarasota 34238, at Westfield Sarasota Square) German cutlery and fine kitchenware; also offers cooking classes.

The Tabletop (941-485-0319; www.thetabletop.com; 205 W. Venice Ave., Venice 34285) Hand-painted and other fun barware, kitchen and table accessories, coffee and espresso paraphernalia, gourmet items.

Tervis Tumbler Outlet (941-966-8614 or 800-237-6688; www.tervis.com; 928 S. Tamiami Trail, Osprey 34229) Floridians know the only way to keep your drinks cool is with Tervis Tumblers, which are made locally. The insulated acrylic tumblers are guaranteed for life, and you can exchange defective or broken merchandise at this outlet.

Shell Shops
Beach Bazaar (941-346-2995; 5211 Ocean Blvd., Siesta Key 34242) A one-stop mart for

seashells, toys, beach clothes, boogie and skim boards, sunglasses, and other vacation must-haves.

Sea Pleasures and Treasures (941-488-3510; 255 Venice Ave. W., Venice 34285) Quantity, not necessarily quality: sea-theme gifts, shells, jewelry, shell craft supplies, and shark's teeth.

Sporting Goods

Note: This listing includes general sports outlets only. For supplies and equipment for specific sports, please refer to "Recreation" in this chapter.

CB's Saltwater Outfitters (941-349-4400; www.cbsoutfitters.com; 1249 Stickney Point Rd., Siesta Key 34242) Fishing gear and sportswear.

Cook's Sportland (941-493-0025; 4419 Tamiami Trail, Venice 34293, next to Basketville) Equipment for archery, golf, camping, and fishing; also fishing licenses, tackle repair, sportswear, shoes, and western clothing.

CALENDAR OF EVENTS

For a complete listing of local cultural events, visit www.sarasota-arts.org, or call 941-365-5118.

January

Arts Day Festival (941-365-5118; downtown Sarasota) A gala confluence of Sarasota's visual and performing arts that spills from the galleries and theaters onto outdoor stages and sidewalks. One day midmonth.

February

Cortez Fishing Festival (941-794-1249; www.cortezfishingfestival.org; village of Cortez) Food vendors, music, net-mending demonstrations, arts and crafts, boat tours, and educational exhibits describing the community of Cortez's hundred-year-old fishing industry. One weekend midmonth.

Greek Glendi Festival (941-355-2616, 877-355-2272; www.stbarbara-church.org/glendi.html; St. Barbara's Greek Orthodox Church, 7671 Lockwood Ridge Rd., Sarasota 34243) Greek food, dancing, arts, and crafts on one weekend near Valentine's Day.

✪ **Ringling Medieval Fair** (877-334-3377; www.renaissancefest.com, Sarasota County Fairgrounds) Two weekends in the month benefits the Ringling Estates by entertaining throngs with kingly entertainment.

Scottish Highland Games & Heritage Festival (941-342-0509; www.sarasotagames.org; held at the Sarasota Fairgrounds, Fruitville Rd.) Traditional dancing as well as competitions and entertainment for one day early in the month.

March

Anna Maria Island Springfest (941-778-2099; Holmes Beach City Hall Park) A celebration of island arts, featuring artist and crafts booths, local entertainment, and food concessions. Two days early in the month.

Manatee Heritage Month (941-749-7165) The entire month is devoted to the celebration of local history and traditions throughout Bradenton and Manatee County. Special tours are arranged by local attractions, and demonstrators weave, quilt, and make baskets and doilies.

PAL Sailor Circus (941-361-6350; www.sailorcircus.org; 2075 Bahia Vista St., Sarasota 34239) Proof that the circus is still in the blood of many Sarasota families. Students from grades 3 to 12 perform professional circus feats during a two-week season. Also Christmastime performances.

Palmetto Heritage Day (941-723-4991; Palmetto Historical Park, 515 10th Ave. W., Palmetto 34221) Live entertainment, a chicken-and-yellow-rice luncheon, and one-day postage cancellations at the historic post office highlight this open house.

Run For the Turtles (941-388-4441; www.mote.org; Siesta Beach Pavilion, Siesta Key) One-day 5K race to benefit Mote Marine Aquarium.

Sarasota Comedy Festival (941-365-1277; www.comedy.org; various locations in Sarasota) A result of Sarasota's large population of cartoonists, the festival takes place for five days midmonth and includes comedy dinner shows with name stand-up comedians.

Sarasota County Fair (941-365 0818; www.sarasotafair.com; Sarasota Fairgrounds, Fruitville Rd.) Traditional county fair, with midway and carnival areas, exhibits, and entertainment.

Sarasota Jazz Festival (941-366-1552; www.jazzclubsarasota.com throughout Sarasota) Big-name jazz players lead a slate of big bands and jazz combos at indoor and outdoor venues. Plus there are jazz appreciation lectures and a jazz trolley route. One week.

April

Sarasota Film Festival (941-364-9514; www.sarasotafilmfestival.com; 1991 Main St., Ste. 108, Sarasota 34236, Courtyard of the Stars next to Regal Cinemas on Main St., downtown Sarasota) Ten days of films, national celebrities, outdoor screenings, and live entertainment.

Florida Heritage Festival (941-747-1998; Bradenton) The monthlong schedule of events (starting at the end of March) includes an illuminated night parade, seafood festival, children's parade, Easter egg hunt, and plastic-bottle boat regatta.

Florida Winefest and Auction (941-952-1109,800-216-6199; www.floridawinefest.com; at various locations in the area) A prestigious event featuring food and wine seminars, tastes from the area's finest restaurants, top entertainment, a black-tie dinner, and a fine-wine auction. Four days.

La Musica International Chamber Music Festival (941-364-8802; www.lamusica festival.org; P.O. Box 5442, Sarasota 34277) Classical music concerts held during two weeks in April.

✪ **Sharks' Tooth & Seafood Festival** (941-412-0402; around the Venice Pier, Venice) A bacchanal of seafood bounty, the festival gets its name also from its reputation among sharks' teeth collectors. One weekend late in the month.

Siesta Fiesta (941-349-3800; Siesta Key) A weekend of crafts shows, food, and live musical and kids' entertainment.

May

New Play Festival (941-366-9000; www.fst2000.org; Florida Studio Theatre, 1241 N. Palm Ave., Sarasota 34236, downtown) Premieres the works of emerging playwrights from Florida and around the nation, launching almost 70 main-stage productions. Late May through early June.

June

Sarasota Music Festival (941-953-3434; www.sarasotamusicfestival.com; Florida West Coast Symphony, 709 N. Tamiami Trail, Sarasota 34236) Presents classical and chamber music by promising musicians from around the world. Sponsored by the Florida West Coast Symphony, the program includes lectures for participants. The public is welcome at the performances. Three weeks.

Savor Sarasota (www.sarasotafl.org/spirit) 10 days of tasting the award-winning fare of 30 local restaurants. Early in the month.

Suncoast Offshore Grand Prix (941-371-8820 ext. 1800; www.suncoastoffshore.org; Sarasota Fairgrounds, Sarasota Bay, and other county-wide locations) A national attraction more than 20 years old, it features fishing and golf tournaments, parties, and fireworks as well as the headline powerboat races. Eleven days at month's end through July 4.

Venice Art Festival (941-484-6722; downtown Venice) Artisans from around the United States gather for one weekend.

August

De Soto Fishing Tournament (941-747-1998; Bradenton Yacht Club, Palmetto) Inshore and offshore divisions. Entry fee and cash prizes. Takes place one weekend midmonth.

October

St. Armands Circle Art Festival (941-388-1554; St. Armands Circle) Features more than 200 national artists for one weekend midmonth.

Stone Crab, Seafood & Wine Festival (941-383-6464, 800-4-COLONY; Colony Beach and Tennis Resort, 1620 Gulf of Mexico Dr., Longboat Key 34228) Celebrates the opening of stone crab season for four days with 2,300 pounds of claws, 700 bottles of wine, dinners, celebrity chef demonstrations, and wine tasting.

November

Blues Fest (941-377-3279; www.sarasotabluesfest.com; Ed Smith Stadium Complex, 2700 12th St., Sarasota 34237) Blues musicians of world renown. One day early in the month.

Sarasota Reading Festival (941-906-1733; www.sarasotareadingfestival.com; P.O. Box 906, Sarasota 34230, at Five Points Park, downtown) The first Saturday of November, this free community event promotes literacy with author appearances and family activities.

Venice Art Festival (941-484-6722; downtown Venice) Artisans from around the U.S. gather for one weekend.

December

Winterfest (941-778-2099; Holmes Beach City Hall Park) Two days of arts and crafts shows, live entertainment, and food.

Winter Wonderland (941-708-6200 ext. 288; Old Main Street, downtown Bradenton) Two mounds of snow, kids' craft fair, lit-boat parade, food, and entertainment. Held three evenings the first weekend of December.

4

Charlotte Harbor Coast

Wild and Watery

As one of Florida's largest bays and its second largest estuary, 270-square-mile Charlotte Harbor supplies a huge gulp of nature and a place to play on many waterfronts—a total of 830 miles of shoreline. The region has remained the most isolated and undeveloped of any in southwest Florida, primarily because its beaches—glorious though they might be—are so far removed from main highways. The fact that 84 percent of Charlotte Harbor shoreline is preserved land ensures that the Charlotte coast will retain its quiet, natural temperament and still hold on to fishing as a way of life and livelihood.

This chapter begins where the last left off, on twisty, out-of-the-way **Manasota Key**, a refuge for wealthy isolationists at its north end and the site of the unpretentious, underappreciated resort community of **Englewood Beach** at its south.

On the mainland Cape Haze peninsula—bounded by the Myakka River and Charlotte Harbor—small residential communities such as ✪ **Englewood**, **Grove City**, **Cape Haze**, **Placida**, and **Rotonda West** hold Amerindian mounds, fishermen, retirees, golf-course communities, and families. Placida is the jumping-off point for **Gasparilla Island**, which has built its reputation and character on one fish in particular: the tarpon. Phosphate shipping and legends of bygone buccaneers first attracted attention to the area. Later the Silver King, prize of the fishing world, drew millionaires to the island community of **Boca Grande**. They're still around; the town reportedly has a median household income of more than $142,000. Privately owned **Little Gasparilla** and **Palm Islands** and mostly state-owned **Don Pedro Island** have run together with shifts of tides and time. They remain three of Florida's most pristine barrier islands.

Inland, across the harbor, **Port Charlotte** is a new city that was built around Tamiami Trail, principally as a retirement community. The town of **Charlotte Harbor** was settled shortly after the Civil War by farmers and cattle ranchers. Facing it across the Peace River's widest point, ✪ **Punta Gorda** boasts a past as deep as its harbor. The southernmost station for the Florida Southern Railroad in 1886, this deepwater port town enjoyed a bustling era of commerce and tourism before railroad builder Henry Plant decided to shut it down in favor of further developing Tampa Bay. Ice making, turpentine stilling, pineapple growing, and especially commercial fishing continued to earn local citizens a living for some time. Today Punta Gorda is working to recover its past glories through downtown and riverfront restoration. Residential-retail developments are replacing old shopping centers and rubble left in the wake of 2004's Hurricane Charley, which hit Punta Gorda squarely.

Photo credit: Lee County Visitor & Convention Bureau

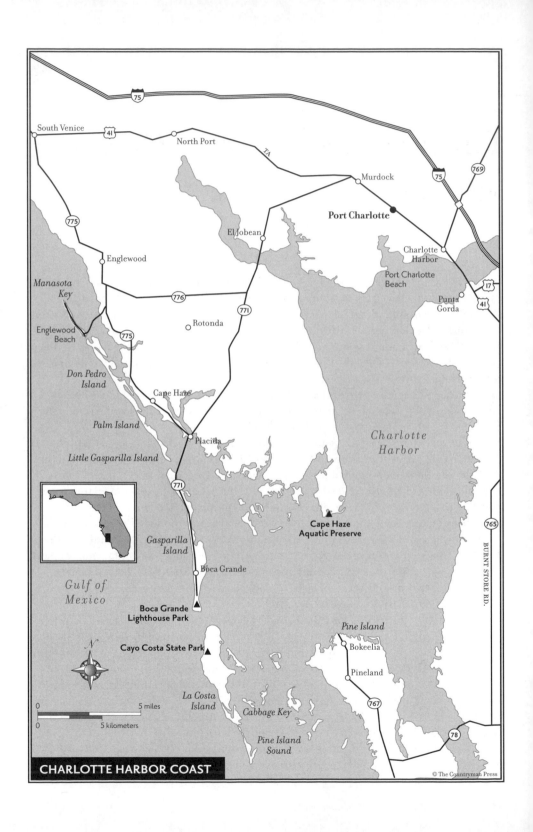

CHARLOTTE HARBOR COAST

© The Countryman Press

Money magazine regularly declares Punta Gorda one of America's most desirable places to live. Home of Ponce de León Park, where the explorer is believed to have met his death, it hosts subdivisions of modern-day youth seekers. Its heyday train depot has been restored to its old glory and today houses a small museum and an antique mall.

LODGING

Accommodations along the Charlotte Harbor coast tend to exude personality. Sure, you have your Best Western and Holiday Inn, but the remainder are either old-money polished, new-money luxurious, or money's-not-the-issue sporting. From beach cottages to the grand old Gasparilla Inn, the Charlotte Harbor coast promises something special in the way of lodging.

During high season, which begins shortly before Christmas and ends after Easter, rates may rise anywhere from 10 to 100 percent above those charged during the off season. Some resorts schedule their rates based on as many as six different seasons, and the highest rates apply from mid-February through Easter. Reservations are recommended during these months. Some resorts and rental services require a minimum stay, especially during the peak season.

The following selection includes some of the coast's greatest lodging characters. Toll-free 800, 888, 866, or 877 reservation numbers where available are listed after local numbers.

Pricing codes are explained below. They are normally per person/double occupancy for hotel rooms and per unit for efficiencies, apartments, and cottages. Many resorts offer off-season packages at special rates. Pricing does not include the 7 percent Florida sales tax or Charlotte County's 5 percent bed tax. Some large resorts add service gratuities or maid charges.

Rate Categories

Inexpensive   Up to $75
Moderate $75 to $150
Expensive $150 to $200
Very Expensive $200 and up

An asterisk after the pricing designation indicates that the rate includes at least continental breakfast in the cost of lodging; one establishment follows the American Plan, pricing all meals into the room rate.

The following abbreviations are used for credit card information:
AE: American Express
MC: MasterCard
D: Discover Card
V: Visa
DC: Diners Club

Note that under the Americans with Disabilities Act (ADA), accommodations built after January 26, 1993, and containing more than five rooms must be useable by persons with disabilities. I have indicated only those small places that do not make such allowances.

Accommodations

BOCA GRANDE
✪ GASPARILLA INN
General Manager: Jack Damioli
941-964-2201
500 Palm Ave., P.O. Box 1088, Boca Grande 33921
At 5th St. and Palm Ave
Price: Very Expensive*
Credit Cards: No
Closed: Mid-June to mid-Dec.

With subtle grandeur the Gasparilla Inn sits on her throne of lush greenery. Dressed in pale yellow clapboard with white columns, Georgian porticos, and Victorian sensibilities, the inn has been a town anchor and social emblem since 1912. The region's oldest surviving resort, the Gasparilla first

opened its doors as a retreat for such families as the Vanderbilts and Du Ponts, whose
descendants still visit, along with the
Bushes and other illuminati. Not that the
accommodations are ultraelegant: The 140
rooms reflect the era of their construction,
with understated, near-institutional furnishings; the cottages are more modern
and roomy. A white-linen dining room, a
beauty salon and spa, an 18-hole golf
course, a croquet lawn, tennis courts, playground, a beach club with fitness facilities,
and two pools provide amenities. It's said
that the Gasparilla Inn in quiet Boca
Grande is where Palm Beach socialites
came to escape charity balls and the per-
petual fashion show of their glittery hometown. Rates include full meal plan in Social
Season (Christmas through Easter), breakfast and dinner only Easter through Tarpon
Season (mid-June), and no meals the rest
of the year.

ISLAND HOUSE INN

General Manager: Tom Knight
941-964-4443
www.bocagranderesort.net
5800 Gasparilla Rd., Boca Grande 33921
At Boca Grande Resort
Price: Very Expensive
Credit Cards: AE, D, MC, V

Formerly Uncle Henry's, this inn has
become part of a new waterside plaza with
owners interested in creating an intimate,
one-of-a-kind experience. Each of its 16
rooms and two two-bedroom suites has
been craftily decorated with Tommy
Bahama furnishings to create a palmy environment. With the new and illustrious Boca
Bistro right on property (see "Dining") and
its more casual downstairs eatery, plus
shops and a food market, the resort's distance from downtown Boca becomes more
asset than disadvantage. Easy water access
and a pleasant little swimming pool add to
the inn's amenities.

The Gasparilla Inn, doyenne of the Gulf Coast

THE INNLET

General Manager: Bill Hinman
941-964-2294
www.innletonthewaterfront.com
1251 Twelfth St. E., P.O. Box 248, Boca
Grande 33921
At 12th St. and East Ave.
Price: Moderate to Expensive.
Credit Cards: AE, MC, V.

Little stepsister to the Gasparilla Inn, the
Innlet is also painted yellow, to fit in with
the family. Fancy lattice touches and renovations pretty up a motel remake. The name
is a double entendre on its sub-inn status
and its bayou location with a ramp and
docking, handy for boating and fishing
types. It has a nice little pool, playground,
restaurant, and 32 rooms and efficiencies
(with stovetop, microwave, and fridge) in
modern, tasteful attire. Guests share communal porches and balconies. An on-site
restaurant is popular for breakfast.

CAPE HAZE

✪ PALM ISLAND RESORT

President: Dean L. Beckstead
941-697-4800, 800-824-5412
www.palmisland.com
7092 Placida Rd., Cape Haze 33946
Price: Expensive to Very Expensive (minimum two-night stay required)
Credit Cards: AE, D, MC, V

A true island getaway in grand style, Palm
Island occupies the northernmost point of a
slab of sand above Gasparilla Island. One
must boat in; a car ferry runs at least every
half hour from the mainland, where the
resort owns one-bedroom harborside condos, in which you can also stay. On the island,
Old Florida–style villas front a wide, isolated
apron of beach and come with fully equipped
kitchens, laundries, one to three bedrooms,
exquisite appointments, and screened
porches overlooking more than 2 miles of
deserted beach. The 160-unit (counting the
mainland accommodations) property has

four pools and 11 tennis courts, plus a restaurant and bar, an island store, a full-service
marina, boat rentals, charter services, nature
programs, kids' programs, playgrounds, plus
bicycles, golf carts (the main mode of trans-
port on the island), kayaks, canoes, and
beach equipment rentals—all the makings for
an "I'm-never-leaving-this-island" vacation.
What it doesn't have is roads, cars (you park
outside resort gates), stress, and rigorous
time schedules.

ENGLEWOOD BEACH

WESTON'S RESORT

Owner: Deborah L. Weston
941-474-3431
www.westonsresort.com
985 Gulf Blvd., Englewood 34223
Price: Inexpensive to Expensive
Credit Cards: D, MC, V

Taking up a good block at Englewood
Beach's southern end, Weston's spreads
from bay to beach to please both fishermen
and sand-loving types. For the former, it
rents boats, motors, and gear and provides
boat slips, fishing docks, and freezer storage. Free for the use of all guests are tennis
courts, barbecue grills, and two swimming
pools. Accommodations on the 83-unit
property range from studio efficiencies
(inexpensive) to three-bedroom apartments (expensive) in cement-block buildings, all modernly outfitted. The rooms are
clean and well kept. In some rooms the
Murphy-style beds flip up into closets for
more space. Kitchens are large and modern. Beach rooms look beyond seawalls to
eroding beach. One pool sits in the middle
of an asphalt parking lot. There's nothing
luxurious about the resort, but its rates and
beach location at the quiet end of the island
make it a good choice for people who love
water and water sports.

MANASOTA KEY

✪ MANASOTA BEACH CLUB

Owners: Robert and Sydney Buffum

Palm Island Resort: the ultimate island hideaway Palm Island Resort

Manager: Sydney Buffum Crampton
941-474-2614
www.manasotabeachclub.com
7660 Manasota Key Rd., Englewood 34223
Price: Very Expensive*
Credit Cards: MC, V

A tiny, low-impact sign whispers MANASOTA
BEACH CLUB. And although it occupies 25
acres of Manasota Key, the resort itself is
just as unobtrusive. The unadvertised
property preserves the island's natural
attributes with a low-key attitude, wooded
paths, and a deserted beach. Guests have
reported seeing 92 bird species about the
grounds. Fifteen cottages, from rustic to
designer in style; the dining room; the bottle club (no alcohol is sold on the premises); and a library display Old Florida
charm. The resort appeals to the "sink into
oblivion" type of vacationer who wishes to
hide out among natural, gnarly vegetation.
(There are no televisions in the units,
unless requested.) The property—which has
a summer-camp feel to it—also appeals to
the sportsperson, with three tennis courts;
a swimming pool; bocce ball, shuffleboard,
and basketball courts; horseshoes; a playground; croquet; bicycling; sailing, windsurfing, and kayaking; a children's
program; and charter fishing. A private 18-
hole golf course nearby is available to

guests. During social season (February
through March), cottage-room guests
receive three meals a day on the American
Plan; a Modified American Plan (two
meals) or Modified European Plan (continental breakfast only) are available
Thanksgiving through January and in April.
May through mid-November, the resort
rents out entire cottages with kitchens and
provides no meals.

PORT CHARLOTTE
BANANA BAY ON CHARLOTTE HARBOR
Manager: Judy King
941-743-4441
www.bananabaymotel.com
23285 Bayshore Rd., Charlotte Harbor
33980
Off U.S. 41
Price: Inexpensive to Moderate
Credit Cards: AE, D, DC, MC, V
No handicap access

Along Bayshore Drive in Charlotte Harbor,
the feeling is Old Florida, relaxed, and
fishy. Across the wide mouth of the Peace
River lies Punta Gorda. Down the way, a
free fishing pier juts into waters flush with
fish. A few inexpensive motels in this
neighborhood serve the stay-away-from-
the-crowds crowd, and Banana Bay is one

Whimsical murals add color to riverfront Banana Bay.

of the prettiest, with its banana-tree murals on its one-story stucco rooms and one-bedroom efficiencies. The 16 rooms, newly renovated after 2004's hurricane damage, have a clean, perky tropical look. Efficiencies have small fridges, stovetops, and microwaves. Along the bay, shuffleboard courts, grills, a little beach, and picnic tables put the focus outdoors on the fetching water view. Families like the mini-golf attraction next door.

HARBOR POINTE RESORT

Resort Manager: Jesse W. Cook
941-627-9930, 877-627-9930
www.resortquestswfl.com/harborpointe
5121 Melbourne St., Port Charlotte 33980
Off U.S. 41
Price: Moderate (Minimum stay is three nights, and housekeeping is extra.)
Credit Cards: AE, D, DC, MC, V

For families or multiple couples, this bargain combines at-home comfort with a central location. Opened January 2006, its 96 three-bedroom units sleep six comfortably or up to eight if you use the sleeper sofa in the spacious living room. Complete, modern kitchens include all your cooking necessities. The complex's six West Indian–style, low-rise stucco buildings huddle around a courtyard that has a heated swimming pool, hot tub, and putting green. Each room contains its own laundry facility, DVD player, balcony, separate shower and bathtub, and wireless Internet access. Many afford views of the Peace River across the street.

PUNTA GORDA
FISHERMEN'S VILLAGE VILLAS

Manager: Patti Pierron
941-639-8721, 800-639-0020
www.fishville.com
1200 W. Retta Esplanade #58, Punta Gorda 33950
Price: Moderate to Expensive

Credit Cards: D, MC, V

This is one of the Gulf Coast's best lodging bargains. These spacious time-share units—all decorated in modern taste and all with a view of the water—contain two bedrooms, a loft, a living area, a big full kitchen with counter bar and stools, and one bath. They are above the shops, restaurants, and courtyard hubbub of Fishermen's Village, but the rooms are well sound-proofed. Guests have free use of a swimming pool, tennis courts, and bicycles. They are close to all the action there is to find in Punta Gorda, on land and on water. Convenient for boat-in guests, Fishermen's Village fronts a yacht harbor and a 111-slip full-service marina.

Home & Condo Rentals

Boca Grande Real Estate (941-964-0338, 866-302-0338; www.bocagranderealestate.com; 430 W. Fourth St., P.O. Box 686, Boca Grande 33921) Large selection of vacation and seasonal accommodations.

Manasota Key Realty (941-474-9536, 800-870-6432; www.manasotakeyrealty.com; 1927 Beach Rd., Englewood 34223) Grand mansions, beachside cottages, and bayside homes.

Place in the Sun Vacation Rentals (941-475-3714; www.placeinthesun.com; 2670 S. McCall Rd. #12, Englewood 34224, at Heron Plaza) Luxury three- and four-bedroom homes.

RV Resorts

Most of the area's RV accommodations lie east of Interstate 75.

Water's Edge RV Resort (941-637-4677, 800-637-9224; www.watersedgervresort.com; 6800 Golf Course Blvd., Punta Gorda 33982) Full hookups, recreation hall, pool, Jacuzzi, fishing lake and dock, convenience store, and rural setting. For adults only.

DINING

Local cuisine smacks of Midwestern influence, but in recent years Floribbean flavors have livened things up. Fishing crews bring just-hooked seafood to the table, but that doesn't mean some restaurants won't try to pawn off frozen products. Here I've tried to include a few eateries that believe in freshness and fanfare at the dining table.

The following listings sample all the variety of Charlotte Harbor Coast feasting in these price categories:

Inexpensive	Up to $15
Moderate	$15 to $25
Expensive	$25 to $35
Very Expensive	$35 or more

Cost categories are based on the range of dinner entrée prices, or, if dinner is not served, on lunch entrées. The following abbreviations are used for credit card information and meals:

AE: American Express
D: Discover Card
DC: Diners Club
MC: MasterCard
V: Visa
B: Breakfast
L: Lunch
D: Dinner
SB: Sunday Brunch

Note: Florida law forbids smoking inside all restaurants and bars serving food. Smoking is permitted only in restaurants with outdoor seating.

BOCA GRANDE
BOCA BISTRO
941-964-8020
5800 Gasparilla Rd., Boca Grande 33921
At Boca Grande Resort
Price: Very Expensive
Cuisine: New American
Children's Menu: No
Liquor: Full
Serving: D (Summer closure schedule varies.)
Credit Cards: AE, D, MC, V
Handicap Access: Yes
Reservations: Yes, recommended for dinner
Special Features: Sea view

Boca Grande's newest rising star on the restaurant horizon takes a daring leap, but with a well-known chef from the Bradenton area, to hopefully ensure success at a location that has lagged in past incarnations. The highly acclaimed Beach Bistro chef has transplanted some of his famed specialties, such as lobsterscargots and "kicker" grilled shrimp appetizers and bouillabaisse. The small menu, abetted by changing nightly specials, also describes extravagant creations such as warm duckling spinach salad, "world's best aged beef," and rack of lamb with port rosemary demi-glace. The bistro's smart red lacquer walls with gold and copper leaf frame a quiet second-story view of mangroves and boats approaching the marina next door. At sea level, a more casual counterpart with pizza ovens and a smoker is more family- and budget-minded and has live music on the weekends.

✪ PJ'S SEAGRILLE
941-964-0806
321 Park Ave., Boca Grande 33921
In the Old Theatre Building
Price: Moderate to Expensive
Cuisine: Seafood
Children's Menu: Yes
Liquor: Full
Serving: L, D (Closed Sun. and mid-July–Sept.)
Credit Cards: AE, DC, MC, V
Handicap Access: Yes
Reservations: Yes, recommended for dinner

PJ's is one of Boca Grande's most popular fine-dining experiences. Family-owned and operated for some 15 years, it exudes an air of island familiarity, and regulars return year after year. Dinners offer linen and candlelight; lunch is more casual, and both are in the setting of unfinished wood and aquariums. The menus change according to fish availability and Chef Jim's creative mood swings. At lunch, you'll find standard fare with sporadic flares of creativity, such as pita chicken sandwich with pesto mayo and grilled black beans and rice with cornbread. At dinner, PJ's shines with an ever-changing menu featuring what the local fishermen caught that day. Some sure bets if you see them: the cucumber-wrapped spicy tuna tartare roll, Thai sweet-and-sour soup (exceptionally well-seasoned), tomato basil bisque with lump crab, char-grilled yellow fin tuna with berry sauce and wasabi, and pan-fried snapper with garlic, lemon, and white wine (much more complex in flavor than it sounds). The sides battle for attention. Try the regularly featured cheese grits or, when available, the curried acorn squash with almonds. Save room for homemade dessert. The key lime pie and chocolate cake with coconut frosting are winners.

Englewood
ZYDECO GRILLE
941-473-7479
www.zydecogrille.net
2639 Placida Rd., Englewood 34223
Price: Moderate
Cuisine: Cajun/Creole
Children's Menu: Kids' items available
Liquor: Full
Serving: L, D (Closed Mon.)
Credit Cards: AE, DC, MC, V
Handicap Access: Yes
Reservations: Yes

Straight from the bayou, complete with New Orleans music and a mess of crawfish, this addition to the local dining scene works a little voodoo magic. Inside, New Orleans–style iron scrollwork and Mardi Gras beads adorn a stylishly decorated but booth-casual, roomy dining room. The bar next door, equally handsome, stays lively into the wee hours. Outdoor seating accommodates smokers. I started my lunch recently with a bowl of the gumbo of the day, which happened to be crawfish and sausage. I also ended my lunch there, because with its scoop of rice and side of bread, the warm, thick stew worked its voodoo. Next visit, I'm going for the crawfish pie, crawfish cakes with tasso ham, or New Orleans barbecue shrimp, and definitely the bourbon bread pudding. The menu stretches beyond its Cajun-Creole mission with charbroiled steaks, grilled seafood, and chicken, but everything has the New Orleans flair. You can have your steak blackened, for instance, or topped with *au poivre* sauce. As for the fresh catch of the day, it can be pan-seared in pecan flour or sautéed with etouffée. Why settle for ordinary? As the menu points out, "life is too short for dull food."

Englewood Beach
GULF VIEW GRILL
941-475-3500
2095 N. Beach Rd., Englewood Beach 34223
www.gulfviewgrill.com
Price: Inexpensive to Expensive
Cuisine: Seafood
Children's Menu: Yes
Liquor: Full
Serving: D, SB
Credit Cards: MC, V
Handicap Access: Yes
Reservations: Yes
Special Features: Window-wall views of beach and gulf; piano bar; early-bird menu.

As my old favorites on Englewood Beach have closed, I was forced to try a more modern restaurant—which, happily, turns out to have more appeal. To start with, there's the drop-dead view from its stilted glass-cage perch. On a recent lunch visit, I was encouraged by the number of locals filling the tables and ultimately thrilled by the chef's special I ordered: spinach and

Gorgonzola tortellini topped with perfectly cooked shrimp and a superb creamy tomato sauce. If this is any indication, I'll be back for dinner, when a multipaged menu features the day's fresh catches simply prepared either grilled and basted with garlic and lemon butter or sautéed in natural pan juices with the chef's sauce of the day. Or choose from specialties such as filet mignon on blue crab meat with portobellos and brandy demi-glace, bouillabaisse, snapper provençal, lamb chops, veal osso buco, or prime rib. For something lighter, try a deep-fried or grilled grouper sandwich or a salad topped with grilled tuna. Sunday brunch features crêpes, baked praline French toast, and "eggs in purgatory" (eggs fried and served atop potato pancakes with marinara sauce and parmesan cheese).

PLACIDA
THE FISHERY RESTAURANT
941-697-2451
www.sunstate.com/fishery
1300 Fishery Rd., Gasparilla Sound, Placida 33946
Price: Inexpensive to Moderate
Cuisine: Seafood

Children's Menu: Yes
Liquor: Full
Serving: L, D (Closed Mon. in summer.)
Credit Cards: AE, DC, MC, V
Handicap Access: Yes
Reservations: Yes

Take a side trip to Old Florida as you drive or boat in to this waterside shanty with a view of mangroves, an old fishing boat, and the rustic fishery next door. Locals and boaters belly up to the bar outdoors on the dock or inside in the plain dining room, where the windows are the focal point. The menu reflects what's fresh from local waters, prepared both in Cracker style and classic Continental. Start with a garlic shrimp appetizer or a bowl of "Famous Fishery Gumbo," then try a basket of gator bites with hush puppies or pan-sautéed grouper with hollandaise and shrimp. For meat-eaters, there are a couple of cuts of steak or chicken picatta. It's all good, hearty, unpretentious fare.

PORT CHARLOTTE
✪ PORTOFINO WATERFRONT DINING
941-743-2800
23247 Bayshore Rd., Port Charlotte 33980

Fishing boats docked out back let you know that what you're gobbling at The Fishery Restaurant is as fresh as can be.

Price: Moderate to Expensive
Cuisine: Italian
Children's Menu: Yes
Liquor: Full
Serving: L, D (Closed for Sun. lunch.)
Credit Cards: AE, D, MC, V
Handicap Access: Yes
Reservations: Yes
Special Feature: River view

Great view: check. Creative Italian cuisine: check. Gorgeous decor: check. Top service: Well, this new sensation on the Peace River could use a little work on that, but one tends to overlook shortcomings in the face of the artistic setting of beautiful wood and tiles. Three-tiered dining allows everyone an eyeful of water as they enjoy the finest ingredients magically worked into a cross-section of Italian favorites. Southern Italy, with its seafood and spice, is well represented with a marriage of local and imported fish: tuna piccante, fried mixed platter, crab cakes, fried grouper with roasted garlic tartar sauce, *frutti di mare fra diavolo*, shrimp and scallops Alfredo with spinach and pancetta crisps, and pan-seared salmon with lemon-caper cream sauce. Traditional dishes include minestrone, lasagna al forno, veal marsala, and chicken parmigiana. To please every palate, the dinner menu also offers fine Angus steaks and some of its own creations, such as a killer wild mushroom ravioli with silky gorgonzola cream sauce and a grilled chicken with portobello mushrooms, caramelized onions, and asiago and mozzarella cheese. The lunch menu, equally extensive, goes from an eggplant parmigiana sandwich and portobello panini to pizza, gorgonzola burger, and pasta primavera.

PUNTA GORDA
AMIMOTO JAPANESE RESTAURANT
941-505-1515
2705 S. Tamiami Trail, Punta Gorda 33950
At Towles Plaza

Price: Moderate to Expensive
Cuisine: Japanese
Children's Menu: No
Liquor: Beer and wine
Serving: L, D (Closed for lunch Sat. and Sun.)
Credit Cards: AE, D, DC, MC, V
Handicap Access: Yes
Reservations: Yes
Special Features: Sushi bar

Soothing and authentic, Amimoto satisfies the spirit as well as the stomach. The decor is simple, contemporary, and clean, decorated with tasteful Eastern art and arranged around the Formica sushi bar. The sushi menu itself presents nearly 50 choices in four categories: raw, vegetable, cooked, and preserved (smoked). I like the *hokkai*—salmon, onions, and radish sprouts or the spicy tuna. Cooked options range from fried shrimp to kobe beef rolls. The steamed *gyoza* dumplings with mustard sauce are also a tasty way to start off the meal. The lunch and dinner menus list dozens more options for appetizers, such as the light miso soup with tofu and enoki, ginger shrimp, fried soft-shell crab, seaweed salad, and scads of exotic combinations involving seafood, tofu, and Oriental vegetables and sauces. *Obento* box combinations, a Japanese improvement on box lunches, are popular midday choices. For entrées, the menus describe a few possible preparations of chicken, pork, and beef, then goes on to list a selection of seafood grilled with wasabi or teriyaki sauce or deep-fried. Sushi combinations are another dinner option.

THE CELTIC RAY PUBLIC HOUSE
941-505-9219
145 E. Marion, Punta Gorda 33950
Downtown
Price: Inexpensive
Cuisine: Irish
Children's Menu: No

Liquor: Beer and wine
Serving: L, D
Credit Cards: AE, D, DC, MC, V
Handicap Access: Yes, but a little cramped.
Reservations: No
Special Features: Live musicians
Wednesday nights

Downtown Punta Gorda's "restaurant row" may be evolving into a trendy, pricey new standard for the area, but ten-year-old Celtic Ray still treads the old affordable and colorful path that makes the town the multitextured enigma it is. Take one of two glider tables out front or duck into the cool, dark sanctuary of a pub that virtually whisks you off to the blarney and conviviality of the Emerald Isle. As you might expect, the beer list satisfies everyone's hankering for lagers, ales, stouts, and a full range of others. Take a seat at the modest collection of wooden tables or pull up a bar stool to peruse the board menu of leek and potato soup; bangers; fish and chips; lamb shank; Guinness pie; cabbage leaves stuffed with sausage, rice, and raisins; and Jamesons bread pudding. All entrées come wreathed with colcannon, a hearty mash of potatoes, leeks, and greens. Customers order at the bar, which skirts a redbrick wall to further the illusion that you're somewhere other than Florida.

✪ THE PERFECT CAPER

941-505-9009
www.theperfectcaper.com
121 E. Marion Ave., Punta Gorda 33950
Downtown
Note: Location is expected to change by mid-2008.
Price: Expensive to Very Expensive
Cuisine: New American
Children's Menu: No
Liquor: Full
Serving: L, D, SB (Closed all day Mon. and for lunch on Tues.)
Credit Cards: AE, D, DC, MC, V
Handicap Access: Yes
Reservations: Yes

Recently moved from its original home on Sullivan Street, this local favorite for fine, creative cuisine now lives in a larger space—a burnished bistro setting with an exhibit kitchen. The duck on my lunch of duck salad came medium-rare as ordered,

The Celtic Ray, the cornerstone of downtown Punta Gorda's Restaurant Row, is a wee corner of Ireland.

tender and juicy, served on greens, and dressed deliciously with cherry vinaigrette. A square of herbed focaccia accompanied. Other intriguing meat-and-greens salads plus an array of entrées and sandwiches, such as ham and brie on a baguette or focaccia, complete the lunch menu. For dinner, a seasonally changing menu offers such delights as a crispy shrimp appetizer fried in shredded phyllo, fig and goat-cheese salad, double truffle chicken, miso black cod with lemongrass ginger broth, and Sichuan green-peppercorn strip steak. The dessert menu presents a tough choice, but you won't regret the chocolate bread pudding with vanilla-caramel sauce or the hand-churned ice cream, sorbet, and gelato of the day. Don't miss this place for Charlotte County's most cutting-edge cuisine.

FOOD PURVEYORS

Bakeries
Boca Grande Baking Co. (941-964-5818; www.bocagrandebakingco.com; 384 E. Railroad Ave., Boca Grande 33921) Homemade breads, creative muffins, scones, pastries, cakes, and other desserts in an inviting setting; complete coffee bar; also pizza, panini, and other eat-in or takeout items.

Breakfast
Loons on a Limb (941-964-0155; 310 E. Railroad Ave., Boca Grande 33921) Open daily for breakfast and brunch; a 21-year Boca tradition, serving typical breakfast fare, smoothies, and mimosas. No credit cards accepted.

Café Ruelle (941-575-3553, www.caferuelle.com; 117 W. Marion Ave., Punta Gorda 33950, downtown) Coffee is the buzzword, but muffins, pastries, quiche, and smoothies with a French accent provide a quick, tasty repast al fresco or inside. Also lunch and weekend dinner.

Candy & Ice Cream
American Pie Ice Cream (941-474-8PIE; 446 W. Dearborn St., Englewood 34223) Beware parents: Besides ice cream and desserts, this old-fashioned-style shop sells classic toys.

The Loose Caboose (941-964-0440; 433 W. Fourth St., Boca Grande 33921, at Park Ave.) Katharine Hepburn, among scores of others, once left her compliments on the bulletin board at this restaurant known for its homemade ice cream and smoothies in many flavors.

Swiss Chocolate (941-639-9484; www.swissconnectionsusa.com; 403 Sullivan St., #112, Punta Gorda 33950) Norman Love Chocolates (see the Sanibel and Fort Myers chapter), imported Swiss chocolate, coffee, mille feuilles, and other European pastries.

Coffee
Café Ruelle (941-575-3553; www.caferuelle.com; 117 W. Marion Ave., Punta Gorda 33950, downtown) Enjoy coffee, tea, espresso, latte, smoothies, muffins, scones, lunch items, and desserts in the little café or its courtyard.

Jitters (941-475-4140; 120 W. Dearborn St., Englewood 34223) In a corner of the Blue Pagoda restaurant, find gourmet java, iced coffee, frozen fruit drinks, and chai.

Village Gifts & Gallery (941-473-2300; 425 W. Dearborn St., Englewood 34233) Roasters Coffee Bar serves fresh roasted coffee and provides free wireless Internet access.

The Village Grind (941-205-5522; www.fishville.com/shops; 1200 W. Retta Esplanade, Punta Gorda 33950, at Fishermen's Village) Specialty coffees (Kona, Jamaican Blue Mountain, Vietnamese spiced), espresso, cappuccino, tea, chai lattes, Italian and French sodas, smoothies, ice cream, luncheon items, and Wi-Fi Internet access.

Deli & Specialty Foods

Gill's Grocery & Deli (941 964 2506; 5800 Gasparilla Rd., Boca Grande 33921, at The Courtyard) Freshly made sandwiches, salads, and heat-up entrées, plus grocery items, ice cream, party trays, and bakery goods. Delivery available.

Grapevine (941-964-0614; 321 Park Ave., Boca Grande 33921, in the Old Theatre Building) Specialty wines, imported cheese, fish, prepared dishes, sandwiches, gourmet products, and baked goods, Monday through Saturday.

Kallis German Butcher Sausage Kitchen (941 627 1413; 2420 Tamiami Trail, Port Charlotte 33952) Wursts of every variety, many of which you've probably never heard of; also fine cuts of meat, rouladen, cheese, hams, and gourmet European imports. This place is a lot of fun.

Presseller Delicatessen (941-639-3990; www.pressellerdelicatessen.com; 209 W. Olympia Ave., Punta Gorda 33950, downtown) Part art gallery, it serves salads, sandwiches named for artists (Renoir, Dalí, and so on), pizza, and soup to eat in or take out. Also sells deli meats, import beer, wine, fudge, and other gourmet groceries.

Internet Cafés

Village Gifts & Gallery (941-473-2300; 425 W. Dearborn St., Englewood 34233) A coffee corner inside with free wireless Internet access.

The Village Grind (941-205-5522; www.fishville.com/shops; 1200 W. Retta Esplanade, Punta Gorda 33950, at Fishermen's Village) Specialty coffees, tea, European sodas, smoothies, ice cream, sandwiches, and Wi-Fi Internet access.

Natural Foods

Reid's Nutrition Center (941-474-1115; 1951 S. McCall Rd., Englewood 34223, at Palm Plaza) Mostly vitamins but also some organic products; vegetable juice and fruit smoothie bar; certified nutritionist on staff.

Pizza & Takeout

Angelo's Pizza (941-474-2477; 2611 Placida Rd., Englewood 34223) Pizza and Italian specialties. Takeout and delivery.

Boca Grande Baking Company (941-964-5818; www.bocagrandebakingco.com; 384 E. Railroad Ave., Boca Grande 33921) Panini, quiche, homemade pizza, lasagna, breads, desserts, and other takeout items.

Oscar's Pizza (941-475-4501; 2960 McCall Rd., Englewood 34223) All-you-can-eat specials when you eat in. Delivery available for takeout.

The Philadelphian (941-766-0555; 2320 Tamiami Trail, Port Charlotte; at Midtown Plaza) Famous, it claims, for its cheese steaks and hoagies, the latter of which come in eight varieties.

Pies & Plates (941-205-3663; www.piesandplates.com; 117 W. Marion Ave., Punta Gorda 33950; downtown) One of those new-wave places where they've prepped so you can go to whip up home-cooked take-home meals.

Seafood

Miss Cindy's Placida Fish Market (941-697-4930; 13010 Fishery Road, Placida, 33946) Besides local and imported fresh and frozen seafood, Miss Cindy's sells homemade soups, salads, and spreads, and gourmet items.

Village Fish Market (941-639-7959; www.fishville.com/shops; 1200 W. Retta Esplanade, Punta Gorda 33950, at Fishermen's Village) A small market featuring New England and Florida seafood, with dining.

CULTURE

The Charlotte Harbor coast is small town—even in its larger, urban-sprawl-infected communities. Long considered a refuge for the retired, the region is not known for a vibrant arts scene or cultural diversity. Overall, it has a Midwestern flavor in coastal areas but is definitely Old Florida in inland rural parts. Awareness of the arts has developed slowly and on a hobby level. For information on local arts and culture, contact the Arts & Humanities Council of Charlotte County, 941-764-8100.

Modern Boca Grande architecture takes cues from Mediterranean styles introduced by the wealthy industrialists who developed and settled the island.

Architecture

In the smaller towns around Charlotte Harbor, single examples of historic character appear serendipitously in the midst of concrete-block homes. **Downtown Englewood**, a destination off the beaten path of the Tamiami Trail, holds a few such treasures that have been reincarnated as shops, boutiques, and galleries.

Punta Gorda sprinkles its architectural prizes—old homes, commercial buildings, and churches—along **Marion Avenue**, **Olympia Avenue**, **Retta Esplanade**, and side streets such as **Sullivan Street** and the developing **History Park on Shreve Street**. Along the **Esplanade**, look for impressive newly restored homes, the jewels of the old riverfront district. In and around the town's historic section, an eclectic array of architecture ranges from old shotgun cigar workers' homes and tin-roofed Cracker shacks to a Victorian mansion and a neoclassical city hall. Watch for historic murals and street sculptures along the way.

Boca Grande's most noteworthy examples of architecture, aside from the grande dame **Gasparilla Inn**, are four historic churches, each with its own style, located in a four-block area downtown. The Catholic church takes its inspiration from Spanish missions; the other three occupy early-20th-century wood-frame buildings and serve Episcopal, Baptist, and Methodist congregations.

A few blocks away, on **Tarpon Avenue**, spruced-up old Cracker homes slump comfortably in a district sometimes called **Whitewash Alley**. For a taste of wealthy eccentricity, check out the **Johann Fust Library** on Gasparilla Road. It was built of native coquina, cypress, and pink stucco.

Cinema

Regal 16 Cinema (941-623-0111; www.regalcinemas.com; 1441 Tamiami Trail, Port Charlotte 33948, in the Port Charlotte Town Center)

Dance

Aki's Dancesport Centre (941-624-4001; 3109 Tamiami Trail, Port Charlotte 33983) Dancing socials, competitions, and lessons in swing, merengue, salsa, lindy, fox-trot, and waltz.

Country Line Dance Lessons (941-575-8188; www.fishville.com; 1200 W. Retta Esplanade, Punta Gorda 33950, in Fishermen's Village) Every Wednesday night 7 to 9; $3 per person for lessons.

Historic Homes & Sites
THE A. C. FREEMAN HOUSE
941-639-2222
311 Retta Esplanade, Punta Gorda 33950.
Open: Hourly winter tours 11–3, Thurs. and Fri., Dec.–Apr.; Fri. only the rest of the year
Admission: Donations suggested

Newly moved to the riverfront, this house was once occupied by Punta Gorda's mayor and mortician. Narrowly escaping the wrecking ball in 1985, the lovely clapboard Queen Anne mansion was saved and restored by the people of Punta Gorda as a memento of gracious pioneer lifestyles.

THE BLANCHARD HOUSE & MUSEUM OF AFRICAN-AMERICAN LIFE & CULTURE
941-639-2914
406 Martin Luther King Blvd., Punta Gorda 33950
Open: Mon, Wed., Fri. 10–2, other times by appointment
Admission: Donations suggested

The 1925 home of an African American steamboat pilot and his mail-order bride, the museum displays photographs, documents, and artifacts relating to Punta Gorda's black population and its history.

BOCA GRANDE LIGHTHOUSE MUSEUM
941-964-0375
www.barrierislandparkssociety.org.
P.O. Box 637, Boca Grande 33921
Gasparilla Island State Park, Gulf Blvd., Boca Grande
Open: 10–4 Wed.–Sun.; extended hours in the height of winter and summer seasons
Admission: $2 for state recreation-area park; donation of $1 requested

This 1890 structure—the most photographed and painted landmark on the island—was renovated in Old Florida style and put back into service in 1986 after 20 years of abandonment. You can self-tour both the lighthouse and the museum, which explores its history and Boca Grande bygones—from ancient Calusa civilizations through railroad and industrial eras to the island's modern-day reputation as a tarpon-fishing mecca. Historic cis-

The Boca Grande Lighthouse is one of the state's most picturesque.

terns, the assistant lighthouse keeper's home, and a struggling native vegetation garden compose the fenced-in complex. It sits within Gasparilla Island State Park.

INDIAN MOUND PARK

210 Winson Ave., Englewood 34223
It's slightly flattened now from age, but this ancient midden mound is still centerpiece to a lovely bay-front park for picnicking, boating, and exploring the trails that crisscross the vegetated mound.

PONCE DE LEÓN HISTORICAL PARK

End of Marion Ave., Punta Gorda
Downsized from a rock shrine encasement to make room for more parking, a chipped-paint statue and historic plaques commemorate Ponce de León's supposed 1513 landing here and his subsequent death caused by an Indian attack. The park has a wildlife and recreational area on the harbor, plus a boat ramp, picnic facilities, a small sea-walled beach, a playground, and a native trail into the mangroves. It is home to the Peace River Wildlife Center rehab facility.

PUNTA GORDA HISTORY PARK

941-639-1887
501 Shreve St., Punta Gorda 33950.
Admission: Free

So far this gathering of historic buildings in a pretty park setting amounts to three old homes. Stop in first at the old Tabue House, where Punta Gorda's founder once lived. It also houses the Peace River Center for Writers and a small exhibit on the history of the two-year-old park and its buildings. Ask for a tour of the Cigar Cottage, where the town's tobacco industry once headquartered, and learn about Punta Gorda's hibiscus-growing fame. The fountain from the old Punta Gorda Hotel also graces the grounds.

PUNTA GORDA TRAIN DEPOT

1009 Taylor St., Punta Gorda 33950
Admission: Free

Signs marked "Colored" and "White" are telltale relics of the late 1920s era when this Atlantic Coast Line station was used. It is the only one of six built in Mediterranean style that survives. You can see historic photographs and the original ticket windows. On the depot's backside, an antique mall raises funds for the historical society (look under "Shopping: Antiques & Collectibles"). Across the street, one of the town's historic murals illustrates its railroad days.

Museums

CHARLOTTE COUNTY HISTORICAL CENTER

941-629-7278
22959 Bayshore Rd., Charlotte Harbor 33980
Open: 10–5 Mon.–Fri.; 10–3 Sat.
Admission: Donation of $2 adults, $1 children ages 12 and under

Located at a gorgeous spot on the river, next to the pier at Bayshore Live Oak Park, the roomy facility is geared toward children with programs, signage, showcases, and interactive exhibits that illuminate facets of local history. Changing exhibits are devoted to the Gasparilla pirate legend, Calusa natives, fishing heritage, fossils, Seminoles, and more.

✪ GASPARILLA ISLAND MARITIME MUSEUM
941-964-GIMM
P.O. Box 100, Boca Grande 33921
At Whidden's Marina, on Harbor Dr.
Open: Hours vary
Admission: By donation

Some might call it a shed full of old junk, but to the citizens of Boca Grande, it represents Americana and a way of life that has survived in contrast to the mansions and yachts that surround it. Part of Whidden's Marina, the museum features photo albums that remember a day when the nation's top industrialists sailed here to fish and winter. Odd parts of boats and fishing gear lie strewn around the old, peeling fish shack, listed on the National Register of Historic Places. Still in operation, the marina and its store make it difficult to tell where the museum ends and the present begins.

Music & Nightlife
BOCA GRANDE
South Beach (941-964-0765; 777 Gulf Blvd., Boca Grande 33921) Contemporary bands play weekend nights. Sunset plays (almost) every evening.

ENGLEWOOD
Englewood Performing Arts Series (941-473-2787) Fine cultural entertainment from around the nation, mid-November through mid-April.

Junior's Cabaret (941-474-8730; 2643 Placida Rd., Englewood 34224) You'll find the locals here—eating, shooting pool, drinking, and dancing.

Saturday Night Live on Dearborn Street (941-473-8782; www.oldenglewood.com; West Dearborn St., Englewood) Live entertainment and free refreshments augment the lively shopping experience here on the second Saturday of the month.

White Elephant Pub (941-475-6801; 1855 Gulf Blvd., Englewood Beach 34223) It hosts live bands on the weekends.

PORT CHARLOTTE
Charlotte County Jazz Society (941-766-9422; www.ccjazz.org ; P.O. Box 495321, Port Charlotte 33949) Sponsors several jazz concerts each year at the Charlotte Center for Performing Arts (see below). Call or visit the Web site for information on jam sessions.

Charlotte Symphony Orchestra (941-625-5996; www.charlottesymphony.com; P.O. Box 495831, Port Charlotte 33949) Performs at the Charlotte Center for the Performing Arts (see below), November through March.

Gatorz Bar & Grill (941-625-5000; 3816 Tamiami Trail, Port Charlotte 33952) Live music—jazz and Top 40—throughout the week.

PUNTA GORDA

Charlotte Center for Performing Arts (941-766-942, 941-505-SHOW for box office; www.cpacc.com; 701 Carmalita St., Punta Gorda 33950) This modern new facility hosts theater, symphony, chamber orchestra, and other performances.

Charlotte County Memorial Auditorium (941-639-5833, 800-329-9988; 75 Taylor St., Punta Gorda 33950) Waterfront host to Broadway plays, big band and swing orchestras, and national stars.

Downtown Punta Gorda Gallery Walk (941-575-9979) The third Thursday of each month, galleries and restaurants host free entertainment. You can tour by foot or trolley.

Fishermen's Village (941-575-3007; www.fishville.com; 1200 W. Retta Esplanade, Punta Gorda 33950) Live entertainment most Tuesday afternoons and Friday and Saturday evenings, with country line dance lessons on Wednesday evenings.

Gilchrist Park (Retta Esplanade) On Thursday nights local musicians gather for impromptu jamming at 7 PM, to which the public is invited.

Theater

Cultural Center of Charlotte County (941-625-4175; www.theculturalcenter.com; 2280 Aaron St., P.O. Box 495129, Port Charlotte 33949) Home of the Charlotte Players (941-255-1022; www.charlotteplayers.org) community-theater group and Charlotte County Jazz Society (see "Music and Nightlife," above).

Lemon Bay Playhouse (941-475-6756; www.lemonbayplayhouse.com; 96 W. Dearborn St., Englewood 34223) Home of the Lemon Bay Players community-theater group. Performances September through July.

Royal Palm Players (941-964-2670; www.royalpalmplayers.com; 333 Park Ave., Ste. 4, P.O. Box 954, Boca Grande 33921) A community-theater group sponsoring plays, guest-artist performances, children's performances, and concerts from November into May.

Visual Art Centers & Resources

Punta Gorda lost many of its 23 historic and educational murals to hurricanes and development, but the Punta Gorda Historical Mural Society is making headway in replacing them. Local artists lend their sculptures for display along the streets.

A listing for commercial galleries is included in the "Shopping" section of this chapter.

Arts & Humanities Council (941-764-8100; 2811-M Tamiami Trail, Port Charlotte 33952, at LaPlaya Plaza) Hosts art displays and events.

Englewood Art Center (941-474-5548; 350 S. McCall Rd., Englewood 34223)

Visual Arts Center (941-639-8810; www.visualartscenter.com; 210 Maud St., Punta Gorda 33950; near Fishermen's Village) Home of the Charlotte County Art Guild. Exhibit halls, gift shops, library, darkroom, and classes.

RECREATION

More behind-the-scenes than the touted playgrounds of its flanking neighbors, the Charlotte Harbor coast's greatest claim to recreational fame is its fishing—particularly for that king of all sport fish, tarpon.

Beaches

You must drive way off the beaten path to find the beaches of Charlotte County. Though less convenient, that keeps them more natural, less trodden.

BLIND PASS (MIDDLE) BEACH

Route 776, mid-island on Manasota Key
Facilities: Restrooms, showers, playground, nature trail, canoe launch

Sixty acres of lightly developed shoreline attract those drawn more to seclusion than to the sports and activities of Manasota Key's other beaches. Low dunes edge wide salt-and-pepper sands. Next door you'll see one of the island's first buildings. Known as Hermitage House, it was once a nudist resort. Today it's a retreat for visiting artists. From the parking lot you can follow a nature boardwalk trail into the mangroves. If there's surf to be found in the area, you'll find it here.

CHADWICK PARK BEACH

941-473-1018
2100 N. Beach Rd., Englewood 34223
Route 776, south end of Manasota Key at Englewood Beach
Facilities: Picnic areas/shelters, restrooms, showers, volleyball, beach wheelchairs
Parking: 50¢ per hour

Many refer to this simply as Englewood Beach, and it is popular with families. Facilities include a boardwalk, pirate-theme playground, a basketball hoop, and picnic shelters. Shops and restaurants huddle around the area, which keeps activity levels high.

✪ DON PEDRO ISLAND STATE PARK

941-964-0375
www.floridastateparks.org/donpedroisland
c/o Gasparilla Island State Park, P.O. Box 1150, Boca Grande 33921
South of Palm Island, accessible only by boat
Facilities: Picnic area/shelters, restrooms, showers, boat docks
Admission: $1 per person

This secluded beach occupies a 129-acre island getaway. Once separated from Palm Island and Little Gasparilla, Don Pedro Island is now connected to the two to form one long, lightly developed barrier island. Don Pedro, the most natural component, is toward the southern end.

LIGHTHOUSE BEACH/GASPARILLA ISLAND STATE PARK

941-964-0375
www.floridastateparks.org/gasparillaisland
P.O. Box 1150, Boca Grande 33921
Along Gulf Blvd., Boca Grande, Gasparilla Island
Facilities: Picnic tables, restrooms
Parking: $2 per car for up to 8 people, $1 for pedestrians and cyclists

Marked by a historic lighthouse with a museum inside, the park edges the deepwater tarpon grounds of Boca Grande Pass. Its plush sands encompass 135 acres, although in some parts the beach gets quite narrow. Swimming is not recommended because of strong currents through the pass. A historic chapel in the same park has been restored for weddings and other private functions.

MANASOTA BEACH

North end of Route 776, Manasota Key
Facilities: Picnic area/shelters, restrooms, showers, lifeguard, historical marker, boat ramp

This lively, 14-acre sunning and shelling venue connects to Venice's Caspersen Beach, about 1 1/2 miles to the north. It also has a reputation—but not as pointed as Venice's—for sharks' teeth. The sands are somewhat narrower here than to the south, and a scenic boardwalk runs along the edge.

PORT CHARLOTTE BEACH PARK

941-625-7529
4500 Harbor Blvd., Port Charlotte 33952
At the southeast end of Harbor Blvd.
Facilities: Picnic areas; restrooms; showers; concessions; bocce, basketball, and two tennis courts; volleyball; playground; horseshoes; boat ramps; fishing pier; canoe and kayak launch; swimming and kiddie pools
Swimming Admission: $2.68 adult, $1.61 children ages 3–15 (Pool phone: 941-629-0170)
Parking: 25¢ per 30 minutes

A highly developed recreational center that sits on Charlotte Harbor along a manmade beach, this is a good place to go if you (or the children) like to keep busy at the beach. It's better for sunning than swimming, however, as bacteria levels are sometimes high. Stick to the swimming pool, which is open daily until 4:45 PM (It opens at 10 AM Monday through

The beach at Boca Grande beckons.

Friday and 11 AM Saturday and Sunday.) A boardwalk runs along the beach and connects to the fishing pier. It looks across the way at Punta Gorda.

✪ STUMP PASS BEACH STATE PARK
941-964-0375
www.floridastateparks.org/stumppass
Barrier Islands State Parks, PO Box 1150, Boca Grande 33921
South end of Gulf Blvd., Englewood Beach on Manasota Key
Facilities: Restrooms, nature trail
Parking: $2 per car, $1 for bikers and pedestrians

This uncrowded beach offers lovely, unspoiled seclusion. Traditionally, the 255-acre park has been a magnet for fishermen who cast into Lemon Bay. Follow the 2-mile wooded trail to the south, and you'll find nice areas to spread a towel and dip your toes. The park stretches all the way to Stump Pass in a skinny strip of black-specked sand fringed by sea oats.

Bicycling

The Charlotte Coast region, with its abundance of back roads and wide-open spaces, gives cyclists an opportunity to pedal in peace. Many of its favored bikeways are on-road or designated bike lanes, which are separated from motor traffic by only a painted white line. According to state law, bicyclists who share the road with other vehicles must heed all the rules of the road. Children under age 16 are required to wear helmets.

BEST BIKING

Glimpse wild turkeys and lake views while pedaling along **Babcock-Webb Wildlife Management Area**'s (941-575-5768; www.myfwc.com; 29200 Tuckers Grade, Punta Gorda 33955) 37 miles of trails.

✪ **Cape Haze Pioneer Trail** (941-743-2425; www.charlottecountyfl.com) runs 5.5 miles parallel to Route 771 along a former rail bed. When completed in 2009, it will total 7 miles.

About a mile past Gasparilla Island's causeway (which can be crossed by bicycle for $1), the **Boca Grande bike path** starts. Here you pedal along old railroad routes. Seven miles of pathway travel the island from tip to tip along Railroad Avenue and Gulf Boulevard. These paths are shared by golf carts, which you can rent and drive about the island as long as you are 14 or older. Many of Boca's downtown streets are also designated golf-cart trails.

Highway 776 through Englewood and Englewood Beach is shouldered with a bike lane that ends at the Sarasota County line. In Punta Gorda, **Gilchrist Park's bike path** runs along green space overlooking the Peace River on Retta Esplanade. Bike riding on city sidewalks is legal throughout the county.

For a map of Charlotte County bikeways, call the Charlotte County–Punta Gorda Metropolitan Planning Organization at 941-639-4676.

RENTAL SHOPS

The Bicycle Center (941-627-6600; 3755 Tamiami Trail, Port Charlotte 33952) All types of bikes, including tandems, children's, and adult tricycles. Free pickup and delivery on weekly rentals within a 10-mile radius.

Bikes and Boards (941-474-2019; 966 S. McCall Rd., Englewood Beach 34223) Bike and kayak rentals, sales, delivery, and service.

Island Bike 'N Beach (941-964-0711; 333 Park Ave., Boca Grande 33921) Rents bikes, golf carts, and beach stuff.

Boats & Boating
Charlotte Harbor Coast offers many waterfronts for adventure: the gulf, the harbor, Peace River, Myakka River, Lemon Bay Aquatic Preserve, and a number of creeks and canals. Charlotte Harbor has been designated in the nation's top 10 sailing destinations by *Sail* magazine.

CANOEING & KAYAKING
For information on paddling trails, contact Charlotte County Parks and Recreation Department at 941-627-1628 or www.charlottecountyfl.com and request a copy of the *Blueway Trails* map and listing. The Woolveton Trail, my favorite, takes you down small, quiet creeks tunneling under mangrove canopies. See Grande Tours under "Wildlife Tours & Charters."

PERSONAL WATERCRAFT RENTAL/TOURS
Island Jet Ski (941-474-1168; 1450 Beach Rd., Englewood Beach 34223, at Englewood Bait House Marina on the south bridge) Hourly and daily rentals.

POWERBOAT RENTALS
Bay Breeze Boat Rentals (941-475-0733; 1450 Beach Rd., Englewood Beach 34223, at Englewood Bait House on the south bridge) Rents pontoon boats and fishing skiffs.

Boca Boat Rentals (941-964-1333, 888-416-BOAT; www.bocaboat.com; 5800 Gasparilla Rd., Boca Grande 33921, at Uncle Henry's Marina) Rents powerboats, kayaks, hydrobikes, and golf carts.

Passengers aboard King Fisher Fleet's Peace River Nature Cruise pop up at an alligator sighting.

Holidaze Boat Rental (941-505-8888; www.holidazeboatrental.com; 1200 W. Retta Esplanade, Punta Gorda 33950, at Fishermen's Village) Rents 17.5- to 21-foot boats and 20- to 26-foot pontoons and deck boats by the hour, half day, or full day. Also jet skis.

PUBLIC BOAT RAMPS

Indian Mound Park (Englewood Recreation Center, 101 Horn St., Englewood 34223, downtown Englewood) On Lemon Bay. Access to Stump Pass, picnic pavilion, restrooms, nature trails.

Laishley Park Marina (Marion Ave. and Nesbit St., Punta Gorda) A newly renovated facility with ship's store, it will soon see an on-site restaurant.

Manasota Beach (Manasota Beach Rd., Manasota Key) One public boat ramp across the street from a county park.

Placida Park (Causeway Blvd.)

Ponce de León Park (west end of Marion Ave., Punta Gorda) One boat ramp on the harbor.

Port Charlotte Beach (941-627-1628; 4500 Harbor Blvd., Port Charlotte 33952, southeast end of Harbor Blvd.) Beach recreational area, access to Charlotte Harbor. Two boat ramps.

SAILBOAT CHARTERS, RENTALS, & INSTRUCTION

Paradise Sailing (941-932-4232; www.paradisesailing.com; 4071 Key Largo Ln., Punta Gorda 33955) Captained cruises, bare boat charters, and American Sailing Association (ASA) sailing courses.

Southwest Florida Yachts/Florida Sailing & Cruising School (239-656-1339, 800-262-SWFY; www.flsailandcruiseschool.com; 3444 Marinatown Ln. N.W., Ste. 19, North Fort Myers 33903) ASA-certification courses and bareboat charters provide excellent adventures out of Burnt Store Marina (southwest of Punta Gorda) into Charlotte Harbor for live-aboard experiences.

SIGHTSEEING & ENTERTAINMENT CRUISES

Look under "Wildlife Tours & Charters" for nature excursions

Boca Boat Cruises & Charters (941-964-1333 or 888-416-BOAT; www.bocaboat.com; 5800 Gasparilla Rd., P.O. Box 294, Boca Grande 33921, at Uncle Henry's Marina) Daily beach and lunch tours, and sunset cruises.

✪ **Grande Tours** (941-697-8825; www.grandetours.com; 12575 Placida Rd., P.O. Box 281, Placida 33946) Tours: sunset, kid fishing, wildlife, and shuttle to Don Pedro State Park. Also kayak nature and fishing tours and rentals and water-taxi service.

✪ **King Fisher Cruise Lines** (941-639-0969; www.kingfisherfleet.com; 1200 W. Retta Esplanade, Punta Gorda 33950, at Fishermen's Village Marina) Excursions to Cayo Costa and Cabbage Key and along the Peace River aboard a double-deck head boat. Also sunset and harbor sightseeing cruises.

Ko Ko Kai Charter Boat Service (941-474-2141; www.kokokai.com; 5040 N. Beach Rd., Englewood Beach 34223) Takes you island hopping to Gasparilla, Palm, Cayo Costa, Cabbage Key, Upper Captiva, and Captiva Islands, as well as on lunch, fishing, and shelling charters.

Fishing

Tarpon reigns as the king of southwest Florida fish—the Silver King, to be exact, named for its silver-dollar-like scales. ✪ **Boca Grande Pass** is one of the most celebrated spots in the world for catching the feisty fighter. But the tarpon is hardly alone on its throne: A National Wildlife Federation study in 2006 reported 256 species of salt and freshwater fish in Charlotte Harbor.

Nonresidents age 16 and older who wish to fish must obtain a license unless fishing from a vessel or pier covered by its own license. You can buy inexpensive temporary-nonresident licenses at county tax collectors' offices and most Kmarts and bait shops. Check local regulations for season, size, and catch restrictions.

FISHING CHARTERS/OUTFITTERS

Boca Grande Fishing Guides Association (941-964-2559; www.bocagrandefishing.com; P.O. Box 676, Boca Grande 33921) Organization of more than 50 qualified charter guides especially knowledgeable about tarpon.

Captain Jack's Charters (941-475-4511; www.sunstate.com/captjack; 1450 Beach Rd., Englewood Beach 34223, at the Englewood Bait House) Half-day, full-day, night, overnight, and weekend trips.

Fishing Unlimited (941-964-0907, 800-4-TARPON; www.4tarpon.com; 431 Park Ave., P.O. Box 1407, Boca Grande 33921) Outfitters, fly shop, guides, and charters. Authorized Orvis dealer.

King Fisher Fleet (941-639-0969; www.kingfisherfleet.com; 1200 W. Retta Esplanade, Punta Gorda 33950, at Fishermen's Village Marina) Deep-sea fishing aboard a 35-foot boat and custom back-bay excursions.

Tarpon Hunter Guide Service (941-743-6622; 265 Lomond Dr. #B, Port Charlotte 33953) Charters aboard the *Tarpon Hunter II* in Charlotte Harbor and backwaters. Specialties include fly and light-tackle fishing.

FISHING PIERS

Bayshore Fishing Pier (22967 Bayshore Dr., Charlotte Harbor) At the mouth of the Peace River in Bayshore Live Oak Park, next to the Charlotte County Historical Center.

Englewood Beach (Anger) Pier (along Beach Rd. east of the drawbridge)

Gasparilla Fishing Pier South (941-627-1628; near Courtyard Plaza, north end of Gasparilla Rd., Gasparilla Island) An old railroad bridge.

Gilchrist Park (Retta Esplanade, Punta Gorda) Cast into the brackish waters where the Peace River empties into the gulf.

Myakka Fishing Pier North & South (941-627-1628; Rte. 776, El Jobean) Two piers into the Myakka River.

Port Charlotte Beach Park (941-627-1628; 4500 Harbor Blvd., Port Charlotte, southeast end of Harbor Blvd.) Part of a beach and pool recreational center.

Golf

PUBLIC GOLF COURSES & CENTERS

Deep Creek Golf Club (941-625-6911; www.deepcreekgc.com; 1260 San Cristobal Ave., Port Charlotte 33983) Semiprivate; 18 holes, par 70; driving range, putting green, and snack bar.

Duffy's Golf Center (941-697-3900; 12455 S. Access Rd., Port Charlotte 33981) An 18-hole executive course (nine holes lit) and lit practice range. PGA professionals, golf shop, and Duffer's Tavern, serving food and beverages.

Lemon Bay Golf Club (941-697-3729; www.lemonbaygolfclub.co; 9600 Eagle Preserve Dr., Englewood 34224) Semiprivate; 18 holes, par 71; restaurant. A certified Audubon Society course.

Port Charlotte Golf Club (941-625-4109; 22400 Gleneagles Terrace, Port Charlotte 33952) Semiprivate; 18 holes; full practice facilities, restaurant, and lounge.

GOLF STORES

Birdie's (941-474-9580; www.birdiesthegolfstore.com; 258 S. Indiana Ave., Englewood 34223) Golf equipment and fairway fashions and accessories.

Health & Fitness Clubs

Charlotte County Family YMCA (941-629629-9622; www.charlottecountyymca.com; 19333 Quesada Ave., Port Charlotte 33948) Aerobics, Trimnastics, body shaping, yoga, volleyball, basketball, golf tournaments, youth sports competition, steam room, and kiddie facilities and programs.

The Punta Gorda Club (941-505-0999; www.puntagordaclub.com; 2905 Tamiami Trail, Punta Gorda 33950) Cardiovascular equipment, golf-enhancement program, free weights, yoga, Tai Chi, weight machines, tennis courts, babysitting, massage, spinal health clinic, and other spa services.

Hiking

Charlotte Harbor Environmental Center (941-575-5435; www.checflorida.org; 10941 Burnt Store Rd., Punta Gorda 33955) Four miles of nature trails depart from this center, part of the State Buffer Preserve.

Fred C. Babcock–Cecil M. Webb Wildlife Management Area (941-575-5768; 29200 Tucker Grade, Port Charlotte 33955) The domain of endangered red-cockaded woodpeckers, this preserve attracts birders along its 37 miles of unpaved hiking and biking trails, once used in logging operations. Sandhill cranes, white-tailed deer, and warblers also favor the diverse habitat found within its 79,013 acres. Avoid trails during peak of the hunting season, late October to mid-November.

Kiwanis Park (941-627-1628; 3100 Donora St., Port Charlotte 33952; at Victoria Ave.) Here's a nice place to hike or jog while the kids entertain themselves on the playground. Nature and fitness trails thread through the woods and alongside a creek where turtles swim.

Hunting

Given southwest Florida's heightened environmental consciousness, most shooting of wildlife is done with a camera. But the Charlotte Harbor coast's wilderness does provide opportunities for hunting various species. The most popular game animals are wild hogs, deer, doves, snipe, quail, turkey, duck, and coot.

For information on hunting licenses, permits, and seasons, visit www.myfwc.com/hunting.

Cypress Lodge at Babcock Wilderness Adventure (941-637-0551, 800-500-5583; www.babcock wilderness.com; 8000 State Rd. 31, Punta Gorda 33982) Experienced guides take guests hunting for wild turkey, quail, and wild hogs.

Fred C. Babcock–Cecil M. Webb Wildlife Management Area (941-575-5768; myfwc .com/huntered/CecilWebb_brochure.pdf; 29200 Tucker Grade, Port Charlotte 33955) With some 79,000 acres, this is one of Florida's 62 designated hunting preserves. Advance permission is required. There is a public shooting range on the property, accessible from Tucker Grade via Rifle Range Road. The range opens daily during daylight hours but closes the fourth Saturday of each month until 2 PM for hunter education training.

Kids' Stuff

Fish Cove Adventure Golf (941-627-5393; 4949 Tamiami Trail, Port Charlotte 33980) Two 18-hole putt-putt golf courses and a bounce house. Open daily 10 AM to 11 PM. Admission for 18 holes of golf is $6.50 to $8.50; $2 for bounce house with golf admission.

KidSpace (941-627-1628; Maracaibo St. and Avacado Rd., Port Charlotte) A county park created by the community expressly for kids, it has a cool fortlike playground, baseball fields, and picnicking.

Kidstar Park (941-235-3131; 18505 Paulson Dr., Port Charlotte, 33954) Go-cart rides, a rock-climbing wall and giant slide, children's rides, laser tag, motion ride, Waltzing Waters, and snack bar and restaurant.

Tringali Recreational Complex Skating (941-473-1018; 3460 N. Access Rd., Englewood 34224) Weekly skate parties for elementary and middle school kids and families; also basketball, tennis, a walking trail, a gym, and picnic grounds.

Racquet Sports

Boca Grande Community Center (941-964-2564; 131 First St. W., Boca Grande 33921) Two lit tennis courts are located on Wheeler Street.

McGuire Park (32236 McGuire Ave., Port Charlotte) Four lit hard-surface tennis courts.

The Punta Gorda Club (941-505-1055; www.puntagordaclub.com; 2905 Tamiami Trail, Punta Gorda 33950) Tennis courts plus other sports and fitness facilities; babysitting available.

Tringali Recreational Complex (941-473-1018; 3460 McCall Rd. S., Englewood 34223) Four outdoor lit tennis courts.

Shelling

You'll find some shells on the beaches along the Charlotte Harbor coast, but if you're a serious beachcomber, you'll head south to the Island Coast.

SHELLING CHARTERS

Ko Ko Kai Charter Boat Service (941-474-2141; 5040 N. Beach Rd., Englewood Beach 34223, at Ko Ko Kai Resort) Shelling excursions on and around the islands of Gasparilla, Palm, Cayo Costa, Cabbage Key, Upper Captiva, and Captiva islands.

Spas

Charles of the Village Salon & Day Spa (941-639-6300, 888-753-6115; www.charles ofthevillage.com; 1200 W. Retta Esplanade, Punta Gorda 33950, at Fishermen's Village) Massage, wraps, polishes, facials, and beauty services. Packages available.

Water Sports

SAILBOARDING & SURFING

Island Bike 'N Beach (941-964-0711; 333 Park Ave., Boca Grande 33921) Rents boogie and skim boards.

SNORKELING & SCUBA

The best underwater sightseeing lies offshore some distance, where divers find a few wrecks and other manmade structures.

Wildlife Spotting

The Charlotte Harbor coast is a haven for many of Florida's threatened and endangered species, including Florida panthers (a relative of the mountain lion that is yellow, not black, and characterized by a kink in its tail), bobcats, manatees, brown pelicans, wood storks, and black skimmers. **Manasota Key** hosts the largest nesting sea turtle population on the Gulf Coast. White pelicans migrate to the region in winter. Look for them on sandbars and small mangrove islands in the bays and estuaries. They congregate in flocks and feed cooperatively by herding fish. The **Cape Haze area** between Englewood and Boca Grande is known for its nesting ospreys and bald eagles. **Lemon Bay Park** and **Cedar Point Environmental Park** afford the best opportunities to see the nests. Look for sandhill cranes on golf courses and in other grasslands.

At **Babcock Ranch**, a massive preserve east of Punta Gorda, you can see native sandhill cranes, reintroduced American bison, and contained Florida panthers, along with lots of alligators (which are farmed there). Adjacent **Babcock-Webb Wildlife Management Area** shelters the endangered red-cockaded woodpecker, among other species of woodpeckers, warblers, and shorebirds. It, along with **Amberjack Environmental Park**, **Cedar Point**, **Charlotte Flatwoods Environmental Park**, **Charlotte Harbor Environmental Center**, **Charlotte Harbor Preserve State Park**, and **Tippecanoe Environmental Park** are plotted on the South Florida section of the **Great Florida Birding Trail** (www.floridabirdingtrail .com).

On **Gasparilla Island** you may spot an iguana in the wild—or trying to cross the road, for that matter. Though they are not native, their numbers have grown to a point where the island is taking measures to control them by trapping.

NATURE PRESERVES & ECO-ATTRACTIONS

CEDAR POINT ENVIRONMENTAL PARK
941-475-0769
www.checflorida.org.
2300 Placida Rd, Englewood 34224
Off Route 775
Admission: Free

Bald eagles, marsh rabbits, bobcats,
gopher tortoises, and great horned owls
are the stars of this 115-acre preserve,
where free guided nature walks are offered
at 10 AM Saturday and other days by
appointment. It borders the Lemon Bay
Aquatic Preserve.

Fluted cypress trees stalk Telegraph Swamp at Babcock Ranch.

CHARLOTTE HARBOR ENVIRONMENTAL CENTER (CHEC) AT ALLIGATOR PRESERVE
941-575-5435
www.checflorida.org
10941 Burnt Store Rd., Punta Gorda 33955.
Hours: 8–3 Mon.–Sat. and 11–3 Sun.; guided trail walks at 10 AM in season and by appointment in summer
Admission: Free

The center conducts guided tours around 4 miles of nature trails that wind through pine
and palmetto flatlands, hammocks, and marshes, where alligators and bobcats live. Its
educational exhibits about local wildlife are geared toward children. Plans call for a new
Calusa Indian display in the nature center. The center conducts various tours and programs both on and off campus. Particularly engaging for adults and children alike is the
Wading Adventure at Ponce de Leon Park.

LEMON BAY PARK & ENVIRONMENTAL CENTER
941-474-3065
570 Bay Park Blvd., Englewood 34223
Admission: Free

Its 195 acres of mangrove forest, wetlands, pinelands, and scrub are home to bald eagles
and other creatures of the sky, woods, and water. Experience its nature trails, butterfly
garden, indoor environmental displays, and educational programs and guided walks.

PEACE RIVER WILDLIFE CENTER
941-637-3830
3400 W. Marion Ave., Punta Gorda 33950
At Ponce de León Park
Hours: 11–3pm daily
Admission: Donations requested

You can self-tour or take a guided tour of the outdoor bird aviary. A board lists the current rehabilitating and recently released patients. It accepts about 1,300 orphaned, displaced, and injured creatures each year.

WILDLIFE TOURS & CHARTERS

✪ BABCOCK WILDERNESS ADVENTURES
941-637-0551, 800-500-5583
www.babcockwilderness.com
8000 SR 31, Punta Gorda 33982
Hours: Tours 9–3 Nov.–May; mornings only June–Oct.
Admission: $17.95 adults, $10.95 children ages 3–12 (plus tax). Advance reservations required.

On a 90-minute swamp-buggy-bus ride through Crescent B Ranch and Telegraph Cypress Swamp you will spot Old Florida wildlife, including white-tailed deer, relocated bison, fenced-in panthers, wild turkeys, sandhill cranes, squirrels, and alligators. The driver gives an onboard demonstration with a live baby gator and leads a boardwalk hike through a cypress swamp. The adventure takes place on an actual ranch that dates back to the cow-hunting era. Cattle are still raised here, as well as alligators. A restaurant, live snake display, gift shop, and a small natural history museum set in a cabin used in Sean Connery's movie *Just Cause* (filmed partly on site) provide other activities at this, one of Charlotte Harbor coast's finest attractions.

✪ GRANDE TOURS
941-697-8825
www.grandetours.com
12575 Placida Rd., P.O. Box 281, Placida 33946
Hours: Most tours arranged daily.

Naturalists lead kayaking tours of Myakka River, Charlotte Harbor Aquatic Preserve, and Blueway Trail. Eco, dusk, and moonlight tours are among those available. The wildlife tour takes you on a pontoon boat in search of dolphin, manatees, and birds.

KING FISHER PEACE RIVER NATURE CRUISE
941-639-0969
www.kingfisherfleet.com
1200 W. Retta Esplanade, Punta Gorda 33950
At Fishermen's Village Marina
Hours: 1 PM daily

You'll likely see alligators, pelicans, egrets, ibises, and cormorants on the 3 1/2 hour journey upriver and back in time. You may also spot manatees, roseate spoonbills, river otters, and great blue herons. Volunteers from Charlotte Harbor Environmental Center knowledgably narrate as the double-decker boat chugs leisurely along.

SHOPPING

Shopping Centers & Malls

Boca Grande (Park Ave.) Despite the millionaires and power brokers who make Boca Grande their winter home, shopping here is low-key and affordable, with shades of historic quaintness. The restored railroad depot houses gift and apparel boutiques; there's more in back at Railroad Plaza. Across the street you'll find an eccentric general store and a department store that's been there forever, both of which set a somewhat funky tone. **Sam Murphy Park** presents a serene place to rest alongside a gentle waterfall pool and under shade trees. Don't visit in August and September, when the town literally closes down.

Downtown Punta Gorda Centered around Marion and Olympia Avenues, both one-way streets, between Nesbit Street and Tamiami Trail South, you'll find a quiet historic downtown that underwent a renaissance in the 1980s and began renovating again after Hurricane Charley in 2004. Restaurants and galleries occupy many of the old buildings. Brick-paved Sullivan Street features old residences under colorful new coats of paint and reborn into decorators and other shops. Streetscaping includes old-fashioned streetlamps, alley arcades, historic murals, street sculptures, and park benches. Two new major residential-retail developments, each taking up a city block, are planned for the near future. Every third Thursday from 5 to 8 PM business owners host a **gallery walk** with live music, art, food, and a chance to meet local artists.

Fishermen's Village (941-639-8721, 800-639-0020; www.fishville.com; 1200 W. Retta Esplanade, Punta Gorda 33950) More than 40 shops and restaurants occupy a transformed fish-packing plant. This is Punta Gorda's most hyper center of activity and the site of festivals and social events. There's docking, lodging, charter boats, and fishing from the docks, besides shopping and dining, geared generally toward seniors. A preponderance of nautical clothing and gifts reflect the motif. ✪ **Olde Englewood Village** (941-473-9795; www.oeva.net) Dearborn Street, Englewood's main drag, has done some sprucing up in the past years. The old historic buildings hold fun-to-browse galleries, gift shops, and restaurants. The second Saturday of the month it hosts the Saturday Nite Live Street Walk from 6 to 9 PM.

Port Charlotte Town Center (941-624-4447; www.simon.com; 1441 Tamiami Trail, Port Charlotte 33948) An indoor megamall with movie theaters and more than 90 commercial enterprises, including Burdines, Sears, and other chain outlets and specialty shops, such as Sam Goody and Old Navy.

Antiques & Collectibles

Antiques on Dearborn (941-475-6737; 447 W. Dearborn St., Englewood 34223) A multi-dealer emporium packed with everything from old coins to jewelry and china.

Blue Pineapple (941-474-1504; 445 W. Dearborn St., Englewood 34223) Unusual, high-end antique and modern home furnishings and accessories from England and Ireland.

Train Depot Antique Mall (941-639-6774; 1009 Taylor St., Punta Gorda 33950) Sales of its wide range of memorabilia benefit the Punta Gorda Historical Society. It also holds flea markets.

Shopping along Olde Englewood Village's Dearborn Street uncovers treasures and surprises.

Books

⭐ **Ruhama's Books in the Sand** (941-964-5800; 333 Park Ave., Boca Grande 33921) Books of local interest and for beach reading; cards, needlepoint supplies, and gifts.

Clothing

A Perfect Day in Paradise (941-964-8188; 420 E. Railroad Ave., P.O. Box 1395, Boca Grande 33921) Sporty, splashy resort wear (think Lilly Pulitzer), including some men's styles.

Captain's Landing (941-637-6000; www.fishville.com/boutiques; 1200 W. Retta Esplanade #24, Punta Gorda 33950, at Fishermen's Village) Men's casual clothing with a nautical and fishing flair; also formal wear.

Courtyard Boutique & Gift Shop (941-637-1226; www.fishville.com/boutiques; 1200 W. Retta Esplanade #9, Punta Gorda 33950, at Fishermen's Village) Kicky women's fashions and accessories for both casual and dressy occasions.

Giuditta (941-639-8701; 322 Sullivan St., Punta Gorda 33950, downtown) Exotic patterns and finely tailored styles for the sophisticated woman; mostly formal and dress-up fashions.

Nichole's Collections (941-575-1911; www.fishville.com/boutiques; 1200 W. Retta Esplanade #12, Punta Gorda 33950, at Fishermen's Village) Fine cotton and casual women's fashions.

Tiki's (941-639-4310; www.tikiclothing.com; 105 W. Marion Ave., Punta Gorda 33950) Distinctive casual and tropical fashions, shoes, and accessories.

Consignment

Carly's Consignment (941-575-1191; 215 W. Olympia Ave., Punta Gorda 33950) Designer clothing, home accessories, and collectibles.

Galleries

Gallery Dragonfly (941-505-0240; www.fishville.com/shops; 1200 W. Retta Esplanade #12, Punta Gorda 33950, at Fishermen's Village) Glass art, fish wall sculptures, paintings, and prints with local appeal.

Grass Roots Gallery (941-473-8782; www.grassrootsfl.com; 411 W. Dearborn St., Englewood 34223) Talented artists' collections of works in metal, fused glass, burlap, ceramics, oils, and photography.

Lemon Tree Gallery (941-474-5700; 420 Dearborn St., Englewood 34223) Bright yellow on the outside, soothing watercolors on the inside, along with art photography, whimsical copper wall sculptures, and jewelry—all tropically inclined and locally created.

Paradise! (941-964-0774; 340 Park Ave., Boca Grande 33921) Small but containing Boca's best selection, this gallery carries works by island artists and artisans and emerging Florida and national artists.

Presseller Gallery (941-639-7776; www.pressellergallery.com; 213 W. Olympia Ave., Punta Gorda 33950, downtown) Punta Gorda's most sophisticated gallery, carrying local photography, paintings, and sculptures—and a deli, to boot.

Sea Grape Artists Gallery (941-575-1718; www.seagrapegallery.com; 113 W. Marion Ave., Punta Gorda 33950) Displays and sells the fine art and affordable paintings, pottery, jewelry, and three-dimensional art of co-op members, who staff the gallery, so you have a chance to meet the artists.

Smart Studio & Art Gallery (941-964-0519; www.smart-studio-fl.com; 370 Park Ave., Boca Grande 33921) Shows and sells paintings of prolific wintering artist Wini Smart as well as other decorative arts. Closed in the off season.

General Stores

Gill's Grocery & Deli Market (941-964-2506; 5800 Gasparilla Rd., Boca Grande 33921, at The Courtyard) Beach needs, clothes, gifts, wine, deli items. Delivery available.

Gifts

Bedbugs (941-474-9054; 475 W. Dearborn St., Englewood 34230) An unique shop carrying a variety of things women love—from fun soaps and unusual tees to hammocks and jewelry.

Laff Out Loud (941-505-2067; www.fishville.com/shops; 1200 W. Retta Esplanade #14, Punta Gorda 33950, at Fishermen's Village) Whimsical toys for all ages: stuffed animals, dolls, puppets, lava lamps, and other nostalgic memorabilia.

Margaret Albritton Gallery (941-698-0603; 13020 Fishery Rd., Placida 33946) After lunch at The Fishery (see "Dining"), browse this delightful shop for everything from kitsch pink flamingo gifts to fine art.

Pirate's Ketch (941-637-0299; www.fishville.com/shops; 1200 W. Retta Esplanade #44, Punta Gorda 33950, at Fishermen's Village) Tasteful nautical clocks and lamps, weather vanes, seashell kitsch, framed sea charts, original art and prints.

Zolyssa (941-474-9072; 479 W. Dearborn St., Englewood 34223) Its self-described line of "shabby chic" includes home accessories, jewelry, and other beachy gifts.

Jewelry

✪ **Al Morgan** (941-637-0946; 119 W. Marion Ave., Punta Gorda 33950, downtown) Showcases of custom, select, one-of-a-kind rings, bracelets, and necklaces—designed with a "chunky philosophy"—for men and women.

Barbara Anne's Jewelry & Repair (941-460-1750; 480 W. Dearborn St., Englewood 34223) Small but well-stocked with affordable silver and gold charms, bracelets, toe rings, necklaces, and earrings.

Fine Things Jewelry (941-964-2166; 321 Park Ave., Boca Grande 33921, at Serendipity Gallery, Old Theater Building) Designer jewelry.

Paradise Jewelers (941-475-2396; 3700 N. Access Rd., Englewood 34224) Custom designs, nautical pieces, diamonds, gems, and repair.

Kitchenware & Home Decor

The Caged Parrot (941-637-8949; www.fishville.com/shops; 1200 W. Retta Esplanade #1, Punta Gorda 33950, at Fishermen's Village) Garden accessories, wood-block models of Punta Gorda buildings, fanciful wall hangings, tin sculpture wall animals, and wind chimes.

Company's Coming (941-205-5520; www.fishville.com/shops; 1200 W. Retta Esplanade #1, Punta Gorda 33950, at Fishermen's Village) Distinctive Florida-style and colorful glassware, pottery, and wooden bowls.

Daylilies (941-473-1840; www.dayliliesfl.com; 477 W. Dearborn St., Englewood 34223) Furniture and decorative items in tropical-jungle and marine-life motifs.

Holly's Home Accessories & Gifts (941-964-2767; www.hollysofbocagrande.com; 383 Park Ave., P.O. Box 1296, Boca Grande 33921) Fun, beachy decorative items, plus jewelry and gifts.

Sporting Goods

Champs Sports (941-627-5556; 1441 Tamiami Trail, Port Charlotte 33948; at Port Charlotte Town Center) Clothes, shoes, and equipment for tennis, aerobics, weight training, and all ball sports.

Fishermen's Village combines the pleasures of water sports and shopping.

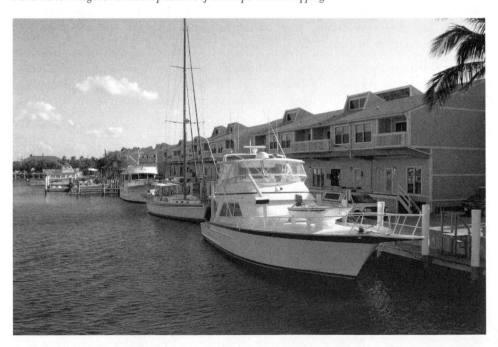

CALENDAR OF EVENTS

February

Black Culture Festival (Gilchrist Park, Punta Gorda) One day midmonth devoted to African, Caribbean, and African American music and dance. Includes kids' activities.

Florida Frontier Days (941-639-7278; www.charlottecounty.com/historical; Charlotte Harbor) Reenactors, artisans, storytelling, old-time games, music, and hands-on activities. One weekend midmonth.

March

Placida Rotary Seafood Festival (941-697-2271; www.seafoodfestival.info; Fishery Restaurant, Placida) Besides fresh fish, there's crab races, sculptures, and arts and crafts. Two days midmonth.

Rotary Spring Fine Arts Festival (941-474-5511; www.englewoodchamber.com; W. Dearborn St., downtown Englewood) A late-month weekend of art from around the U.S., live entertainment, and refreshments.

May

Oh Boy! Oberto Redfish Cup & Festival (888-698-2591; www.RedfishCup.com; Laishley Park Marina, Punta Gorda) In addition to world-class fishing for participating anglers, the festival brings three days of activities for all ages early in the month.

April

Punta Gorda Block Party (941-639-3200; www.puntagordablockparty.org; Punta Gorda) Community celebration, with music, food, crafts, and a variety of events. Late in the month.

May

Charlotte Harbor–Florida Fishing Tournament (941-625-0804) Thousands of dollars in prizes. Monthlong.

Ladies' Day Tarpon Tournament (941-964-0568) All-woman, all-release competition held on Mother's Day.

Taste of Charlotte (Fishermen's Village, Punta Gorda) Feast on food, art, and music and this restaurant cook-off. One day early in the month.

December

Christmas Peace River Lighted Boat Parade (941-639-3720) A procession of vessels in holiday attire. Saturday evening early in the month.

5

Sanibel Island & the Fort Myers Coast

Sand, Shells, and Serenity

A dreamy, tropical land adorned with a necklace of islands, this slab of coastline resembles, more than any of its neighboring regions, the laid-back islands of the Keys, Bahamas, and Caribbean. Tourism pundits brand it "The Beaches of Sanibel & Fort Myers" to capitalize on its most reputable parts. More developed than its Charlotte Harbor neighbors and more relaxed than what lies to the south and at the Sarasota end of things, the Island Coast gives us the leafy greenery for the southwest Florida sandwich. It is considered one of Florida's most ecology-minded resort areas. How it balances its dual roles as wildlife preserver and tourism mecca has served as a model for state ecotourism.

At their northern extreme, the islands are mired in an Old Florida time frame. **Cabbage Key**, **Useppa Island**, **Cayo Costa**, and **Pine Island** gave birth to the Gulf Coast's legacy of fishing lifestyles, back when the Calusa lived off the sea. On Pine Island, fishing, crabbing, and shrimping are still a way of life and survival. Many commercial fishermen have turned to charter captaining in the wake of the net-ban legislation in the 1994. In 2003, *Field & Stream* editors named Pine Island among the 25 hottest American fishing destinations, but unfortunately agricultural and other chemical runoff in recent years has altered the balance with accelerating algae growth; solutions are being sought. Protected from rampant resort development by its lack of beaches, Pine Island clings to an older way of life like a barnacle to a mangrove prop. **Cayo Costa** and **North Captiva**, both largely state owned, remain the uncut jewels in the Fort Myers coast necklace. **Useppa Island** and Cabbage Key preserve another era of island bygones, days graced by celebrity sporting types in search of escape, adventure, and tarpon.

Out in San Carlos Bay, to the south, the islands of Sanibel and Captiva developed quietly but steadily through the years. At various times in the past, the islands have supported a government lighthouse reservation, citrus and tomato farms, communities of fishermen (who sometimes dealt in rum-smuggling on the side), and a coconut plantation. From 1910 through 1940, wealthy notables made their way to the islands, intent on the relative anonymity that the wilds afforded them. Teddy Roosevelt discovered Captiva Island in 1914. Charles Lindbergh and his wife, Anne Morrow Lindbergh, visited often, inspiring her to pen her well-loved seashell analogies in *Gift From the Sea*. Pulitzer Prize–winning cartoonist and conservationist Jay N. "Ding" Darling gained national attention for Captiva

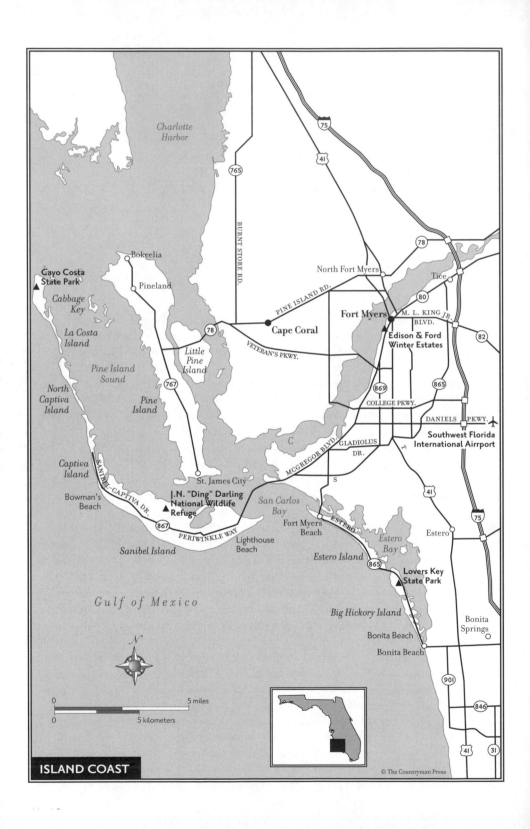

ISLAND COAST

© The Countryman Press

and Sanibel islands by fighting for the preservation of their natural attributes during his winter visits. His efforts sparked the development of the coast's environmental conscience.

Fort Myers Beach on San Carlos and Estero islands is synonymous with gulf shrimp, beach bustle, and spring breakers. Most of the bustle happens around Times Square, a pedestrian zone where retail meets the beach. The square's restaurants and shops are undergoing a renaissance.

Southward, the maze of islands that includes **Lovers Key** and **Mound Key** is reminiscent of the coast's earliest times, with primeval estuaries, intact shell mounds, whispers of buried pirate treasure, and fishing lifestyles.

On the mainland, **Cape Coral** once served as a hunting refuge for steel magnate Ogden Phipps, who vacationed in Naples. The second largest Florida city in the area, it was something of a developer's folly. The young city was cleared, canalled, and platted in 1970 and is slowly growing into itself. A downtown revitalization effort is currently under way, and a huge new marina, housing developments and resorts are in the works. **North Fort Myers**, rural in character, borders it on the east, and the Caloosahatchee River lines it on the south.

Across the river from North Fort Myers and Cape Coral, **Fort Myers** has evolved from its fort status of Seminole War time into the hub of communications, government, and transportation for the region. Cattle barons gave the community its early wild temperament; Thomas Edison and his class of successful entrepreneurs elevated it above its cow-trail streets.

Most unusual circumstances created the small community named **Estero**, along Tamiami Trail south of Fort Myers. The 19th-century religious cult that called itself the Koreshan Unity first settled there, led by Cyrus Teed, or Koresh (the Hebrew version of his name). The Koreshans believed that the earth clings to the inside of a hollow globe like coconut meat to its shell. Members practiced celibacy and communal living. They also experimented with tropical gardening, bringing to southwest Florida the mango and avocado. The site of their brief stay has been preserved and recreated by the state, together with their buildings and the natural Florida that they discovered there.

Between Fort Myers and Estero, **San Carlos Park** escalated to booming status with the genesis of a state university a decade ago. On its shirttails came massive shopping centers, restaurants, and other commercial enterprises that fill in the gap that once existed between quiet towns.

Thomas Edison put Fort Myers on the map when he built his winter home there in the late 1880s. Edison & Ford Winter Estates

LODGING

Maine may boast its bed-and-breakfasts, Vermont its historic inns, and Colorado its ski lodges. But when vacationers envision Florida, it's the beachside resorts that flash first through the mental slide projector. The Fort Myers/Sanibel coast has perfected this image of sun-and-sand abandon. Megaresorts are designed to keep guests (and their disposable income) on property. Not only can you eat lunch, rent a bike, and get a tennis lesson, you can hire a masseuse, charter a boat for a sunset sail, play golf, and enroll your child in Sandcastle Building 101. These destination resorts are in business to fulfill fantasies, and they spare no effort to achieve that goal.

Side by side with the resorts, you'll also find homey little cottages that have held their ground against buyouts and takeovers. Existing between the two extremes are a wide variety of high-rise condos, funky hotels, retirement resorts, mom-and-pop motels, fishing lodges, and inns. The 2004 hurricane season took its toll on the area's lodging landscape, most notably South Seas Island Resort on Captiva Island, which remained closed for more than two years. It and others that sustained heavy damage are all up and running, for the most part, better than ever. The resort collection of South Seas and its sister resorts on Sanibel Island were recently sold and continue to undergo massive changes and renovations that elevate them in the luxury market.

Privately owned second homes and condominiums provide another source of upscale accommodations along the coast. For families and other groups, these can often be a better value than hotel rooms. Timeshare rental was practically invented on Sanibel Island, and you'll find plenty of these options still around. Vacation brokers who match visitors with such properties are listed under "Home & Condo Rentals" at the end of this section.

The highlights of Lee County hospitality listed here—alphabetically by town—include the best and freshest in the local industry. While spanning the range of endless possibilities, this list concentrates on those

properties that break out of the skyscraping, wicker-and-floral mold. Toll-free 800, 888, or 877 reservation numbers, where available, are listed after local numbers.

Pricing codes are explained below. They are normally per unit/double occupancy. The range spans low- and high-season rates and standard to deluxe accommodations. Many resorts offer off-season packages at special rates and free lodging for children. Pricing does not include the 6 percent Florida sales tax. Some large resorts add service gratuities or maid charges, and Lee County imposes a 5 percent bed tax, as well, which goes toward beach and environmental maintenance.

Rate Categories

Inexpensive	Up to $75
Moderate	$75 to $150
Expensive	$150 to $200
Very Expensive	$200 and up

(An asterisk after the pricing designation indicates that the rate includes at least a continental breakfast in the cost of lodging and occasionally other meals as described in the listing.)

The following abbreviations are used for credit card information:

AE: American Express
MC: MasterCard
D: Discover Card
V: Visa
DC: Diners Club

Note that under the Americans with Disabilities Act (ADA), accommodations built after January 26, 1993, and containing more than five rooms must be useable by persons with disabilities. I have indicated only those small places that do not make such allowances.

Accommodations

CABBAGE KEY
❂ **CABBAGE KEY INN**
Innkeeper: Rob Wells

239-283-2278
www.cabbagekey.com
P.O. Box 200, Pineland 33945
Price: Moderate to Expensive
Credit Cards: MC, V

Cabbage Key appeals to vacationers seeking an authentic Old Florida experience. Built on an unbridged island atop an ancient shell mound, the inn and its guest accommodations are reminiscent of the 1930s, when novelist Mary Roberts Rinehart used native cypress and pine to construct a home for her son and his bride. Six cypress-paneled guest rooms in the inn and six cottages (two of them historic) accommodate overnighters. Four of the cottages have kitchens, and four have their own private docks. A couple of the cottages date back to the Rinehart era; the others are modern homes. The restaurant and its currency-papered bar attract boaters and water tours for lunch, but the island shuts down to a whisper come sundown. The inn can give you a list of boat charters from Captiva or Pine Island for transportation to and from the island. Boat rentals are available for day use.

CAPE CORAL
CASA LOMA MOTEL
Owners: Karen and Bob Bothwell, Brenda and Rick Fioretti
239-549-6000, 877-227-2566
www.casalomamotel.com
3608 Del Prado Blvd., Cape Coral 33904
Price: Inexpensive to Moderate.
Credit Cards: AE, D, MC, V

Cape Coral doesn't currently offer a lot in the way of resorts, but if you're looking for a place to stay while enjoying the town's family attractions or somewhere less costly than the beaches, this tidy little property does have its own charm—and canal-front views and docks in the bargain. Its 49 efficiencies are each stocked with a kitchenette containing a microwave, minifridge, and stovetop. Reclining chairs in some rooms and stylish motel furnishings provide comfort. Some porches and balconies overlook the canal and paved sundeck. Nicely landscaped grounds complement the Spanish villa architecture, with its red roof and arched balcony openings. Waterside tables, loungers, and a tiki-covered deck offer scenic places to relax.

CAPTIVA ISLAND
✪ JENSEN'S TWIN PALM COTTAGES & MARINA
Owners: David, John, and Jimmy Jensen
239-472-5800
www.gocaptiva.com
1507 Captiva Dr., P.O. Box 460, Captiva Island 33924
Price: Moderate to Very Expensive.
Credit Cards: AE, MC, V

One of Captiva's most affordable lodging options is also one of its homier places. You get an immediate sense of neighborliness on the grounds. Perhaps it has to do with its partiality to fisherfolk, demonstrated by its bayside docks, fishing charters, boat rentals, and bait supplies. I expected to find the accommodations in that same vein, where what's out in the water matters more than what's indoors. The 14 units look plain enough from the outside: white stucco cottages with tin roofs and a splash of blue trim. Each screened-in porch holds a plain picnic table. Inside, the one- and two-bedroom cottages are entirely cheery, with immaculate white board-and-bead walls, perky curtains, and simple, sturdy wooden furniture. The full kitchens are modern and spotless—nothing fishy about 'em. Just charming old-island style dressed up comfortable. The owners are known to make some music and entertain the local fishermen in the evenings.

SOUTH SEAS ISLAND RESORT
General Manager: Craig Schwan

239-472-5111, 800-965-7772
www.southseas.com.
5400 Plantation Rd., Captiva Island 33924
Price: Very Expensive
Credit Cards: D, DC, MC, V

South Seas is historically one of the great destination resorts of Florida, where you can enter through the security gates and leave one week later without ever having gone off property. In 2006, it reopened after a two-year makeover following the 2004 hurricane season with added panache, but still a sea-oriented, islandy style. Celebrities have always craved its privacy and discretion. South Seas offers any type of getaway dwelling you could imagine, from tennis villas to beach cottages to harborside hotel rooms—nine different types of accommodations in all. Rooms are furnished with stylish, high-quality pieces, 32-inch LCD televisions, pillow-top beds, and other luxury appointments. The property monopolizes a third of the island with about 550 guest units—mostly privately owned—six poolside eateries; formal lounges; shops; a gorgeous gulfside, nine-hole golf course; a fitness center and spa (with a new expanded spa in the works); a yacht harbor; 19 swimming pools; 18 tennis courts; boating; fishing; water-sports equipment rentals and lessons; excursion cruises; a recreation program for children; and 2.5 miles of beach. A free trolley takes guests around the 330-acre property, which is embraced on three sides by water.

'TWEEN WATERS INN
General Manager: Jeff Shuff
239-472-5161, 800-223-5865
www.tween-waters.com
15941 Captiva Rd., P.O. Box 249, Captiva Island 33924
Price: Moderate to Very Expensive*
Credit Cards: AE, D, MC, V

'Tween Waters spans the gap between beach cottage lodging and modern super resort.

Built early in the 1930s, when wildlife patron Jay N. "Ding" Darling kept a cottage there, the property shows glints of Old Florida architecture (some of it rather unglamorous) and easygoing attitudes. Compact but complete, it holds 149 rooms, restored historic cottages, efficiencies, and apartments as well as restaurants, a bustling marina, tennis courts, a fitness center, and a swimming pool. Named for its location between two shores at Captiva's narrowest span, the inn lies across the road from a length of beach that is usually lightly populated because it lacks nearby public parking. Its marina, one of its best features, is the island's top water-sports center, with charters, tours, boat and canoe rentals, and the Canoe & Kayak Restaurant. The Crow's Nest lounge provides the island's best nightlife. Continental breakfast is included in the rates.

FORT MYERS
AMBASSADOR RIVERFRONT HOTEL
239-337-0300, 800-833-1620
www.ambassadorfl.com
2500 Edwards Dr., Fort Myers 33901
Price: Moderate
Credit Cards: AE, D, DC, MC, V

Unfortunately, this 25-story hotel overlooking downtown's riverfront has always struggled to keep alive. A couple of years ago, it came under new ownership for yet another time and seems to be holding its own with the convention crowd. The view and the affordability of its rooms should ensure success, but alas, downtown undergoes its reinvention pains, and such businesses suffer along with it. The rooms could use some reinvention themselves, because they're still decorated in an Art Deco style introduced when the hotel first opened a decade ago. Free covered parking and wireless Internet throughout the property, two swimming pools, a restaurant, a lounge, and a fitness center add value. Right now it's the only hotel in the historic district, and I hope it can survive and upgrade in the coming years.

CROWNE PLAZA FORT MYERS
General Manager: Jim Larkin
239-482-2900, 877-227-6963
www.cpfortmyers.com
13051 Bell Tower Dr., Fort Myers 33907
At Bell Tower
Price: Expensive to Very Expensive
Credit Cards: AE, D, DC, MC, V

In 2006, this popular Holiday Inn—close to the airport, shopping, dining, and movie theaters—got a $5 million upgrade to the chain's Crowne Plaza status. The biggest change was the relaxation factor of the rooms, where sleep masks, sleep CDs, lavender spray, nightlights, massage show-erheads, and more are provided. As part of the bustling Bell Tower entertainment area, Shoeless Joe's, the hotel's sports bar/restaurant, draws in a lively crowd to its outdoor porch area and indoor pool-table scene off the spacious marble-floored lobby. Abstract metal and glass sculptures, a baby grand piano, and black-and-white checkered marble and granite flooring add touches of highbrow elegance to the entry-way. Priority Club guests enjoy complimentary continental breakfasts, evening appetizers, cookies and milk at night, and drink specials in the fifth-floor concicrgc lounge. All 226 rooms have minifridges. Airport transportation is free to all guests. High-speed and wireless Internet access, a waterfall outdoor pool, and a small cardio fitness center are available.

✪ SANIBEL HARBOUR RESORT & SPA
Managing Director: Brian Holly
239 466 4000, 800-767-7777
www.sanibel-resort.com
17260 Harbour Pointe Dr., Fort Myers
33908

Sanibel Harbour Resort & Spa makes an elegant waterfront statement.

Price: Expensive to Very Expensive
Credit Cards: AE, D, DC, MC, V

Stunningly beautiful for a property its size, the Sanibel Harbour Resort, which completely renovated after 2004's hurricanes, capitalizes on Florida style and a spectacular location. Not actually on Sanibel Island as the name suggests, the resort's 400 rooms, suites, and condos are located on a chin of land across San Carlos Bay from the island, on an inlet known as Sanibel Harbour. Half the units have water views of either the bay or nearby estuaries. A concierge-style inn holds 107 of the rooms and suites, which are decorated in European style and shiny brass and are more intimate than tower accommodations. The suites feature heavy four-poster beds and oversized bathtubs. The property encompasses four restaurants, a buffet-dining yacht, five outdoor swimming pools, lit Har-Tru tennis courts, a complete spa offering more than 60 services, and a small bayside beach. Charley's Cabana Bar has a 280-degree view of the sea and a lovely, breezy cocktail patio. Dining runs the gamut from a coffee and pastry stand to a steakhouse and an intimate fine-dining venue. The fitness center, canoe/kayak trail, and water-sports charters and rentals provide guests with a well-rounded menu of fitness and recreation options. Kid's Klub takes youngsters on nature hikes and a variety of other activities, and special children's menus come in Viewmaster format.

FORT MYERS BEACH
THE OUTRIGGER BEACH RESORT
General Manager: Dianne F. Major
239-463-3131, 800-655-8997
www.outriggerfmb.com
6200 Estero Blvd., Fort Myers Beach 33931
Price: Moderate to Very Expensive
Credit Cards: AE, MC, V

The Outrigger Beach Resort occupies the quiet south end of Fort Myers Beach, where the sand flares wide and gorgeous and is protected by a sandbar that's a bird hangout. The 30-year-old, 144-room resort boasts a casual, unstructured vacationing style that works well for families. Activity centers around its white-fenced pool and tiki bar deck area, where guests can sun and mingle. Or you can rent water-sports equipment through the front desk. Rooms are compact, modern, and furnished simply. Five types of accommodations range from the traditional to efficiencies with full kitchens. Prices also depend on whether they're on the first or second floor and the quality of the view. Shuffleboard, a putting green, beach volleyball, a little café, and live weekend and Wednesday night entertainment keep the place vivacious.

PINK SHELL BEACH RESORT & SPA
General Manager: Brij Misra
239-463-6181 or 888-847-8939
www.pinkshell.com
275 Estero Blvd., Fort Myers Beach 33931
Price: Moderate to Very Expensive
Credit Cards: AE, D, DC, MC, V

After $70 million in renovations, this resort barely resembles the longtime beach institution of its former self. Set between bay waters and 1,500 feet of beach, the 12-acre property has, in the past couple of years, gotten rid of its Old Florida cottages to build more high-rises, an Octopool fantasy water feature with an underwater theme, and a world-class spa. To the original Sanibel View Villas of 60 gulfside kitchenette suites and Beach Villas of 28 two-bedroom condos, the White Sand Villas added 92 one- and two-bedroom units with floor-to-ceiling gulf-facing windows and a central reception area with a mammoth stylized banyan tree "growing" through it. Captiva Villas, the fourth and newest building, contains another 43 units, replacing two older low-rises. All accommodations are privately owned and decorated in tasteful tropical style with a view of the wide, powdery beach and gulf. When completed, the property will have four pools. Three restaurants, a coffee shop/deli, boat docking, two tennis courts, a kids program, and a slew of water-sports rentals and tours complete Pink Shell's reputation as a destination resort at the northern tip of Fort Myers Beach, away from the bustle of the Times Square area.

SILVER SANDS VILLAS
Owner: Andrea Groves
239-463-2755, 800-603-0501
www.silversands-villas.com
1207 Estero Blvd., Fort Myers Beach 33931
Price: Moderate to Expensive
Credit Cards: AE, MC, V

In Fort Myers Beach, not much can be found that one could describe as charming. I discovered this notable exception by getting lost. Its assemblage of 20 one- and two-bedroom, circa-1935 cottages caught my attention from a side street. With their pale yellow paint jobs and tin roofs, they make a strong personality statement. Inside they are simple but in character, with white wainscoting and yellow walls, full kitchens in all but two units, and Old Florida–style porches. The compact property, bordered by a canal and within walking distance of the beach, holds complimentary docking for guests, a small pool, a fountain court-yard, a huge shady banyan tree, canal-front views, tables covered by chikee thatching, and laundry facilities—all behind a picket fence and hibiscus hedge right on the happening strip of Estero Boulevard, from where you hardly notice it. It's very congenial and convenient while feeling deliciously hidden away.

PINE ISLAND
BRIDGE WATER INN
General Manager: Gloria Conroy
239-283-2423, 800-378-7666
www.bridgewaterinn.com
4331 Pine Island Rd., P.O. Box 457, Matlacha 33909
Price: Moderate to Expensive
Credit Cards: AE, MC, V

In fish-frenzied Pine Island, Matlacha has its share of fishing cottages where what matters is what's biting. Fishing types will also like this tropically bright nine-unit roadside lodge because its wraparound covered deck hangs over the water. Rooms and efficiencies, decorated with distinct style and comfort, open up onto the deck, so you can step right out the door and cast. Suites 2 and 3 have the best views. With leather furniture and eye-catching colors (check out the hanging tropical bird planters made in Colombia from old tires), Bridge Water is a step up from other Matlacha accommodations. Restaurants, fish markets, shops, and galleries are within walking distance.

SANIBEL ISLAND
✪ GULF BREEZE COTTAGES AND MOTEL
Owners: Sandi and Charley Hutchings
239-472-1626, 800-388-2842
www.gbreeze.com
1081 Shell Basket Ln., Sanibel Island 33957
Price: Moderate to Very Expensive (for up to 6 people)
Credit Cards: MC, V

The address is Shell Basket Lane, and this place is just that delightful and seashell oriented. A dozen classic cottages, efficiencies, and duplexes make for the ideal barefoot beach vacation. Shuffleboard, a picnic pavilion with barbecue grills, and a station where you can clean your shells and fish provide outdoor-time amenities. The grandma and grandpa who have owned Gulf Breeze for more than 20 years love children and treat their guests like family. This property blends old island with new, holding its ground amid low-rise, concrete neighbors. Sea grapes, bougainvillea,

Island Inn wears its 100-plus years graciously.

Bahama shades, carved balustrades, lattice, and fish-scale siding add a fairy-tale quality.

✪ ISLAND INN

General Manager: Pegge Ford
239-472-1561, 800-851-5088
www.islandinnsanibel.com
3111 W. Gulf Dr., P.O. Box 659, Sanibel Island 33957
Price: Moderate to Very Expensive* (minimum stay for cottages and condos)
Credit Cards: AE, D, MC, V

Sanibel's only historic lodging—more than 100 years old—displays all the refinement of Florida's great old inns and hotels but without the snobbery. It has the same congenial and relaxed atmosphere that Granny Matthews, a Sanibel matriarch of renown, created at the turn of the 20th century when she entertained the whole island (including guests from other resorts) at Saturday night barbecues. She also initiated the Sanibel Shell Fair as a way to keep guests busy; she hosted it in the lobby, where white wicker, French doors, a windowed dining room, a fireplace, and shell displays now give an immediate impression of immaculate spaciousness and island graciousness. Renovations after Hurricane Charley in 2004 resulted in finding a beautiful hardwood floor beneath old carpeting. During the winter season (November 15 to April 15) a Modified American Plan is available, including breakfast and dinner at the Continental cuisine–inclined Traditions Restaurant. In summer, rates include continental breakfast. Cottages and lodges house 54 units, including three one-bedroom condos—all with a view of gentle gulf waves lapping at a shell-covered beach. Cottages have one to three bedrooms; lodges contain hotel rooms, with either full kitchens or refrigerators only. The hotel rooms can be combined into suites. The resort doesn't pretend to furnish extravagantly; all is done in uncontrived old-island style. That does not translate into shoddiness, however. The Island Inn is owned by shareholders who reinvest profits for constant upgrading. Decor is cheerful, comfortable, and impeccably maintained. Outside lodge room doors sits a wooden table where guests display their shell finds for others to peruse and admire. It's an Island Inn tradition. The atmosphere is saturated with conviviality. Dinner is announced by the blowing of a conch shell. Outdoors, native vegetation is landscaped around tin-roofed structures. A butterfly garden frames a croquet court, a swimming pool sits squarely on the beach, and tennis and shuffleboard provide recreation. As a recent nod to technology, the inn now provides free Internet access in the lobby.

SANIBEL'S SEASIDE INN

General Manager: Jack Reed
239-472-1400, 800-965-7772
www.seasideinn.com
541 E. Gulf Dr., Sanibel Island 33957
Price: Expensive to Very Expensive*
Credit Cards: AE, D, DC, MC, V

I recommend this place to visitors looking for intimacy on the beach without great extravagance. A measure of Key West—banana yellow tints, tin roofs, and gingerbread-trimmed balconies—creates Seaside Inn's old-island charm. It's the kind of place where you kick off your shoes the first day and don't find them again until you're packing to leave. Kitchen facilities and VCRs come in every studio, beach cottage, and one , two-, and three-bedroom suite, of which there are 32 in all. A swimming pool, brick-paved deck, complimentary continental breakfast (delivered to your door if you so desire), a video- and book-lending library, complimentary bike use, and tropical appointments complete the picture of seaside coziness. Use of facilities and amenities at Seaside Inn's sister resorts, including Sundial Beach Resort and Sanibel Inn, is available free of charge to guests. An inter-resort trolley provides transportation.

✪ SUNDIAL BEACH RESORT

General Manager: David Shepherd
239-472-4151, 800-965-7772
www.sundialresort.com
1451 Middle Gulf Dr., Sanibel Island 33957

Price: Expensive to Very Expensive
Credit Cards: AE, D, DC, MC, V

Sundial promises the perfection of a worry-free vacation. Sanibel's fine shelling beach is the focus of the 20-acre resort, which takes its name from a species of shell. In the stunning lobby, a sundial shell mosaic is inset on a marble floor. The resort provides extensive recreation, with 12 tennis courts, five heated swimming pools, bike and beach rental concessions, a fitness center, game room, recreation programs, and an eco-center complete with touch tank. The lavish main building houses one of two bar-and-grills; the second is located poolside. Less stylish, low-rise condo buildings are camouflaged by well-maintained vegetation and hold 270 fully equipped units. Decorated in tropical array and natural rattan, the units take advantage of gulf or garden views. Given its high level of service, the Sundial is one of the area's least pretentious and most comfortable properties, especially for families.

WEST WIND INN

General Manager: René Affourtit
239-472-1541, 800-824-0476
www.westwind.com
3345 W. Gulf Dr., Sanibel Island 33957
Price: Very Expensive
Credit Cards: AE, D, DC, MC, V

"Friendliness and cleanliness" is its motto—old-fashioned values for a Sanibel resort that started in the late 1960s. But this casual favorite looks anything but worn-out. The four lodging buildings of the two-story low-rise cluster beachside, and most of its 103 rooms have at least a glimpse of the gulf. Many overlook the pool and its fun-time pool bar, which, like the rest of the buildings, show a bit of Mediterranean flair with tile embellishments and red barrel-tile roofs. The pool bar serves lunch, or guests can get out of the weather and dine in the Normandie restaurant for breakfast, lunch, and, on weekends, dinner. Rooms, decorated demurely in plantation prints, come with a kitchenette or small refrigerator and microwave oven. All rooms have DVD players and free access to wireless Internet service. For recreational purposes, there are two tennis courts, free use of balls and racquets, a fish- and shell-cleaning tiki hut, a lovely butterfly garden, and 500 feet of gorgeous beach.

USEPPA ISLAND
✪ COLLIER INN & COTTAGES
General Manager: Vincent Formosa
239-283-1061, 888-735-6335
www.useppa.com
P.O. Box 640, Bokeelia 33922

The Collier Inn has been welcoming by-boat travelers since the early 20th century.

Price: Moderate to Very Expensive* (minimum stay on weekends and holidays)
Credit Cards: AE, MC, V

Used to be that only club members could enjoy the delicious privacy and historic elitism of Useppa Island. Once an escape for turn-of-the-20th-century celebrities, the island remains exclusive and aloof from the world. Now, if you can afford the price, you can be admitted onto the carefully guarded island by checking into the Collier Inn. The 100-year-old building, the original circa-1900 home of Barron Collier's Izaak Walton Club, holds seven elegant rooms and suites, individually designed for classic mood and comfort; historic cottages and the marina reception building add another four units. Plus, there are privately owned two- and three-bedroom cottages with kitchens available. Guests have access to the Useppa Island Club's full-service marina, Har-Tru tennis courts, swimming pool, manmade beach, croquet, outdoor chess, and fitness center. The pink-paved walkway around the island takes you past historic cottages, bounteous gardens, an ancient shell mound, and the 100-acre island's intriguing historical museum. Collier Inn Restaurant serves daily meals; a continental breakfast buffet is included for accommodations without kitchen facilities.

Home & Condo Rentals
Leisure American Vacation Rentals (239-463-3178; www.leisureamerican.com; 2450 Estero Blvd., Fort Myers Beach 33931) Condos and homes in and around Fort Myers Beach.

Sanibel Accommodations (239-472-3191, 800-237-6004; www.sanibel-captiva.com; 2341 Palm Ridge Rd., Sanibel 33957) Has available an online catalog of condo and home rentals on Sanibel and Captiva islands.

RV Resorts

Fort Myers–Pine Island KOA (239-283-2415, 800-562-8505; www.pineislandkoa.com; 5120 Stringfellow Rd., St. James City 33956) 371 sites, cabins, pool, saunas, hot tub, exercise room, tennis court, shuffleboard, horseshoes, lake fishing, and free bus to the beach a couple of times a week.

Red Coconut RV Resort (239-463-7200, 888-262-6226; www.redcoconut.com; 3001 Estero Blvd., Fort Myers Beach 33931) Right on the beach but packed in a bit tightly; 250 full hookup sites, on-site trailer rentals, laundry, shuffleboard, cable TV, and car rentals. Write for reservations.

DINING

The Island Coast is home to two of the nation's shellfish capitals. Shrimp—that monarch of edible crustaceans—reigns in Fort Myers Beach, where a fleet of shrimp boats is headquartered and an annual festival pays homage to America's favorite seafood. The sweet, pink gulf shrimp is the trademark culinary delight of the town and its environs. The fish markets of Pine Island, an important commercial fishing and transshipment center, sell all sorts of fresh seafood—oysters, shrimp, scallops, snapper, catfish—but the signature seafood is the blue crab and stone crab that come from local waters.

The following listings cover the variety of Island Coast feasting in these price categories:

Inexpensive	Up to $15
Moderate	$15 to $25
Expensive	$25 to $35
Very Expensive	$35 or more

Cost categories are based on the range of dinner entrée prices, or, if dinner is not served, on lunch entrées. Those restaurants listed with "Healthy Selections" usually mark such on their menu.

Note: Florida law forbids smoking inside all restaurants and bars serving food. Smoking is permitted only in restaurants with outdoor seating.

The following abbreviations are used for credit card information and meals:
AE: American Express
D: Discover Card
DC: Diners Club
MC: MasterCard
V: Visa
B: Breakfast
L: Lunch
D: Dinner
SB: Sunday Brunch

CABBAGE KEY
✪ CABBAGE KEY INN
239-283-2278
www.cabbagekey.com
P.O. Box 200, Pineland 33945
Price: Expensive
Cuisine: American
Children's Menu: Yes
Liquor: Full
Serving: B, L, D
Credit Cards: MC, V
No handicap access
Reservations: Yes, required for dinner
Special Features: Historic inn with walls papered in dollar bills left by visiting boaters; accessible only by boat.

Still funky after all these years, Cabbage Key has a reputation among boaters as a safe haven for a beer, a cheeseburger, and all-around friendliness. Everyone's in a good mood at Cabbage Key, particularly the bartender and waitstaff. Lunch—the most popular meal—consists of shrimp, salads, stone crab in season, burgers, sandwiches, and key lime pie. Tour boats bring in crowds, so it can get crazy, and waits for a table are often a beer-sodden affair. (If you're driving the boat, you may wish to opt for a walk around the nature trail instead.) Dinner is much quieter, and the local grouper couldn't get any fresher. I recently had it with a chipotle sauce drizzle and nearly swooned; it ruined me for grouper anywhere else. The scampi shrimp on pasta is another good bet. So are the Bloody Marys.

CAPE CORAL
ESQUISITO
239-540-8910
4721 Vincennes Blvd., Cape Coral 33904
Price: Inexpensive to Moderate
Cuisine: Italian
Children's Menu: No
Liquor: Beer and wine
Serving: L, D
Credit Cards: MC, V
Handicap Access: Yes
Reservations: Yes
Special Features: Outdoor seating

Cape Coral has a reputation for Italian restaurants, and this newest on the scene makes, as its names suggests, an exquisite statement at reasonable prices. Decorated in rich Tuscan tones and wine racks, with an antique horse carriage as centerpiece, Esquisito serves classics from all regions of Italy with great aplomb. Don't miss the mussels Esquisito, swimming in a creamy, buttery, and garlicky broth with bits of onion and tomato, for an appetizer. You'll be dipping the crusty Italian bread in the bowl to sop up every last bit. For entrées, pick from a wide selection of pastas (the lobster ravioli is divine), veal and seafood dishes, and grilled meats. House specialties include lasagna, lobster fra diavolo, and paella Valenciana. Either pasta fagioli soup or a green or Caesar salad come with the meal. Frank Sinatra, Dean Martin, and Italian tunes play in the background, and smart dangling lights over each linen-draped table create an atmosphere of romance.

IGUANA MIA
239-945-7755
www.iguanamia.com

1027 E. Cape Coral Pkwy., Cape Coral 33904
Price: Inexpensive to Moderate
Cuisine: Mexican American
Children's Menu: Yes
Liquor: Full
Serving: L, D
Credit Cards: AE, D, MC, V
Handicap Access: Yes
Reservations: No

This, the original Iguana Mia, spawned others in Fort Myers and Bonita Springs, but we like this one best, even if it means we have to cross the bridge to Cape Coral and pay a toll to get there. It's the most down-to-earth of the three. Sure, it's just as flashy, with its electric-green exterior paint job and nicely rendered interior Mexican frescos, but it retains some of the unpretentious lunchroom ambiance it started out with. Stacked cases of Mexican beer still count as decor elements. And most importantly, the food is flat-out better. Things seem more rushed at the newer places; here it's mañana paced. My husband invariably orders the sour cream chicken chimichanga, a specialty. I—usually already half full from shoveling in huge gobs of the salsa I can't resist with warm, crunchy tortilla chips—like the veggie burrito, nachos, or quesadilla. You're bound to find something you like on the menu—it's huge and lets you do some of your own meal engineering.

RUMRUNNERS
239-542-0200
At the Cape Harbour Marina
5848 Cape Harbour Dr., Cape Coral 33914
Price: Inexpensive to Moderate
Cuisine: New American
Children's Menu: Yes
Liquor: Full
Serving: L, D
Credit Cards: AE, D, MC, V
Handicap Access: No

Rumrunners caters to boat- and drive-in guests looking for creative cuisine and fine views.

Reservations: Yes
Special Features: Waterfront setting with outdoor seating

One of Cape Coral's newest restaurants happens to be one of the most enjoyable in its culinary history. Opened by the people who wow us at Bistro 41 in Fort Myers, it has its own imaginative style and overlooks a mangrove waterway in the midst of new upmarket development. Even better: prices are surprisingly affordable for such specialties as seafood potpie—chockful of shrimp, scallops, and crab with a creamy lobster sauce and a flaky pastry sitting atop it. We sampled a wide variety of starters, main courses, and desserts besides the potpie and had no complaints except that the calamari could be crispier. In the "loved it" category: chicken quesadilla with blackened tomato "jam," salsa fresca, and cumin-scented crème fraîche; spinach and blue cheese salad; vodka penne; angel hair pasta generously decorated with shrimp, scal-lops, mussels, and torn basil; warm chocolate bread pudding (did I detect a splash of rum in there?), and Rumrunners cobbler with a biscuit crust, five berries, diced mango, and vanilla ice cream (totally wonderful). Pasta dishes are available in full and half portions. The building at first seems cold and oversized, but once you're sitting in the glassed room or on the deck overlooking the water, you immediately warm to the location.

✪ SIAM HUT

239-945-4247
4521 Del Prado Blvd., Cape Coral 33904
Price: Inexpensive
Cuisine: Thai
Children's Menu: No
Liquor: Beer and wine
Serving: L, D (Closed Sun. and lunch Sat.)
Credit Cards: MC, V
Handicap Access: Yes
Reservations: No

A long-standing favorite in Cape Coral, Siam Hut's affordability is matched by its versatility and authentic goodness. You basically can design your own meal from the noodles, stir-fried, curry, and fried rice sections. For instance, I recently chose the pad kee mao, a stir-fried rice-noodle dish of basil, colorful and crunchy veggies, and chili paste. I had a choice of tofu, beef, pork, chicken, shrimp, or squid to centerpiece that, and I chose the latter—tender, tasty rings set afire by the seasonings. (You also get to pick your degree of spiciness.) The meal was flavorful, filling, and a bargain with the inclusion of fried strips of wonton, soup, and a small iceberg and carrot salad dressed in a tasty peanut vinaigrette. House specialties include fried-crispy frog legs with garlic and black pepper, fried whole fish in a variety of preparations, and Thai entrée salads. Go traditional and sit at a floor table on pillows that support your back, or choose one of the more plentiful booths or standard tables and chairs.

Captiva Island
THE BUBBLE ROOM
239-472-5558
www.bubbleroomrestaurant.com
15001 Captiva Dr., Captiva Island 33924
Price: Moderate to Expensive
Cuisine: American
Children's Menu: Yes
Liquor: Full
Serving: L, D
Credit Cards: AE, D, DC, MC, V
Handicap Access: Limited
Reservations: No
Special Features: Museum-like displays of '30s and '40s memorabilia

The Bubble Room is so Captiva—and something you have to experience once. It's especially fun to take kids there. The quirkiness begins outside, where bubbles bedeck the kitsch-cottage structure and lawn gnomes greet you. Inside, the tables are glass-topped showcases filled with jacks, Monopoly money, comic books, dominoes, and assorted toys from the past. A Christmas elves scene, circus plaques, Betty Boop, celebrity photos, a plaster hippo's mouth, and other nostalgic memorabilia fill every wall, phone booth, bathroom door, nook, and cranny. A toy train runs under the ceiling, and servers—Bubble Scouts—wear goofy hats. So that's the atmosphere—and you've gotta see it for yourself. The menu continues the frivolity. At lunch, Mae's West is a charbroiled chicken breast sandwich. The Piggly Wiggly barbecued pork sandwich I ordered was delicious, from the sweet bun to the coleslaw heaped on the messy meat. Dinner's Duck Ellington is a tasty rendition of roasted duck with orange and banana sauce. Other snappily titled dishes include Beignet Goodman (crispy light grouper fingers), the Scarlett O'Hara (macadamia-crusted red snapper), and Eddie Fisherman (grouper topped with Ritz cracker crumbs and pecans, then steamed in a bag). The service is exceptional, considering the tight quarters and volume of business. Other things for which the Bubble Room is known are its basket of bubble bread (yum! cream cheesy), its sticky buns with dinner, and its fabulous desserts. You must leave room for a huge slab of moist and delicious red-velvet cake, the rich almond-studded orange crunch cake, or any of the other many tempting selections.

KEYLIME BISTRO
239-395-4000
www.captivaislandinn.com
11509 Andy Rosse Ln., Captiva Island 33924
Price: Moderate to Expensive
Cuisine: American
Children's Menu: Yes
Liquor: Full
Serving: B, L, D, SB
Credit Cards: AE, D, MC, V

Handicap Access: Yes
Reservations: No
Special Features: Outdoor patio and live
music

KeyLime Bistro evokes a Caribbean–Key
West setting with brightly painted oversized
booths indoors, a tiki hut stage outdoors,
and a prevailing sense of whimsy. The patio
overlooks historic "downtown" Captiva, a
quirky, bustling corner of the world. As
part of a small inn, the bistro serves all
meals, plus Sunday Jazz Brunch. Musicians
entertain nightly. As if the 30-plus-entrée
set dinner menu doesn't give you enough
choices, a specials menu with about
another 15 options clouds decision-
making. Time for a key lime martini or
pineapple cosmo while pondering, nibbling
sesame crackers with cheese and grapes,
and watching life go by on the other side of
the white-picket fence. Seafood and pasta
are the clear favorites, though the menus
stretch to chicken, steak, and prime rib. On
a recent visit, our meals peaked with the
salad course—one decorated with artichoke
hearts, hearts of palm, and asparagus and
dressed with a tomato-orange vinaigrette,
which was too scarce; the other composed
of spinach, grilled portabella, roasted red
pepper, and strawberry cider vinaigrette.
We both ordered the small version, which
could have served as meals regardless. Our
fish dishes—grouper piccata and snapper
scampi—were nicely sauced but woefully
overcooked. At breakfast, there are huevos
rancheros, Belgian waffles, and eggs Benedict with key lime hollandaise. Interesting
salads, including those we ordered for dinner, star on the lunch menu.

ESTERO
✪ BLUE WATER BISTRO

239-949-2583
www.gr8food.net
23151 Village Shops Way, Ste. 109 Estero
33928
At Coconut Point Center

Price: Inexpensive to Expensive
Cuisine: Seafood
Children's Menu: Yes
Liquor: Full
Serving: D
Credit Cards: AE, MC, V
Handicap Access: Yes
Reservations: Yes
Special Features: Outdoor seating

Successful Naples restaurateur Skip Quillen
opened Blue Water Bistro with an old concept, but one new for him: seafood. He's put
his thumbprint on it by using sauces and
products with zing. From the centerpiece of
the stretch menu, guests choose their
brand of grilled seafood, its sauce, and a
side dish. Again, not a new concept, but the
difference here is the quality of the choices,
the global novelty of the fish selections, and
the other stuff that fills in the menu to offer
enough diversity to satisfy the whims of the
restaurant's large indoor and outdoor
capacity. Begin with the long, tall drink
menu, filled with the expected to the unexpected in beers, wines, martinis, shots, and
other fun quaffs. The bar dominates the
modern, semicircular space, so it's no surprise that drinking is as much a priority
here as dining. For me, the pomegranate
Cosmo seemed like a good place to start; my
husband ordered a microbrew from Dog
Fishhead, which tasted quite sweet until
our appetizer of hickory-barbeque bacon-
wrapped scallops arrived to balance its
honey-saffron tones. The barbeque sauce,
which we sampled again later with a side of
crunchy thin onion rings, proves the skill
of the kitchen's *saucier*. The menu promised
a bed of cheesy grits, which tasted more
like mashed potatoes, but that did not
detract. Our second appetizer, tequila-
roasted oysters with a "cha-la-peño" and
pepper-jack topping, proved a deliciously
piquant interpretation of oysters
Rockefeller. For entrées, my partner chose
off the mix-and-match section—Costa

Rican yellowtail snapper with chipotle hollandaise and the wonderful aforementioned onion rings. The sauce, like much about Blue Water, had a nice spark of spice, and the fish was grilled simply to retain its moisture and flavor. I ordered off the specials section, which ranges from grouper kung pao and king crab Alfredo to burgers and baby-back ribs. The blackened salmon with bourbon and brown sugar glaze sounded sweet, but I was pleasantly surprised at the subtleness of the flavors, particularly when combined with the buttery jalapeno-pecan sauce. For dessert, we greedily devoured a pineapple upside-down cake with rum raisin ice cream and Blue Mountain coffee caramel, and an achingly creamy version of key lime pie with splotches of tequila blueberry sauce and mango coulis.

FORT MYERS
BISTRO 41
239-466-4141
www.bistro41.com
13499 S. Cleveland Ave. #143, Fort Myers 33907
At Bell Tower Mall
Price: Moderate to Expensive
Cuisine: New American
Children's Menu: No
Liquor: Full
Serving: L, D (Closed for Sun. lunch.)
Credit Cards: AE, MC, V
Handicap Access: Yes
Reservations: Yes
Special Features: Outdoor seating

Whether you choose a sidewalk table looking out at Saks Fifth Avenue or an indoor booth between brightly painted walls, Bistro 41 feels festive and chic. The regular dinner menu highlights oak-grilled specialties such as signature rosemary-marinated rotisserie chicken and filet mignon with a gorgonzola pesto crust and sun-dried cherry demi-glace. Other eclectic offerings include mussels simmered with

smoked lemon, snapper tartare, meat loaf and blue cheese mashed potatoes with wild mushroom demi, and miso-glazed salmon. To further complicate decision-making, a separate menu comprises a tableau of specials, from which we typically order and are always pleasantly surprised. For lunch, ready-to-drop shoppers renourish on the grilled lobster melt half sandwich with tomato-parmesan soup, smoked salmon salad with boursin and bacon, barbecued chicken pizzetta, and sweet and spicy Vietnamese noodles. This is a favorite of ours both for dinner à deux and girl's gatherings.

✪ BLU SUSHI
239-489-1500
13451 McGregor Blvd., Ste. 23, Fort Myers 33919
At Cypress Square
www.blusushi.com
Price: Inexpensive
Cuisine: Sushi/Japanese
Children's Menu: No
Liquor: Full
Serving: L, D (Closed Sat. and Sun. lunch)
Credit Cards: AE, MC, V
Handicap Access: Yes
Reservations: No

So popular in Fort Myers, it has spun off into a Naples location and will soon be opening in Estero. Blu Sushi is as blue and cutting edge as its name. Local businesspeople crowd the bar and outdoor waiting areas to score one of a dozen tables or sushi-bar chairs in the blue-walled dining room. Hydraulic bar chairs, a cool water wall, and fun martinis (in blue-stemmed glasses, of course), sakes, and saketinis make the wait part of the adventure. Try the mango X-rated martini or the Asian pear sake for something exotic. You can order from the full menu, which consists largely of sushi rolls and sashimi, in the bar. Appealing to even the less-than-enthusiastic sushi fan, the rolls fuse Japanese and American favorites for the tastiest, most creative sushi this town has ever seen. The clear winner, Blu Special, makes a perfect meal with its balance of starch, protein, vegetables, and rich creaminess. Inside out with cucumbers tucked into sushi rice and thinly wrapped with avocado, it wears a luxurious blanket of mayo-bound cooked scallops and shrimp. Other recommendations from the 18 varieties of specialty rolls: Storm Safe (eel, crab, avocado, crunchy flakes of tempura for great taste and texture, and eel sauce), the Bahama (spicy conch, cucumber, and smelt roe), and Fire Dragon (spicy tuna inside out with whitefish and avocado on top). The seaweed salad is tasty and proportioned to share as an appetizer; the king miso soup adds crab meat to the traditional. Or try the tuna tataki, carpaccio-thin slices of lightly seared top-quality tuna wading in a pool of ponzu sauce. Dessert comes liquid and spiked only and includes such offerings as bananas foster, crème brûlée, and butterfly kisses (chocolate vodka, butterscotch, and toffee liqueur).

BLUE PEPPER

239-939-4700
www.bluepeppergourmet.com
7091-14 College Pkwy., Fort Myers 33907
At College Parkway Center
Price: Inexpensive to Moderate
Cuisine: New American
Children's Menu: No
Liquor: Beer and wine
Serving: L, D (closed Sun.)
Credit Cards: AE, MC, V
Handicap Access: Yes
Reservations: No

What started out as a gourmet market selling prepared foods, desserts, meats, seafood, wine, and cheese has evolved into a café within a scaled-down market. In other words, its prepared dishes were so popular,

it became a menu for eating out rather than in, and affordably so. Lunch and dinner menus have an air of cunning and intrepidness about them. For instance, my key lime snapper on a recent visit came aboard a puddle of thick mango vinaigrette and with a side of mashed sweet potatoes and roasted asparagus. Every element was prepared correctly and boosted with creative insight. The meal begins with salt-encrusted ciabatta bread and components for making your own olive oil dip. Tasty, but the herb shaker is also salted, resulting in way too much sodium. That was our sole complaint. The dinner menu leans heavily on seafood, with crab cake and seared ahi tuna appetizers, a blackened sea scallop salad, and entrées such as Caribbean seafood stew and citrus-crusted grouper. Light dinners borrow from the lunch menu to offer options such as a vegetarian wrap, crab cake sandwich, and shrimp scampi over ditalini pasta. The lunch menu brings fresh alternatives to the local scene with the likes of a roast beef and boursin sandwich and bacon-wrapped meat loaf. The market still specializes in wine (with regular tastings) and desserts, and the selections in both arenas cap the Blue Pepper experience with delight.

CRÜ

239-466-3663
www.crufoodandwine.com
13499 S. Cleveland Ave. #241, Fort Myers 33907
At Bell Tower Mall
Price: Moderate to Very Expensive
Cuisine: New American
Children's Menu: No
Liquor: Beer and wine
Serving: D
Credit Cards: AE, MC, V
Handicap Access: Yes
Reservations: Yes
Special Features: Outdoor seating

The Bell Tower shops have become headquarters for cutting-edge dining in Fort

Myers. At Crü, we sat down to a white porcelain tray holding two spoon-shaped crackers of a soft Swiss cheese and two white porcelain shot glasses of carrot and strawberry juice—a delightful amuse-bouche to start the experience. The white china contrasts with everything black about Crü's interior: walls, tablecloths, deeply coved booths, servers' uniforms. A compact display kitchen and a huge, bright abstract painting provide splashes of color—that and the uplifting menu. "Lush wines and pure foods" is the motto, and the wine list makes up in originality for what it lacks in size. The menu is unusual in its think-outside-the-box format, where diners can share such appetizers as the Grand Crü (beef tartar, beef hand rolls, big eye sashimi, seared foie gras, and imported cheese) or the three-game entrée (elk, buffalo tenderloin, and duck breast with foie gras potatoes and goat cheese). We went slightly more traditional with the wonderful roasted red pepper and crab bisque off the nightly special menu and escargot off the regular menu. The latter twisted classic style with a shell-less presentation of the mild little snails in garlic butter with wild mushroom, proscuitto bits, and chunks of boursin cheese—an inspired combination. We ordered our entrées also from the specials menu. Pan-seared yellowtail snapper topped with lime-flavored corn chow-chow on a bed of smoky-flavored tomato and okra ragout won favor over the pork tenderloin, grilled to medium rare and served with wilted spinach, wild mushrooms, and a veal reduction. Both were complex creations—nicely executed and flavored. What you won't find on a Crü table is salt or pepper or a breadbasket. You won't miss any of the above. Our server described several dessert dishes in a stream of ingredients that left us reeling. Rather than have him repeat it all, we zeroed in on something with blueberries and were thrilled with an artistically multilayered confection of ricotta cheese, fresh blueberries, blueberry mousse, candied pecans, and brandied cherries. Something tells me there's nothing you could order here that would fail to overimpress.

EL PATIO RESTAURANT
239-278-3303
4444 Cleveland Ave., Fort Myers 33901
At Regency Square
Price: Inexpensive
Cuisine: Peruvian
Children's Menu: Yes
Liquor: Beer and wine
Serving: L, D
Credit Cards: D, MC, V
Handicap Access: Yes
Reservations: No

This place packs 'em in—Peruvians, gringos, families alike—for an exotic taste of Peruvian cuisine, known for the invention of ceviche, its great variety of corn, and its Asian influence. El Patio's extensive menu sweeps the country's specialties, starting with exotic soups such as hen broth with noodles, potatoes, and eggs and a green rice and seafood soup. Appetizers include tamales, avocado stuffed with chicken or seafood, giant white corn with cheese, and mashed potatoes stuffed with seafood. Ceviche—seafood marinated in lime juice, which causes a chemical reaction that seems to cook the fish—comes as an entrée instead of an appetizer, as we are increasingly seeing it in mainstream restaurants. Varieties include fish, octopus, shrimp, and combinations thereof. I chose the fish and, when given a choice by our charming Peruvian waiter, asked for it hot (as in spicy, the dish itself is always served chilled). It came with two cold, yam-like vegetables and a lettuce leaf filled with corn fries—roasted and salted large-kernel corn, somewhat akin to corn nuts but not as hard and starchier. They're a favorite bar snack in Peruvian eateries. The ceviche, garnished simply with red onion slices, was outstanding. My husband ordered a steak dish with sautéed sweet onions and a side of beans. The thinly sliced steak was tender and flavorful. Other entrées span seafood and beef realms and include a specialty marinated fish dish with spicy cream sauce, stir-fried rice with beans and steak, paella, and Peruvian-style spaghetti with beef. The Peruvian purple corn pudding intrigued us, but unfortunately they weren't serving it that evening so we settled on the quatro leches cake. With its caramel core and rich moistness—not too sweet, as tres leches tends to be—it vied with all the other yums our Peruvian adventure delivered.

CHILE RANCHERO

239-275-0505
11751 S. Cleveland Ave. #18, Fort Myers 33907
In Family Thrift Center
Price: Inexpensive
Children's Menu: Yes
Cuisine: Mexican
Liquor: Beer and wine
Serving: L, D
Credit Cards: AE, D, MC, V
Handicap Access: Yes
Reservations: No
Special Features: Live Mexican music weekends

A refreshing departure from Tex-Mex chains, it serves home-cooked, fresh-tasting, affordable specialties designed for the local Hispanic population. Tongue or liver taco, anyone? That aside, most dishes are suited also to less adventurous gringo palates: homemade nachos with a tongue-tingling peppery salsa, calamari, bean soup, huge burritos, sautéed sirloin with tomatillo sauce, grilled chicken and romaine salad with avocado vinaigrette,

fried tilapia sandwich, shrimp à la diabla, and flan. Try the nacho de ccviche, topped with slices of avocado, for a change of pace and taste. Wash it down with a Modelo Especial or Pacifico beer. Mexican music plays in the background, and Spanish-speaking staff efficiently attends at the spacious, pleasant café. Mariachi bands perform on weekends.

FRENCH ROAST CAFÉ

239-936-2233
www.frenchroastcafe.com
12995 S. Cleveland Ave., Ste. 118, Fort Myers 33907
At Pinebrook Park
Price: Moderate to Expensive
Cuisine: French/Vietnamese
Children's Menu: No, but appropriate items available
Liquor: Beer and wine
Serving: B, L, D, SB Credit Cards: AE, D, DC, MC, V
Handicap Access: Yes
Reservations: Yes

Don't write this off as a coffee shop, although uncommon brews are a specialty. The fine French food is delightfully afford-able, but the best deal is the lunchtime Vietnamese specials. I favor the grilled beef wrapped in grape leaves (exquisitely seasoned with garlic, ginger, and lemongrass) over rice vermicelli—one of the 10 selections. For $8.95, I also got an excellent egg-drop chicken soup, not so impossibly salty like many renditions, and delicate spring rolls with a light sweet-sour dip, prettily cut pickled veggies, and all that the menu promised in flying flavors. The rest of the lunch menu, with the exception of its crêpes, offers a typical and full complement of salads, sandwiches, and burgers. Dinner in this cozy, elegant setting of fireplace, arches, and columns offers Vietnamese and classic French dishes such as tablesideflamed steak Diane, snapper provençal, breast of duck Chambord, and crêpes à la Grand Marnier (made tableside). Despite its elevated view of a parking lot, this place exudes romance and excels at all it prepares.

MILLE SAPORÉ

239-437-5040
15880 Summerlin Rd., Fort Myers 33908
Price: Inexpensive to Expensive
Cuisine: Mediterranean
Children's Menu: Yes
Liquor: Full
Serving: L, D (Closed for Sun. lunch and for lunch in the summer.)
Credit Cards: AE, D, MC, V
Handicap Access: Yes
Reservations: Yes
Special Features: Outdoor seating

The beauty of this place is you can go in and have a nice seafood or steak dinner or just an inexpensive pizza. Either way, it will surprise you. Nothing is ordinary here. Pizzas come in varieties such as the pepata (with shrimp, mussels, black peppers, and light cream) and the melanzane (with mozzarella and marinated eggplant). Order a 9-inch or a 16-inch for appetizers or entrées. Otherwise, go for the red snapper with sour oranges and red onions, pesto linguine, or veal flank with smoked salmon green peppercorn sauce—winners all. Tucked unassumingly into a supermarket strip mall, Mille Saporé has wowed the local dining-cognizant community with a tastefully decorated bar and dining room, both feeling like mild refuges from outside bustle. The bartender is congenial, and the hosts fitted with the proper accent to make this feel like an Old World experience in a thoroughly modern cadre.

PATIO 33

239-337-2846
33 Patio de Leon, Fort Myers 33901
At Hendry and First streets, downtown
Price: Moderate
Cuisine: New American Grill
Children's Menu: No
Liquor: Full
Serving: L, D (Closed Sun. and lunch on Sat.)
Credit Cards: AE, MC, V
Handicap Access: Yes
Reservations: Yes, for dinner
Special Features: Outdoor patio seating and an indoor-outdoor bar upstairs

A catalyst in downtown Fort Myers' comeback, it occupies a historic Spanish-style building with a notched parapet roofline. The bouquet of rotisserie meat seduces you first thing in the door—that and the self-assured look of faux unfinished walls painted bright ochre, black exposed ductwork, glossy cement floors, and safari-suggestive accents. Off the rotisserie, there's chicken, duck, teriyaki pork, and short ribs. Other entrées, luncheon sandwiches and starters show the same bold confidence. Don't miss the tomato and basil soup gratinée with Gorgonzola and Swiss, Parma and spinach salad with black olive pesto vinaigrette, baked goat-cheese sandwich with sun-dried tomatoes, meatloaf-stuffed tomato, seafood pasta, and wild mushroom and truffle risotto. Nightly specials off the grill include suckling pig, baby lamb, and leg of veal. After a chocolate fondant or tarte tatin dessert, head upstairs for mingling and cocktailing rooftop.

PLAKA II

239-433-5404
15271-27 McGregor Blvd., Fort Myers 33908
At McGregor Point Shopping Center
Price: Inexpensive
Cuisine: Greek
Children's Menu: Appropriate items on regular menu
Liquor: Beer and wine
Serving: L, D

The Veranda infuses creativity into Southern cuisine.

Credit Cards: D, MC, V
Handicap Access: Yes
Reservations: No

The food is genuine Greek here and so is
the atmosphere—colorful, borderline tacky
(think the front yard in *My Big Fat Greek
Wedding*), decorated with rope-light-
framed paintings and Greek bric-a-brac.
The dinner menu doesn't lower itself to
American standards, although the lunch
menu offers burgers and other staples.
Wash down pickled octopus or tzatziki-dip
appetizers and moussaka or pastitso with
a glass of retsina wine. My favorite is the
dolmathes, cooked so the grape leaves
melt away in your mouth and topped with
a wonderful, traditional egg-lemon sauce.
One entire section of the dinner menu
offers seafood with Greek preparation,
from squid and smelt to shrimp, grouper,
and snapper. And of course, there's
baklava to wrap up the meal with honey
and phyllo.

✪ THE VERANDA

239-332-2065
www.verandarestaurant.com
2122 Second St., Fort Myers 33901
Price: Moderate to Expensive
Cuisine: Florida/Southern
Children's Menu: No.
Liquor: Full
Serving: L, D (Closed for Sat. lunch, Sun.
lunch and dinner.)
Credit Cards: AE, MC, V
Handicap Access: Yes
Reservations: Yes, recommended
Special Features: Garden/courtyard dining,
piano bar

My husband and I had our first "big" dinner date at the Veranda, so it will always be
one of my favorites—but not solely for sen-
timental reasons. Victorian trappings and
Southern charm create an atmosphere of
romance in a historic-home setting.
Occupying two early 20th-century houses,
the Veranda is a place for business lunches

and special-occasion dinners. The dining room huddles around a two-sided redbrick fireplace and looks out on a cobblestone garden courtyard, separated from traffic by showy greenery and a white fence. Historic Fort Myers photos and well-stocked wine cases line the dark-wood bar. Start with something unusual from the Veranda's appetizer board—perhaps the superb blue crab cakes, artichoke fritters with blue crab and béarnaise sauce, or Southern grit cakes with pepper jack cheese and grilled andouille sausage. Entrées are traditional but exceed the ordinary. Tender medallions of filet are dressed Southern style, in a rich, smoky sour-mash whiskey sauce. Rosemary merlot sauce complements the rack of New Zealand lamb. Tender crawfish top pan-seared yellowtail snapper. Daily specials typically include fresh seafood catches, and the menu changes to reflect the seasons. Lunches span the spectrum from specialties such as Cajun chicken or baked tomato pasta to fried green tomato salad or grouper sandwich. Desserts wilt willpower with such temptations as chocolate pâté on raspberry coulis, peanut-butter-fudge pie, and Baileys cheesecake.

FORT MYERS BEACH

Locals go to Fort Myers Beach expecting fresh seafood and reasonable prices. It's known more for fun dining and waterfront views than for culinary innovation, and menus are fairly predictable.

MATANZAS INN

239-463-3838
www.matanzasrestaurant.com
416 Crescent St., Fort Myers Beach 33931
Price: Inexpensive to Moderate
Cuisine: Seafood/American
Children's Menu: Yes
Liquor: Full
Serving: L, D
Credit Cards: AE, D, MC, V
Handicap Access: Yes
Reservations: No
Special Features: Waterside view, open-air dining

When I think of Fort Myers Beach, I think of three things: shrimp, boats, and water. Matanzas Inn embodies the laid-back, free-spirited soul of the "the Beach" with its ramshackle look and landmark position in the shadow of the high bridge, where boat traffic and aerial bird shows provide entertainment whether you're sitting inside or out. I invariably order fried shrimp when I sit down to a meal here, despite the fact that the menu comprehensively stretches beyond Fort Myers Beach's trademark dish. I can depend on its crunch and freshness. It appears on both the lunch and dinner menu. Other worthy considerations: the steamer platter, grouper stuffed with seafood and provolone, crunchy grouper, barbeque shrimp, and baby-back ribs. The key lime pie is well worth the calories—creamy, and, like Fort Myers Beach, just tart enough.

SOUTH BEACH GRILLE

239-463-7770
7205 Estero Blvd., Fort Myers Beach 33931
At Santini Marina Plaza
Price: Moderate to Expensive
Cuisine: Seafood
Children's Menu: Yes
Liquor: Full
Serving: D
Credit Cards: AE, D, MC, V
Handicap Access: Yes
Reservations: Yes

To break away from Fort Myers Beach's typical fried shrimp mold, this one—despite some service problems—takes you to a higher level of culinary daring. Our last visit found the bright, open dining room packed to the gills, so to speak, which perhaps explains the lapses in service. The ambitious menu tends tropical in theme, starting you out with such choices as fried calamari with banana molasses ketchup, coconut fried shrimp with rum-plum dip, crab cakes with mango, roasted pepper vinaigrette, and seafood chowder. We stuck to seafood entrées, which tasted fresh but with a few disappointments. With the shrimp scampi, for example, the promised butternut squash risotto was just regular rice (not Arborio) flavored (too) subtly with squash. The blackened ahi tuna with sweet coconut curry sauce proved a better choice—quite tasty and well executed. Other entrée choices include pork porterhouse with smashed sweet potatoes, grilled salmon glazed with honey mustard and horseradish, parmesan encrusted grouper, and frenched rack of lamb. An early dining menu from 4:30 to 5:30 offers seven entrées in the $15 to $17 range, including soup or salad. The sautéed mussels provençal with basil angel hair pasta sounds tempting and appears also on the regular menu. Eight desserts sound equally so—from Florida-inspired confections such as orange cake and key lime tart to universal standards such as carrot cake and banana split.

PINE ISLAND
RED'S FRESH SEAFOOD HOUSE & TAVERN
239-283-4412
www.redsfreshseafoodhouse.com
10880 Stringfellow Rd., Bokeelia 33922
Cuisine: Seafood
Price: Inexpensive to Moderate
Children's Menu: Yes
Liquor: Full
Serving: L, D (Closed for lunch in summer.)
Credit Cards: AE, D, DC, MC, V
Handicap Access: Yes
Reservations: No

This newest barn red, red-hot Pine Island sensation gives you page after page of options, highlighting seafood but covering all bases from a chipotle cheeseburger and burritos to steak and balsamic onion salad, seafood pasta dishes, steamer platters, and filet mignon. If you doubt that any one restaurant can do justice to more than 100 entrées, not counting salads and sandwiches, you haven't seen the nightly crowds at Red's. Locals crowd around the L shaped bar and fill tables and booths that are all dressed in red. Begin with an unusual martini off the extensive drink and wine list—something in root beer or strawberry cheesecake, perhaps? Two pages of starters include steamed shellfish, baked oysters, tuna carpaccio, and popular finger foods such as nachos, fried cheese, and ribs. Dinners come the old-fashioned way—with a choice of two salads or sides. The house salad with the ginger scallion vinaigrette and mashed butter pecan sweet potatoes are clear winners. For an entrée, I can highly recommend the linguine with shrimp and spinach-gorgonzola sauce or the grouper provençal, which comes in a garlic butter and wine sauce. Everything tastes fresh and properly cooked, and the atmosphere bubbles with happy customers and servers.

TARPON LODGE RESTAURANT
239-283-2517
www.tarponlodge.com
13771 Waterfront Dr., Pineland 33945 Price: Moderate to Expensive
Cuisine: New Continental
Children's Menu: Yes
Liquor: Full
Serving: L, D
Credit Cards: AE, MC, V
Handicap Access: Yes
Reservations: Yes, suggested
Special Features: Historic setting

Before there was Tarpon Lodge, Pine Island dining projected an Old Florida-meets-the-Midwest image. Now there's a creative, gifted force to reckon with. Set in a 1926 fishing lodge, banked with vintage wavy-glass windows looking out on the water, the restaurant brings on the freshness in every sense of the word. For lunch, the marinated portobello mushroom and goat-cheese sandwich, quesadilla, crab cake sandwich, or shrimp and crab fettuccini gratify. Imaginative dressings and sides make the dishes; for example, a tasty garlic mayonnaise, potato salad, and coleslaw accompanied the crab cake sandwich, which was slightly heavy on breading but nicely seasoned. Try the hearty and fresh-tasting crab and roasted corn chowder for lunch or dinner. The succinct menu's 10 dinner entrées include vegetarian pasta, veal piccata, and beef tenderloin medallions wrapped in bacon and finished with demiglace, plus the day's fresh catch and nightly specials. Here in this seafood kingdom, with its steep fishing heritage, you can't go wrong ordering the catch, or—thanks to the chef's savvy—anything else, for that matter.

SANIBEL ISLAND
BEACHVIEW STEAKHOUSE & SEAFOOD
239-472-4394
www.beachviewgolfclub.com
110 Parview Dr., Sanibel Island 33957
Price: Moderate to Expensive
Cuisine: Steak
Children's Menu: Yes
Liquor: Full
Serving: L, D
Credit Cards: AE, D, MC, V
Handicap Access: Yes
Reservations: Yes

"Horrifying Vegetarians since 1995," its motto boasts. But thrilling meat-lovers, I might add. Its chef, Mike Price, knows his way around a good steak; if the bone-in filet mignon is being offered on your visit,

and you can afford it, go for it. The Cowboy Steak (bone-in prime rib) and marinated T-bone steak are also sure winners. In the seafood department, the Sanibel "Hot Pot" gives you a medley of shellfish over linguine, and the tilapia has a sun-dried tomato crust. Wednesday night is German Night, with wiener schnitzel, sauerbraten, sausages, and other appropriate selections. During lunch hours, golfers and others stop in for hot and cold sandwiches such as the turkey cordon bleu wrap and grouper reuben. If you're so inclined, the martinis are perfectly mixed and chilled, and the service is always spot on.

✪ DOLCE VITA
239-472-5555
www.dolcevitaofsanibel.com
1244 Periwinkle Way, Sanibel Island 33957
Price: Moderate to Expensive
Cuisine: Mediterranean
Children's Menu: No
Liquor: Full
Serving: D
Credit Cards: AE, D, MC, V
Handicap Access: Yes
Reservations: Yes, recommended
Special Features: Live music

This reigns as one of Sanibel's most glamorous and popular fine-dining experiences. The large, open dining room is at the same time elegant and convivial. Its baby grand piano is the centerpiece of its live entertainment. The menu is extensive, yet each dish is well crafted with Mediterranean and other Continental and global influences. Old-fashioned flavors infuse dishes modernized with nouveau nuances. For starters, there's everything from wok-steamed mussels and wonderfully spicy shrimp pill-pill to Absolut gravlax and a flavorful, soupy mariscadas—shellfish in a garlic-fish-tomato broth (you may want to ask for a spoon). The cassoulet of escargot gets an injection of individuality from mushrooms and herbs to supplement the garlic. We like the scallops fettuccine, Angry Lobster Arrabiata (blanketed in a spicy Tuscan pomodore sauce—not too hot, just to the point of zingy), and veal chop Calvados from among the dizzying choice of entrées, which also includes roasted duck "au figs," Texas wild-boar saddle (tamarind-honey glazed with black currant coulis), tequila smoked salmon with vodka penne, jerk chicken fettucine, and porterhouse béarnaise, to name a sampling. Because you are eating in a place whose name translates as "sweet life," you must have dessert, which is another highlight. The Black Forest cake comes with an unlikely but oddly complementary scoop of passion fruit sherbet. It is dark, rich, and delightful. For another chocolate treat, skip dessert and order the chocolate martini.

THE JACARANDA

239-472-1771
1223 Periwinkle Way, Sanibel Island 33957
Price: Expensive
Cuisine: Continental
Children's Menu: Yes.
Liquor: Full.
Serving: D
Credit Cards: AE, D, MC, V
Handicap Access: Yes
Reservations: Yes

Restaurants come, go, and change formats quickly on Sanibel Island, but "the Jac" has remained constant and consistently fine for more than 20 years. Its menu—a modernized version of Continental with a strong lean toward seafood—gets tweaked to abide with the times, but the quality of execution puts this longtimer at the top of the island restaurant list. Islanders and visitors alike first get to know its bar, which is famous for its live music and dance floor. In the restaurant, the extensive drink and martini

menu successfully segues from the bar scene to the creativity one finds from the kitchen. The Sanibel Rain martini kicked off our recent soiree with refreshing of Rain Vodka and Cointreau. We led off with the SanCap Shrimp appetizer, a delightful threesome wallowing in spiced rum, coconut cream, and orange juice. From the dinner menu, divided between pasta (shrimp Alfredo, linguine DiMare, and so on), seafood specialties, and meat (such as cowboy steak, veal Rockefeller, and roast duckling)—we relished crab cakes with honey mustard and plum sauce, and sesame crusted yellowfin tuna, done perfectly rare to my specifications and sided with wakame salad. Everything was fresh, flavorful, and just how it was supposed to be. The service was professional while entertaining, and all in all we enjoyed one of our most pleasurable meals in a very long time out on Sanibel.

LAZY FLAMINGO

239-472-5353
www.lazyflamingo.com
6520-C Pine Ave., Sanibel Island 33957
At Blind Pass
Price: Inexpensive to Moderate
Cuisine: Seafood/American
Children's Menu: Yes
Liquor: Beer and wine
Serving: L, D
Credit Cards: AE, D, MC, V
Handicap Access: No
Reservations: No

This is the original Lazy Flamingo, which has spawned another on Sanibel's south end and others in the region. Look for a Pepto Bismol—pink building at Blind Pass, just before the bridge to Captiva. Neighborhood and nautical are the concepts behind this first Flamingo, where you order and pick up your own food at the counter, eat off plastic plates in the shape of scallop shells, and wipe your hands with paper towels from a roll at the table. The menu and ambiance have an essence of the Florida Keys—the owners even lifted the idea of a popular ring-and-hook game from a bar down there. Conch fritters, clam pot, mesquite-grilled grouper, wings, prime-rib sandwich, Caesar salad, and choco-late—key lime cheesecake are some of the most popular menu items. Avoid the Dead Parrot Wings; they are inedible to all but the most callused, but the regular chicken wings rank highest on the island. Most of the meals come with fries, but you can sub-stitute a small Caesar salad, which is usually tasty. The place is small: about a dozen counter seats and a few booths plus some outdoor tables. For the same food but more room, shrimp-boat decor, and table serv-ice, try the Lazy Flamingo at 1036 Periwinkle Way (239-472-6939).

GRAMMA DOT'S SEASIDE SALOON

239-472-8138
634 N. Yachtsman, Sanibel Island 33957
At Sanibel Marina
Price: Inexpensive to Expensive
Cuisine: Seafood
Children's Menu: Yes
Liquor: Beer and wine
Serving: L, D
Credit Cards: MC, V
Handicap Access: Yes
Reservations: No

I have finally found it: the island's (perhaps all of Lee County's) best key lime pie. Flecks of lime zest give this creamy version its pucker power, and now I'm afraid I'm addicted. That's not all that makes this place popular among locals and visitors. Take in the view of luxury yachts in the har-bor and savor the freshness of the seafood dishes to get the full picture. The curried lobster salad is top choice on the lunch menu, which is available until the little screened-porch eatery closes at 7:30 PM.

(After 5 PM, lunch items go up $1 in price.) Winning entrées include the mesquite grouper, coconut shrimp, bacon-wrapped shrimp with pineapple sauce, and fried oysters. Portions are generous and accom-panied by a tasty potato croquette, the house tartar sauce, fresh sautéed veggies, and fruit served in a chocolate cup molded in the shape of a scallop shell. Nightly spe-cials, such as the blackened salmon with cucumber-dill sauce I recently enjoyed, give fresh options for regular customers. Just don't forget to leave room for the pie.

TRADERS STORE & CAFÉ

239-472-7242
1551 Periwinkle Way, Sanibel Island 33957
Price: Moderate to Expensive.
Cuisine: American/Bistro
Children's Menu: Yes
Liquor: Full liquor
Serving: L, D
Credit Cards: AE, D, MC, V
Handicap Access: Yes
Reservations: Yes
Special Features: A restaurant embedded in the setting of a gallery-like import store; live music two nights a week

This is the equivalent of performance art, where you become a part of the store. You sit among wooden tribal masks on imported chairs, eating terrific crusty bread out of hand-woven baskets. The café occupies the front section of this unusual store, owned by the founders of the Chico's clothing store dynasty (see "Shopping," below). The food rivals the surrounding artifact-quality furnishings and objets d'art. It's become *the* place for islanders to meet for lunch, with its succinct menu of sandwiches, pastas, and small plates. The soup of the day is usually a good bet, and the seafood gumbo, fortified with rice, could be a meal. I also can recommend the grilled marinated portobello sandwich and the sesame-seared tuna with Asian slaw and wasabi vinaigrette. The dinner menu describes such masterworks as macadamia-crusted grouper with Thai peanut sauce, bourbon-glazed lollipop pork chops, poached salmon and spinach-artichoke ravioli with dill vinaigrette, and parmesan sea bass with avocado coulis. Nightly specials dazzle. Cutting edge aside, Traders is also known for its burgers and barbecue baby-back ribs.

Food Purveyors

Bakeries

Bara Bread Bistro (239-334-8216; 1520 Broadway, Fort Myers 33901) A charming bistro-*boulangerie* specializing in French bread by the loaf, quiche, coffee, and luscious French pastries. There's a large seating area in the store and out in its courtyard, where you can enjoy your purchase or have French-style lunch.

European American Baking Co. (239-694-7964 or 800-200-BAKE; www.eabake.com; 12450 Metro Pkwy., Fort Myers 33966) Wholesale, retail, and café operation with the most tempting international treats: éclairs, scones, strudel, Italian butter cookies, cheesecake, napoleons, tarts, turnovers, and artisan breads. Also specialty coffees and deli foods.

Les Lavandes French Bakery (239-482-2011; Bridge Plaza, 12901 McGregor Blvd., Fort Myers 33919) Small but chockful of treats français: baguettes, great olive bread, cookies, meringues, cheesecake, and pastries.

Mason's Bakery (239-334-4525; www.masonsbakery.com; 1615 Hendry St., Fort Myers 33901) A fixture on the downtown scene, it lures shoppers with coffee, yummy cakes, cookies, breads, bagels, danishes, cinnamon rolls, and more. Also prepares box lunches.

Breakfast

✪ Amy's Over Easy Café (239-472-2625; 630-1 Tarpon Bay Rd., Sanibel Island 33957) Islanders are happy to have an alternative (and a better one at that!) to breakfast at Lighthouse Café, a tourist favorite long touted for its breakfasts. Cheerful and creative, Amy's menu does standard along with unusual dishes such as my favorites: egg Reuben sandwich, vegetarian Benedict, and portobello and spinach omelet. Also lunch.

Frankie's 2 Family Restaurant (239-454-4430; 16541 San Carlos Blvd., Fort Myers 33908) Breakfast, served until 3 PM, features international omelets—Greek, Polish, and German—and hearty country fare. Also lunch and dinner.

Candies & Ice Cream

Chocolate Expressions (239-472-3837; 2075 Periwinkle Way #37, Sanibel Island 33957, at Periwinkle Place) Homemade chocolates (including sugar-free varieties), hand-scooped ice cream, smoothies, nonalcoholic daiquiris, and other treats.

Kilwin's (239-463-4500; www.kilwins.com; 50 Old San Carlos Blvd., Fort Myers Beach 33931, at Times Square) A respected name in sweets, it sells fudge, chocolates, and ice cream in many flavors. Pop in for a free sample or a turtle sundae after a hard day on the beach.

Love Boat Ice Cream (239-466-7707; 16229 San Carlos Blvd., Fort Myers 33908) Homemade ice cream at a longtime favorite at the crossroads leading to Fort Myers Beach and Sanibel Island.

Pan American Coffee House (239-472-7787; 2006 Periwinkle Way, Sanibel 33957, at Tahitian Gardens) Queenie's Real Homemade Ice Cream, a locally produced boutique ice cream, is served in a half-dozen local flavors such as key lime pie and toasted coconut. Also shakes, smoothies, and—if you haven't guessed—coffee.

Pinocchio's Ice Cream (239-472-6566; 362 Periwinkle Way, Sanibel Island 33957) Homemade Italian ice cream and yogurt, cappuccino, espresso, and frozen coffee drinks.

Coffee

Blackhawk Fine Coffee & Provisions (239-433-7770; 13499 S. Cleveland Ave. #137, Fort Myers 33907, at Bell Tower Shops) An inviting setting of easy chairs, coffee tables, and backgammon boards, where you can enjoy coffee, lattes, desserts, flavored ice tea, and other goodies. Wireless Internet access available.

Latté Da (239-472-0234; www.captivaislandinn.com/village/la.htm; 11508 Andy Rosse Ln., Captiva Island 33924) Sells Seattle's Best brand coffees and espresso, plus locally homemade Queenie's Real Ice Cream.

Origins Coffee Roasterie & Café (239-542-6080; 1021-A Cape Coral Pkwy. E., Cape Coral 33904) Have a seat at a sidewalk table for specialty coffees, a pastry, hot breakfast, lunch, and a Wi-Fi connection.

Sanibel Bean Island Coffees (239-395-1919; www.thebeanofsanibel.com; 2240-B Periwinkle Way, Sanibel Island 33957; also at Southwest Florida International Airport and

---

The Queen of Ice Cream

When Vanessa "Queenie" Viglione talks ice cream, she begins to sound like a true junkie. By the time she's finished, you're rushing to the nearest vendor of Queenie's Real Homemade Ice Cream for a fix of your own.

"I had a $260 a month habit," she says of her pattern of ordering premium ice cream by overnight shipping when she couldn't find a suitable product locally. That was before her boyfriend sent her to ice-cream-making school for her birthday. She returned after the two-week course and eventually opened her little factory in Fort Myers. Ice cream connoisseurs covet her handcrafted ice cream at select shops and eateries on Sanibel and Captiva islands.

Year-round flavors include butter pecan, pure vanilla, Dutch chocolate, toasted coconut, black raspberry chip, mint chocolate chip, very strawberry, fresh banana, "Cup O' Joe" coffee, cookies and sweet cream, and key lime pie. Queenie also scoops up seasonal delights such as Pine Island mango, cinnamon, candy cane, and pumpkin pie.

"I saw so many misguided youth that actually thought ice cream was the fat-free-sugar-free-soft-serve-stuff that was being offered in 100 flavors pumped continuously from two dispensers," says Queenie, who generously donates her ice cream to local blood donor and family events. "My philosophy was to perfectly produce a dozen superior flavors that I would be proud to serve to my own family."

in Cape Coral) Sanibel's wildly popular buzz shop, it serves the usual espresso, cappuccino, and latte selections, plus fresh-squeezed juice, smoothies, ice cream, bagels, breakfast, sandwiches, and salads.

Deli & Specialty Foods

Blue Pepper Gourmet Market & Café (239-939-4700; www.bluepeppergourmet.com; 7091-14 College Pkwy., Fort Myers 33907) Part of a café-retail operation, it sells import cheeses, wines, luscious desserts, sauces, and other gourmet culinary products and implements. Wine tastings and cooking classes.

Cheese Nook (239-472-2666; Periwinkle Place, 2075 Periwinkle Way, Sanibel Island 33957) A longtime favorite of locals for not only cheese but also wine, fresh bread, and gourmet hot sauces, preserves, and soups.

Francesco's Italian Deli and Pizzeria (239-463-5634; 7205 Estero Blvd., Fort Myers Beach 33931, at Santini Marina Plaza) Homemade breads, calzones, deli sandwiches, pizza whole or by the slice, Italian dishes for reheating, ice cream, gourmet cheeses and groceries.

India Bazaar (239-939-0797; 5228 Bank St., Fort Myers 33907) A shop filled with exotic smells, foods, and gifts from India, Thailand, the Middle East, and Britain. Fresh, packaged, and frozen ethnic ingredients plus premade meals.

Kim Orient Mart (239-275-8812; 1910 Boy Scout Dr., Fort Myers 33907) Adjacent to a Chinese restaurant, this Oriental market sells fresh, packaged, frozen, and canned goods in bulk or small packages; everything from soy sauce to dried fungus.

✪ **Mario's Italian Meat Market & Deli** (239-936-7275; 12326 Cleveland Ave., Fort Myers 33907) Fresh homemade sausage, braciola, and other meats; delicious homemade Italian cheeses, sauces, pastas, soups, sandwiches, and hot and frozen prepared Italian specialties. Limited seating.

Petra Middle Eastern Food (239-939-3090; 1916 Boy Scout Dr., Fort Myers 33907) Stop here for feta cheese, flat breads, gyros, and unusual processed items such as rose jam, stuffed eggplant, and exotic candies.

✪ **Sandy Butler Gourmet Market** (239-482-6765, www.sandybutler.com; 17650 San Carlos Blvd., Fort Myers Beach) A new, spacious culinary dream filled with wonderful cheeses, wines, bakery goods, prepared dishes, fresh produce, and gourmet products.

Fruit & Vegetable Stands

For the freshest produce, visit the plentiful roadside stands along the coast. Some feature U-Pick options, especially for tomatoes and strawberries.

Downtown Farmers' Market (239-332-6813; Fort Myers, near Centennial Park, under the bridge) Look for fresh fruit, vegetables, flowers, herbs and live plants, arts, and crafts every Thursday, 7–2.

Mango Street Market (Estero Blvd. at Mango St., Fort Myers Beach) Roadside stand selling fresh produce.

Oakes Brothers Produce (239-466-4464, 800-413-6881; 16758 McGregor Blvd., Fort Myers 33908) My personal favorite for locally grown tomatoes, citrus, and other fresh fruit, vegetables, and preserves. They also ship fruit.

Sunburst Tropical Fruit Company (239-283-1200; 7113 Howard Rd., Bokeelia 33922) One of the oldest island groves, Sunburst specializes in mangoes but also grows carambolas, litchis, and other exotics and sells fruit products. It's best to call ahead.

Sun Harvest Citrus (239-768-2686, 800-743-1480; www.sunharvestcitrus.com; 14810 Metro Pkwy. S., Fort Myers 33912, at Six Mile Cypress) Part tourist attraction, part citrus stand, Sun Harvest offers free samples, tours, demonstrations, a playground, and a gift shop.

Internet Cafés

Mo's Deli & Ice Cream (239-437-7135l 9299 College Pkwy., Fort Myers 33917) Free wireless Internet; ice cream, breakfast and lunch menus.

Sanibel Bean Island Coffees (239-395-1919; www.thebeanofsanibel.com; 2240-B Periwinkle Way, Sanibel Island 33957) Free Wi-Fi and computer use; coffee drinks, smoothies, ice cream, bagels, breakfast, sandwiches, and salads.

Natural Foods

Ada's Natural Foods Market (239-939-9600; www.adasnatural.com; 4650 S. Cleveland Ave., Fort Myers 33907) Extensive line of organic produce and other healthy food products. A deli/juice bar with seating produces tasty meatless sandwiches, salads, and hot dishes.

Healthy Habits (239-278-4442; 11763 S. Cleveland Ave., Fort Myers 33907) Organic produce, dairy products, and other natural groceries.

Island Nutrition Center (239-472-4499; www.islandnutritioncenter.com; 1633C Periwinkle Way, Sanibel Island 33957) Small but well stocked with refrigerated and packaged organic, low-fat, low-carb, and low-sodium products.

Jayne's Victorian Garden (239-482-2466; 12901-13 McGregor Blvd., Fort Myers 33919) Hard to place in one category, this establishment also qualifies as a teacup-sized restaurant and an unusual gift shop. Shelves are stocked with organic products and homemade preserves. Stay for a healthy lunch served on antique china. Also vegan, gluten-free, and other special diet catering.

Pizza & Takeout

Andrea's Gourmet Market & Delicatessen (239-472-9990, www.andreasgourmet market.com, 2430 Periwinkle Way, Ste. A, Sanibel Island 33957) Operated by the owner of Dolce Vita (see above), this new-in-2006, handsome market sells fresh meats, seafood, and baked breads, plus hand-cut farmstead cheeses, wine, and creative sandwiches, soups, and salads to go.

El Mambo Cuban Restaurant (239-542-9995; 4716 Del Prado Blvd. S., Cape Coral 33904) Serving Cape Coral's Hispanic population and those who love the food, it sells Cuban bread, desserts, fresh fruit juices, Cuban sandwiches, and other sandwiches and Cuban specialties.

The Flying Pig (239-337-3744, www.theflyingpig.net, 7970 Summerlin Lakes, Ste. 101, Fort Myers 33907;) Fresh, creative sandwiches and salads for lunchtime takeout; also catering and order-ahead prepared meals.

Mozella's Food Works (239-472-2555; 2330 Palm Ridge Rd., Sanibel Island 33957) Luncheon sandwiches and homemade dinners for takeout.

Plaka I on the Beach (239-463-4707; 1001 Estero Blvd., Fort Myers Beach 33931) Gyros, spinach pie, moussaka, and baklava to go or eat in a screened-in dining room near the beach.

Starz Restaurant & Pizzeria (239-482-STAR, 16740 McGregor Blvd., Fort Myers 33908) Close to the islands, its pizzas, calzones, subs, and Italian specialties have a faithful following.

Taste of New York Pizzeria (239-432-0990; 13499 S. Cleveland Ave., Fort Myers 33907; at Bell Tower Shops) Declared to be among the best takeout or eat-in for regular or gourmet pizza—white, vegetarian, tropical, pesto, garlic—and other New York–Italian specialties. Free delivery available.

Tropical Beach Grill (239-454-0319; 17260 San Carlos Blvd., Fort Myers Beach 33931) Better-than-average drive-up takeout for burgers, chicken sandwiches, and more.

Seafood

Beach Seafood (239-463-8777, 800-771-5050; 1100 Shrimp Boat Ln., P.O. Box 2490, Fort Myers Beach 33932, on San Carlos Island) Fresh seafood at its source, specializing in shrimp—fresh, frozen, steamed, and dinners. This is a locals' hot spot for lunch, by the way.

Skip One Seafood (239-482-0433; 15820 S. Tamiami Trail, Fort Myers 33908) The freshest and best-priced shrimp, stone crab (in season), lobster tails, clams, and fish on the mainland; join the crowds who have discovered the quality and value of its food for lunch and dinner. Shipping service available.

Timbers Fish Market (239-472-3128; 703 Tarpon Bay Rd., Sanibel 33957) Located inside a popular seafood restaurant, Timbers has the best selection, prices, and freshness on the island for all types of seafood fresh, steamed, and smoked.

CULTURE

For many years the region was considered a cultural limbo, void of strong artistic or regional identity except for a certain retiree/Midwestern influence. Still lagging behind Sarasota and Naples in that department, the region nonetheless is making inroads toward "artsification." The population, furthermore, is diversifying in terms of ethnicity and age.

The residents of Cape Coral and North Fort Myers include many nationalities that share their customs at social clubs, restaurants, festivals, and other venues. Throughout Fort

Myers, African-Americans, Asians, East Indians, Europeans, and other ethnic groups heighten the cosmopolitan flavor. Flashes of Southern and Cracker spirit survive in the less resortlike areas of North Fort Myers and Pine Island.

The islands along the coast have inspired their share of creativity. Singer Jimmy Buffett has frequented Cabbage Key and Captiva Island. His brand of beachy folk song is the closest thing the Gulf Coast has to homegrown music. A Sanibel musician named Danny Morgan affects that same style and has been entertaining the islands for decades.

One of the few arts that residents can truly call their own is shell art, a form that flourishes on Sanibel Island, Florida's ultimate shell island. In its highest form, shell art can be stunning and delicate; its lowest can result in some pretty tacky shell animals.

Wealthy visitors to Sanibel and Captiva have exerted an influence on the fine arts through the years. The illustrious roll call began in the 1920s with Charles and Anne Morrow Lindbergh. Edna St. Vincent Millay's original manuscript for *Conversation at Midnight* burned in a Sanibel Island hotel fire. Today Robert Rauschenberg, a maverick in the field of photographic lithography, is the region's impresario.

Architecture

Fort Myers is home to some lovely architecture downtown and along McGregor Boulevard. Thomas Edison's home was perhaps Florida's first prefab structure: Because wood and materials were scarce (most newcomers made do with palmetto huts), Edison commissioned a Maine architect to draw up plans and construct sections of the home to be shipped down and pieced together on site. Downtown, the **Richard Building**, circa 1924, boasts an Italian influence, while the courthouse annex superbly represents Mediterranean Revival. So do the Miles Building, built in 1926 by Dr. Franklin Miles, the "Father of Alka-Seltzer," and **Patio De Leon**, a restored and burgeoning entertainment and shopping complex on First Street. The newer Harborside Convention Center and other recent constructions echo the motif.

Once a one-room schoolhouse, Captiva's Chapel-by-the-Sea hosts interdenominational services and many a wedding.

Pine Island possesses the best, most concentrated collection of preserved vernacular architecture, especially in ✪ **Matlacha**. Pineland's mound-squatting homes are also prime examples, occasionally dressed up with latticework and vivid paint jobs. In **Bokeelia**, the entire Main Street is designated a historic district. Notice especially the Captain's House, a fine example of slightly upscale folk housing of the early 1900s, with French Provincial elements. Nearby Turner Mansion represents a higher standard of living and is reminiscent of New England styles. The club at **Useppa Island** exhibits another prime collection of Old Florida styles, both traditional and revival.

Koreshan's historic village preserves and recreates a time when a religious community grew up along the banks of the Estero River.

Cinema

AMC Merchants Crossing 16 (239-995-1191; 15201 N. Cleveland Ave., North Fort Myers 33903) State-of-the-art movie complex.

Beach Theater (239-765-9000; www.ftmyersbeachtheater.com, 6425 Estero Blvd., Fort Myers Beach 33931) A new theater with four screens, serving a full-meal (and slightly overpriced) menu, beer, and wine.

Gulf Coast Town Center (230-267-0783; www.gulfcoasttowncenter.com; 9903 Gulf Coast Main St., Fort Myers, at Interstate 75 and Alico Rd.) Sixteen Regal theaters.

Island Cinema (239-472-1701; 535 Tarpon Bay Rd., Sanibel Island 33957, at Bailey's Shopping Center) A two-screen theater showing first-run films.

Marquee Cinema Coralwood Mall (239-458-2543; 2301 Del Prado Blvd., Cape Coral 33909, at Coralwood Shopping Center) Ten screens for first-run films.

Regal Bell Tower 20 (239-590-9696; Daniels Pkwy. and U.S. 41, Fort Myers 33907) A modern megacomplex of theaters in the form of an airport hangar.

Dance

Dance Theatre Academy (239-275-3131; 2084 Beacon Manor Dr., Fort Myers 33907) Ballet, pointe, tap, jazz, and interpretative dance for adults and children.

Gulfshore Ballet (239-590-6191; www.gulfshoreballet.org; 2155 Andrea Ln., Ste. C 5–6, Fort Myers 33912) Ballet instruction.

The Spa at Sanibel Harbour (239-466-2153; Sanibel Harbour Resort, 17260 Harbour Pointe Dr., Fort Myers 33908) Salsa classes on Tuesday evenings, ballroom dancing of Thursdays.

Gardens
FRAGRANCE GARDEN OF LEE COUNTY
239-432-2034
www.leeparks.org
7330 Gladiolus Rd., Fort Myers 33908
In Lakes Regional Park
Open: 8–6 daily
Parking: $1 per hour or $5 per day

The garden was designed primarily for the visually and physically impaired, although the general public will also enjoy this one-of-a-kind attraction. For the visually impaired there are pungent herbs and fragrant plants such as frangipani and gardenias. Paved paths with vegetation planted at wheelchair height accommodate the physically challenged. A gazebo is built wide enough for easy wheelchair access.

Historic Homes & Sites
CHAPEL-BY-THE-SEA
239-472-1646
11580 Chapin Ln., P.O. Box 188, Captiva Island 33924

This quaint church is a popular spot for interdenominational Sunday services (during season), weddings, and seaside meditation. Many of the island's early pioneers were laid to rest in its cemetery.

✪ EDISON & FORD WINTER ESTATES
239-334-7419
www.efwefla.org
2350 McGregor Blvd., Fort Myers 33901
Open: Continuous tours daily 9–4; open until 5:30
Admission: $20 adults, $11 children ages 6–12; laboratory and museum tour only $11 adults, $4.50 children.

Nowhere in the U.S. will you find the homes of two such important historical figures sitting side by side. This site is so much more than just a couple of preserved houses—it's a slice of Floridiana, Americana, and Mr. Wizard, all rolled into 26 riverside acres. The 75-minute guided or audio self-guided tour begins across the street under the nation's largest banyan tree, a gift from tire mogul Harvey Firestone. The tree, 400 feet around, poses outside a museum that contains many of Edison's 1,093 inventions—including the phonograph, the movie camera, the lightbulb, children's furniture, and cement—as well as the 1907 prototype Model T Ford his friend and wintertime neighbor, Henry Ford, gave him. Edison's late-1880s home hides in a tangle of tropical flora with which Edison experimented. (Special garden and in-depth botanical tours are available.) Mina's Moonlight Garden, named for Edison's wife, is a serene highlight. Actually there are two homes, identically built and connected with an arcade. One contained the Edisons' living quarters, the other, guest quarters and the kitchen. His laboratory, full of dusty bottles and other ancient gizmos, sits across the street behind the museum. The Friendship Gate separates Edison's estate from Ford's. The Mangoes, as it was called, in honor of the fruit orchards the car manufacturer so loved, seems humble compared to its neighbor. Its furnishings are true to the era and the Fords' simple tastes. Often, actors portraying America's geniuses circulate around the grounds. In 2006, the estates reopened after a massive, three-year, $9 million overhaul, which included the debut of the Caretaker's House, the oldest building on the property, dating to the 1860s. Forthcoming improvements will include restoration of Fort Myers' first swimming pool, which is on the property, and a research garden restoration near the banyan tree.

FISHING SHACKS
Pine Island Sound at Captiva Rocks, east of North Captiva

The last artifacts of the region's early commercial fishing enterprises have braved weather and bureaucracy to strut the shallows along the Intracoastal Waterway. The shack at the mouth of Safety Harbor on North Captiva is the most noticeable. It once served as an ice-house. If you look east, you'll spot several others where fishermen and their families used to live. Privately owned and maintained as weekend fishing homes for local enthusiasts, most are listed in the National Register of Historic Places and serve as picturesque reminders of days gone by.

✪ KORESHAN STATE HISTORIC SITE
239-992-0311
www.floridastateparks.org/koreshan
P.O. Box 7, Estero 33928
Tamiami Trail, U.S. 41 and Corkscrew Rd
Open: 8 AM–sunset; narrated tours 10 AM Sat. and Sun.
Admission: $4 per vehicle with up to 8 passengers, $3 per single driver, $1 per cyclist, pedestrian, or extra passenger; tours $2 for adults, $1 for children

Contained within a state park, this site has restored the customs and ways of a turn-of-the-last-century religious cult that settled on the banks of the Estero River. Under the leadership of Cyrus Teed, whose Hebrew name was Koresh, members of Koreshan Unity were well versed in practical Christianity, speculative metaphysics, functional and aesthetic gardening, art, occupational training, and cellular cosmogony. The latter, their most unusual theory, held that the earth lined the inside of a hollow globe and looked down into the solar system. Teed and his followers envisioned an academic and natural utopia of 10,000 followers. They planted their settlement (home for only 250 at its peak) with exotic crops and vegetation. Before losing their momentum upon the death of their charismatic leader in 1908, the Koreshans built a theater, a communal mess hall, a store, and various workshops, all of which have been restored or reconstructed to tell their strange story. Archives are kept at the library of the Koreshan Unity Foundation across the road from the park (239-992-2184).

MOUND HOUSE

239-765-0865
289 Connecticut St., Fort Myers Beach 33931
Open: Dig site open 8–noon Tues.–Sat.

One of two of its kind in the nation (the other is at Historic Spanish Point in Sarasota), an archaeology exhibit of artifacts currently being excavated from a Calusa shell mound, dating back more than 2,000 years, will open at this historic site by fall 2008. In the meantime, visitors can watch excavations. Eventually, they will be able to descend stairs to an underground room and observe the mound's layers. Mound House, a 5,000-square-foot cultural museum and environmental center, was built in 1906 atop the 3-acre mound.

MOUND KEY STATE ARCHAEOLOGICAL SITE

239-992-0311
www.floridastateparks.org/moundkey
P.O. Box 7, Estero 33928
c/o Koreshan State Historic Site

The only way to reach this adjunct of the Koreshan site (see above), where Calusa Indians and Spanish missionaries have set up camp in eras past, is by boat. Many do it by canoe or kayak from Koreshan, Lovers Key State Park (launch only, no rentals), or Estero River Outfitters. A path weaves through the native shell mounds, one of which reaches 32 feet high, qualifying as the county's highest geologic elevation. The 133-acre island was formed from years of shellfish eating as the Calusa piled the discarded shells on a sandbar that grew into the seat of their kingdom. Farmers settled years later, and modern-day explorers can find remnants of the centuries' habitation. It is illegal to take any artifacts from the island, which is under excavation by archaeologists.

RANDELL RESEARCH CENTER

239-283-2062
www.flmnh.ufl.edu/rrc/
13810 Waterfront Dr., P.O. Box 608, Pineland 33945
On Pine Island
Open: Daily 10–4; guided tours Wed. 10 AM Jan.–Apr.
Admission: Suggested donation $7 adults, $4 children; Village of Pineland tour $57

Archaeologists from Gainesville's Florida Museum of Natural History meet here at the time-stilled village of Pineland to discover the lifestyles of the lost Calusa tribes. In 2005, the center finished its 3,700-foot Calusa Heritage Trail with modern interpretative signage that tells of Pineland's importance as a center of Calusa culture for more than 1,500 years. The short trail climbs to the top of an ancient shell mound. On certain days archaeologists are digging at the site. Volunteers are welcome, but call in advance. Randell also offers a land and sea tour that includes lunch at nearby historic Tarpon Lodge and a two-hour boat cruise to smaller islands in the Calusa kingdom. Calusa Ghost Tours (239-938-5342, www.calusaghosttours.com) takes you into the haunting past aboard a 14-seat canoe and two smaller vessels.

SANIBEL CEMETERY
Off the bike path on Middle Gulf Dr.; not accessible by car

No signs direct you to it. Just follow the path, and you'll come across a fenced plot with wooden headstones announcing the names of early settlers—a wonderful, quiet place to ponder times past.

SANIBEL LIGHTHOUSE
Southeast end of Periwinkle Way, Sanibel Island

Built in 1884, the lighthouse was the island's first permanent structure. Once vital to cattle transports from the mainland, it still functions as a beacon of warning and welcome. The lighthouse and Old Florida–style lightkeeper's cottage were renovated in 1991.

Kids' Stuff
BROADWAY PALM CHILDREN'S THEATRE
239-278-4422
www.broadwaypalm.com
Royal Palm Square, 1380 Colonial Blvd., Fort Myers 33907

Each year, Broadway Palm Dinner Theatre puts on three or four plays geared toward families and served up with kids'-fare lunch.

✪ IMAGINARIUM
239-337-3332
www.cityftmyers.com/imaginarium
2000 Cranford Ave., P.O. Box 2217, Fort Myers 33902
At Dr. Martin Luther King Jr. Blvd. and Cranford Ave.
Open: 10–5 Mon.–Sat., Sun. 12–5
Admission: $8 adults, $7 seniors, $5 for children ages 3–12

I have visited many of the new-wave interactive science museums that have hit Florida in the past decade, and I'm happy to say this is among my favorites. It is not overwhelmingly huge, like some, but it is colorfully attractive and varied in its approach to teaching about everything from Florida environment to the world of finance. Emphasis is on weather and water (it occupies a former city water plant). The Hurricane Experience will, as they like to say, "blow you away." You can feel a cloud, tape yourself on location broadcasting a tornado, and walk through a thunderstorm. Aquariums, a touch tank, a swan lagoon, and alligator feedings acquaint visitors with local water creatures. The animal lab exhibits dramatic critters such as tarantulas, a kinkajou, snakes, and a juvenile alligator. A new Sporty Science Exhibit opened in 2006 and allows visitors to try their hand at baseball and hockey. Other displays appeal to all ages with gadgets, toys, and computers; special 3-D movies and hands-on shows are part of the fun.

Museums
✪ BAILEY-MATTHEWS SHELL MUSEUM
239-395-2233, 888-679-6450
www.shellmuseum.org
3075 Sanibel-Captiva Rd., P.O. Box 1580, Sanibel Island 33957
Open: 10–5 daily
Admission: $7 ages 17 and up, $4 children ages 5–16, free for ages 4 and under

The only one of its kind in the U.S., this museum reinforces Sanibel's reputation as a top shell-collecting destination. It uses nature vignettes and artistically arranged displays to demonstrate the role of shells in ecology, history, art, economics, medicine, religion, and other fields. The centerpiece of the museum is a two-story globe surrounded by shells of the world. Outside is a memorial devoted to the late actor Raymond Burr, who helped establish the museum. The Children's Science Lab provides games and hands-on learning experiences in colorful reef-motif surroundings, but oddly with a touch tank you can't touch. The newest exhibit explores the role of shells in the lives of the Calusa Indians. The museum holds more than two million specimens in the showroom and catalogued upstairs, representing a third of the world's 150,000 species of living mollusks.

CAPE CORAL HISTORICAL MUSEUM
239-772-7037
www.capecoralhistoricalmuseum.org
544 Cultural Park Blvd., P.O. Box 150637, Cape Coral 33990
Open: 1–4 Wed., Thurs., Sun.
Closed: July and Aug.
Admission: $2 donation per adult

Exhibits include a new Cracker kitchen model to complement the existing Cracker house model, seashell and model boat collections, and a replicated burrowing owl nest. A mural depicting Cape Coral's old rose gardens attraction brightens up the spot. Outside, a blossoming garden continues the link between the town and roses.

LEE COUNTY BLACK HISTORY SOCIETY WILLIAMS ACADEMY MUSEUM
239-332-8778
www.lcbhs.ebmnet.com
1936 Henderson Ave., Fort Myers 33916
Open: 10–4 Tues.–Fri., Sat. by appointment
Admission: $5 adults, $2.50 for students up to age 18, free for children ages 5 and younger

Once part of a school for the African American population, this circa-1942, clapboard, tin-roofed building in Clemente Park houses artifacts and exhibits illuminating the local experience for persons of African descent. Displays include a permanent audio timeline titled "Chronology of the African American Presence in Lee County."

MUSEUM OF THE ISLANDS
239-283-1525
www.museumoftheislands.com
5728 Sesame Dr., Pine Island Center 33922; mail: P.O. Box 305, St. James City 33956.

ON PINE ISLAND
Open: Nov. 1–Apr. 30, Tues.–Sat. 11–3, Sun. 1-4; May 1–Oct. 31, Tues.–Thurs, Sat. 11–3
Admission: $2 adults, $1 children

Occupying the old Pine Island library at Phillips Park, the museum concentrates on the area's Calusa and fishing heritage. Continue on to the settlement of Pineland to see time standing still on intact Native American mounds.

SANIBEL HISTORICAL VILLAGE & MUSEUM
239-472-4648
950 Dunlop Rd., Sanibel Island 33957
Near City Hall
Open: Nov.–May, 10–4 Wed.–Sat.; June–mid-Aug., 10–1, Wed.–Sat.
Admission: $5 donation per adult requested

The village began with a historical Cracker-style abode, once the home of an island pioneer. The museum focuses on Sanibel's modern history of homesteading, citrus farming, steamboating, and tourism, with photos and artifacts. It recalls the Calusa era with a dugout canoe and other relics of the times. The island's original Bailey's General Store, circa 1927, was moved to the site in 1993 as a kickoff to establishing a pioneer village on the grounds. Since then a 1920s post office, a teahouse, and other vintage homes have been added. One houses a lens that outfitted the Sanibel Lighthouse in the 1960s.

SOUTHWEST FLORIDA MUSEUM OF HISTORY
239-332-5955
www.cityftmyers.com/museum
2300 Peck St., Fort Myers 33901
At Jackson St.
Open: 10–5 Tues.–Sat.
Admission: $9.50 adults, $8.50 seniors, $5 students, free for children under age 3; walking tours of downtown 10 AM Wed. and Sat., Jan.–Apr., $5, $3 for children

The displays in this museum—housed in a handsome Spanish-style railroad depot—take you back to the days of prehistoric mammals and ancient civilizations and up through the eras of the Calusa Indians, Spanish exploration, fish camps, cattle driving, gladiolus farming, and World War II training. Well-arranged scale and life-sized models, graphic depictions, videos, changing exhibits, and interactive historical games illuminate the past. Outdoors, tours examine a replica of a local early 1900s Cracker house and the world's last and longest Pullman private railcar, circa 1930. (Don't miss the Pullman tour; it's truly a highlight if you have a good guide.)

BARBARA SUMWALT HISTORICAL MUSEUM
239-283-1061
Useppa Island Club, Useppa Island 33922
Admission: $4 donation requested for visitors over age 18

The wee island of Useppa is stuffed to the gills with history, a fact that calls for a historical museum. This one is exceptionally well presented for such a small place. (It helps that wealth outmeasures square footage on the island.) Dioramas are interpreted via taped presentations that you hear from small tape recorders and headsets. They describe the island's Calusa history, its fishing and resort eras, and its role in training revolutionaries for the Cuban Bay of Pigs confrontation in 1960. Its newest exhibits deal with damage the island suffered in 2004's Hurricane Charley. Since the island is owned by a private club, visitors must be island guests or guests aboard the *Lady Chadwick* luncheon cruise to the island (see Captiva Cruises under "Boats & Boating: Sightseeing & Entertainment Cruises" in this chapter).

Music & Nightlife

Downtown Fort Myers is trying to metamorphose into a hot entertainment district, featuring jazz bars, bistros, nightclubs, and street festivals. As for the islands, Fort Myers Beach is definitely the most hopping. On Sanibel and Captiva you'll find a quieter brand of partying; nightlife there is focused on theater and more highbrow forms of music. Friday's *Gulf Coasting* supplement to the *News-Press* covers the region's entertainment scene.

Cape Coral

Jimbob's (239-574-8100; 1431 SE 16th Place, Cape Coral 33904) Live music on weekends.

La Venezia (239-945-0034; 4646 SE 11th Place, Cape Coral 33904) Dance every Wednesday from 7 to 10 PM.

Captiva Island

✪ **Crow's Nest Lounge** (239-472-5161; 'Tween Waters Inn, 15951 Captiva Rd., Captiva Island 33924) Live contemporary dance bands Tuesday through Sunday; entertaining crab races on Monday and Thursday. The islands' hottest spot.

Fort Myers

Fat Cats Drink Shack (239-226-9272; 1512 Hendry St., Fort Myers 33901) Casual and lighthearted with pool tables and occasional live music.

Fort Myers Community Concert Association (239-939-3236; P.O. Box 606, Fort Myers 33902) Highbrow musical entertainment—from brass ensembles to ballet—at the Barbara B. Mann Performing Arts Hall (see "Theater" below).

Jazz Alliance (239-939-2787; 10091 McGregor Blvd., Fort Myers 33919, at the Lee County Alliance for the Arts headquarters, www.artinlee.org) Sponsors a series of three springtime outdoor concerts featuring name artists, fine wine, and specialty foods.

Liquid Café (239-461-0444; 2236 First St., Fort Myers 33901, downtown) A sophisticated eatery with artsy entertainment, open-mike nights, and beer and wine.

The Loft @ Patio 33 (239-337-2846; www.patio33; 33 Patio de Leon, Fort Myers 33901, downtown) Live or DJ entertainment on the rooftop, weekends and Wednesdays.

Neo Lounge (239-878-5995; 1528 Hendry St., Fort Myers 33901) Live entertainment includes Friday Latin Night with happy hour specials 8 to 9 PM.

Southwest Florida Symphony (239-418-1500; www.swflso.org; 4560 Via Royale, Ste. 2, Fort Myers 33919) Performs classical and pops series November through May at the Barbara B. Mann Performing Arts Hall in Fort Myers, BIG ARTS on Sanibel Island, and local churches.

FORT MYERS BEACH

If you can't find nightlife in Fort Myers Beach, better check your eyes and ears.

The Beached Whale (239-463-5505; 1249 Estero Blvd., Fort Myers Beach, 33931 Party from the rooftop to live music nightly in the heart of Times Square.

The Bridge Waterfront Restaurant (239-765-0050; www.thebridgerestaurant.com; 708 Fisherman's Wharf, Fort Myers Beach 33931) A popular spot with boat-in and drive-in barflies, featuring lively dance music outdoors on the docks, including a reggae party every Sunday afternoon and evening.

Junkanoo (239-463-6130; www.junkanoo-anthonys.com, 3040 Estero Blvd., Fort Myers Beach 33931) You don't have to wait until dark to party in Fort Myers Beach. Here's a popular spot "where the party never ends," and young people headquarter their day at the beach with drinks, food, pool tables, water sports, volleyball, and music and dancing indoors and out.

Lani Kai Island Resort (239-463-3111; www.drfun.com/lani-kai; 1400 Estero Blvd., Fort Myers Beach 33931) *The* premier collegiate party spot on the beach, with live entertainment nightly and during the day on weekends, on the rooftop Aloha Deck or on the beach.

The Shanty (239-463-4343; www.snugharborrestaurant.com; 1131 First St., Fort Myers Beach 33931, at Snug Harbor Waterfront Restaurant) Upstairs overlooking the bay, with live music and a typical Fort Myers Beach crowd—which is to say "rowdy."

PINE ISLAND

Bert's Bar & Grill (239-282-3232; www.bertsbar.com; 4271 Pine Island Rd., Matlacha 33993) Florida funk at its finest, with a salty attitude, good munchies, waterfront stance, and live music during season (see Web site for schedule).

Starboard Lounge and Grill (239-282-1131; 3421 Stringfellow Rd., St. James City 33956) Also known as the Ragged Ass Saloon, its Banana Tree Stage hosts concerts under the stars every Friday night, usually showcasing local talent.

Tarpon Lodge (239-283-3999; www.tarponlodge.com; 13771 Waterfront Dr., Pineland 33945) Midweek music series from February into early April features live local entertainers from 6 to 9:30 PM Tuesday through Thursday. No cover charge.

SANIBEL ISLAND

BIG ARTS (239-395-0900; www.bigarts.org; 900 Dunlop Rd., Sanibel Island 33957) Hosts classical musical quartets and trios and orchestras November through April.

Jacaranda (239-472-1771; www.sanibelsteakhouse.org/jacaranda; 1223 Periwinkle Way, Sanibel Island 33957) Top-40 hits, reggae, and island music performed live.

Specialty Libraries

For regional reference information by phone, call 239-479-INFO.

Sanibel Public Library (239-472-2483; www.sanlib.org; 770 Dunlop Rd., Sanibel Island 33957) Contains an identification collection of seashells, wireless Internet access, and Internet access computers by reservation.

Florida Repertory Theatre performs professional productions in a historic movie theater.

Talking Books Library (239-995-2665; 13240 N. Cleveland Ave., North Fort Myers 33903) This library for the visually and physically impaired has books on tapes or records.

Theater

The Arcade Theatre/Florida Repertory Theatre (239-332-4488, 877-787-8053; www .floridarep.org; 2267 First St., P.O. Drawer 2483, Fort Myers 33902, downtown) The glory of the 1920s, this Victorian playhouse has been restored and advanced to the 21st century. Home to an energetic professional company that brings new life to old boards.

✪ **Barbara B. Mann Performing Arts Hall** (239-481-4849; www.bbmannpah.com; Edison College, 8099 College Pkwy. SW, Fort Myers 33919) Hosts major Broadway shows, musical performers, and dance troupes. Broadway season runs November to late April.

Broadway Palm Dinner Theatre (239-278-4422; www.broadwaypalm.com; 1380 Colonial Blvd., Fort Myers 33907, at Royal Palm Square) Lunch and dinner musical performances, starring professional actors, in a made-over grocery store that seats and serves 448. Each year a few of the shows, such as *Charlotte's Web*, are geared toward families. Its Off-Broadway Palm Theatre presents cabaret-style shows in an adjacent, intimate 90-seat playhouse. Lunch and dinner shows or shows only. Both theaters are closed Monday year-round and Tuesday from May through October.

Claiborne & Ned Foulds Theater (239-936-3239; www.artinlee.org; 10091 McGregor Blvd., Fort Myers 33919, at Lee County Alliance for the Arts headquarters) An indoor and outdoor stage for recitals, concerts, and workshops. Theatre Conspiracy, a cutting-edge professional troupe that occasionally stages family shows, performs part of its season here.

Cultural Park Theatre Company (239-772-5862; www.culturalparktheatre.org; 528 Cultural Park Blvd., Cape Coral 33990) A 186-seat theater that hosts community theater.

Performances run from mid-September through mid-May. Also acting classes for kids and adults.

Germain Arena (239-948-7825; www.germainarena.com; 11000 Everblades Pkwy., Estero 33928) Home of the Everblades hockey team, this venue also hosts touring entertainers.

Schoolhouse Theater (239-472-6862; www.theschoolhousetheater.com; 2200 Periwinkle Way, Sanibel Island 33957) Relocated from its former historic one-room schoolhouse setting into a newer facility across the street (the original schoolhouse was moved to the Sanibel Historical Village), it now represents a professional troupe that concentrates on comedies, musicals, and musical revues.

Visual Art Centers & Resources

Flocks of wildlife art and other eclectic galleries make a name for Sanibel Island in cultural circles, while smaller communities support their own offbeat galleries and art associations. On Pine Island, national artists come to hide out and nourish their souls, sparking a growing art colony of sorts that's centered in Matlacha. The following entries introduce you to opportunities for experiencing art as either a viewer or a practicing artist. A listing of commercial galleries is included in the "Shopping" section.

Alliance for the Arts (239-939-2787; www.artinlee.org; 10091 McGregor Blvd., Fort Myers 33919) This not-for-profit conducts classes and workshops and operates a public gallery, members' gallery, 175-seat indoor theater, and outdoor stage. It is home base for the Frizzell Gallery of Fine Art and most local arts and cultural groups.

Barbara B. Mann Performing Arts Hall creates drama even in its lobby spaces.

BIG ARTS (239-395-0900; www.bigarts.org; 900 Dunlop Rd., Sanibel Island 33957) Home of Barrier Island Group for the Arts, an energetic multidisciplinary organization that includes Phillips Gallery. Art shows and classes are scheduled regularly at the facility.

Cape Coral Arts Studio Rubicond Park (239-574-0802; 4533 Coronado Pkwy., Cape Coral 33904) Classes, exhibitions, and sales.

Fort Myers Beach Art Association (239-463-3909; www.fortmyersbeachart.com; Donora St. and Shell Mound Blvd., P.O. Box 2359, Fort Myers Beach 33932) Member and other exhibits; workshops and classes.

Bob Rauschenberg Gallery (239-489-9313, Edison College, 8099 College Pkwy. SW, Fort Myers 33919) Exhibits works of nationally and internationally renowned artists.

RECREATION

Shelling, island-hopping, fishing, sailboarding, and warming chilled bones on hospitable beaches: These are a few of the favorite things to do in the Fort Myers–Sanibel area.

Beaches

The region's 50 miles of local beaches are known for their natural state and abundance of shells. *Family Fun* magazine recently rated this stretch of beach the "#1 beach in the southeast U.S." In recent years, red algae drift periodically washes up on the beaches. It is not pretty and is often smelly, but it is no risk to your health. Red tide, however, is a different problem, causing dead fish to wash up on the beach from time to time and people to have allergic reactions to the algal blooms.

Most beaches charge for parking. Sanibel Island beach stickers can be purchased from the police department at City Hall and allow you to park for free at most accesses. Along the Gulf Drives you'll see signs at beach accesses designating resident sticker–only parking. Cyclists and walk-ins, however, can take advantage of these accesses without stickers.

Bonita Beach
BAREFOOT BEACH PRESERVE COUNTY PARK
239-591-8596
www.colliergov.net
3300 Santa Barbara Blvd., Naples 34116
Entrance at Hickory Blvd. and Bonita Beach Rd., south end of Little Hickory Island
Facilities: Restrooms, showers, nature learning center, aquatic butterfly garden, snack bar
Parking: $6 per day

Actually within neighboring Collier County but accessible from Bonita Beach, the 342 acres in this preserve contain a coastal hammock and 8,200 feet of beach and low dunes. Sea grapes, cabbage palms, and other native vegetation landscape the grounds. Gopher tortoises often lumber across the road and footpaths. Rangers give nature walks and shell talks at the chikee learning center.

✪ BONITA BEACH PARK
239-229-0632
www.leeparks.org

27954 Hickory Blvd., south end of Little Hickory Island
Facilities: Picnic table shelters, restrooms, lifeguard, water-sports and beach rentals, volleyball, nearby restaurants
Parking: $1 per hour; $5 per day

The only true public park on Bonita Beach, it becomes lively during the high season and on weekends. Water sports and volleyball, plus a hamburger and bar joint, create a youthful spirit. Vegetation is sparse; there's nothing hidden about this beach. Parking fills up early in season and on weekends year-round. About 10 other accesses with free but limited parking line Hickory Boulevard to the north.

Cape Coral
CAPE CORAL YACHT CLUB COMMUNITY PARK
239-574-0806
www.capecoral.net/citydept/parks/pks_yachtclub.cfm
5819 Driftwood Pkwy., Cape Coral 33904
Facilities: Restrooms, showers, picnic shelters, swimming pool, marina, shuffleboard, outdoor racquetball courts, fishing pier, bait shop, food concession
Open: Swimming pool (239-542-3903) 10–5 daily
Admission: Free. Pool admission $4.50 ages 18 and up, $3.50 for ages 10–17, and $2.50 for ages 9 and younger

The manmade beach on the Caloosahatchee River is part of a large park that sponsors recreational and other programs and exudes a true sense of community. The groomed beach is better for sunning than swimming, for which the pool fills the void. The first

Sanibel Island's beaches are known not only for their seashells but also for their birding opportunities.

Wednesday of every month, the park hosts Sunset Celebration on the Pier with live music and entertainment, food, and arts and crafts.

Captiva Island
CAPTIVA BEACH
North end Captiva Rd., Captiva Island
Facilities: Portable restrooms
Open: 6 AM–11 PM
Parking: $2 per hour

Only early arrivals get the parking spots for this prime spread of deep, shelly sand, newly widened in 2005. It's a good place to watch a sunset.

Fort Myers
LAKES REGIONAL PARK
239-839-8656, 239-267-1905 for train
www.leeparks.org
7330 Gladiolus Dr., Fort Myers 33908
Facilities: Picnic areas, restrooms, showers; playgrounds, climbing wall, model railroad ride, fitness trail, bike path, water-sports rentals, snack concession
Parking: $1 per hour or $5 per day.

This land of freshwater lakes features a small sand beach with a roped-off swimming area. Newly renovated since Hurricane Charley with all native vegetation, this is a great place for the family to spend the day. The 279-acre park offers a new interactive water playground, canoeing, paddleboating, fishing, nature and bike trails, an exercise course, a miniature

A sculpture at Lakes Park captures childhood abandon.

train ride (admission), kayaking, biking, and terrific playground facilities. The second and fourth Saturday of each month, the park hosts an introduction to fishing for kids ages 7 to 12. Nature walks take place the first Saturday of the month.

Fort Myers Beach
BOWDITCH POINT REGIONAL PRE-SERVE
239-432-2127
www.leeparks.org
50 Estero Blvd., Fort Myers Beach 33931
At the north end of the island
Facilities: Picnic shelters, restrooms, showers, nature trails
Parking: $1 per hour or $5 per day

This pretty, green, 17-acre park fronts Estero Bay and the gulf. It's a nice, quiet beach, underutilized and unspoiled, and a favorite of boat-ins.

LOVERS KEY STATE PARK
239-463-4588
www.floridastateparks.org/loverskey
8700 Estero Blvd., Fort Myers Beach 33931
Route 865 between Fort Myers Beach and Bonita Beach
Facilities: Picnic area, restrooms, showers, boat ramps, fishing, food concession, beach shop
Parking: $5 per vehicle with up to 8 passengers, $3 for single passengers, $1 for extra passengers, bicyclists, and pedestrians

Ride a truck-pulled tram through the natural mangrove environment to South Beach or walk to secluded North Beach. The area between Estero and Little Hickory Island consists of natural island habitat populated by birds, dolphins, and crabs. On the barrier island of Lovers Key, Australian pines provide shaded picnicking along a narrow, natural stretch of sand that is due for renourishing in coming years. South of the park entrance, Dog Beach is the county's only designated off-leash dog beach. (Most beaches on Sanibel Island allow pets on leash.) A gazebo provides a picnic shelter and a popular wedding venue. Away from the beach, shaded picnic grounds line estuarine inlets; there is a launch for canoes and kayaks, and a path accommodates hikers and cyclists. In 2005 and 2006, Lovers Key was named the most visited and top income-generating Florida state park.

✪ LYNN HALL MEMORIAL PARK
239-463-1116
www.leeparks.org
950 Estero Blvd., Fort Myers Beach.
In the Times Square vicinity
Facilities: Picnic areas, grills, restrooms, showers, playground, fishing pier, water-sports rentals; nearby restaurants, bars, and shops.
Parking: In lot for $1 per hour (Warning: Park only in designated areas, or your car will be towed at great expense.)

Part of the pedestrian Times Square plaza, this park attracts college students in the spring and families the rest of the year. A rocking, rollicking place, it appeals to beach barhoppers, crowd watchers, and those interested in water sports. It features volleyball, a fishing pier, beachwear stores, restaurants, ice cream shops, beachside drinks, parties, parasailing, jet skiing. For thinner crowds, hit public accesses, marked with banners, on the south end of Estero Boulevard.

SANIBEL ISLAND
✪ BOWMAN'S BEACH
Bowman's Beach Rd. off Sanibel-Captiva Rd., Sanibel Island
Facilities: Picnic area, restrooms, fitness trail
Parking: $2 per hour

Bowman's is Sanibel's most natural beach. Long, coved, and edged by an Australian pine forest, it's on an island all its own. It can be reached by footbridges from the parking lot (a rather long walk, so go lightly on the beach paraphernalia). Shells are plentiful here—in some places a foot or more deep along the high-tide mark.

LIGHTHOUSE PARK BEACH

239-472-6477
South end of Periwinkle Way, Sanibel Island
Facilities: Picnic area, restrooms, nature trail, fishing pier, mobile food concession in season
Parking: $2 per hour

Skirting Sanibel Island's historic lighthouse is an arc of natural beach fronting both the gulf and San Carlos Bay. One of Sanibel's most populated beaches, it features a nature trail and a popular fishing pier. Strong currents forbid swimming off the point. The wide beach gives way to sea oats, sea grapes, and Australian pine edging. I like the neighborhood around it, because it is historic and more laid-back than other parts of the island.

SANIBEL CAUSEWAY BEACH

Sanibel Causeway Rd.
Facilities: Picnic area, restrooms

Historically, windsurfers and fishermen favor this packed-sand roadside beach. In 2007, the bridge was reconstructed, which cut down on some of the recreational use. Beach lovers in RVs and campers often pull up here to picnic and spend the day in the sun.

TARPON BEACH

239-472-6477
Middle Gulf Dr. at Tarpon Bay Rd., Sanibel Island
Facilities: Restrooms, mobile food concession in season
Parking: $2 per hour

Another popular beach, this one is characterized by sugar sand and a nice spread of shells. It's a bit of a hike from the parking lot to the beach, and the area gets congested on busy days. RVs can park here. Great for swimming.

Sanibel's Lighthouse Beach features a historic structure, a fishing pier, and beaches on two waterfronts.

On Florida's gulf coast, where surfing waves are rare, skimboarding appeals to young beachgoers.

TURNER BEACH

239-472-6477
South end Captiva Rd., Captiva Island
Facilities: Restrooms, foot shower, nearby restaurants, water sports, and store
Parking: $2 per hour

A pretty beach with wide, powdery sand, Turner tends to get crowded, and parking is limited. The entrance is on a blind curve, which can be dangerous. More bad news: Riptides coming through the pass make this taboo for swimming. Park your beach towel far north or south of the pass for calmer, swimmable waters. We like to come here in the evening to watch the sunset and walk the beach. Surfers like the waters to the north in certain weather. It's also a hot spot for fishermen, who line bayside shores and the bridge between Sanibel and Captiva.

Upper Islands
✪ CAYO COSTA STATE PARK

941-964-0375
www.floridastateparks.org/cayocosta
La Costa Island, accessible only by boat
Facilities: Picnic ground, restrooms, showers, nature trails, camping, cabins
Admission: $1 per person

The Lee County coast is blessed with some true getaway beaches, untamed by connection to the mainland. On these, one can actually realize that romantic fantasy common to beach connoisseurs: sands all your own. Cayo Costa stretches for 9 miles and is most secluded at its southern extremes. A larger population of beachgoers congregates at the north end, where docks, a picnic and camping ground, and primitive cabins attract those who seek creature comforts with their sun and sand. A tram transports boaters from docking on the bay side to facilities on the beach side. Or you can walk the short distance, on a path that is part of a 5-1/2-mile trail system. Shelling is superb in these parts, particularly at Johnson Shoals, which surfaces at the island's north end during low tide.

NORTH CAPTIVA
Across Redfish Pass from South Seas Resort and Captiva Island; accessible only by boat

Like Cayo Costa, here's a place to go for private beaching. Though it's narrow at the south end, the sand is like gold dust. You'll find no facilities unless you venture across the island to the bay, where restaurants and civilization inhabit the north end. The hurricane of 2004 split a section off the island's south end to form a small, separate island.

Bicycling
The bikeways of the Fort Myers–Sanibel region come in two varieties. Bicycle paths, the most common, are separated from traffic by distance and, ideally, a vegetation buffer. Bicycle lanes are a designated part of the roadway. Cyclists also take to the road in rural areas, where no bikeways exist but traffic is light. By law they must abide by the same rules as motor vehicles. Children under age 16 are required to wear helmets.

BEST BIKING
More than two miles of bike trails run through **Lakes Park**, where bike rentals are also available (239-332-2453). Long stretches of bike path in **Fort Myers** follow **Daniels Parkway**, **Metro Parkway**, **Colonial Boulevard**, and **Summerlin Road**. The **Summerlin path** leads to the Sanibel causeway (cyclists cross for $1), to connect with island paths. **McGregor Boulevard**'s sidewalk provides another popular and scenic circuit. Design is under way for **Ten Mile Linear Park**, which will follow Ten Mile Canal from downtown Fort Myers to Estero. Far-reaching plans could eventually hook up the system with the West Coast Greenway extending from Tampa to Naples. More than 5 miles of bike paths also wind through **Lovers Key State Park**, and a ranger leads guided bike tours; call 239-463-4588 for a schedule.

Many of **Cape Coral**'s city streets designate bike lanes.

✪ **Sanibel**'s 23-mile path covers most of the island and occasionally leaves the roadside to plunge you into serene backwoods scenery. Segments along busy Periwinkle Way have recently been widened and moved away from roadside. The Sanibel Historical Society (239-472-4648) distributes brochures at Sanibel Historical Village and Museum (950 Dunlop Road) on Pedaling Periwinkle Way and exploring, by bike or foot, Old Sanibel around the lighthouse at the east end. Cyclists also pedal 4-mile, paved Wildlife Drive through J. N. "Ding" Darling National Wildlife Refuge and its unpaved but hard-packed Indigo Trail.

The 17-mile **Pine Island** bike path, 20 years in the making, was completed in 2007 to stretch along Stringfellow Road from St. James City to Bokeelia.

BMX bikers can use the **Sanctuary Skate Park** (see "Kids' Stuff," below) on Monday evenings. Cape Coral also has a dedicated BMX park.

RENTAL/SALES

Billy's Rentals (239-472-5248; www.billysrentals.com; 1470 Periwinkle Way, Sanibel Island 33957) Bicycles, surrey bikes, and equipment for family biking. Also scooters and Segway tours. Rentals by the hour, day, or week.

Fun Rentals (239-463-8844; 1901 Estero Blvd., Fort Myers Beach 33931) Rentals start at $12 for two hours. Per-day to per-week rates are available.

Nature Recreation Management (239-314-0110; www.naturerecreationmanagement .com; 8720 Estero Blvd., Fort Myers Beach 33931) rents bikes at Lovers Key State Park.

YOLO Watersports (239-472-1296 or 866-YOLO-JIMS; www.yolo-jims.com; 11534 Andy Rosse Ln., Captiva Island 33924) Rentals by the half day, full day, and 24 hours. Also motor scooters, golf carts, and water-sports equipment.

Boats & Boating

With its procession of unbridged islands and wide bay, the region begs for outdoor types to explore its waters. Island-hopping constitutes a favorite pastime of adventurers.

Canoeing & Kayaking

In addition to those outlets listed below, many resorts and parks rent canoes and kayaks.

Adventures in Paradise (239-472-8443, 239-437-1660; www.adventureinparadiseinc .com; 14341 Port Comfort Rd., Fort Myers 33908, at Port Sanibel Marina, east of Sanibel toll booth) Naturalist- or self-guided tours through a marked mangrove trail. Rentals available. Free pickup from hotels and condos on Sanibel.

Cape Coral Yacht Club is a recreational hub with everything from a marina and fishing pier to a swimming pool and racquetball courts.

Captiva Kayaks & Wildside Adventures (239-395-2925 or 877-395-2925; www.captiva
kayaks.com; McCarthy's Marina, 11401 Andy Rosse Ln., Captiva Island 33924) Sea-kayaking
tours for beginning to experienced paddlers focus on natural history and sea life. Kayak
and canoe rentals are available.

Estero River Outfitters (239-992-4050; www.esteroriveroutfitters.com; 20991 S.
Tamiami Trail, Estero 33928, opposite Koreshan Historic Site) Rents and sells quality
kayaks and canoes for a 4-mile adventure down the natural Estero River to Estero Bay.
Guided tours are available.

GAEA Guides (239-694-5513, 866-256-6388; www.gaeaguides.com; mail only: 340
Kingston Dr. W., Fort Myers 33905) Guides kayaking tours at Lovers Key State Park, Estero
Bay, and up the Caloosahatchee River for birding. Also teaches kayak clinics on the Orange
River and conducts archaeological tours for Randell Research Center from Pine Island.

✪ **Great Calusa Blueway** (239-461-7400; www.thegreatcalusablueway.com) This paddling trail along the island Intracoastal Waters extends more than 100 miles, from Cayo
Costa to Bonita Springs and up the Caloosahatchee River. Using GPS technology, it takes
paddlers to Mound Key, Lovers Key State Park, Bunche Beach, and other dynamic birding,
archaeological, and beaching destinations. You can view maps or request a free map at the
site or by calling phone number listed above.

Gulf Coast Kayak (239-283-1125; www.gulfcoastkayak.com; 4530 Pine Island Rd.,
Matlacha 33993, on Pine Island) Morning nature and sunset trips in ✪ **Matlacha Aquatic
Preserve** and other local natural areas; full moon and nature ventures (Thanksgiving
through St. Patrick's Day only). All guides are naturalists and kayak instructors. Rentals
available for self-guided tours.

Lakes Park (239-839-8656; www.leeparks.org; 7330 Gladiolus Dr., Fort Myers 33908)
Kayak rentals for paddling on a freshwater lake.

Captiva Cruises' Lady Chadwick *anchors at Useppa Island.*

✪ **Manatee Park** (239-432-2038, 239-694-3537; 10901 Route 80, Fort Myers 33905) Kayak among the manatees with a double kayak rental (November through March only).

Nature Recreation Management (239-314-0110; www.naturerecreationmanagement .com; 8720 Estero Blvd., Fort Myers Beach 33931) Rents canoes and kayaks at Lovers Key State Park.

Tarpon Bay Explorers (239-472-8900; www.tarponbayexplorers.com; 900 Tarpon Bay Rd., Sanibel Island 33957) Rents canoes and kayaks for use in ✪ **Tarpon Bay** and on the "Ding" Darling refuge's Commodore Creek Canoe Trail. Also guided canoe/kayak tours. *Canoe & Kayak* magazine has rated Tarpon Bay among the top ten places to paddle in the U.S.

Tropic Star Cruises (239-283-0015; www.tropicstarcruises.com; 16499 Porto Bello St., Bokeelia 33922, on Pine Island) Rent single and double kayaks for half- and full-day trips from Bokeelia and Cayo Costa.

DINING CRUISES

Big M Casino (239-765-7529, 888-373-3521; www.bigmcasino.com; Moss Marine, 450 Harbor Ct., Fort Myers Beach 33931) Gambling cruise with live entertainment and buffet and à la carte dining.

J. C. Cruises (239-334-7474; modernsurf.com/jccruises; Fort Myers Yacht Basin, P.O. Box 1688, Fort Myers 33902, downtown) Lunch, dinner, Sunday brunch, and sightseeing cruises up the Caloosahatchee River aboard the *Capt. J.P.,* a three-deck paddle wheeler.

Sanibel Harbour Princess (239-466-2128; www.Sanibel-resort.com/Dining/Princess _Harbour_Dining_Cuisine.asp 17260 Harbour Pointe Dr., Fort Myers 33908, at Sanibel Harbour Resort, off Summerlin Rd., before Sanibel Island causeway) Sunset dinner buffet and Sunday brunch cruises aboard a sleek, elegant luxury yacht.

PERSONAL WATERCRAFT RENTALS/TOURS

Holiday Water Sports (239-765-4386; www.watersportsrentals.net; Pink Shell Beach Resort, 250 Estero Blvd. Fort Myers Beach 33931; and 239-463-6778, Best Western Beach Resort, 684 Estero Blvd., Fort Myers Beach 33931) Waverunner rentals and dolphin-spotting tours.

POWERBOAT RENTALS

Adventures in Paradise (239-472-8443, 239-437-1660; www.adventureinparadiseinc .com; 14341 Port Comfort Rd., Fort Myers 33908, at Port Sanibel Marina, east of Sanibel toll booth) Rent Grady White bow riders and center consoles or deck boats by half day, day, and week.

Bluewater Vacations (239-995-0585; www.bluewatervacations.com; 3444 Marinatown Ln., N., Fort Myers 33903) Rent 37- to 41-foot air-conditioned houseboats for one- to seven-day cruises out of Marinatown. Full galley and fishing gear included.

The Boat House (239-472-2531; Sanibel Marina, 634 N. Yachtsman Dr., Sanibel Island 33957) Powerboats for trips into intracoastal waters only.

Fish-Tale Marina (239-463-3600; www.fishtalemarinagroup.cc; 7225 Estero Blvd., Fort Myers Beach 33931) Rents Grady Whites, pontoons, and skiffs.

Four Winds Marina (239-283-0250; www.fourwindsmarina.com; 16501 Stringfellow Rd., Bokeelia 33922, on Pine Island) Rent 20- to 22-foot fishing and deck boats.

Jensen's Marina (239-472-5800; www.gocaptiva.com; 15107 Captiva Dr., Captiva Island 33924) A colorful, locals' corner where fishermen hang out to tell lies. Rent a skiff, center console, or pontoon boat for half- or full-day rates. Water taxi transportation to the upper islands is also available.

Southwest Florida Yachts (239-656-1339, 800-262-SWFY; www.swfyachts.com, www .flsailandcruiseschool.com; 3444 Marinatown Ln., Ste. 19, North Fort Myers 33903) Offers power-yachting lessons and rentals in the 32- to 42-foot range.

PUBLIC BOAT RAMPS

Bokeelia Boat Ramp (239-283-4110; 7290 Barrancas Ave., Bokeelia 33922)

Cape Coral Yacht Club (239-574-0815; 5819 Driftwood Pkwy., Cape Coral 33904) Two free public ramps on the Caloosahatchee River, with bait shop, marina, and recreational facilities.

Lovers Key State Park (239-463-4588; www.floridastateparks.org/loverskey; 8700 Estero Blvd., Fort Myers Beach 33931, at Route 865 between Fort Myers Beach and Bonita Beach) Access to Estero Bay and the gulf, with picnicking facilities.

Matlacha Park (239-283-4110; 4577 Pine Island Rd. NW, Matlacha 33993, on Pine Island) Playground and fishing pier.

Punta Rassa (18500 McGregor Blvd., Fort Myers 33908, at Summerlin Rd., before the Sanibel causeway) Picnic facilities and restrooms.

Sanibel (Causeway Rd.) Two ramps at the west end of the Sanibel causeway.

SAILBOAT CHARTERS

New Moon (239-395-1782 or 888-472-7245; www.newmoonsailing.com; 'Tween Waters Inn Marina, 15951 Captiva Dr., P.O. Box 352, Captiva Island 33924) Up to six passengers aboard a 40-foot sloop. Sailing lessons for kids and adults, three-hour cruises, and extended custom sails.

SAILBOAT RENTALS & INSTRUCTION

✪ **Offshore Sailing School** (239-454-1700, 800-221-4326; www.offshore-sailing.com; 16731 McGregor Blvd., Fort Myers 33908, at South Seas Island Resort Marina on Captiva Island and Pink Shell Beach Resort on Fort Myers Beach) Weeklong and three-day certification (US SAILING) instruction offered, from beginning women's-only and mixed sailing courses to family learning vacations, advanced racing, and coastal navigation; operated by an Olympic and America's Cup veteran. Course instructors are knowledgeable, experienced, and easygoing ("no yelling" is the rule). Accommodation packages with resorts available.

Southwest Florida Yachts/✪ Florida Sailing & Cruising School (239-656-1339, 800-262-SWFY; www.flsailandcruiseschool.com; 3444 Marinatown Ln. NW, Ste. 19, North Fort Myers 33903) American Sailing Association (ASA) certification courses and bareboat charters provide excellent adventures into Charlotte Harbor for live-aboard experiences. Also powerboat courses.

SIGHTSEEING & ENTERTAINMENT CRUISES
Look under "Wildlife Tours & Charters" for nature excursions

✪ **Captiva Cruises** (239-472-5300; www.captivacruises.com; P.O. Box 580, Captiva Island 33924, at McCarthy's Marina) A complete menu of upper island sightseeing, beach, and luncheon trips is offered aboard the finely fitted 150-passenger *Lady Chadwick* and a 48-passenger pontoon, and guides share history and lore along the way. For a nonguest, these cruises are the only way to see private Useppa Island, where you can enjoy lunch at the Collier Inn restaurant.

J. C. Cruises (239-334-7474, 239-334-2743; www.modernsurf.com/jccruises; P.O. Box 1688, Fort Myers 33902, at Fort Myers Yacht Basin) Sightseeing jungle/manatee cruises and dinner-boat tours.

Nature Recreation Management (239-314-0110; www.naturerecreationmanagement .com; 8720 Estero Blvd., Fort Myers Beach 33931) Conducts one-hour ecological, shelling, and sunset cruises that depart from Lovers Key State Park.

Stars & Stripes (239-472-2531; www.irelandyachtsales.com; Sanibel Marina, 634 N. Yachtsman Dr., Sanibel Island 33957) Ninety-minute sightseeing and wildlife tours depart three times daily, plus one sunset/cocktail cruise with complimentary beverages.

Tropic Star Cruises (239-283-0015; www.tropicstarcruises.com; 16499 Porto Bello St., Bokeelia 33922, on Pine Island at Knight's Landing) Full-day nature and Boca Grande cruises and ferry service to Cayo Costa (ferry/kayak package available). Plus a land-sea Calusa Heritage Trail & Mound Tour at Randell Center.

Fishing
Snook and tarpon are the prized catch of local anglers. Snook, which is a game fish and can't be sold commercially, is valued for its sweet taste.

Redfish is another sought-after food fish. More common catches in back bays and waters close to shore include mangrove snapper, spotted sea trout, shark, sheepshead, pompano, and ladyfish. Deeper waters offshore yield grouper, red snapper, amberjack, mackerel, and dolphinfish. Most fish are released in these days of environmental consciousness. Check local regulations for season, size, and catch restrictions.

Nonresidents age 16 and older must obtain a license unless fishing from a vessel or pier covered by its own license. Inexpensive, temporary nonresident licenses are available at county tax collectors' offices and most Kmarts, marinas, and bait shops.

DEEP-SEA PARTY BOATS
Getaway Deep Sea Fishing (239-466-3600 or 800-641-3088; www.getawaymarina.com; Getaway Marina, 18400 San Carlos Blvd., Fort Myers Beach 33931) All-day or half-day excursions.

FISHING CHARTERS/OUTFITTERS
Competent fishing guides work out of the region's major marinas. If it's your first time fishing these waters, I recommend hiring someone with local knowledge.

Captain Mike Fuery (239-466-3649; www.sanibel-online.com/fuery; P.O. Box 1302, Captiva Island 33924) Located at 'Tween Waters Inn Marina, he has a good reputation for finding fish.

Captain Pat Hagle Charters (239-283-5991; P.O. Box 245, Pineland 33945) Fish excursions into Pine Island Sound; also nature, history, shelling, beachcombing, and water-taxi cruises.

Sanibel Marina (239-472-2723; www.sanibelmarina.com; 634 N. Yachtsman Dr., Sanibel Island 33957) Several experienced fishing guides operate out of the marina. Captain Dave Case (home phone 239-472-2798) has been at it a long time.

SoulMate Charters (239-851-1242; www.soulmatecharters.com; 17544 Lebanon Rd., Fort Myers 33967) Captain Rob Modys takes you fishing or shelling from Punta Rassa and Port Sanibel Marina, east of the Sanibel Causeway.

FISHING PIERS

Plans are to adapt part of the old causeway bridge to Sanibel Island as a fishing pier. In the meantime, the following are available.

Cape Coral Yacht Club (239-574-0815; 5819 Driftwood Pkwy., Cape Coral 33904) The 620-foot lit fishing pier is part of a boating/recreational complex, which includes a bait and tackle shop.

Centennial Park (Edwards Dr. near Yacht Basin, downtown Fort Myers) Complete park with playgrounds and other facilities.

✪ **Fort Myers Beach Pier** (1000 Estero Blvd., Fort Myers Beach 33931, at Lynn Hall Memorial Park, www.leeparks.org, at Times Square) The concrete T-pier with wooden

Surf fishing combines two of the coast's greatest outdoor pleasures.

Arrive early for a prime spot on Sanibel's popular Lighthouse Beach pier.

railings offers lots of casting room and hungry pelicans. It holds a tin-roofed bait shop, which also rents rods.

⭐ **Manatee Park** (239-432-2038, 239-694-3537; www.leeparks.org; 10901 Route 80, Fort Myers 33905) A great place for visitors to learn more about the endangered West Indian manatee that is native to the region. On the Orange River.

Matlacha Park (Matlacha, Pine Island) Playground and boat ramps.

Sanibel Lighthouse Park Beach (Southeast end of Periwinkle Way, Sanibel Island) A T-dock into San Carlos Bay.

Golf
Home of such golfing greats as Patty Berg and Nolan Henke, the region keeps pace with the growing popularity of golf.

PUBLIC GOLF COURSES
Alden Pines (239-283-2179; 14261 Clubhouse Dr., Bokeelia 33922; on Pine Island) A semiprivate, 18-hole, par 71 course, with affordable rates year-round. Snack bar.

Bay Oaks Disc Golf (239-765-4222; www.leeparks.org; Bay Oaks Recreation Center, 2731 Oak St., Fort Myers Beach 33931) A new twist on golf: an 18-"hole" course you play with Frisbees.

Beachview Golf & Tennis Club (239-472-2626; www.beachviewgolfclub.com, 1100 Parview Dr., Sanibel Island 33957) Public 18-hole, par 71 course with steakhouse grill, pro shop, rentals, and lessons.

Dunes Golf & Tennis Club (239-472-2535; www.dunesgolfsanibel.com; 949 Sandcastle Rd., Sanibel Island 33957) Semiprivate 18-hole, par 70 course. Restaurant and bar. Lush, Audubon-preserve links. High rates, especially in season.

Eastwood Country Club (239-275-4848; www.cityftmyers.com/attractions/golf/eastwood .htm; 4600 Bruce Heard Ln., Fort Myers 33994) One of the region's favorites; 18 holes, par 72, located away from traffic.

Fort Myers Beach Golf Club (239-463-2064; www.fmbgolfclub.com; 4200 Bay Beach Ln., Fort Myers Beach 33931, off Estero Blvd.) An 18-hole executive course, par 60, surrounded by condo communities yet rife with birdlife. Affordable rates.

Fort Myers Country Club (239-936-2457; www.cityftmyers.com/attractions/golf/ fmcc.htm; 3591 McGregor Blvd., Fort Myers 33901) Fort Myers's oldest; 18 holes, par 71. Restaurant and lounge.

Summerlin Ridge Golf Course (239-432-0000; 16750 Pine Ridge Rd., Fort Myers 33908) A lit 18-hole executive course, popular during hot summer days. Driving range and snack bar.

Health & Fitness Clubs

Asylum (239-437-3488; www.asylumfitnessclub.com; 13211 McGregor Blvd., Fort Myers 33919) Memberships start at one month; fully equipped aerobic and weight studios plus classes.

Gold's Gym (239-549-3354; 1013 Cape Coral Pkwy. E, Cape Coral 33904) Classes in spinning, step aerobics, body flex, yoga, and karate. Personal training.

The Omni Club (239-931-6664; www.theomniclub.com; 1755 Boy Scout Dr., Fort Myers) More than 100 cardio machines, a separate women's-only facility, classes, and club-style locker rooms with free towel service.

Sanibel Fitness Center (239-395-2639; www.sanibelfitnesscenter.com; 975 Rabbit Rd., Sanibel Island 33957) Newly expanded with full cardiovascular and weight-training studios, aerobic classes, personal training, and seniors program. Short-term memberships (one to six days) available.

Hiking

Cayo Costa State Park (941-964-0375; www.floridastateparks.org/cayocosta; P.O. Box 1150, Boca Grande 33921, at Barrier Islands GEO Park, Cayo Costa) Six miles of trail take you through barrier island ecology, a pioneer cemetery, and remnants of a circa-1904 quarantine station.

Corkscrew Regional Ecosystem Watershed (CREW) Marsh (239-657-2253; mailing address: 2301 McGregor Blvd., Fort Myers 33901; 23998 Corkscrew Rd., Estero 33928, 18 miles east of Interstate 75, exit 123) Five miles of hiking trails through peri-Everglades environment—pine flatwoods, oak and palm hammock, and sawgrass marsh—to a 12-foot observation tower. Free guided tours the second Saturday of every month, from October through May.

✪ **J. N. "Ding" Darling National Wildlife Refuge** (239-472-1100; www.fws.gov/ darling, www.dingdarlingsociety.org; 1 Wildlife Dr., Sanibel Island 33957, off Sanibel-

Captiva Rd.) Its longest hike, the Indigo Trail, travels for more than 4 miles from the refuge education center, across a boardwalk, and along bird-rich ponds. A shorter trail takes you to a protected Calusa shell mound.

Estero Bay State Buffer Preserve (239-463-3240; mailing address: 700-1 Fisherman's Wharf, Fort Myers Beach 33931, off W. Broadway in Estero) Provides about 8 miles of nature trails through scrubland along the Estero River and bay marshes.

Sanibel-Captiva Conservation Foundation (239-472-2329; www.sccf.org; 3333 Sanibel-Captiva Rd., P.O. Box 839, Sanibel Island 33957) Nearly 5 miles of trails through natural habitat along the Sanibel River. The majority of wildlife consists of birds, lizards, alligators, and insects.

Kids' Stuff

Fort Myers Beach Pool (239-463-5759; 2600 Oak St., Fort Myers Beach 33931) Not your ordinary city pool, this one has a two-story slide and the toddler Tad Pool. Admission is $4 for ages 12 and older, $2 for ages 3 to 11.

Fort Myers Skatium (239-461-3145; www.fmskatium.com; 2250 Broadway, Fort Myers 33901) Open indoor ice skating. Hours vary. Cost for public ice skating sessions is $5 adults, $4 seniors and children ages 12 and younger, plus $2 for skate rental.

Germain Arena (239-948-7825; www.germainarena.com; 11000 Everblades Pkwy., Estero 33928, exit 123 off Interstate 75, at Corkscrew Rd.) The public can ice skate at one of the two indoor, NHL-sized rinks daily (times vary). Admission is $6 for a regular session. Skate rental is $3. Sunday family skating is $3 each, including rentals, plus there are special late skate and pizza-and-pop sessions. There are learn-to-skate classes, an ice-hockey league, in-line teams, and a figure-skating club. A video arcade and snack counter complete the family amenities.

✪ Greenwell's Bat A Ball and Family Fun Park (239-574-4386; www.greenwells familyfunpark.com; 35 NE Pine Island Rd., Cape Coral 33909) Named after the city's favorite sports son, Red Sox player Mike Greenwell, this facility contains batting cages, a miniature golf course, a small playground, a maze, a video arcade, four go-cart tracks, and snack concessions. Kids really love it here, but be prepared to lay out a lot of money if you spend much time—especially in the arcade room.

Periwinkle Park (239-472-1433; 1119 Periwinkle Way, Sanibel Island 33957) The owner of this trailer park raises and breeds exotic birds and waterfowl. He daddies roughly 600 birds of 133 species, specializing in African and Asian hornbills.

Shell Mound Trail at J. N. "Ding" Darling National Wildlife Refuge provides a quiet boardwalk stroll into a hardwood hammock.

Flamingoes, parakeets, cockatiels, cockatoos, and others occupy the park and 15 aviaries. During the off season, visitors can drive through; in season, biking is recommended. A few of the birds raised here can be seen more easily at Jerry's Shopping Center (1700 Periwinkle Way). Take the children in the evening, when the birds are most talkative.

Sanctuary Skate Park (239-337-5297; www.sanctuaryskateparks.com; 2277 Grand Ave., Fort Myers 33901, downtown, behind the Skatium) Skateboarders and in-line skaters love this city-owned outdoor facility with its cool ramps and half-pipes. Skate and pad rentals are available. Admission is $7 for a two-hour session. On Monday evenings the park is open for BMX riders.

Sanibel Skate Park (239-472-0345; 3840 Sanibel-Captiva Rd, Sanibel Island 33957) Opened in 2007 at the city's redeveloping park next to the Sanibel School, it offers skating classes within its compact confines.

The Shell Factory (239-995-2141, 800-282-5805; www.shellfactory.com; 2787 N. Tamiami Trail, N. Fort Myers 33903) A shell shop on steroids, this longtime attraction has grown into a megacomplex. Though still old-fashioned, it now includes restaurants, a fun park, a nature park, new re-created life-size dinosaurs, Waltzing Waters lit fountain show, aquariums, video games, a seafood restaurant, and gifts from fine to tacky. Admission to the Shell Factory is free; admission to the nature park is $10 for adults and $6 for children ages 4 to 16. The Waltzing Waters costs $5 for anyone older than 12. Bumper boat rides and miniature golf are $5, water wars $2, and the pitching cage is $1 for three balls. Fun park hours are 11 to 7 daily. Special events such as Gumbo Fest and Chili & Rib Fest are fun for the whole family and feature live entertainment.

Strausser BMX Sports Complex (239-458-1943; www.capecoralbmx.org; 1410 SW Sixth Pl., Cape Coral 33991) A bicycle motocross track is provided for practice and weekly races. also picnic grounds, a playground, a softball field, and a sand volleyball court.

✪ **Sun Splash Family Waterpark** (239-574-0557; www.sunsplashwaterpark.com; 400 Santa Barbara Blvd, Cape Coral 33991) This spot offers wet fun in a dozen varieties and includes pools, slides, flumes, a log roll, cable drops, a river ride, volleyball, food, lockers, and special events. Admission is $14.95 for guests 48 inches or taller, $12.95 for shorter children, $8.95 for senior citizens, and $4.95 for children ages 2 and younger (plus tax). Parking is $1. The park is open early March through September, but schedule varies according to time of year and day; it is open daily from late May through mid-August.

Racquet Sports

Cape Coral Yacht Club Community Park (239-574-0806; www.capecoral.net; 5819 Driftwood Pkwy., Cape Coral 33904) Five lit tennis courts and two outdoor racquetball courts.

Fort Myers Racquet Club (239-278-7277; www.cityftmyers.com/departments/public works/recreation/tennis.aspx; 1700 Matthew Dr., Fort Myers 33907) Newly renovated, eight clay courts and two hard courts (eight lit), lessons, and tournaments. Admission.

Hancock Bridge Community Park (239-565-7748; 2211 Hancock Bridge Pkwy., Cape Coral 33990) The Lee County Community Tennis Association (www.leecountytennis.com) conducts classes and league play on five lit courts.

Rutenberg Community Park (6500 S. Pointe Blvd., Fort Myers 33907) Eight lit courts.

Signal Inn Resort (239-472-4690; www.signalinn.com; 1811 Olde Middle Gulf Dr., Sanibel Island 33957) Two racquetball courts. Admission.

STARS Complex (239-332-6671; 2980 Edison Ave., Fort Myers 33916, downtown) Two lit tennis courts.

Shelling

Welcome to shelling heaven. Sanibel Island, in particular, is known for its great pickings. Be aware that a state of Florida law prohibits the collection of live shells on Sanibel Island, to preclude the possibility of dwindling populations. Collecting live shells is also prohibited in state and national parks. Elsewhere in the county, live collecting is also discouraged. Any shell with a creature still inside is considered a live shell. Shellers who find live shells washed up on the beach—a common occurrence after storms—are urged to gently return (no flinging!) the shell to deep water.

HOT SHELLING SPOTS

Big Hickory Island (northwest of Little Hickory Island, accessible only by boat) An unhitched crook of beach favored by local boaters and shellers.

✪ **Bonita Beach** (Little Hickory Island) Look north of the public beach.

✪ **Cayo Costa State Park** (between North Captiva and Boca Grande, accessible only by boat) Because it takes a boat ride to get there, these sands hold caches of shells merely by virtue of their remoteness. North-end Johnson Shoals provides a thin strip of sandbar for good low-tide pickings.

Sanibel Island Known as the Shelling Capital of the Western Hemisphere, the island even has its own name for the peculiar, shell-bent stance of the beach collector: the Sanibel Stoop. Unlike the other Gulf Coast barrier islands, Sanibel takes an east-west heading. Its perpendicular position and lack of offshore reefs allow it to intercept shells that arrive from southern seas. Its fame as a world-class shelling area has made Sanibel a prime destination for shell collectors for decades. With shell-named streets, store shelves awash in shells and shell crafts, an annual shell fair, and a shell museum, one risks suffering shell shock just by visiting there. Best gulfside shelling spot: Bowman's Beach, midisland, away from the paths leading to the parking lot.

SHELLING CHARTERS

Adventures in Paradise (239-472-8443, 239-437-1660; www.adventureinparadiseinc .com; 14341 Port Comfort Rd., Fort Myers 33908, at Port Sanibel Marina, east of Sanibel toll booth) Shelling and snorkeling excursions to Cayo Costa aboard power catamarans.

Captain Mike Fuery's Shelling Charters (239-466-3649; www.sanibel-online.com/ fuery; P.O. 1302, Captiva Island 33924) A local shelling expert takes small groups to Cayo Costa, Johnson Shoals, and other shelling hot spots.

Captiva Cruises (239-472-5300; www.captivacruises.com; P.O. Box 580, Captiva Island 33924, at McCarthy's Marina) Full- and half-day shelling trips, with experienced instruction, to Cayo Costa and North Captiva.

Spas

Aquagene (239-463-6181; www.pinkshell.com; Pink Shell Resort, 275 Estero Blvd., Fort Myers Beach 33931) The area's newest resort spa takes its cues from the sea in design and spa treatments, which include a red algae marine wrap, Sea of Life facial, and Dead Sea Salt Glow. Seashells and waves set the motif for its fashionable locker and waiting areas.

Sanibel Day Spa (239-395-2220, 877-695-1588; www.sanibeldayspa.com; 2075 Periwinkle Way #24, Sanibel Island 33957, at Periwinkle Place, upstairs) Long-established and well-reputed place of pampering offering extensive à la carte and spa package services, including hair care, manicures, pedicures, men's treatments, facials, oxygen therapy, ayurvedic wellness treatments, scrubs, and massage.

Sanibel Harbour Resort & Spa (239-466-4000, 800-767-7777; www.sanibel-resort.com; 17260 Harbour Pointe Dr., Fort Myers 33908, directly before the Sanibel causeway) Sanibel Harbour was a spa before it became a resort (see "Lodging"). Guests, members, and day visitors can take advantage of the swimming pool, whirlpools, training room, aerobics and Tai Chi classes, saunas, steam rooms, and racquetball courts. Renovated in 2003 and again after Hurricane Charley, the spa offers special services that capitalize on the resort's important archaeological Calusa location: a living wishing-shell mound, interactive couples treatments, herbal wraps, aromatherapy massage, a new flexibility studio and relaxation bistro, personal training, facials, and the unique BETAR musical and sound relaxation system.

Spada (239-482-1858; www.spadasalonanddayspa.com; 13161 McGregor Blvd., Fort Myers 33919) Full line of classic and creative body and skin care treatments, including prenatal and couples massages, chocolate massage, acupuncture, salt glows, facials, cranberry spa manicure, and microdermabrasion.

Touch Spa Salon (239-454-9933; www.touch-spa-salon.com; 13499 S. Cleveland Ave., Fort Myers 33907) Facials are its strong suit and come in flavors of European, pumpkin chiffon, pearl and ginseng, and more. Also massage and hair and nail services.

Spectator Sports

Crab Races

✪ **'Tween Waters Inn Crow's Nest** (239-472-5161; 15951 Captiva Dr., Captiva Island 33924) and **Parrot Key** (239-462-3257; www.myparrotkey.com; 2500 Main St., Fort Myers 33931, at Salty Sam's Marina) Participate or watch. The early session is geared toward families. Captiva's races take place at 6 and 9 every Monday and Thursday night; Fort Myers Beach's at 6 and 8 every Wednesday night.

PRO BASEBALL

City of Palms Park (239-334-4700, 877-RED-SOX9; www.redsox.com; 2201 Edison Ave., Fort Myers; 33901, downtown at Jackson St.) Home of the Boston Red Sox's spring exhibition games, starting in March and played into April.

Hammond Stadium (239-768-4210; 14100 Six Mile Cypress Rd., Fort Myers 33912) Hosts the Minnesota Twins (239-768-4270, 800-33TWINS; www.twinsbaseball.com) for spring training in March. From April through August, the Miracle Professional Baseball team

(239-768-4210; www.miraclebaseball.com), a member of the Florida State League, competes here.

PRO FOOTBALL
Florida Firecats (239-390-CATS; www.floridafirecats.com; Germain Arena, off Interstate 75, exit 123, at Corkscrew Rd., 11000 Everblades Pkwy., Estero 33928) Part of the arenafootball2 league, they play April through July.

PRO HOCKEY
Florida Everblades (239-948-7825; www.floridaeverblades.com; Germain Arena, off Interstate 75, exit 123, at Corkscrew Rd., 11000 Everblades Pkwy., Estero 33928) Southwest Florida's professional ice hockey team plays its October–April season at Germain Arena. The public can skate at the rink daily (times vary) for a fee. (See "Kids' Stuff," above.)

WATERSKIING
Southern Extreme Waterski Show Team (239-571-4957; www.southernextreme .com) Puts on a free show every Sunday during season at Miromar Outlets (see "Shopping").

Water Sports
DIVE SHOPS & CHARTERS
Underwater Explorers (239-481-4733; www.underwaterexplorers.net; 12600 McGregor Blvd., Fort Myers 33919) National Association of Underwater Instructors (NAUI) certification courses and equipment, plus dive trips out of the region. This operation has been

around for years. Others come and go throughout the region, but this is the most dependable.

PARASAILING & WATERSKIING

Holiday Water Sports (239-765-4FUN; www.watersportsrentals.net; 250 Estero Blvd., at Pink Shell Beach Resort; also 239-463-6778; 684 Estero Blvd., Fort Myers Beach 33931, at Best Western Beach Resort) Hobie Cat, kayak, aquacycle, parasailing, and Waverunner rentals available.

Ranalli Parasail (239-542-5511; www.ranalliparasail.com; 2000 Estero Blvd., Fort Myers Beach 33931) Rides along Fort Myers Beach and Waverunner rentals.

YOLO Watersports (239-472-9656 or 866-YOLO-JIMS; www.yolo-jims.com; 11534 Andy Rosse Ln., P.O. Box 1150, Captiva Island 33924) Parasailing rides from 600 to 800 feet high.

The Boston Red Sox come out swinging each spring in Fort Myers. Boston Red Sox

SAILBOARDING & SURFING

Winter and summer storms bring the sort of waves that surfers crave, but in general, gulf waves are too wimpy for serious wave riders. Strong winds, however, provide excellent conditions for sailboarders in several locations throughout the region. Sanibel Causeway is the most popular windsurfing spot.

Ace Performer (239-489-3513; www.aceperformer.com; 16842 McGregor Blvd., Fort Myers 33908) Rents and gives lessons for windsurfers, kite boards, and kayaks. Free delivery to the Sanibel causeway.

SNORKELING & SCUBA

Florida's west coast has no natural reefs, but several have been built to provide homes for marine life and make divers and fishermen happy. Nearly 20 of these artificial reefs lie along the Sanibel Island–area coast. The Edison Reef, one of the largest, was created from the sinking of a former Fort Myers bridge in 42 feet of water 15 nautical miles off the Sanibel Lighthouse. The Belton Johnson Reef, constructed of concrete culvert, lies about 5 nautical miles off Bowman's Beach on Sanibel. Other popular sites include the Redfish Pass Barge, lying in 25 feet of water less than a nautical mile from Redfish Pass between Captiva and North Captiva, and the Doc Kline Reef, a popular tarpon hole less than 8 nautical miles from the Sanibel Lighthouse. Cayo Costa State Island Preserve offers snorkelers nice ledges in 2 to 5 feet of water alive with fish, sponges, and shells.

Wilderness Camping

Cayo Costa State Park (941-964-0375; www.floridastateparks.org/cayocosta; P.O. Box 1150, Boca Grande 33921, at Barrier Islands GEO Park, La Costa Island) You'll need boat transportation to reach this unbridged island (see Tropic Star Cruises under "Boats & Boating: Sightseeing & Entertainment Cruises"), which is home to wild pigs and myriad birds. Bring your own fresh drinking water and lots of bug spray. And don't expect to plug in the camcorder. There are showers, picnic grounds, boat docks, nature trails, a tram that runs cross-island, tent sites, and some very primitive cabins. Call ahead to reserve the latter. Camping was once allowed anywhere on the 2,225-acre island, but today it's restricted to a specific area.

Koreshan State Historic Site (239-992-0311; www.floridastateparks.org/koreshan; P.O. Box 7, Estero 33928) Koreshan's 60 campsites circle a volleyball court and are built fairly close together; a few face the Estero River. The park contains a nature trail, canoe trail, boat ramp, and 12 buildings in the historic compound. For reservations call 800-326-3521 or visit www.reserveamerica.com.

Wildlife Spotting

Loggerhead turtles lumber up on local beaches each summer to lay their cache of eggs. (Only vigilant night owls actually see them, but you can find their tracks in the morning light and see their nests, which patrols stake off.) Brown pelicans swarm fishing piers for handouts. Black skimmers nest on uninhabited sandy islands, while hundreds of other birds visit or stay in local habitats. The Fort Myers–Sanibel area is a vital area for wildlife, and many opportunities exist to spy on animals in their natural setting.

ALLIGATORS

Once endangered, the alligator population sprang back in recent decades, only to be decimated in past years by fear gone overboard. Thanks to organizations and laws that fought to protect the prehistoric reptiles, the jawsome creatures were taken off endangered lists. Sanibel Island paved the way by pioneering a no-feeding regulation that later became state law. (Hand-fed alligators lose their fear of people.) Then in 2004, after a couple of deadly attacks on Sanibel, the City began open harvesting of the creatures; when a gator trapper is called, he is allowed to take as many gators as he wishes at that outing. Now the alligator, once a common sight, especially at J. N. "Ding" Darling National Wildlife Refuge, is rarely seen. Concerned citizens and naturalists continue to cry for reform, but for now the slaughter continues.

Innate homebodies, alligators usually leave their home ponds only during spring and summer mating. That's when you're most likely to spot them. You will hear the bellow of the bull gator in the night and sometimes see both males and females roaming from pond to pond in search of a midsummer night's romance. They can do serious damage to a car, so be alert. And never approach one on foot.

When it's cold, alligators stay submerged to keep warm. When they're in the water, you first spot their snouts, then their prickly, tire-tread profiles. Once your eye becomes trained to distinguish them from logs and background, you'll notice them more readily. On sunny days throughout the year you may spot them soaking up rays on the banks of freshwater rivers and streams.

BIRDS

Roseate spoonbills are the stars of the J. N. "Ding" Darling National Wildlife Refuge, but hundreds of other species live among the sanctuary's wiry mangrove limbs and shallow estuarine waters, including ibises, brown and white pelicans, tricolor herons, red-shouldered hawks, snowy egrets, anhingas, and ospreys. In 2002 *Birder's World* magazine listed "Ding" Darling as third among its Top 15 Birding Hot Spots.

DOLPHINS

Playful bottle-nosed dolphins cruise the sea, performing impromptu acrobatic shows that it's hard to believe aren't staged. When the next performance will be is anybody's guess, but if you learn their feeding schedules, you have a better chance of catching their act. They often like to leap out of the wake of large boats. Out in the gulf I've been surrounded by their antics to the point where I suffered minor whiplash from spinning around to keep track of them all. Don't expect them to get too close—take some binoculars—and forget seeing them in captivity around here. Locals once staged a protest in Pine Island Sound when collectors tried to take some of their dolphins. And when a swim-with-the-dolphins facility was proposed near Sanibel Island, citizens again rose up in arms against animal exploitation.

MANATEES

In east Fort Myers—where warm waters discharged from the Florida Power & Light Company have always attracted the warm-blooded manatees to so-called Yankee Canal in the winter months—✪ **Manatee Park** (see "Nature Preserves & Eco-Attractions") has opened to provide a manatee viewing area, exhibits, and other recreational and educational assets on the wild and natural Orange River.

Pine Island's backwaters offer a good venue for manatee spotting. Check out the bay behind Island Décor & More, a popular sea-watch site, just before the Matlacha Bridge. If you're around South Seas Island Resort on Captiva Island, watch the marina waters for surfacing manatees.

Visit Manatee Park November through April to see its eponymous loveable, blubbery sea mammals live.

NATURE PRESERVES & ECO-ATTRACTIONS

CALUSA NATURE CENTER & PLANETARIUM

239-275-3435
www.calusanature.com
3450 Ortiz Ave., Fort Myers 33905
Open: 9–5 Mon.–Sat., 11–5 Sun. Call for astronomy and laser show times.
Admission: Museum, trails, and planetarium $8 adults, $5 children ages 3–12, children under 3 free

This multifaceted environmental center offers three wildlife trails with a butterfly aviary, a native plant garden, a caged bobcat and white-tailed deer, and an injured-bird aviary. Join a guided walk of the

Sizing Up a Shrimp

Gulf shrimp are graded by size and assigned all sorts of vague measurements, such as jumbo, large, medium-sized, and boat grade. The surest way to know what size shrimp you are ordering is to ask for the count-per-pound designation. This will be something like "21–25s," meaning there are 21 to 25 shrimp per pound. "Boat grade" normally designates a mixture of sizes, usually on the small side.

Cypress Swamp Boardwalk every Tuesday and Friday at 9:30 AM. Indoors you can see more live animal exhibits—snakes, tarantulas, alligators, turtles, and bees—and demonstrations. Daily programs allow visitors to get up close and personal with some of the fascinating creatures of Southwest Florida, plus the center hosts special kids and adult nature programs every month. Snakes are fed every Sunday at 11:15 AM. The planetarium uses telescopes, laser lights, and astronomy lessons in its presentations.

CAYO COSTA STATE PARK

941-964-0375
www.floridastateparks.org/cayocosta
P.O. Box 1150, Boca Grande 33921
Barrier Islands GEO Park, Cayo Costa Island, accessible only by boat
Admission: $1 per person

A wildlife refuge occupies about 90 percent of this 2,225-acre island. Cayo Costa preserves the Florida that the Native Americans tried to protect against European invasion. Besides the occasional feral hog that survives on the island, egrets, white pelicans, raccoons, ospreys, and black skimmers frequent the area. The path across the island's northern end features a side trip to a pioneer cemetery. Blooming cacti and other flora festoon the walk, which is sometimes a run when the weather turns warm and uncontrolled mosquito populations remind us of the hardships of eras gone by.

C.R.O.W.

239-472-3644
www.crowclinic.org
3883 Sanibel-Captiva Rd., Sanibel Island 33957
Open: Programs at 11 AM Mon.–Fri. and, in Nov.–Apr., also 1 PM Sun.
Admission: $5 adults, free for children ages 12 and under

C.R.O.W. is the acronym for Clinic for the Rehabilitation of Wildlife. This hospital complex duplicates natural habitats and tends to sick and injured wildlife: birds, bobcats, raccoons, rabbits, and otters. The facility cares for more than 3,000 patients a year. Daily programs introduce you to C.R.O.W.'s mission and are the only times visitors are allowed, for now. Work has begun on a new nature center, so that may change.

✪ J. N. "DING" DARLING NATIONAL WILDLIFE REFUGE

239-472-1100

www.fws.gov/dingdarling, www.dingdarlingsociety.org

1 Wildlife Dr., Sanibel Island 33957

Off Sanibel-Captiva Rd.

Open: Refuge, sunrise to sunset (closed Fri.); education center, 9–5 Jan.–Apr., 9–4 May–Dec.

Admission: Free to education center; parking $5 per car for refuge, $1 per cyclist or pedestrian

More than 6,000 acres of pristine wetlands and wildlife are protected by the federal government, thanks to the efforts of Pulitzer Prize–winning cartoonist and politically active conservationist J. N. "Ding" Darling, a regular Captiva visitor in the 1930s. A 4-mile drive takes you through the refuge, once a satellite of the original Everglades National Wildlife Refuge. To really experience "Ding," get out of the car. At the very least follow the easy trails into mangrove, bird, and alligator territory. Look for roseate spoonbills, yellow-crowned night herons, white pelicans, painted buntings, and dozens of other life-list prizes. Narrated tram and guided canoe tours are available (239-472-8900). The new education center holds hands-on wildlife displays, realistic habitat vignettes, bird sculptures, a birders' room, and a peek into the world of the refuge's namesake. Naturalist programs take place throughout the week in season.

FOUR MILE COVE ECOLOGICAL PRESERVE

239-549-4606

At the end of SE 23rd Terrace, north of Midpoint Memorial Bridge in Cape Coral (follow the signs off Del Prado Blvd. north of Coralwood Mall at SE 21st Ln.)

Open: 8–sunset daily

Admission: Free

An urban preserve runs parallel to the bridge and allows exploration of 365 acres of wetlands along a 4,500-foot boardwalk. Nature trails take you away from the bustle of traffic. Interpretative center, restrooms, picnicking, guided nature walks, and kayak rentals are available on the weekends (October through May only).

LAKES REGIONAL PARK

239-839-8656

www.leeparks.org

7330 Gladiolus Dr., Fort Myers 33908

Open: 8–sunset daily; train village open 10–1:45 Mon.-Fri., 10–3:45 Sat., noon–3:45 Sun.

Admission: Free; parking $1 per hour, $5 per day; mini-train rides $3 for ages 6 and older, $1 for ages 1–5

Making a grand comeback from severe hurricane damage in 2004, Lakes Park has reinvented itself not only as a family picnic-and-play park, but also as a prime birding spot. It hosts birding tours the first Saturday of every month and holds its annual Birdfest in March. For the family, there's a sand beach on the lake (a former quarry), a water fountain park, playgrounds with a climbing wall, a miniature train to ride, a fragrance garden, walking and biking trails, and pedal boat and kayak rentals.

✪ MANATEE PARK

239-690-5030
www.leeparks.org
10901 Route 80 (Palm Beach Blvd.), Fort Myers 33905
Open: 8–sunset daily
Admission: Free; parking $1 per hour, $5 per day

A well-kept, 16-acre recreational park feeds our fascination with the loveable manatee, teddy bear of the water world. In addition to a manatee viewing area, it provides polarized filters for peeping underwater, habitat exhibits, a nature boardwalk, a canoe and kayak launch (and rentals and clinics in winter), nature programs (in winter), wildlife habitat areas (including a butterfly garden), an information center, and picnic facilities. The park also serves as a rescue and release site for injured and rehabilitated manatees. For manatee viewing updates, call 239-694-3537.

MATANZAS PASS PRESERVE

239-432-2127
www.leeparks.org
199 Bay Rd., Fort Myers Beach, at School St.
Open: Dawn to dusk
Admission: Free

A quiet respite from vacationland action, this 56-acre preserve provides a 1.25-mile loop trail and boardwalks through mangroves and maritime hammocks to out-of-the-way bay waters.

J. N. "Ding" Darling National Wildlife Refuge, the nation's second-most-visited refuge, draws birders from around the world.

OSTEGO BAY FOUNDATION'S MARINE SCIENCE CENTER

239-765-8101
www.ostegobay.org
718 Fisherman Wharf, Fort Myers Beach 33931
Open: 10–4 Wed.– Fri., 10–1 Sat.
Admission: By donation

Primarily a marine-science education and research facility, Ostego Bay maintains a show-room of local sea life for visitors to tour. Aquariums hold local species in various habitats, such as sea grass, estuarine, and gulf. Manatee, loggerhead, and other kiosks explain the plight of endangered species and the workings of the local shrimping industry. Interactive displays include a dry-touch table, microscopes, and a touchable shark's skin and blue marlin's bill. The foundation has built a boardwalk along the bay where the shrimp boats dock off Main Street. Here you can learn yet more about shrimping, estuaries, and local maritime heritage. The three-hour Wednesday Working Waterfront Tour takes you along the boardwalk beginning at 9 AM, October through May; the cost is $15 per person.

SANIBEL-CAPTIVA CONSERVATION FOUNDATION CENTER

239-472-2329
www.sccf.org
3333 Sanibel-Captiva Rd., P.O. Box 839, Sanibel Island 33957
Open: 8:30–3 Mon.–Fri. during summer; 8:30–4 Mon.–Fri., mid-Oct.–mid-May; 10–3 Sat., Dec.–Apr.
Closed Sun. and Sat., May–Nov.
Admission: Nature Center admission is $3 for visitors ages 17 and older.

This research and preservation facility encompasses more than 1,800 acres. A guided or self-guided tour introduces you to indigenous flora and natural bird habitats. Indoor displays and dioramas further educate and include a touch tank. Guest lecturers, seminars, and workshops address environmental issues during the winter season. The weekly beach walk is fun and informative. A native plant nursery and butterfly house are also on the premises.

SIX MILE CYPRESS SLOUGH PRESERVE

239-432-2004
www.leeparks.org/sixmile
7751 Penzance Crossing, Fort Myers, on Six Mile Cypress Pkwy.
Open: 8–5 daily, Oct.–Mar.; 8–8 daily, Apr.–Sept.
Admission: Free, parking $1 per hour (maximum $5)

Egrets, herons, ibises, and cormorants come to feed at this shallow waterway. Take a guided or self-guided tour around the more than 1-mile-long boardwalk through cypress stands and wetlands. Guided walks are at 9:30 AM daily (Wednesdays only from May through October); an extra 1:30 PM tour is available from January through March. A new interpretative center was in progress at press time.

WILDLIFE TOURS & CHARTERS

Adventures in Paradise (239-472-8443, 239-437-1660; www.adventureinparadiseinc

.com; 14341 Port Comfort Rd., Fort Myers 33908, at Port Sanibel Marina off Summerlin Rd., before the Sanibel causeway) Sea-life-encounter excursions led by a marine biologist, who throws a seine net, aboard a 40-foot power catamaran. Also shelling and snorkeling quests.

Canoe Adventures (239-472-5218; Sanibel Island 33957) Guided tours with a noted island naturalist in J. N. "Ding" Darling National Wildlife Refuge, on the Sanibel River, and in other natural areas.

Manatee World (239-693-1434; www.manateeworld.com; 5605 Palm Beach Blvd., Fort Myers 33905, on Route 80 at Interstate 75 exit 141, Coastal Marine Mart, East Fort Myers) Specializes in one-hour tours up the Orange River to spot manatees. Educational video viewing. Closes from mid-April through October.

Sanibel-Captiva Conservation Foundation Center (239-472-2329; www.sccf.org; 3333 Sanibel-Captiva Rd., Sanibel Island 33957) Hosts guided nature-trail, beach-walk, and island-boat tours.

Tarpon Bay Explorers (239-472-8900; www.tarponbayexplorers.com; 900 Tarpon Bay Rd., Sanibel Island 33957) Naturalist-guided kayak, pontoon boat, and tram tours through J. N. "Ding" Darling National Wildlife Refuge and ✪ **Tarpon Bay**. Also canoe and kayak rentals, bike and boat rentals, and free lunchtime wildlife talks.

SHOPPING

Shopping Centers & Malls

Two new mega shopping-entertainment malls have opened and continue to expand in the fast-growing Estero–San Carlos Park area south of Fort Myers, near Florida Gulf Coast University. They are Coconut Point, a residential-retail development, and Gulf Coast Town Center, which includes a Bass Pro Shops Outdoor World sportsman shopping attraction.

Bell Tower Shops (239-489-1221; www.thebelltowershops.com; 13499 S. Cleveland Ave., Fort Myers 33907) Saks Fifth Avenue anchors this alfresco, Mediterranean-style plaza of one-of-a-kind shops, upscale chains (Victoria's Secret, Brookstone, Williams-Sonoma), terrific restaurants, and movie theaters.

Captiva Island Like Captiva in general, the shopping scene here is quirky and beach oriented. Hurricane Charley in 2004, however, set it back a few years, and it is still struggling to make a comeback.

Coconut Point (www.coconutpointretail.com, Tamiami Trail and Coconut Point Rd., Estero) New in 2007, the fashionable mall within a planned community includes major chains such as Victoria's Secret and Johnny Rockets and some local venues, including Blue Water Bistro.

Coralwood Mall (2301 Del Prado Blvd., Cape Coral 33909) An outdoor mall of restaurants and chain stores, including Bealls Department Store.

Downtown Fort Myers (First Street) Downtown is slowly looking up as a three-year redevelopment project puts utility lines underground and paves streets and sidewalks with brick. More business- and government-minded than commercial, it does harbor some interesting book and cigar stores and unusual antique and whatnot shops. Urban renewal emphasis is on entertainment and dining, so most shops are utilitarian.

Edison Mall (239-939-5464; www.simon.com; 4125 Cleveland Ave., Fort Myers 33901) An entirely commercial, enclosed, and air-conditioned mall with major department stores such as Macy's, Dillard's, JCPenney, and Sears, plus about 150 smaller clothing and gift shops and a food court.

Fort Myers Beach Shop in your bikini, if you wish, at Times Square, a hub of ultracasual island activity. You'll find a profusion of swimsuit boutiques, surf shops, and food outlets at this pedestrian mall. At the island's south end, Villa Santini Plaza has some interesting shops and food stops.

Gulf Coast Town Center (230-267-0783; www.gulfcoasttowncenter.com; 9903 Gulf Coast Main St., Fort Myers; at I-75 and Alico Rd.) Opened in 2007, its Market Plaza serves as a family entertainment hub and its University Plaza caters to university students with free wireless Internet access. Among its 60-plus stores and restaurants are a Bass Pro Shops outlet (239-461-7800; www.basspro.com).

Matlacha (Pine Island) Sagging old fish houses, cracker-box shops, quirky art galleries, and fishing motels heavily salt the flavor of this island village. Knickknack historic structures painted in candy-store colors give the town an artistic, Hansel-and-Gretel feel. Sea-themed gifts, art, and jewelry make up the majority of merchandise.

McGregor Antiques District (Fort Myers) A nucleus of 17 shops spread around five small strip centers at College Parkway.

Page Field Commons (www.pagefieldcommons.com; Cleveland Ave. at Fowler Ave., Fort Myers) A conglomeration of mega-marts such as Old Navy, Toys "R" Us, Best Buy, Books-A-Million, and Michael's Crafts.

Sanibel Island Periwinkle Way and Palm Ridge Road constitute the shopper's routes on Sanibel, which is known for its galleries (specializing in wildlife art), shell shops, and resort-wear stores. These are clustered in tastefully landscaped, nature-compatible outdoor centers, the largest being Periwinkle Place (www.periwinkleplace.com) on Periwinkle Way.

Antiques & Collectibles

Albert Meadow Antiques (239-472-8442; 15000 Captiva Dr., Captiva Island 33924) Turn-of-the-20th-century decorative arts by Tiffany, Gorham, and Steuben, plus antique jewelry, lamps, Navajo weavings, and Art Deco and Art Nouveau pieces.

Fancy Flamingo Antiques (239-334-1133; 2259 Peck St., Fort Myers 33901) It nicely displays a wide variety of clothing, housewares, dolls, toys, and knickknacks between vintage red brick interior walls.

Judy's Antiques (239-481-9600; 12710 McGregor Blvd., Fort Myers 33919) One of the oldest in the McGregor Antiques District, this establishment is well organized and sells quality sterling, porcelain, and crystal, specializing in estate jewelry.

McGregor Antique Mall (239-433-0200; 12720 McGregor Blvd., Fort Myers 33919) In the same neighborhood as Judy's but more folksy and nostalgic in its considerable offerings—household goods, books, toys, country-style furnishings, and more.

The Vintage Emporium (239-936-4888; 1927 Suwannee Ave., Fort Myers 33901) This off-the-beaten-path shop is fun any time of the year, but especially at Halloween or June weddings. It deals entirely in vintage clothing, carrying everything from tuxes and wedding gowns to gaudy bell-bottom jumpsuits and fur-trimmed hats.

Books

Beach Book Nook (239-463-3999; 7205 Estero Blvd., Fort Myers Beach 33931, at Santini Marina Plaza) New and used paperback exchange; a nice selection of new local guides, adult books, and kids' books.

✪ **MacIntosh Books & Papers** (239-472-1447; www.sanibelbooks.com; 2365 Periwinkle Way, Sanibel Island 33957) A tiny shop packed full of books of local and general interest, plus stationery.

Clothing

Brown Bag (239-472-1171; 2075 Periwinkle Way, Sanibel Island 33957, at Periwinkle Place) Tropical shirts, T-shirts, and other casual menswear.

Chico's (239-472-3773; 2330 Palm Ridge Rd., Sanibel Island 33957, at Palm Ridge Place) I prefer this Chico's store to the original on Periwinkle because it's more low key, with less hustle and bustle.

Francesca's Collections (239-267-5050; 13499 Cleveland Ave., Fort Myers 33907, at Bell Tower Shops) Young, fun, affordable women's fashions, accessories, and gifts.

Giggles (239-395-0700; 1987 Periwinkle Way, Sanibel 33957, at Tahitian Gardens) Cute Florida-appropriate clothing for kids.

H2o Outfitters and Footloose of Captiva (239-472-8890; 2075 Periwinkle Way, Sanibel Island 33957, at Jerry's Shopping Center) Name-brand men's and women's beach and marina fashions, shoes, quality souvenir T-shirts and sweatshirts.

Jos. A. Banks Clothiers (239-454-3543; 13499 Cleveland Ave., Fort Myers 33907, at Bell Tower Shops) Fine sporting, casual-tropical, and formal wear for men.

Lucky Dog of Sanibel (239-395-3733; 2359 Periwinkle Way, Sanibel Island 33957) Select, pricey threads for trendsetters.

Mr. Pants and Michelle's Resortwear (239-463-1515; 7205 Estero Blvd. #712,

Mutlacha Art Gallery creates its own microcosm of fantasy.

Fort Myers Beach 33931, at Santini Marina Village) Fine casual, Florida-fit fashions for men and women.

Peach Republic (239-472-8444; www.peachrepublic.com; 2075 Periwinkle Way #16, Sanibel Island 33957, at Periwinkle Place) Stylish cotton and other tropical resort wear for women, plus shoes and jewelry.

Pier Peddler (239-765-0660; 1000 Estero Blvd., Fort Myers Beach 33931) At the base of the Fort Myers Beach Fishing Pier, it carries beach and tropical fashions for men and women, including the Tommy Bahama line for men.

Trader Rick's (239-489-2240; 13499 U.S. 41 #217, Fort Myers 33907, at Bell Tower Shops; and 239-472-9194, 2075 Periwinkle Way #38, Sanibel 33957, at Periwinkle Place) Creative-casual Florida wear for women plus unusual and handmade jewelry, toiletries, and other accessories.

Consignment

Buying secondhand on the Island Coast is not the embarrassment it is in some places. Because of the wealthy and transient nature of its residents, the area offers the possibility of great discoveries in its consignment shops.

Classy Exchange (239-278-1123; 12791 Kenwood Ln. #B1, Fort Myers 33907) Designer women's fashions and housewares.

Designer Consigner (239-472-1266; 2330 Palm Ridge Rd., Sanibel Island 33957, at Tarpon Bay Center) Clothing, furniture, and household items.

Elite Repeat (239-936-1001; 12955 Cleveland Ave. #156, Fort Myers 33907, at Pinebrook Park) Formal, career, and casual wear, including shoes and jewelry, for women.

Once Again Boutique (239-482-5445; 12721 McGregor Blvd., Fort Myers 33919) Nicely arranged women's clothing and shoes with brand names, including a rack of Chico's.

Perennials (239-275-8838; 7051 Crystal Dr., Fort Myers 33907) Baby furniture, toys, and children's and women's clothes.

Second Hand Rose (239-574-6919; 1532 SE 14th St., Cape Coral 33990, at Del Prado Mall) Extensive selection of fashion, jewelry, household items, furniture, and collectibles.

Factory Outlet Centers

Miromar Outlets (239-948-3766; www.miromaroutlets.com; 10801 Corkscrew Rd., Estero 33928, at exit 123 off Interstate 75) An above-average assortment of factory shops, designer outlets, and eateries, including Adidas, Nike, Reebok, Harry and David, Nautica, Coach, and Pottery Row. Watch the Southern Extreme Waterski Show Team (239-571-4957; www.southernextremewaterski.com) on Sunday in season or replenish (so you don't drop) at one of several restaurants.

Sanibel Tanger Factory Outlets (239-454-1974, 888-471-3939; www.tangeroutlet.com; 20350 Summerlin Rd., Fort Myers 33908, at McGregor Blvd.) Sitting at Sanibel's doorstep are more than 45 outlets for Samsonite, Maidenform, Gap, Reebok, OshKosh, Polo Ralph Lauren, and Bass Shoes.

Flea Markets & Bazaars

Fleamasters Fleamarket (239-334-7001; www.fleamall.com; 4135 Dr. Martin Luther King Jr. Blvd., Fort Myers 33916) Some 400,000 indoor square feet of produce, souvenirs, and novelties in more than 900 shops and eateries; open Friday through Sunday.

McGregor Boulevard Garage Sales (Fort Myers) Drive the boulevard early—the earlier you go, the better the pickings—every Friday and Saturday morning and watch for garage sale signs directing you to private sales.

Ortiz Fleamarket (239-694-5019; 1501 Ortiz Ave., Fort Myers 33905) Smaller than Fleamasters, this market convenes every Saturday and Sunday, from 6 AM to 4 PM.

Galleries

During season, hit Pine Island's Matlacha, a thriving artists' community, for Art Night the second Friday of the month. Besides gallery tours, visitors get entertainment, food, and Pine Island's special brand of fun.

Arts for ACT Gallery (239-337-5050; 2265 First St., Fort Myers 33901) Local artists and traveling exhibits to benefit abused women. Prices range from one to four figures for original paintings, jewelry, pottery, painted furniture, artistic clothing, and more.

Crossed Palms Gallery (239-283-2283; www.crossedpalmsgallery.com; 8315 Main St., Bokeelia 33922, on Pine Island) A delightful gallery facing the sea, it occupies two restored 1950s fishermen's cottages built around a cistern, which has become part of the gallery. Its rooms are filled with original fine arts, glasswork, pottery, and jewelry by local and national artists.

Jungle Drums (239-395-2266; www.jungledrumsgallery.com; 11532 Andy Rosse Ln., P.O. Box 368, Captiva Island 33924) On the outside, dolphins and birds are carved into the stair rail and floor studs. Inside, local and national artists depict wildlife themes in various media, much of it whimsical, all of it delightfully creative.

Matlacha Art Gallery (239-283-6453; www.seaweedgallery.com; 4639 Pine Island Rd., Matlacha 33993) Recently bought by the owners of Seaweed Gallery (see below), it's still both fun and serious about art and features the work of locals. Stay for a cup of coffee in the waterfront Oz gallery garden in back.

Portfolio (239-489-4333; 13499 S. Cleveland Ave., Fort Myers 33907, at Bell Tower Shops) Affordable original art, prints, and posters, framed or unframed.

Seaweed Gallery (239-472-2585; www.seaweedgallery.com; 11513 Andy Rosse Ln., Captiva Island 33924; and 239-395-3328, 1989 Periwinkle Way, Sanibel Island 33957, at Tahitian Gardens) Fun and colorful painted furniture, tropical oil paintings, fused glass jewelry, palm-pattern pottery, and other works with a sense of place.

Space 39 Gallery, 239-690-0004; www.spacethirtynine.com; 39 Patio de Leon, Fort Myers 33901) Downtown's leading gallery for national traveling exhibitions.

Tower Gallery (239-472-4557; www.towergallery-sanibel.com; 751 Tarpon Bay Rd., Sanibel Island 33957) In its charming Caribbean-motif old-beach-house digs, this artists' cooperative specializes in fine tropical art by area artists: masterful black-and-white photography by Charles McCullough, Sanibel scenes, pottery, and glass.

WildChild Gallery (239-283-6006, www.WildChildArtGallery.com; 4625 Pine Island Rd. NW, Matlacha 33993) Part of Pine Island's quirky art scene, it has wares ranging from jewelry and pottery to original oils and sculptures by local artists. On weekends, you can usually find artists at work or demonstrating.

General Stores

Bailey's General Store (239-472-1516; 2477 Periwinkle Way, Sanibel Island 33957, at Bailey's Shopping Center, corner Tarpon Bay Rd.) An island fixture for ages, it stocks mostly hardware and fishing and kitchen supplies and has an attached grocery, bakery, and deli.

Island Store (239-472-2374; 11500 Andy Rosse Ln., P.O. Box 907, Captiva Island 33924) Here's where you can buy those necessities you forgot—but try not to forget too much, because the prices reflect the location, here at the end of the earth.

Gifts

Bubble Room Emporium (239-472-6545; www.bubbleroomrestaurant.com/gift.html; 15001 Captiva Dr., Captiva 33924) Find some of the same zany buttons and hats that the Bubble Room servers wear (see "Dining"), plus toys and baubles for you and your home.

Cheshire Cat Toys (239-482-8697; 13499 S. Cleveland Ave., Fort Myers 33907, at Bell Tower Shops) Brio, Playmobil, stuffed animals, puppets, fine dolls, books, arts and crafts, and learning toys.

Discovery Bay (239-463-4715; 7205 Estero Blvd., Fort Myers Beach 33931, at Santini Marina Plaza) Whimsical, tasteful nautical and tropical gifts and home accessories, plus crystal.

Enjewel (239-415-4023; 2214 First St., Fort Myers 33901, downtown) Affordable and stand-out costume jewelry and decorative bags.

Local Color (239-463-9199; 1021 Estero Blvd., Fort Myers Beach 33931, at Times Square) This tiny shop packs in a little of everything—clothing, jewelry, tableware, toiletries, cards, and more—all with an artistic flair:.

Needful Things (239-472-5400, 1995 Periwinkle Way, Sanibel 33957, at Tahitian Gardens) Kids especially love this place, although the novelties, toys, and cards also appeal to the teens' and adults' sense of fun and budgets.

Pandora's Box (239-472-6263; 2075 Periwinkle Way #1, Sanibel Island 33957, at Periwinkle Place) Delightful decorative items, creative jewelry, potpourri, specialty children's gifts, soaps, yard art, and the best selection of greeting cards on the island.

Sanibel Surf Shop (239-472-8185; 1700 Periwinkle Way, Sanibel Island 33957, at Jerry's Shopping Center) Collections of T-shirts, beach toys, jewelry, and shells all under one roof, selling affordable mementos of the island. Formerly Jerry's Bazaar.

A Swedish Affair (888-867-9567 or 239-275-8004; www.swedensfinest.com; 1400 Colonial Blvd., Fort Myers 33907, at Royal Palm Square) Scandinavian gifts from funny to fine: amusing cards, old-fashioned toys, lingonberry preserves, folk art, candles, glassware, Christmas ornaments, and fine pewter serving pieces.

Toys Ahoy (239-472-4800; 2075 Periwinkle Way, Sanibel Island 33957, at Periwinkle Place) Old-fashioned and learning-focused toys, puppets, books, stuffed toys, and more.

Jewelry

✪ **Congress Jewelers** (239-472-4177, 800-882-6624; www.congressjewelers.com; 2075 Periwinkle Way, Sanibel Island 33957, at Periwinkle Place) Dolphin, mermaid, bird, sandals, sand bucket, and shell gold pendants, plus other fine jewelry.

Enjewel (239-415-4023; 2214 First St., Fort Myers 33901) Artistic sterling silver pieces, Polish-made amber jewelry, and unique Murano-glass jewelry from Italy.

Friday's, The Sanibel Diamond Store (239-472-1454, 800-850-6605; www.sanibel diamond.com; 1700 Periwinkle Way, Sanibel 33957, in Jerry's Shopping Center) Specializes in diamonds; home of the "Sanibel Diamond."

Mayors (239-590-6166; 13499 S. Cleveland Ave., Fort Myers 33907, at Bell Tower Shops) Swiss watches and pens, rings, bar- and tableware, and elegant baubles of all sorts in a spacious setting.

Scruples (239-463 0500; 7205 Estero Blvd., Fort Myers Beach 33931, at Santini Marina Plaza) I like this shop for its interesting heirloom-style pieces and its affordable jewelry.

Kitchenware & Home Decor

Cheese Nook (239-472-2666; 2075 Periwinkle Way, Sanibel Island 33957, at Periwinkle Place) Fun and tropical placemats, towels, and dishware; also gourmet food items, including a wide selection of hot-pepper sauces and select wines.

International Design Center (239-390-5111; www.idcfl.com; 10800 Corkscrew Rd, Ste. 382, Estero 33928, at Interstate 75, across from Miromar Outlets) This new, ultra-sophisticated facility gathers high-end furniture stores, tile and fixtures merchants, flooring, rugs, and art galleries under one elegant roof. Valet parking and one complimentary hour of designer-on-call service.

Island Decor & More (239-283-8080; 4206 Pine Island Rd., Matlacha 33993) Affordable decorative home art and accessories with an islandy appeal.

Island Style (239-472-6657; 2075 Periwinkle Way, Sanibel Island 33957, at Periwinkle Place) Whimsical, artistic, and one-of-a-kind decorative elements with a Sun Belt motif: hand-painted chairs, carved wooden mobiles and stabiles, brightly colored dishware, Caribbean-inspired pieces.

Sanibel Home Furnishings (239-472-5552; www.sanibelhomefurnishings.com; 1618 Periwinkle Way, Sanibel 33957) Sophisticated and tasteful island-style furnishings and decoration ideas.

Traders (239-395-3151; www.tradersstoreandcafe.com; 1551 Periwinkle Way, Sanibel Island 33957) This restaurant-and-store combo excels at both (see "Dining"). Warehouse-sized, the shop brims with objets d'art, candles, hats, scarves, and imported gifts.

Wilford & Lee (239-395-9295; 2009 Periwinkle Way, Sanibel 33957, at Tahitian Gardens) Affordable (for Sanibel) and distinctive home decorations, including lamps, marine-life wall sculptures, and tableware.

Shell Shops

Island Decor & More (239-283-8080; 4206 Pine Island Road, Matlacha 33993) The focus at this longtime shell shop has changed to home decor (see above), but it still carries an aisle of specimen shells. Bonus: a good location for spotting dolphin and manatees.

Sanibel Seashell Industries (239-472-1603; www.seashells.com; 905 Fitzhugh St., Sanibel 33957, just off Periwinkle Way) Serious shell junkies and shell artisans should head here for the best specimens at the best price. In front of the warehouse-like outlet at 1544 Periwinkle Way, the same family has opened a smaller, more gifty shop.

She Sells Seashells (239-472-6991; 1157 Periwinkle Way, Sanibel 33957; and 239-472-8080; 2422 Periwinkle Way, Sanibel 33957) The island's oldest shell dealer has everything you need for shell crafts and displays.

The Shell Factory (239-995-2141, 800-282-5805; www.shellfactory.com; 2787 N. Tamiami Tr., North Fort Myers 33903) A palace of Florida souvenirs, tacky to fine, the Shell Factory is built like a bazaar. In addition to shells, it sells jewelry, art, clothes, and knickknacks. Also at the complex (can't miss it; look for the giant conch shell on the sign) are restaurants, an arcade, a kids' entertainment center, and a nature park.

Showcase Shells (239-472-1971; 1614 Periwinkle Way, Sanibel Island 33957,at Heart of the Islands Center) As elegant as a jewelry store, this boutique adds a touch of class to sifting through specimen shells by putting them under glass and into artistic displays.

Sporting Goods

Note: For supplies and equipment for specific sports, please refer to "Recreation."

Sports Authority (239-418-0281; 2317 Colonial Blvd., Fort Myers 33907) Full line of equipment, sportswear, and shoes.

CALENDAR OF EVENTS

January

Caloosahatchee Celtic Festival (239-338-2287; Centennial Park, downtown Fort Myers) One day at the end of the month devoted to Irish and Scottish music, dance, and food.

Cape Coral Festival of the Arts (239-945-1988; www.capecoralfestival.com; Cape Coral Pkwy., Cape Coral) This main thoroughfare closes down for a weekend arts street festival midmonth.

February

✪ **Edison Festival of Light** (239-332-4786; www.edisonfestival.org; Fort Myers) Commemorates the birthday of Thomas Edison and culminates in a spectacular lighted night parade. Two weeks early in the month.

March

Fort Myers Beach Lions Club Shrimp Festival (239-463-6986; Lynn Hall Memorial Park, Fort Myers Beach) Kids' run, 5K run, parade, and shrimp boil. Two days midmonth.

Greek Fest (239-481-2099; www.greekfestfortmyers.com; Greek Orthodox Church, 8210 Cypress Lake Dr., Fort Myers 33907) Ethnic food and music. Three days early in the month.

Lee County Reading Festival (239-461-2914; www.lee-county.com/library/ readingfestivalhome.htm; Centennial Park, downtown Fort Myers) One day midmonth to celebrate literacy; features prominent authors and related activities.

Sanibel Music Festival (239-336-7999; www.sanibelmusicfestival.org; Sanibel Island) Features concerts by classical artists from across the nation. Most events held at Sanibel Congregational Church, 2050 Periwinkle Way. Monthlong.

Sanibel Shell Fair and Show (239-472-2155; www.sanibelcommunityhouse.com/Shell Fair.htm; Sanibel Community House, 2173 Periwinkle Way, Sanibel Island 33957) Showcases sea life, specimen shells, and shell art. Four days in early March. Admission to show.

April
Earth Day (239-472-2329; Sanibel-Captiva Conservation Foundation, 3333 Sanibel-Captiva Rd., Sanibel Island 33957) Participants can ride free trams to this midmonth homage to Mother Earth.

River & Blues Festival (239-229-9825; Centennial Park, Fort Myers) One day, midmonth, of live music, local food, and activities for kids.

May
Kayak Fishing Classic (239-671-9347; www.kayakfishingclassic.com; Lovers Key State Park and environs) Fish from a kayak for prizes in youth and adult divisions, to benefit the local Boy Scouts.

June
Caloosa Catch & Release Fishing Tournament (239-671-9347; South Seas Island Resort, Captiva Island) Four-day event that kicks off a four-event fishing series throughout the summer.

July
✪ **MangoMania Tropical Fruit Fair** (239-283-4842; www.mangomaniafl.com; German-American Social Club, 2101 SW Pine Island Road, Cape Coral) Celebrates Pine Island's favorite fruit with music and stands selling mangos, mango trees, mango drinks, mango cookies, and other local delicacies. Good, honest community fun, one weekend in mid-July. Admission.

August
Cape In-Shore Redfish Challenge (239-573-3125; Yacht Club Community Park, Cape Coral) A fishing tournament for all anglers. Cash prizes totaling $10,000 and other awards for kids and adults. Two days at the beginning of the month.

Summer Slam (239-671-9347; South Seas Island Resort, Captiva) Two days of slam-bang fishing competition limited to 75 boats and awarding more than $20,000 in cash and prizes; this is the third leg of the Caloosa Catch & Release Fishing Tournament (the second leg takes place in Naples).

October

The Calusa Blueway Paddling Festival (239-433-5909; www.calusabluewaypaddling festival.com; Pine Island) One week, late in the month, for paddling the Great Calusa Blueway trail and learning about kayaking, fishing, and more.

"Ding" Darling Days (239-472-1100; J. N. "Ding" Darling National Wildlife Refuge, Sanibel Island) One week in October is devoted to birding, exploring the refuge, and celebrating the birthday of its namesake.

Friendly Forest (239-275-3435; www.calusanature.com; Calusa Nature Center, 3450 Ortiz Ave., Fort Myers 33905) Two weekends of family-friendly trick-or-treating on the nature trails, plus a special Halloween laser show in the planetarium.

Jazz on the Green (239-477-4683; www.jazzonthegreen.com; Florida Gulf Coast University, Fort Myers) A weekend of soothing alfresco jazz by well-known artists. Admission.

Oktoberfest (239-281-1400; www.gasc-capecoral.com; German-American Social Club, Cape Coral) Cape Coral celebrates its strong German heritage with Oktoberfest music, food, and activities. Two weekends.

Pirate Festival (239-454-7500; www.fmbchamber.com; Old San Carlos Blvd., Fort Myers Beach) Treasure hunts, a walking pub crawl, and pirate look-alike contests. One weekend early in the month.

Granny Matthews started the Sanibel Shell Fair tradition 70 years ago. Island Inn

November

American Sandsculpting Contest (239-454-7500; www.sandfestival.com; Outrigger Beach, GullWing, and Holiday Inn resorts, Fort Myers Beach) Amateur and masters divisions. One weekend in mid-November.

BIG ARTS Fair (239-395-0900; www.bigarts.org; BIG ARTS, 900 Dunlop Rd., Sanibel Island) Juried arts and crafts exhibits. Thanksgiving weekend.

Cape Coral CoCoNut Festival (239-573-3125; Sunsplash Family Water Park) Tropical food, live music, and a carnival. One weekend midmonth.

December

Christmas Luminary Trail (239-472-1080; Sanibel and Captiva islands) More than 3 miles of luminary candles line the main roads of Sanibel's and Captiva's commercial areas, where businesses stay open and dole out free drinks and food. One weekend early in the month.

Holiday House (239-334-7410; www.efwefla.org/hh.asp; Edison & Ford Winter Estates, 2350 McGregor Blvd., Fort Myers) Period and seasonal exhibits and miles of light strings draw crowds to this popular attraction. Admission.

Cape Coral Boat-a-Long (239-573-3125; Four Freedoms Park, Cape Coral) Decorated boat parade with live entertainment, Santa, Christmas crafts, food, and more.

6

Naples & the South Coast

Precious Commodities

Perched on alabaster sands at the edge of Florida's Everglades, meticulous Naples transcends its wild setting like a diamond in the rough. Settled by land developers late in its life, this cultural oasis historically has appealed to the rich and the sporting. Today the state's final frontier is known for its million-dollar homes, great golfing, art galleries, posh resorts, world-class shopping, and fine dining. In the spirit of its Italian namesake, Naples has in the past decade undergone a sort of renaissance that has included a highly successful urban renewal project on Fifth Avenue South and various new cultural venues, including Sugden Community Theatre, von Liebig Art Center, and the world-class Naples Museum of Art. In 2006, the developing Naples Botanical Gardens opened a major new phase. In its northern reaches the city spreads into the quiet residential district of **North Naples**, seaside **Vanderbilt Beach**, and the town of **Bonita Springs**, and it continues to grow now eastward, where a new Catholic college community is being built.

Bonita Springs still adheres to an early agricultural heritage with its reputation for tomatoes, citrus, and other cash crops. Citrus freeze-outs farther north, plus the town's navigable Imperial River, created the community, first called Survey, in 1893. Here Henry Ford maintained a hunting lodge to which he and his Fort Myers friends, including Thomas Edison, traveled by horseback. Today, where the tomato fields end, upscale golfing communities begin, all surrounding a neighborly little town left frozen in time by dint of the Tamiami Trail's rerouting. These days Bonita Springs starts to blend in with north Naples, both physically and in its character. New residential, hotel, and shopping developments boost it upward like an overachieving tomato vine climbing above its stake.

At the South Coast's southern and eastern extremes, the civility is balanced with swamp-buggy mud races, agriculture, Native American villages, fishing lodges, Florida panthers, and the unvarnished wilderness of the Everglades.

Neighboring **Marco Island** introduces the labyrinthine, mysterious land of Ten Thousand Islands. It was once an important center of the ancient Calusa culture, and the carved Key Marco Cat archaeological find (now exhibited at the Smithsonian Institution) has become an island icon. Tempered in a rough-and-tumble history, the island also boasts contemporary upscale resorts and good manners. Ancient Indian mounds, clam canneries, and pineapple plantations color the past of its three communities: **Isles of**

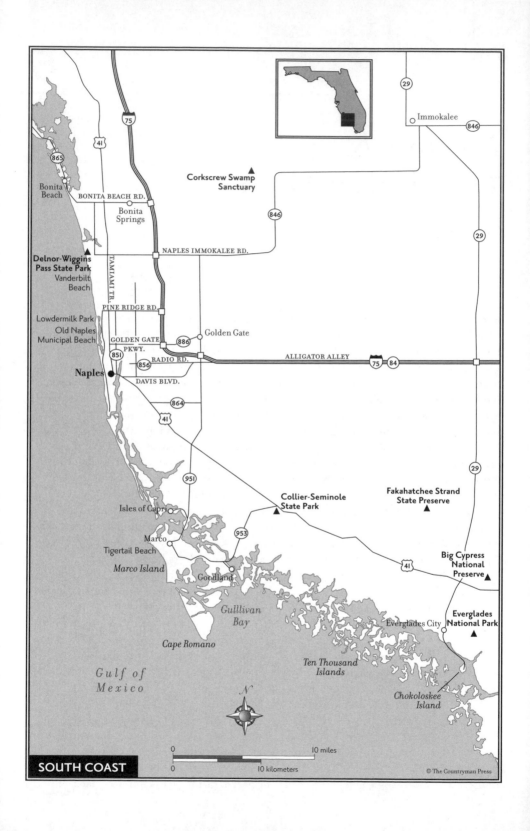

SOUTH COAST

Everglades City's riverfront—festooned with crab traps, nets, and buoys—still reflects its fishing roots.

Capri, **Marco**, and ✪ **Goodland**. First settled by the clan of William Collier (no relation to Barron Collier) in 1871, Marco Island has done most of its growing in modern times. Between 1960, when plans for a modern bridge were being formed, and 1980, the population increased by 755 percent. Goodland, so named because its land provided fertile soil for avocado farming, purposely kept itself behind the times—giddily stuck in a good-time, catch-fish mode—for most of its life. But these days signs of upscaling appear on the laid-back horizon.

✪ **Everglades City**—the county seat until Naples took over—languishes in its wilderness setting at the doorstep to Big Cypress Swamp and Ten Thousand Islands. Its settlers have always kept a step ahead of the law, doing what they must to survive, whether it was fishing, alligator poaching, or pot smuggling. Today, with a population of about 500, commercial fishing restrictions have channeled the town's orientation toward stone crabbing and tourism. A new coat of paint on the town has meant a surge in growth and property values. Speaking of a new coat of paint, check out the boat crane-turned-art in front of the Rod & Gun Club, designed and executed in bright colors in 2006 by world-renowned artist Kenneth Noland. Just goes to show the little town attracts a select artsy crowd. Across a long, narrow causeway, **Chokoloskee Island** remains relatively untouched by change. It's a haven for RV campers and fishermen.

LODGING

The South Coast was once a place for roughing it and low-key vacationing. The old wooden Naples Hotel, built in the 1880s by town developers, was as posh as it got. In 1946 Naples became a forerunner in the golf-resort game when the Naples Hotel was bought and converted. In 1985, the Ritz-Carlton came to town and set a new tone. Naples changed forever. The Registry, recently renamed Naples Grande, and other smaller luxury hotels followed the Ritz. Downtown, new properties continue to rise and tend toward intimacy and European style, giving Naples a well-rounded menu of options, from cottages and inns to golf meccas and grandes dames. Bonita Springs, to the north, is growing into its own as a destination with fine lodging, including a

Hyatt Regency that opened in fall 2001. Nearby Marco Island lines up high-rise after high-rise resort and condo community along its coveted beaches. Privately owned second homes and condominiums provide another source of upscale accommodations along the South Coast. (Vacation brokers who match visitors with such properties are listed under "Home & Condo Rentals" at the end of this section.) Away from the metropolitan airs of Naples and Marco, lodging options reflect the simple, primitive nature of the Florida Everglades.

The highlights of South Coast hospitality listed here include the best and freshest in the local industry. Toll-free 800, 877, 866, or 888 reservation numbers, where available, are listed after local numbers.

Pricing codes are explained below. They are normally per unit/double occupancy. The range spans low- and high-season rates and standard to deluxe accommodations. Many resorts offer packages at special rates. Prices do not include the 6 percent Florida sales tax, and some large resorts add service gratuities or maid charges. Collier County imposes a 4 percent tourist bed tax, as well, proceeds from which are applied to beach and environmental maintenance.

Rate Categories

Inexpensive	Up to $75
Moderate	$75 to $150
Expensive	$150 to $200
Very Expensive	$200 and up

(An asterisk after the pricing designation indicates that at least a continental breakfast is included in the lodging rate.)

The following abbreviations are used for credit card information:
AE: American Express
MC: MasterCard
D: Discover Card
V: Visa
DC: Diners Club

Note that under the Americans with Disabilities Act (ADA), accommodations built after January 26, 1993, and containing more than five rooms must be useable by persons with disabilities. I have indicated only those small places that do not make such allowances.

Accommodations

BONITA SPRINGS
✪ HYATT REGENCY COCONUT POINT RESORT & SPA

Managing Director: Joe Murgalo
239-444-1234, 800-55-HYATT
www.coconutpoint.hyatt.com
5001 Coconut Rd., Bonita Springs 34134
Price: Moderate to Very Expensive
Credit Cards: AE, D, DC, MC, V

Opened defiantly soon after 9/11, this tower of luxury has succeeded against the odds to make a glamour statement on shores where fish camps and pristine estuary formerly dominated. Despite its high-rise contrast to the surrounding low-key landscape, the resort strives to blend with its Florida setting wherever possible. The elegant Italian marble and mahogany lobby is localized with Florida-look terrazzo, and the colors of the the public spaces and 450 rooms and suites reflect the sea, sand, and verdure. All rooms and suites are outfitted with minifridges, CD and DVD players, robes, safes, and coffeemakers. The Tarpon Bay restaurant resembles old fish-shack architecture and serves local seafood. To make up for the lack of readily available beach (guests must take a boat shuttle to a private island for sand), Hyatt's signature water features fill in with a waterslide kiddie pool, a lazy river, a toddler's pool, adult pools, and stunning fountains and a reflecting pool. Many guests are more interested in golfing, anyway, and the Hyatt pleases them with 18 top-notch holes. A kids' camp, a spa with one of Florida's few Watsu (water + shiatsu) pools, tennis, and a medley of bars and casual eateries make this a full destination resort for those who don't mind being a short drive away from the beach, shopping, and nightlife that's getting the Bonita-Naples area noticed.

✪ TRIANON BONITA BAY

General Manager: Darren Robertshaw
239-948-4400, 800-859-3939
www.trianon.com
3401 Bay Commons Dr., Bonita Springs 34134
Price: Moderate to Very Expensive*
Credit Cards: AE, D, DC, MC, V

The name implies "a special place," in the spirit of the Grand Trianon and Petit Trianon on the grounds of Versailles near Paris. Heavy on European influence, the hotel's lobby displays both elegance and intimacy, with an inviting fireplace, polished marble, and high-arched ceilings. The dramatic entryway segues into a cozy lounge–breakfast nook, where there is a fireplace and baby grand piano and where tropical iced tea and fruit are on hand to refresh guests. Attention to detail is a hallmark of Trianon, which is a spin-off of a Naples Fifth Avenue South prototype. In its 100 spacious guest rooms and suites you'll find the same refinement previewed in the lobby: dark-wood armoires, sliding French doors to a balcony, gourmet European coffee service, roomy all-white bath, and space enough to dance. Continental breakfast, served in the lounge, is included in the rates. A small pool lies in the back yard of the four-story, chateaulike structure, and the new Lake House Bar & Grill overlooks the pool and a lake. Shoppers will like the Trianon's walking-distance proximity to the fine stores and restaurants of Promenade.

EVERGLADES CITY
THE IVEY HOUSE

General Manager: Sandee Harraden
239-695-3299
www.iveyhouse.com
107 Camellia St., Everglades City 34139
Price: Inexpensive to Expensive*
Credit Cards: MC, V
Closed: June–Sept.

The family-run Ivey House is tailor-made for outdoor enthusiasts. The original Ivey House Lodge, a born-again boardinghouse from the 1920s, offers 10 simple B&B rooms. The 17-room Ivey House Inn opened in 2001, plus there's the Ivey House Cottage (two-night minimum stay), which has two small bedrooms. Smoking and alcohol is not allowed in the rooms. In the original B&B, men's and women's bathrooms are separate from the rooms, dorm style. The new inn rooms, which encircle the courtyard swimming pool, have private baths and offer added style and comforts, including TVs and phones. Breakfast is included in all room rates. Ivey's main attraction is its proximity to Everglades waterways and partnership with North American Canoe Tours. You could call this a BB&B: bed, breakfast, and backcountry. North American Canoe Tours leads tours into the Ten Thousand Islands by canoe, kayak, or boat; rents equipment; and provides shuttle service to launching and landing sites. Sightseeing, birding, and other excursions are available.

ROD & GUN CLUB

Innkeeper: Patricia Bowen
239-695-2101
200 Broadway, P.O. Box 190, Everglades City 34139
Price: Inexpensive to Moderate
Credit Cards: None
No handicap access

Steeped in both history and outdoorsmanship, this circa-1850 lodge crowns a modest town that serves as the South Coast's gateway to the Everglades. The club's main building was built as luxury pioneer housing; the Old South–style mansion came under the ownership of the county's developer and namesake, Barron

Collier, who turned it into a fishermen's and hunters' haven during the 1920s. A sportsman's lodge in the finest sense, it has cypress walls that are still decorated with mounted tarpon, a gator hide, and tools of the fishing trade. Seventeen rooms in tin-roofed cottages scatter around the white-clapboard lodge, which has a wraparound veranda and yellow-striped awnings. The rooms are furnished for function rather than pampering—TV and air-conditioning are the extent of luxury. The club's restaurant, which has a screened porch facing the river, specializes in local delicacies and will cook your catch for a nominal fee. The swimming pool lies off the dining room and is decorated with banana trees, lattice, and rock waterfalls.

MARCO ISLAND
THE BOAT HOUSE
General Managers: Desiree and Nick Buhelos
239-642-2400, 800-528-6345
www.theboathousemotel.com
1180 Edington Place, Marco Island 34145
Price: Moderate to Expensive
Credit Cards: MC, V

At Marco Island's north end, known as Olde Marco, things are a-changing. Once quiet and immune to the resort activity along the beach, the area now sees the completion of a large, fancy resort adjunct to the historic Marco Inn. If you're seeking something less upscale and expensive than Marco's trademark resort scene, drive past the new Olde Marco Inn and turn the corner to this waterfront gem. Twenty rooms, studios, condos, and the two-bedroom gazebo house (expensive to very expensive) line boat docks, and a small pool lies in a two-story strip among the giants. The rooms are nicely appointed and designed for easy, breezy waterfront living. Wireless Internet access is available throughout the resort.

✪ MARCO BEACH OCEAN RESORT
General Manager: Phillip Starling
239-393-1400, 800-260-5089
www.marcoresort.com
480 S. Collier Blvd., Marco Island 34145
Price: Very Expensive
Credit Cards: AE, D, DC, MC, V

If you want the same wide beach but wish to knock it up a cha-ching from the Marriott, try this exclusive relative newcomer just a couple of doors south. Compared to the Marriott, it is more compact, more intimate (though still 12 stories with 103 one- and two-bedroom suites), and more elegant. Its greatest asset may be Sale e Pepe, its Tuscan-style restaurant that overlooks the beach. The sumptuous rooms all face the gulf. The swimming pool and its pool bar are elevated to a fifth-floor rooftop, and parking is in a covered valet ramp. Guests have club privileges at a nearby golf and tennis facility.

MARCO ISLAND LAKESIDE INN
General Manager: Marcia Mandel
239-394-1161, 800-729-0216
www.marcoislandlakeside.com
155 First Ave., Marco Island 34145
Price: Moderate to Expensive
Credit Cards: AE, D, MC, V

Escape from the madhouse traffic and high-rises along the beach to this Superior Small Lodging gem on Marco Lake. Renovation by new owners in 2003 gave the 17-year-old property a perky new attitude, which is enhanced by its acclaim-gathering Sushi Blues & Steaks restaurant. Its 10 suites offer either lakeside views from screened porches (or, on the second floor, balconies) or poolside ground-level accommodations with a shared patio. The lakeview rooms have full kitchens and one or two bedrooms (expensive to very expensive for the two-bedrooms), while those around the pool have kitchenettes and no separate sleeping quarters. In all, deluxe amenities such as pillow-top chiropractic mattresses, French doors, and white spic-and-span tiled bathrooms lend a boutique feel. A small sand beach that edges the lake and nicely maintained landscaping have raised the once motel-like structure into something soothing and special.

✪ MARCO ISLAND MARRIOTT RESORT, GOLF CLUB & SPA

General Manager: Rick Medwedeff
239-394-2511, 800-438-4373
www.marcoislandmarriott.com
400 S. Collier Blvd., Marco Island 34145
Price: Very Expensive
Credit Cards: AE, D, DC, MC, V

In 2007, the Marriott completed a three-year renovation that brought to the long-stretching beachfront property a magnificent new spa with an outdoor Watsu therapy pool, a pool with slides, and an infinity pool overlooking the Gulf of Mexico. Restaurants have changed, and the lobby area has been modernized, but it remains a sprawling complex on the beach—an extra-wide, shell-cluttered, sandbar-sheltered beach—and still provides a fantasy playground for vacationers of all ages. Families enjoy water-sports rentals, a pizza parlor, a game room and ping-pong tables, and a remarkable kids' program. Adults can shop in the marble-floored arcade, golf at an off-site Marriott course, dine grandly or beach style, and act like a kid when the mood strikes. The 735 rooms and 62 suites—which all got a new palm/plantation look—each provide a minifridge, coffeemaker, hair dryer, and minibar. Historic photography and beach sculptures adorn the walls; blond-wood furniture pieces in the guest rooms are decorated with carvings of palm fronds. In the new spa building, which replaces an 18-hole miniature golf course, a state-of-the-art fitness center extracts a fee from guests; they can also use the original fitness room for free.

NAPLES
✪ BELLASERA HOTEL

General Manager: John Gruelich
239-649-7333, 888-612-1115
www.bellaseranaples.com
221 Ninth Street S., Naples 34102
Price: Expensive to Very Expensive
Credit Cards: AE, DC, MC, V

Feel the warmth of Tuscany as you splash in the tiled fountain pool and sup on Italian specialties from Zizi, the poolside restaurant. Inside the lobby, a sweeping staircase and rich Tuscan tones introduce a motif that carries through in the hotel's 100 studios and one- to three-bedroom suites. In the studios, plantation shutters in the bathroom open onto the living area so you can watch TV from the jetted tub. The spacious suites include all the comforts and modern conveniences of home, plus full kitchens and porches and balconies overlooking the beautifully landscaped courtyard and grounds. A small fitness center fits into a room near the pool. Location-wise, the hotel sits steps away from the action and smart social scene of downtown Naples but is tucked away to ensure peace and romance. A free shuttle whisks you off to the beach, minutes away.

COVE INN

General Manager: Carol Nerone
239-262-7161, 800-255-4365
www.coveinnnaples.com
900 Broad Ave. S., Naples 34102
Price: Moderate to Expensive.
Credit Cards: AE, D, DC, MC, V

Back before the Ritz-Carlton and Naples Grande, Naples was about water, boating, and fishing. Cove Inn persists in the old tradition by focusing on the harbor that it edges at Naples's original, circa-1915 settlement of fishermen and builders of Tamiami Trail. Accommodations range from hotel rooms to efficiencies to one- and two-bedroom units with separate living/dining areas. The 85 balconied units are individually owned and decorated; most have a view of the harbor, and even the hotel rooms come equipped with a refrigerator, coffeemaker, microwave, and ironing board and iron. An old-fashioned coffeehouse serves breakfast and lunch, and the marina-side chikee bar slaps down cold ones for sunbathers around the pool. Part of the Crayton Cove and city docks community, Cove Inn is close to casual waterfront restaurants, shops, and marina services.

THE EDGEWATER BEACH HOTEL

General Manager: Matthew LaVine
239-403-2000, 800-821-0196
www.edgewaternaples.com
1901 Gulf Shore Blvd. N., Naples 34102
Price: Expensive to Very Expensive
Credit Cards: AE, D, DC, MC, V

The Edgewater hints at New Orleans style with lacy, white-iron balustrades on two of its three buildings, all of which face the gulf-lapped beach. You can't stay much closer to the sand than at this appropriately named hotel. Its 124 one- and two-bedroom suites are spacious, convenient, and handsomely appointed with clay tiles, designer furnishings, and thick bedspreads. The floor plan of each includes a full kitchen with microwave, living/dining area, and private patio or balcony. Guests can dine in the chic new lobby restaurant, Coast, or poolside under stylish market umbrellas. There's an on-site exercise room, spa services, and opportunities for other recreation nearby, including golf at the Naples Grande Golf Club. Guests have privileges at the Naples Grande sister resort.

LEMON TREE INN

General Manager: Rob DeCastro
239-262-1414, 888-800-LEMON
www.lemontreeinn.com

250 Ninth St. S., Naples 34102
Price: Moderate to Expensive*
Credit Cards: AE, D, MC, V

Despite its lemon-pulp-yellow paint job and free lemonade in the lobby, this property, recently converted to a condo-hotel operation, is anything but a lemon. At the edge of downtown's fashionable drags, it retains a humble charm, dressed in white-tin roofs and flowering plants. The 34 rooms with porches (most are screened) are named Periwinkle, Plumosa, Poinciana, and such, after local flowers. Spacious, simple, and cottage style in decor, they are individually decorated and outfitted with tiled kitchens containing a microwave, toaster, coffeemaker, and minifridge. Around the pool and a gazebo in the courtyard, thick foliage and stylish globe streetlamps create character. At the poolside breakfast nook you can help yourself to continental goodies. Shopping is steps away, and the beach is a short drive.

NAPLES BEACH HOTEL & GOLF CLUB

Owners: the Watkins family
General Manager: Jim Gunderson
239-261-2222, 800-237-7600
www.naplesbeachhotel.com
851 Gulf Shore Blvd. N., Naples 34102
Price: Expensive to Very Expensive
Credit Cards: AE, D, DC, MC, V

The doyenne of Naples resorts, this combines the best of the area—its beaches and its golf—into a three-generation tradition in the heart of town. The 18-hole golf course hosts the Florida State PGA Seniors Open and other major golf tournaments. Its stand-alone spa and clubhouse complex overlooks the greens. The spacious facility also holds meeting rooms, a fitness center, and Broadwell's, an elegant dining room. Har-Tru tennis courts, a heated pool, the Beach Klub 4 Kids, and water-sports equipment rentals vie for off-the-course recreational hours. The hotel's spacious lobby and Everglades Room, where a breakfast buffet is served, communicate old Florida vacationing ease. Its 329 guest rooms, efficiencies, and suites are done in Florida decor and display some lingering classic trademarks of yesteryear. Accommodations overlook the wide, palm-studded beach or the lush golf course. Golf, tennis, and other packages are available.

✪ NAPLES GRANDE RESORT & CLUB

Managing Director: Hunter H. Hansen
239-597-3232, 800-247-9810
www.naplesgrande.com
475 Seagate Dr., Naples 34103
Price: Very Expensive
Credit Cards: AE, D, DC, MC, V

Formerly the Registry, Naples Grande recently came under new management and benefited from a major facelift, which included the addition of a stand-alone Golden Door Spa. The resort's distinctive red-capped tower, villas, and 15 Har-Tru tennis courts dominate north Naples's pristine, mangrove-fringed estuaries. Luxurious but with beach casualness, the resort's style impresses from the moment you walk through the front door into the newly redesigned sleek, chic lobby with its smart bar and Aura restaurant. Outside, the family pool has a Flintstones feel with a 100-foot on-the-rocks waterslide and private cabanas. Also for families is a fine kids' program. Tram service is available along the boardwalk that traverses estuaries to Clam Pass Recreation Area, a 3-mile stretch of plush sands with all manner of water-sports rentals. Fifty luxury bungalows edge the tennis courts; another 424 rooms and 29 suites overlook the gulf. All of these are spacious and furnished with a dry bar, walk-in shower, soaking tub, and class. Naples Grande owns a nearby 18-hole golf course and provides a golf concierge. Five heated pools include Jacuzzis. Restaurants range

from poolside casual to a steakhouse and Aura's fashion-forward breakfast, lunch, and dinner. Covered parking and fitness room use is included in a resort fee.

PARK SHORE RESORT

Resort Manager: Steve McIntire
238-263-2222, 800-548-2077
www.sunstream.com
600 Neapolitan Way, Naples 34103
Price: Expensive to Very Expensive
Credit Cards: AE, D, DC, MC, V

Its 156 one- and two-bedroom condos stack up a couple stories high in buildings that encircle a lake. A tropically landscaped island in the middle of the lake, accessible by several wooden footbridges, holds a swimming pool with a craggy waterfalls backdrop. The pool complex includes barbecue and sunning decks and a poolside café serving fun martinis, frozen drinks, and Caribbean-inspired dishes. Cobblestone paths encircle the pool complex and lead to racquetball, volleyball,

Park Shore Resort boasts its own island in a luxuriant green setting.

tennis, and basketball courts. Free shuttles are available to the beach, which is only minutes away. Tucked into one of Naples' exclusive neighborhoods, the resort is also convenient to shopping and dining. On property, guests enjoy free Internet access, laundry facilities, and a friendly atmosphere and homelike accommodations, complete with fully equipped kitchens.

THE RITZ-CARLTON GOLF RESORT

Hotel Manager: Michael McMahon
239-593-2000, 800-241-3333
www.ritzcarlton.com/resorts/naples_golf
_resort
2600 Tiburón Dr., Naples 34109
Price: Very Expensive
Credit Cards: AE, D, DC, MC, V

Making Naples the only city in the world with two Ritz-Carltons on the same street, the golf resort opened amid 27 holes of lush, Greg Norman–designed greens in 2002. The Rick Smith Golf Academy, a putting course and practice area, and a clubhouse with pro shop make this a complete golf resort. Its sybaritic relationship with its elder sister out on the beach gives both properties the most complete menu of leisure activities possible. Guests at the golf resort have access via shuttle to the beach resort's spa, beach, kids' program, and fine restaurants. Its own Lemonia restaurant gives guests a reason to stay right on property for a fabulous Tuscan feast overlooking the links. A gourmet pastry shop, pool grill, cigar bar, room service, and other lounges help fill the dining-entertainment bill. The golf resort also has an on-property fitness center, four lit tennis courses, and a pool. Kids from both resorts learn golf and golf etiquette at the newer resort. Overlooking the greens with private balconies, 295 rooms and suites have it all, from cuddly robes and oversized marble bathrooms to high-speed and wireless Internet access

and safes large enough to hold laptop computers.

✪ THE RITZ-CARLTON NAPLES

Hotel Manager: Ed Staros
239-598-3300, 800-241-3333
www.ritzcarlton.com/resorts/naples
280 Vanderbilt Beach Rd., Naples 34108
Price: Very Expensive
Credit Cards: AE, D, DC, MC, V

The gold standard for regal accommodations, the Ritz-Carlton melds Old World elegance with Old Florida environment. The hotel's facade looms majestically classic. Inside, oversized vases of fresh flowers, massive chandeliers, cabinets filled with priceless china, 19th-century oil paintings, vaulted ceilings, and crystal lamps detail Ritz extravagance. Each of the 465 units in the U-shaped configuration faces the gulf. Guest rooms and suites are dressed in fine furniture, plush carpeting, and marble bath areas. Accommodations include an honor bar, a refrigerator, bathrobes, hypoallergenic pillows, telephones in the bathroom, clothes steamers, and private balconies overlooking the hotel's backyard, where wilderness and civility meet. In the courtyard, fountains and groomed gardens exude European character. Classic arches, stone balustrades, and majestic palm-lined stairways lead to a boardwalk that takes you through mangroves. At the end of the boardwalk lie golden sands, where Gumbo Limbo restaurant serves daytime fare and water-sports rentals are available. Other amenities and services that earn the Ritz its five stars include a formal dining room, afternoon tea service, a fine steak grill, two cafés, a gourmet coffee shop, an elegant spa, a lap pool and free-form family pool, a lounge, a ballroom, tennis courts, sister-property golf facilities (see above), a fitness center, a beauty salon, children's programs, a nature walk, bicycle rentals, shops, transportation services, and twice-daily maid service. New poolside cabanas are equipped with all relaxation necessities—from high-speed Internet and a flat-panel TV with DVD player to fresh fruit and a cabana butler.

VANDERBILT BEACH
✪ LAPLAYA BEACH & GOLF RESORT
General Manager: Ron Vuy
239-597-3123, 800-237-6883
www.laplayaresort.com
9891 Gulf Shore Dr., Naples 34108
Price: Very Expensive
Credit Cards: AE, D, DC, MC, V

LaPlaya's gracious, Southern-style lobby, Thai spa, exercise room, rocky waterfall pool, pool bar, and trendy restaurant menu (see **Baleen** under "Dining" below) put it on par with Miami Beach's boutique hotels. Rooms show a meticulous attention to detail; some sport Jacuzzis with sea views, and all are luxurious with four-poster beds, Frette linens, goose-down pillows, private balconies, and marble baths. Of its 189 units, 141 are beachfront with private balconies. The "golf" part of the name refers to privileges on a course 15 minutes away. The "beach" part is obvious—a delicious slice of sands that gives way to the property's lush tropical garden and Colonial-style public areas.

VANDERBILT BEACH RESORT
General Manager: Mick Moore
239-597-3144, 800-243-9076
www.vanderbiltbeachresort.com
9225 Gulf Shore Dr. N., Naples 34108
Price: Moderate to Very Expensive
Credit Cards: AE, D, DC, MC, V

This longtime fixture on the barefoot-casual Vanderbilt Beach scene comes in two parts: a two-story, Old-Florida beach motel with a small swimming pool in the shadow of next door's towering high-rise and, across the street, a four-story bayside condo building. The efficiencies and apartments in the older beach building have an easygoing feel, while the condos sport a bit more elegance. All 34 units come with fully equipped kitchens, but plan on at least one dinner at the inimitable and highly hailed Turtle Club restaurant on property. It serves lunch and dinner inside or outside on the patio or in the sand. A private fishing dock and a tennis court add to the convenience of the compact property.

Home & Condo Rentals
Resort Quest Southwest Florida (239-992-6620; www.resortquest.com; 26201 Hickory Blvd., Bonita Springs 34134) Rentals from Fort Myers Beach to Marco Island.

RV Resorts
Chokoloskee Island Park (239-695-2414; www.chokoloskee.com/cip.html; P.O. Box 430, Chokoloskee, 34138) Rustic fishing paradise with easy access to the Everglades and the gulf. Full-service marina, tackle shop, guide service, ramps, and docks. Overnight or seasonal tent and RV sites with complete hookups; mobile home rentals.

Outdoor Resorts of Chokoloskee Island (239-695-3788; www.outdoor-resorts.com; 150 Smallwood Dr., P.O. Box 39, Chokoloskee 34138). Marina, boat rentals, a bait-and-tackle shop, and guide service for fishing and touring. Pull into one of 283 full-service sites or stay in the motel. Either way you can take advantage of the resort's three pools, health spa, lit tennis and shuffleboard courts, and restaurant.

Rock Creek RV Resort (239-643-3100; www.rockcreekrv.com; 3100 North Rd. at Airport Rd., Naples 34104) Full hookups for 221 RVs, pool, laundry, and shade trees. Limited pet area.

Dining

Everglades City considers itself a fishing and stone-crab capital, so figure you can expect some highly fresh seafood in these parts. Stone crab, in fact, was discovered as a food source in the Everglades—at least that's the way some of the old-timers tell it. Before a couple of locals began trapping stone crabs and selling them to a Miami restaurant, the delicate, meaty flavor of these crustaceans went unappreciated. Along with stone crab, alligator, frog legs, and other local delicacies make up the substance of Everglades cookery.

Marco Island, too, is known as a good market for buying stone crab, which gets quite expensive farther from the source. With more than 100 restaurants on the island, Marco covers every genre of cuisine. Its trademark is its Old Florida style of no-nonsense, trend-resistant seafood preparation, particularly in Goodland.

Naples's dining reputation is staked on hauteur and creativity. Even the old fish houses dress up their catches in the latest fashion, which ranges from redesigned home cooking and continental nouvelle to Floribbean, Pacific Rim, and fusion styles. Naples is a dining-out kind

Downtown Naples' gator art goes culinary on Fifth Avenue South.

of place. The renovation of downtown's Fifth Avenue South brought restaurants out into the street and sparked the genesis of what has been termed Naples' "café society."

The following listings sample all the variety of South Coast feasting in these price categories:

Inexpensive	Up to $15
Moderate	$15 to $25
Expensive	$25 to $35
Very Expensive	$35 or more

Cost categories are based on the range of dinner entrée prices, or, if dinner is not served, on lunch entrées. The following abbreviations are used for credit card information and meals:

AE: American Express
D: Discover Card
DC: Diners Club
MC: MasterCard
V: Visa
B: Breakfast
L: Lunch
D: Dinner
SB: Sunday Brunch

Note: Florida law forbids smoking inside all restaurants and bars serving food. Smoking is permitted only in restaurants with outdoor seating.

Bonita Beach
BIG HICKORY SEAFOOD GRILLE

239-992-0991
www.bighickorygrille.com
26107 Hickory Blvd., Bonita Beach 34134
Price: Inexpensive to Expensive
Cuisine: Old and new Florida
Children's Menu: Yes
Liquor: Beer and wine
Serving: L, D (Closed Mon. during the summer.)
Credit Cards: AE, D, DC MC, V
Handicap Access: Yes
Reservations: No
Special Features: Indoor and outdoor seating on the harbor, where Old Blue, the little

blue heron, and arriving fishing boat catches entertain.

A masterful blend of fish-shack chic and contemporary tropical Florida style have remade this longtime marina-side favorite into a sure keeper. Its all-day menu adheres to its roots with fresh seafood prepared in both traditional and creative modes. One entrées section devotes itself to "Cracker style"—deep-fried seafood baskets of oysters, grouper fingers, shrimp, and belly-on clams. The other, along with the weekly changing special menu, goes gourmet to a Caribbean beat. The Cubana Grouper is a catch in all senses of the word—a generous supply of pan-seared, banana-crusted fish swimming in a creamy banana-liqueur sauce with the fresh veggie of the day, which is usually nice and garlicky. On Lobster Nights, usually Tuesday and Wednesday, the first lobster dinner costs $20, the second $14, but you must reserve ahead.

DOC'S BEACH HOUSE

239-992-6444
www.docsbeachhouse.com
27980 Hickory Blvd., Bonita Beach 34134
Price: Inexpensive
Cuisine: American
Children's Menu: No, but plenty of appropriate options on the regular menu
Liquor: Beer and wine
Serving: B, L, D
Credit Cards: None (ATM available)
Handicap Access: Yes
Reservations: No
Special Features: On the beach, with outdoor and indoor seating

This is the kind of place where Gidget and Moondoggie would hang out (if there were surfable waves, that is). It's all about being on the beach—Bonita's colorful, action-packed beach. If you can't bear leaving the sands, you can just grab a quick burger or dog and get back to it. If you need a break from the sun, duck inside. Downstairs is

open and barefoot casual. Upstairs is blessedly air-conditioned and has huge picture windows so you won't miss any of the beach action. Both levels have bars and sports TVs. The menu makes no pretense of fine dining, but the food is solidly good. Grab-and-go items include Sand Dollar Burgers, Chicago-style pizza, tacos, chili, and sandwiches of all sorts. For dinner or a heartier lunch, add a choice of grilled seafood, strip steak, and a fried seafood combo basket.

BONITA SPRINGS
✪ CHOPS CITY GRILL

239-992-4677
www.chopsbonita.com
8200 Health Center Blvd., Bonita Springs 34134
U.S. 41 and Coconut Rd. at Brooks Grand Plaza
Price: Expensive to Very Expensive
Cuisine: Steaks, Asian
Children's Menu: No
Liquor: Full
Serving: D
Credit Cards: AE, D, MC, V
Handicap Access: Yes
Reservations: Yes
Special Features: Courtyard dining

A spin-off from its original downtown Naples success, Chops's name is a double entendre for the food it does unerringly well: steaks and Pacific Rim—style dishes. Seriously fashionable, with a burnished copper bar and modern kitchen-theater dining room, Chops's ambience sets a tone of nouvelle sophistication that the food follows. The menu rhapsodized my pan-seared grouper's sauce, for instance, as "screaming hot rock shrimp with tomatoes, garlic, and white wine." The "screaming hot" was overstated, but certainly not the garlic, which was apparent in crunchy slices throughout the sauce and the gooey-good wild-mushroom risotto. We discovered a clear penchant for garlic here, for in my husband's mound of arugula whipped potatoes, the chef had buried treasures of whole roasted garlic cloves. Creative sushi rolls and other Asian and eclectic inspirations (big eye tuna tartare, beef satay, shrimp- and hoisin-spiced beef spring rolls) start the meal out right. Meat-lovers can order the unadulterated finest in steaks, while more adventurous palates will choose from day's specials and a selection of imaginative entrées, such as mango-chili-glazed tuna with wasabi mashed potatoes, teriyaki roasted sea bass with lobster stir fry and coconut sticky rice, or Asian-glazed pork porterhouse with smoked gouda potato cake. For dessert, the banana spring rolls wrap up the meal in proper motif and exotic sweetness.

✪ DIXIE MOON CAFÉ

239-495-0023
27755 Old 41 Rd., Bonita Springs 34134
Downtown Bonita Springs
Price: Inexpensive
Cuisine: Southern
Children's Menu: No, but appropriate items on regular menu
Liquor: Beer and wine
Serving: B, L, D (Closed for lunch and dinner on Sun.)
Credit Cards: AE, D, MC, V
Handicap Access: Yes
Reservations: No

It looks old on the outside—like from the Alamo "old"—but in reality it's been around for only 10 years. During that time, it has built its reputation for "Southern food with an attitude" by winning various local awards for its burgers, Southern cooking, chicken wings, and fried chicken. Obviously, no awarders have tasted its peach blossom cake—a buttery transgression topped with caramel sauce and served hot in a pool of real cream. Wooooe! But let's not jump ahead. If you can't find something that warms the cockles of your heart, soul, and stomach off this comfort-

food menu, you've never tasted home cooking. Despite their Culinary Institute degrees, the cooks stick to Dixie like collard greens to ribs. Choose from 10 varieties of burgers, including voodoo (blackened) and jalapeno; five deviations of cheese-steak sandwiches; and a slew of traditional and quirky specialties, such as chicken gizzards with cream sauce, grit cakes, chicken-fried steak, meatloaf, fried crawfish, pot roast, smelt, and fried green tomato sandwich with bacon. Relish your meal at the worn, curved Formica counter or a table covered with chili-pepper-decorated oilcloth. Talk friendly to the folks who work the warped wood floor. Just whatever you do, don't fill up before your peach blossom cake arrives.

TARPON BAY RESTAURANT

239-444-1234
www.coconutpoint.hyatt.com
5001 Coconut Rd., Bonita Springs 34134
At the Hyatt Regency Coconut Point Resort & Spa
Price: Expensive
Cuisine: Seafood
Children's Menu: Yes
Liquor: Full
Serving: D
Credit Cards: AE, D, MC, V
Handicap Access: Yes
Reservations: Yes
Special Features: Patio seating overlooking a fountain pond

White-clapboard fish houses were once the architectural icon of this just-lately developed area. The Hyatt Regency designed its casual resort restaurant to pay homage to the old Florida it replaced. Considerably more well dressed than the real thing, the ambiance nonetheless feels cottage comfortable. (Outdoor seating overlooks a pond containing a fountain and a floating golf hole, which can provide its share of entertainment.) Local and imported seafood get a tropical zing. My favorite reason for dining there is the ceviche raw bar. Besides the typical shellfish, you can sample one of seven types of raw seafood "cooked" in various citric marinades. Can't make up your mind? Try the sampler for $28. From the menu's entrée selections, crispy fried red snapper is a visual and gastronomic masterpiece. Unusual ingredients and exquisite freshness make the meal: cilantro-lime-and-chipotle crab cakes, brown butter–basted scallops with saffron vegetable risotto, warm grilled vegetable terrine with lemon-thyme-champagne vinaigrette, and pan-roasted chicken with Peruvian purple potatoes are just some examples.

WYLDS CAFÉ

239-947-0408
www.wyldscafe.com
4271 Bonita Beach Rd., Bonita Springs 34134
Price: Moderate
Cuisine: Continental
Children's Menu: Yes
Liquor: Beer and wine
Serving: D
Credit Cards: AE, MC, V
Handicap Access: Yes
Reservations: Yes

If I were to describe Wylds in a word, it would be "buttery." So leave home the diet and prepare to be slathered. It began with the buttery, garlicky, herby spread between the crusty bread and ended with cinnamon bread pudding crusted with pecan praline and sauced with warm caramel and crème anglaise. Wow! In between, we sampled an appetizer of pan-seared scallops, cooked to perfection and majestically throned upon bread, maple creamed spinach, and toasted prosciutto. The Enigma Salad was a romaine-based creation with avocado, shiitakes, shredded duck, capers, and a rich, creamy parmesan-peppercorn dressing.

The parmesan-crusted walleye wore a shawl of impeccable tomato-basil beurre blanc and came with a gooey side of roasted shallot risotto. The chef has a definite affinity for butter sauces, and an orange beurre blanc accompanied my husband's grilled swordfish. Mango-pineapple chutney supplied an added flavor boost (and, hey, even a measure of health!). Both entrées came with young unshelled peas that were so flavorful we guessed butter and meat broth, if not bacon fat, must have been an accomplice in the sautéing process. Other starters range from chicken tortilla soup and an interesting cheese plate to calamari tossed with crimini mushrooms and roasted red peppers in a scampi soy broth. Entrées are seafood heavy with some intriguing concessions to meat-lovers (duck and foie gras sausage with roasted duck over pasta in a sage butter sauce, braised cranberry barbecue boneless short ribs, and grilled heirloom pork chop) and vegetarians (pasta pomodoro and asparagus wrapped in falafel with gorgonzola polenta). In a simple setting of linen and russet-textured walls and with service that was right on, the Wylds experience is as soothing as it is rich.

EVERGLADES CITY
ROD & GUN CLUB

239-695-2101
200 Broadway, P.O. Box 190, Everglades City 34139
Price: Moderate to Expensive
Cuisine: Florida
Children's Menu: Sometimes, dinner only
Liquor: Full
Serving: L, D
Credit Cards: No
Handicap Access: Yes
Reservations: No
Special Features: Historic waterfront setting

Dining here on a screened porch overlooking the Barron River, with the mangroves on the other side, always triggers the relaxation mechanism in my body, mind, and spirit. Paddle fans twirl from pressed-tin ceilings, and white columns, a rounded portico, a porch with wicker chairs, and there are yellow-and-white striped awnings at the lodge's entrance. The inside dining room, the antithesis of the patio's lightness, is all dark pecky-cypress wood, polished wood floors, and mounted fish and fowl—remnants of the lodge's sporting past. From the 1890s to 1960 the club hosted presidents, movie stars, and other intrepid Everglades hunters and fishermen. Back then guests dined on frog legs, alligator tail, and fresh fish. They still do. Menus also offer more conventional fare—Reubens, burgers, New York strip steak, shrimp linguine, and stone crab in season—but the ultimate Everglades City experience requires sitting back, taking in the view, enjoying local hospitality, and dining on Everglades specialties. The frog legs are incredibly tasty; the onion rings, the crunchiest and lightest imaginable; the gator nuggets, well tenderized but salty and a tad greasy; and the key lime pie, simply divine.

GOODLAND
✪ OLD MARCO LODGE CRAB HOUSE
239-64-CRABS
1 Papaya St., Goodland 34140
Price: Inexpensive to Moderate
Children's Menu: Yes
Cuisine: Seafood/Florida
Liquor: Full
Serving: L, D (Closed Mon. during off season, plus the month of Sept.)
Credit Cards: AE, MC, V
Handicap Access: Yes
Reservations: Yes, for dinner
Special Features: Waterfront dining, salad bar, live entertainment

Goodland is a town where a more modest pace of tourism has allowed folks to remain proudly hometown. A long-ingrained fishing tradition means you'll find both the freshest catches and people who know how to prepare them. Old Marco Lodge has been doing it longer than anyone, in a waterfront restaurant built in 1869. Specialty of the house is—no surprise—crab, served in soft-crab sandwiches, in the incredibly full-flavored vegetable-crab soup, and, most popularly, steamed and presented simply with a hammer or nutcracker. Hammer

Casual and waterside, Old Marco Lodge is all about what's good in Goodland.

away at a bowl of signature garlic crabs—blue crabs (when they're in stock) in butter and garlic—or try stone (in season), king, or snow crab. The extensive all-day menu embraces everything seafood-lovers and landlubbers want: crab cakes, grouper sandwich, seafood pasta, famous crab Imperial, lobster tail, and much more. The key lime pie makes you pucker, just like it should, and the Bloody Marys are among the best I've tasted.

MARCO ISLAND (SEE ALSO GOODLAND)
✪ SALE E PEPE
239-393-1600
www.sale-e-pepe.com
480 S. Collier Blvd., Marco Island 34145
At Marco Beach Ocean Resort
Price: Expensive to Very Expensive
Cuisine: Tuscan Italian
Children's Menu: Yes
Liquor: Full
Serving: B, L, D
Credit Cards: AE, D, DC, MC, V
Handicap Access: Yes
Reservations: Yes
Special Features: View of beach and gulf; terrace dining

Whether it's your fantasy to dine under the Tuscan sun or the Florida moon, Sale e Pepe brings it to reality in a replicated, palace-proportioned, Italian-villa setting with an outdoor terrace. Perched on the second floor, it affords an elevated perspective of sand and sea. Inside, you can choose a formal frescoed dining setting (jackets required) or a more casual lounge setting. All serve the same finely crafted, award-winning, Tuscan-based creations. Everything's made fresh, from the crusty olive and rustic herb breads to the pasta, soups, sausage, and tiramisu. The menu adapts to the seasons, always paying tribute to the main Tuscan food groups: beans, fish, meat, and pasta. You may find a chestnut and roasted shrimp in Italian bacon soup. In the pasta department I can recommend the addicting agnolotti stuffed with spinach and ricotta cheese and topped with silky mascarpone and parmesan cream or the Maine lobster over fettucine—entire meaty tail and claw sections atop a subtly spicy tomato sauce, flavor-bolstered by strips of dried tomato. I've also raved about the seared yellowfin tuna, masterfully complemented with a tangle of caramelized onions and grained mustard sauce. The veal tenderloin with rosemary sauce is a specialty. The formal dining room also offers a four- or five-course tasting menu for about $55 (or $85, including wine pairings). Lunch and breakfast on the terrace and in the lounge are prepared by a different operation and not as impressive. Stop in the huge gaslit bar, a shrine to artist Toulouse-Lautrec, for an after-dinner drink. Or take the staircase down to the beach to walk off the dinner in which you've undoubtedly overindulged.

NAPLES
✪ BHA! BHA!
239-594-5557
www.bhabhapersianbistro.com
847 Vanderbilt Rd., Naples 34108
At Pavilion Shopping Center
Price: Moderate to Expensive
Cuisine: Middle Eastern
Children's Menu: No
Liquor: Beer and wine
Serving: L, D, SB (closed Mon.)
Credit Cards: AE, MC, V
Handicap Access: Yes
Reservations: Yes, for dinner

A merger of creativities results in a sleek, bright, and sunny setting of ocher and key lime green walls, ottomans, a fountain, and Turkish tapestries. They call it a Persian bistro. In an Iranian dialect the name means "Yum! Yum!" And that's where Chef Michael Mir comes in. He fuses his native background with his experience in fine American kitchens to present an intriguing menu that maintains the authenticity and boldness of Middle Eastern cuisine while employing a few tricks of classic Continental and experimental new American styles. Prepare your palate for a magic carpet ride. Aash, a peasant-style herbed bean soup, starts out simple but, as you nibble into the center garnish of Persian noodles, becomes more and more complex and extraordinary. In the appetizer of eggplant and artichoke, we could discern an orchestra of flavors: distinctive Bulgarian feta, dill, and a hint of sweetness in the mustard sauce, and the peanut oil in which the eggplant was sautéed. Yum, yum. From the lunch menu, the marinated portobello mushroom stuffed with grilled vegetables and feta is divine. The dinner menu is divided between classic and innovative Persian cuisine and *khoreshes* (specialties). I recommend the spicy kermani beef, its dark saffron sauce enlivened by pepperoncini and cucumber yogurt; charbroiled lamb (incredibly beautiful and tasty); garlic eggplant chicken (wonderful!); and duck fesenjune, braised in orange saffron stock and served with pomegranate walnut sauce (a bit heavy sweet). Turkish coffee comes served in a delicate espresso service with an ornamental wooden box full of rock candy and sugar. Try the unusual, rose-scented hibiscus-lemon sorbet or gooey baklava for dessert.

BISTRO 821

239-261-5821
www.bistro821.com
821 Fifth Ave. S., Naples 34102
Price: Moderate to Expensive
Cuisine: American Bistro
Children's Menu: Yes
Liquor: Full
Serving: D
Credit Cards: AE, D, DC, MC, V
Handicap Access: Yes
Reservations: No
Special Features: Sidewalk dining

Bistro 821, the maverick of Fifth Avenue South and trendsetter in the local bistro

craze, still leads today, despite a swell of competition in its wake. The menu benefits from an injection of fearless creativity. Small plates range from the familiar escargot, oysters Rockefeller, and shrimp cocktail to the inventive wild-mushroom bisque and rock-lobster satay. Salads come in appetizer and full portions (be sure to indicate "appetizer" even if you order it as a first course). One menu section is devoted to pasta and risotto, also as appetizer and full options, with such tempters as shrimp-and-prosciutto macaroni and cheese and seafood risotto. Entrées, too, wax from such traditional bistro fare as chicken pot pie and bouillabaisse to house specialties: sugarcane-skewered prawns, steak au poivre with goat-cheese-stuffed potato cake, seafood paella, and grilled ostrich tenderloin. The coconut, ginger, and lemongrass—encrusted snapper with coconut-ginger jasmine rice and coconut butter sauce will dazzle any sweet tooth. On the specials menu, chefs flex even further with such adventures as the elk rib chop crusted with maple-caramelized pistachio nuts that I recently relished. A robust wine list and intriguing dessert menu (try the wonderfully complex ope'ra cake) round out the reasons Bistro 821 will always remain at the Fifth Avenue forefront.

ESCARGOT 41

239-793-5000
www.escargot-41.com
4229 N. Tamiami Trail, Naples 34103
At Park Shore Shopping Center
Price: Moderate to Expensive
Cuisine: French
Children's Menu: No
Liquor: Wine
Serving: D (closed Sun.)
Credit Cards: AE, D, MC, V
Handicap Access: Yes
Reservations: Required

Who would have thought: near-perfect French cuisine in a corner next to Kmart and having only a dozen tables? The wine list, nearly as big in size as the restaurant itself, came as the first surprise. Our white Bordeaux, Chateau Peyruchet 2002, started out light but opened up marvelously to meet the rich creaminess of our appetizers, which followed a charming amuse-bouche of pureed eggplant and goat cheese. Escargot, we felt, we must try and so opted for the night's special appetizer in cognac cream. They were as divine as our mussels appetizer in their soup of wine, tomato and red pepper coulis, and basil, with a touch of cream. If you're on a splurge and visiting in winter, you might want to go for the black truffle and foie gras appetizer with proscuitto, morels, and spinach in phyllo dough for $79 or caviar, priced $25 to $95. Otherwise, smoked salmon, foie gras, onion soup, lobster bisque, and Caesar salad kick off the meal. The *fruits de mer aux morilles* delightfully surprised us next by sheer nonstingy volume of the morel strips tucked among shrimp, scallops, and mushrooms—all luxuriously napped in a champagne cream sauce with a subtle thyme undertone. The yellowtail snapper was fresh, lightly pan-fried, and served in a shallot–white wine cream sauce flecked with fresh tomatoes and marjoram. Other entrées wander into meat categories: tournedos sautéed with wild escargots, duck in plum port wine sauce, veal scaloppini in Calvados cream sauce, and, with 24-hour advance notice, a white bean cassoulet containing duck confit, smoked pork, and French sausages. For dessert, the vanilla crème brûlée came heavily caramel crusted in a heart-shaped dish. The velvety smooth underlie was a creamy counterpoint, and we toasted it with a small glass of port and bubbly kir royale. It was the perfect wrap to a perfect dining experience.

BRICKTOP'S

239-596-9112
www.bricktops.com

Waterside Shops, 5555 Tamiami Trail N., Naples, Naples 34108
Price: Inexpensive to Moderate
Cuisine: American
Children's Menu: No
Liquor: Full, but limited
Serving: L, D
Credit Cards: AE, D, MC, V
Handicap Access: Yes
Reservations: Yes

At the bar we got our first inkling of the quirky selectiveness of BrickTop's. The menu does not try to be all things to all people, but just the best at what it does. My husband didn't appreciate that fact when he couldn't get his preferred brand of Manhattan and then to find only a half dozen available beers. But by the time we scraped up the last bit of key lime pie, we had both come to appreciate BrickTop's brand of perfectionism. The all-day menu is deceivingly simple, like a diner's: sandwiches, burgers, steak and fries, baby-back ribs, jumbo lump crab cakes, filet mignon, grilled pork chops. Rotisserie chicken is a specialty; we could smell and see dozens of plump birds spinning over flames near our table. The three flatbreads showed promise of creativity, so we decided to split the seared beef tenderloin version as an appetizer. The crisp lavosh crust was spread thinly with mashed potatoes and topped with tender bits of meat, blue cheese, caramelized red onion, and capers. We had to force ourselves to stop nibbling to save some room for entrées. He ordered the rotisserie chicken sandwich—juicy breast meat between soft rolls and loaded with jack cheese, tomato, and red onion. He raved equally about the sandwich and the pile of skinny-cut French fries. My pan-fried snapper special was heavier on breading than I like, but the tartar sauce was flavored nicely with fresh sprigs of dill. A side of wild-rice salad presented an extraordinarily original mélange of white and wild rice, fresh corn, grapes, blue cheese, walnuts, and red bell pepper in a light, sweet vinaigrette. The key lime pie was built upon a macadamia-studded crust flavored with a hint of cinnamon; it was tart and creamy beyond belief and topped generously with fresh-made and slightly sweetened whipped cream. So it turns out that BrickTop's menu simply understates its fresh quality. It lets the food itself do the sales job, at which it succeeds marvelously.

CILANTRO TAMALES

239-597-5855
10823 Tamiami Trail N., Naples, 34108
Price: Inexpensive to Moderate
Cuisine: Mexican
Children's Menu: Yes
Liquor: Beer and wine
Serving: L, D
Credit Cards: MC, V.
Handicap Access: Yes
Reservations: No

Cilantro Tamales touts "modern Mexican food" in a bright bistro setting. With a slab of clay tile for a placemat and two bottles of chili sauce on the table, you're ready to dip into a Mexican dining experience that's as authentic as it is creative. I knew this the minute the cursory presentation of chips and salsa hit the table. An earthenware throne held two types of sauces: a fresh pico de gallo and a spicier red tomatillo sauce, its recipe straight from Mexico, our server said. Full of flavor, its heat played backup to the first burst of flavor. This is how Mexican food is supposed to be: zest, then zing. We ordered a side of guacamole—my barometer for truth in Mexican—and a cup of sopa de tortilla to get things rolling. The guac passed the litmus test with flying colors, neither pureed nor mashed and dressed lightly in a garlic-seasoned tomato sauce. We ended up eating it out of its flowerpot dish with a spoon. The tortilla soup also carried off that homemade flavor, full

of the goodness of chicken and cilantro. For entrées try the house specialty: cilantro tamales, what else? The smoked Gouda cheese stuffing lends an unusual, worldly quality to the bell pepper and onions inside. Tamales also come in pork and chicken varieties, plus the menu carries many other Tex-Mex standards and a few surprises, such as the Mexican rice bowl and Mexican chicken wings. All in all, Cilantro Tamales lives up to its menu promise: "cooked with Old World know-how seasoned and plated with modern imagination." It proved so popular when it opened in Naples a few years back that two others in Bonita Springs and Marco Island have cropped up.

✪ THE DOCK AT CRAYTON COVE

239-263-9940
www.dockcraytoncove.com
845 12th Ave. S., Naples 34102
Price: Moderate
Cuisine: Seafood/American
Children's Menu: Yes
Liquor: Full
Serving: L, D
Credit Cards: AE, D, MC, V
Handicap Access: Yes
Reservations: No
Special Features: Open-air view of the marina

The Dock remembers what Naples is about—clear down to its roots—while keeping up with what Naples has become. The roots part is reflected in the fun, casual, waterlogged atmosphere exuded from its breeze-through setup and location along Naples's original, circa-1915 fishing harbor. Opened in 1976, the fish-house-style eatery has kept abreast of Naples's sophistication with remakes and menu upgrades. Once a purveyor of typical fried seafood fare, today it makes a serious stance among the town's tough culinary standards. Seafood still reigns in traditions such as grouper and chips, Ipswich clams, and Maine smelts, but island and Cajun influences have washed in to give us such offerings as Red Stripe baby-back ribs with guava sauce, key lime–grilled grouper, and pineapple-glazed sea bass. Chefs execute the creative offerings with complexity. Crafty salads, sandwiches, and specials complete the luncheon offerings, plus the all-day menu offers six fresh catches prepared just with olive oil. Or choose from a select menu of oysters imported from several seasonal locations.

✪ HANDSOME HARRY'S THIRD STREET BISTRO

239-434-6400
www.handsomeharrys.com
1205 Third St. S., Naples 34102
Price: Moderate to Very Expensive
Cuisine: American steakhouse, Italian bistro
Liquor: Full
Serving: L, D
Credit Cards: AE, D, MC, V
Handicap Access: Yes
Reservations: Yes

Every detail about Handsome Harry's Third Street Bistro lives up to its name. But don't let the attention to the cover sway your opinion about the book. Beauty goes much deeper than the chic black-and-white floor, booths, and tables, accented by rich tones. The food is as smart as the place is pretty. Both the ambiance and menu take their cue from classic steakhouses and contemporary bistros. Starting with the drink menu, Harry's creative spirit and eye for quality shows in a selection of above-average wines and fun martinis blended with top-shelf spirits. Lunch prices put it into the special-occasion category, but it's well worth it. Starters on both lunch and dinner include the extraordinary: baked onion soup topped with a heavy, luscious head of creamy Gruyère cheese, lemon cream of

lobster bisque, a chunky king crab cake, and filet mignon stems crusted with peppercorns and skewered on a rosemary blade. At lunchtime, the Maine lobster salad is a winner—loaded with sweet, tender claw and tail chunks tossed lightly with citrus aioli and softly bedded upon Bibb lettuce with spears of avocado and mango and splotches of two types of dressing. At dinner, meat and pasta receive top billing: fine grilled meats, lamb loin chops, "white glove" spare ribs with apricot glaze, pork rib chop stuffed with prosciutto and provolone, portobello and eggplant lasagna, beef tenderloin and rapini with cognac cream sauce over farfalle, and lobster fra diavolo. For dessert, choose the incredibly moist and large serving of carrot cake or Blackout Chocolate.

NAPLES TOMATO

239-598-9800
www.naplestomato.com
14700 Tamiami Trail N., Naples 34120
Price: Moderate to Expensive
Cuisine: Italian
Children's Menu: No
Liquor: Wine
Serving: L, D
Credit Cards: AE, D, MC, V
Handicap Access: Yes
Reservations: Yes

The word "grocery" on the sign is your first clue. You enter through an Italian market. People actually are eating at tables in the grocery store, right in front of the cheese case, next to the fancy mustards. The main dining room creates a little more atmosphere, offsetting black industrial exposed ductwork with grand glass bowl and wrought iron chandeliers. Black granite tabletops are free of cloths or placemats. Everything is pared down to basics because the food is what Naples Tomato is about. Like its name, it takes the fundamentals of fine cuisine and turns them ripe and juicy.

Tony Ridgway, Naples' godfather of cuisine, conducts cooking classes at his eponymous restaurant.

Wine is a huge focus and calls for experimentation. My Avalon Cabernet Sauvignon opened up beautifully to the gazpacho martini I ordered as an appetizer. We passed up on the antipasto buffet table, which one can choose for entrée or appetizer. For the main course, I went with the house special, osso bucco with truffle risotto. I expected the risotto would be flavored with truffle paste but there were visible black truffle shavings on top, and the dish held the telltale earthy appeal of the coveted fungus. The lamb shank fell off the bone, as it should, and the sauce was a masterpiece of simplicity: pan juices in which diced carrots, onions, and celery had simmered. Pasta dominates the menu and presents a quandary for its fans. Will it be something classic such as lasagna or fettuccini with vodka sauce? Or something whimsical and experimental, like the butternut squash raviolinni with porcini sauce, the spinach and gorgonzola ravioli, or linguine with house-smoked salmon and brandy flambé? My husband settled on the Maine Event, ravioli stuffed with lobster meat seasoned (a bit heavily) with onions and royally crowned with the house seafood-stock pink sauce. Those watching carbs can choose from rare ahi tuna with tangerine sesame salad; shrimp stuffed with hearts of palm, proscuitto, and parmesan; veal chops; and salmon stuffed with grilled zucchini and anchovies and topped with champagne beurre blanc. The lunch menu offers some of the same, plus interesting salads and sandwiches.

RIDGWAY BAR & GRILL

941-262-5500
www.ridgwaybarandgrill.com
1300 Third St., Naples 34102
Price: Moderate to Very Expensive
Cuisine: New Continental
Children's Menu: Yes.
Liquor: Full
Serving: L, D
Credit Cards: AE, D, DC, MC, V
Handicap Access: Yes
Reservations: Yes, recommended
Special Features: Alfresco porch seating

The name has changed a few times since Chef's Garden set a new standard for Naples dining in the 1970s. But its ownership and wicker-and-linen ambiance have remained constant. Naples has continually raised the restaurant bar in the past decade, leaving Chef's Garden in the flour dust, in need of reinvention. First came Mediterranean-style Terra, now Ridgway, named for constant chef-owner Tony Ridgway. With Tommy Bahama drawing the casual crowd down the street, Tony has kept true to a higher-reaching cuisine with such nice turns as crab cakes with corn and sweet red pepper cream, grilled pork chop with Swiss chard and pancetta, mustard- and herb-glazed rack of lamb, and seared grouper with lemon confit vinaigrette. For lunch, try the prime burger, fried goat cheese, chicken potpie, chicken and grapes salad, or salad Nicoise. The luscious desserts, another constant hallmark, come from next door at Tony's Off Third. Pastries and are the highlight of well-executed meals with, unfortunately, typically lax service.

TROPICAL REEF SEAFOOD RESTAURANT

239-591-4385
8050 Tamiami Trail N., Naples 34103
Price: Moderate to Expensive
Cuisine: Floribbean seafood
Children's Menu: Yes
Liquor: Beer and wine
Serving: L, D
Credit Cards: AE, D, MC, V
Handicap Access: Yes
Reservations: Yes

Tropical Reef adheres to the two somewhat contrary characteristics of Caribbean cooking: total freshness of exotic ingredients and resourceful, labor-intensive, flavor-intensive preparation. Take for instance what has become my new favorite indulgence: grilled sea scallops with passionfruit beurre blanc and mango pico de gallo. The scallops were flash grilled to draw out the sea saltiness and crust the custardy, medium-rare centers with a slightly caramelized sheath. The pretty pastel puddle around them reflected a careful, patient reduction of a fruit that doesn't easily give up its juice. Its pleasant tartness was perfectly balanced with sweet and thickened exactly to a point where it lightly coated the scallops, each topped with its chop of tomatoes and mango. Seafood is the emphasis here. Crab packed the deep-fried crab cakes, but the highlight of this appetizer was what lay underneath, not inside—namely a charred pineapple vinaigrette and mound of black bean salsa. Living next to Naples Cheesecake elevates the significance of dessert at the Reef. Besides all the varieties you have to choose from at Naples Cheesecake, Tropical Reef lists its own impossible-to-deny selections. Try the Zach's Killer Brownie—share it to survive—or the coconut panna cotta in passion fruit soup.

VANDERBILT BEACH
BALEEN

239-597-3123
www.laplayaresort.com
9891 Gulf Shore Dr., Naples 34108
At LaPlaya Beach & Golf Resort
Price: Moderate to Very Expensive
Cuisine: Seafood
Children's Menu: Yes
Liquor: Full
Serving: B, L, D
Credit Cards: AE, D, DC, MC, V
Handicap Access: Yes
Reservations: Yes
Special Features: Indoor and outdoor seating with gulf view

Monkeys have become the motif of fashion these days in Florida, and here you see their likeness hanging from chandeliers and poking their noses out of the earthy tropical decor. The round crusty loaf of bread is even called "monkey bread," why I'm not sure. (I'm also a bit confused by the whale reference in the restaurant's name.) Outdoors, heavy teak tables and chairs provide a front-row seat to the sunset and the percussion of the surf. The menu allows you to order your seafood simple—roasted, grilled, or sautéed—or dressed in all the trappings of creative New World cuisine. My roasted grouper was elevated to gourmet status with an excellent garlic-caper sauce and superb accompaniment of artichoke-bacon mashed potatoes. A couple of meat dishes round out the menu, and the Roquefort-crusted filet mignon we sampled demonstrated the kitchen's expert handling in that department. It was done to the perfect degree of wellness as ordered, and its red wine sauce anointed it like a blessing. For lunch try the chopped BLT salad or lobster burger with mango remoulade.

FOOD PURVEYORS

Bakeries

Bakeries today are often combined with delis, grocery stores, and even wine shops.

Naples Cheesecake Co. (239-598-9070, 800-325-6554; www.naplescheesecake.com; 8050 Trail Blvd., Naples 34108) Up to 15 different flavors, including key lime, amaretto, and Baileys Irish Cream.

Tony's Off Third (239-262-7999; 1300 Third Ave. S., Naples 34102) Dessert bakery featuring legendary cakes, pastries, and tarts and a well-respected selection of wine and coffee, plus deli items and sandwiches.

Breakfast

First Watch (239-434-0005; www.firstwatch.com; 225 Banyan Blvd., Naples 34102, at Charleston Square; and 239-566-7395; 1000 Immokalee Rd., Naples 34110, at Granada Shoppes) A popular upscale chain that has reinvented breakfast with such terminology such as "crepeggs," "chickichanga," and the "bacado" (bacon and avocado) omelet. Also serves lunch.

✪ **Manna from Heaven** (239-593-4948; 835 Vanderbilt Beach Road, Naples 34108, at Pavilion Shopping Center) European-style breakfast offering crêpes, interesting eggs Benedict varieties (including Tuscan style with chargrilled portobello mushroom, Asiago cheese, and sweet pepper hollandaise) and specialties such as "Moo and Cluck"—bacon-wrapped filet mignon with sautéed mushrooms and poached eggs. Also serves lunch.

✪ **Skillets Café** (239-262-3788; www.goodbreakfast.com; 4170 Tamiami Trail N., Naples 34103; 239-566-1999; 5461 Airport Rd., Naples 34109; and 239-992-9333; 9174 Bonita Beach Rd.; Bonita Springs 34135) A cheery way to wake up, it offers a menuful of Belgian waffles, pancake platters, Irish oats, Benedicts, frittatas, and healthy options. Don't skip the Skillets potatoes—hash browns baked with sour cream and scallions. Also serves lunch.

Susie's Diner (239-642-6633; 1013 N. Collier Blvd., Marco Island 34145, at Marco Town Center) Belgian waffles are a favorite; omelets come in creative varieties such as one stuffed with corned beef hash and another made with egg whites with spinach and other veggies. It's open daily for breakfast and Monday through Saturday for lunch.

Candy & Ice Cream

The Chocolate Strawberry (239-394-5999; 123 S. Barfield Dr., Marco Island 34145, at Shops of Marco) The specialty is strawberries hand dipped in various types of chocolate; also offers seahorse-shaped lollipops, ice cream, smoothies, coffee, and chocolates in the shape of turtles, shells, dolphins, and other local critters.

Everglades Scoop (239-695-0375; 203 S. Copeland, Everglades City 34139) Cheerful, bright ice cream parlor serving 16 flavors of hand-dipped ice cream, plus shakes, sundaes, and homemade key lime pie.

Ice Cream Parlor (239-597-4043; 829 Vanderbilt Beach Rd., Naples 34108, at Pavilion Shopping Center) Join the Ice Cream Club and savor unusual flavors such as Superman, Kahlua almond fudge, and blueberry cheesecake.

Olde Naples Chocolate (239-262-3975; www.oldenapleschocolate.com; 1305 Third St. S., Naples 34102) An old-fashioned chocolate and ice-cream fantasy with sidewalk tables.

Regina's Ice Cream (239-434-8181; 824 Fifth Ave. S., Naples 34102) An old-fashioned soda fountain with modern frozen yogurts, sorbets, and sugar-free and name-brand ice cream.

The Serious Cookie Company at Tin City Sweets (239-263-3382, 877-263-3383; 1200 Fifth Ave. S., Naples 34102, at Tin City) Just try to pass this place by without succumbing. Besides their trademark half-pound cookies, they make brownies, saltwater taffy, chocolates, turtles, chocolate pretzels, cordial creams, rugelach, and other irresistible goodies.

Sweet Annie's Ice Cream & Candy (239-642-7180; 692 Bald Eagle Dr., Marco Island 34145) Old-fashioned-style parlor with black-and-white tiled floor, counter, and chrome-legged stools. It serves 45 flavors of ice cream, including sugar free, frozen yogurt, gelato, and frozen custard. Its video arcade holds 20 games.

Coffee

Big House Coffee (239-695-3633; www.chokoloskee-island.com; 238 Mamie St., Chokoloskee Island 34138) Organic espresso, tropical-fruit smoothies, luncheon snacks, scones and creative desserts, high-speed Internet access, and gifts

Fifth Avenue Coffee Company (239-261-5757; 599 Fifth Ave. S., Naples 34102) Hot and iced coffee and tea, cappuccino, caffe latte, macchata, bakery goods. Seating indoors and out with high-speed and wireless Internet connections.

Roberto's (239-394-8388; 1031 N. Collier Blvd., Marco Island 34145, at Marco Town Center Mall) Espresso bar, fresh cakes, cookies, and other bakery goods, light breakfast and lunch, ice cream, smoothies, key lime pie, and other desserts. Seating indoors and out.

The Villaggio Café (239-643-0004; 4350 Gulf Shore Blvd. N., Naples 34103, at the Village on Venetian Bay) Coffee, cappuccino, espresso, chai latte, iced coffee and tea, milk shakes, frozen daquiris.

Deli & Specialty Foods

Artichoke & Co. (239-263-6979; 4370 Gulf Shore Blvd. N., Naples 34103, at the Village on Venetian Bay) Gourmet takeout, soups, breads, cheeses, pastries, salads, coffee, and wines. Serves breakfast and lunch.

Crayton Cove Gourmet (239-262-4362, 800-743-1480; www.craytoncovegourmet.com; 800 12th Ave. S., Naples 34102) Old-fashioned purveyor of Florida goodies, specializing in citrus shipping, fresh orange juice, homemade fudge, key lime pie and other citrus sweets, and orange-blossom honey.

✪ **Evoo Market** (239-444-2020; www.evoomarket.com; 13240 Tamiami Trail N., Naples 34110) Following the new trend for restaurant-gourmet market combos, this one, whose name is an acronym for extra virgin olive oil, is highly hailed for its ready-made dinners to go, meats, cheeses, and prepared products, including its own sauces and jams.

Irish Pub (239-642-6206; 591 S. Collier Blvd., Marco 34145) Deli sandwiches.

Pepper's Fine Food (239-643-2008; 4165 Corporate Square, Naples 34104) Butcher shop with every kind of sausage, plus fresh sauerkraut, potato salad, and other German products.

Ródes Fresh & Fancy (239-992-4040; 3756 Bonita Beach Rd., Bonita Beach 34134) Fresh produce and local seafood market. Also sells fresh breads and gourmet groceries.

Tony's Off Third (239-262-7999; 1300 Third St. S., Naples 34102) Sandwiches, prepackaged deli salads, and a selection of entrées for quick warm-up meals in.

Wynn's on Fifth (239-261-0901; 745 Fifth Ave. S., Naples 34102) Since 1945 the Wynn family has operated this Fifth Avenue landmark, most famous for its fine selection of wine, fresh bakery goodies, desserts, and hot-and-cold prepared deli foods.

Fruit & Vegetable Stands
Third Street South Farmers' Market (www.naplesfarmersmarket.com; parking lot at Third St. S. and 13th Ave., Old Naples) Every Saturday 7:30–11:30 AM, October through April.

Internet Cafés
Big House Coffee (239-695-3633; www.chokoloskee-island.com; 238 Mamie St., Chokoloskee Island 34138) High-speed Internet access, coffee, smoothies, and snacks.

Fifth Avenue Coffee Company (239-261-5757; 599 Fifth Ave. S., Naples 34102) Seating indoors and out with high-speed and wireless Internet connections, plus coffee and coffee drinks.

Natural Foods
Food & Thought (239-213-2222; 2132 Tamiami Trail N., Naples 34102, at Gateway Plaza) Smoothies and juice bar; fresh, prepared, and preserved organic food; indoor and outdoor seating.

For Goodness Sake (239-992-5838; www.forgoodnesssake123.com; 9118 Bonita Beach Rd. E., Bonita Springs 34135, at Sunshine Plaza, and 2464 Vanderbilt Beach Rd., Naples 34109, at Naples Walk) Full line of health groceries, including local honey, fresh produce, frozen products, and a menu of salads, sandwiches, and fruit or protein smoothies.

Summer Day Market and Café (239-394-8361; 1027-1/2 N. Collier Blvd., Marco Island 34145, in Marco Town Center) Inviting market with full line of fresh, frozen, bulk, and processed organic and low-carb products, including baby food. Sandwich and smoothie-juice bar with outdoor tables.

Pizza & Takeout
5 Brothers Pizza (239-394-5100; 599 S. Collier Blvd., Marco Island 34145, at Marco Walk Plaza) New York–style pizza, subs, and Italian dinners delivered all day.

Aurelio's (239-403-8882; 590 N. Tamiami Trail, Naples 34102) Since 1959 pizza, pasta, and other Italian specialties to eat in or to go.

Big House Coffee (239-695-3633; www.chokoloskee-island.com; 238 Mamie St., Chokoloskee 34138) Sandwich takeout and homemade desserts.

Cilantro Tamales (239-597-5855; www.cilantrotamales.co; 10823 Tamiami Trail, Naples 34108; 239-949-9955; 25301 Tamiami Trail, Bonita Springs 34134; and 239-394-6555; 1069 N. Collier Blvd., Marco Island 34145) Modern Mexican food for takeout and delivery. See listing above.

Kitchen 845 (239-593-6966; 835 Vanderbilt Beach Road, at Pavilion Shopping Center) Tomato dill bisque, Caesar wrap, coconut tilapia, and other such delights to go.

Seafood

Captain Jerry's Seafood (239-262-7337; 141 9th St. N., Naples 34102, inside Wynn's Market) Shrimp, stone crab, fish, and live Maine lobster.

City Seafood (239-695-4700; 702 Begonia St., Everglades City 34139) Find all that's fresh and special about Everglades cuisine: stone crab in season, alligator tail, frog legs, lobster, grouper, and key lime pie. Serves lunch and early dinner dockside.

Kirk's Fresh Seafood Market (239-394-8616; 417 Papaya Dr., Goodland 34140) Right on the fish docks, with crab traps piled around it, selling wholesale and retail.

Paradise Shrimp (239-949-6001; www.paradiseshrimpcompany.com; 24851 Tamiami Trail S., Bonita Springs, 34134) The pick of local gourmet cooks, it sells seafood and limited meat products fresh, frozen, and prepared with bottled and boxed products to complement.

Ródes Fresh & Fancy (239-992-4040; 3756 Bonita Beach Rd., Bonita Springs 34134) Fresh produce and local seafood market.

CULTURE

The affluent residents of Naples—many of them transplanted CEOs and captains of industry from lands to the north—share their county with impoverished migrants who work in Immokalee, the nearby agricultural center. The influences of Haitian, Puerto Rican, Jamaican, and other Caribbean cultures are finding their way into the mainstream, while flashes of southern spirit and Cracker charm surface in Goodland, Everglades City, and Chokoloskee.

The Miccosukee and Seminole Indians inhabit reservations in the Everglades. They celebrate their culture each year at the Green Corn Ceremony, during the first new moon in June. They contribute the South Coast's only authentic, indigenous art: colorful weaving, stitching, jewelry, dolls, and other age-old handicrafts.

Highbrow art has become a trademark of Naples and its long roll of galleries and performance spaces. For information on cultural events, contact the United Arts Council of Collier County at 239-263-8242 or visit www.collierarts.com.

Architecture

In **Naples**, commercial architecture is marked by style and panache, not to mention the architectural beauty of homes and resorts. Banks and insurance companies seem to compete for virtuosity. It's truly a land of visual allure. **Pelican Bay** developments provide examples of a new residential style and provide a contrast with old-money **Port Royal**.

The architecture of the Village on Venetian Bay shopping district contributes to the Italian flavor of America's Naples.

Old Naples, that neighborhood in the vicinity of the pier and Fifth Avenue South, has held on to some real treasures, including the tabby-mortar **Palm Cottage**, the old **Mercantile**, and the **Old Naples building** at Broad and Third. In the same neighborhood, on **Gordon Drive**, pay attention to the charming board-and-batten Cracker survivors.

In **Everglades City** and **Chokoloskee Island**, recreational vehicles and cement-block boxes typify the fishing-oriented community's traditional style, though that is changing with a trend toward gentrification. The **Rod & Gun Club**, built in 1850, stands out and dresses the town in southern flair. The style of thatch housing, perfected by the Indians, known as chikee (pronounced *chi-KEY*) prevails in the Everglades and serves as a trendy beach-bar motif at the ritziest resorts throughout the coastal region.

Cinema
Bonita Springs 12 Regal Cinemas (239-949-2600; 25251 S. Tamiami Trail, Bonita Springs 34134)

Marco Movies (239-642-1111; www.marcomovies.com; 599 S. Collier Blvd., Marco Island 34245, at Marco Walk) Four screens with first-run movies, food, beer, and wine service.

Pavilion Cinema (239-596-0008; Vanderbilt Beach Rd., Naples 34108, at Pavilion shopping center) 10 theaters

Regal Hollywood Cinema 20 Cinemas (239-597-9494; 6006 Airport Pulling Rd., Naples 34109, at Pine Ridge Rd.)

Gardens
NAPLES BOTANICAL GARDEN
239-643-7275
www.naplesgarden.org
4820 Bayshore Dr., Naples 34112

Open: 10–4 Wed.–Sat., 12–4 Sun., Nov–Apr.; 9–1 Thurs.–Sat., July–Sept.; 9–1 Wed.–Sat.
other months.
Admission: $6 adults, $4 children ages 6–12

Developing in phases its 160 acres of subtropical and tropical gardens with plants from
many warm lands, it currently has three acres open to the public, including a Pollination
Pavilion containing butterflies, Madagascar geckoes, lorikeets, and hummingbirds. A 1-
mile loop trail explores uplands habitat, including cypress swamp, wetlands, and oak
scrub. Additions slated for 2011 completion will include Children's, Asian, Caribbean, and
Brazilian gardens.

NAPLES ZOO AT CARIBBEAN GARDENS

239-262-5409
www.napleszoo.com
1590 Goodlette-Frank Rd., Naples 34102
Open: 9:30–5:30 daily (last ticket sold at 4:30)
Admission: $15.95 adults, $9.95 children ages 4–15

These tropical gardens, today the setting for a nicely proportioned zoo (see "Kids' Stuff" in
this section), were planted in 1919 by Dr. Henry Nehrling, a botanist who brought his private collection to Naples. After he died, Julius Fleischmann, a developer, restored and

expanded the doctor's 3,000-plus specimens and opened the gardens to the public
in 1954. Besides native vegetation, exotics
such as magnificent creeping figs, birds of
paradise, and monkey-puzzle, calabash,
mango, and kapok trees flourish in wetlands and on hammocks.

*Palm Allée royally greets visitors to Naples
Botanical Garden.*

Historic Homes & Sites
INDIAN HILL
Scott Drive, Goodland

Marco Island is rich in natural and historic
heritage, but hides it well among 20th-
century trappings. Witness Indian Hill. On
your own you'll have to search to find it,
and when you do, only a barely noticeable
plaque marks the spot. (Or take a trolley
tour—**Marco Island Trolley**, 239-394-
1600—to get there.) Southwest Florida's
highest elevation at 58 feet above sea level,
built up by ancient Calusa Indian shell
mounds, it now holds a ritzy neighborhood
called the Heights, which feels the tiniest
bit like San Francisco.

A Madagascar gecko goes for a drink from a palm boot in Naples Botanical Garden's Pollinators Pavilion.

OTTER MOUND PRESERVE

239-213-2957
1831 Addison Ct., Marco Island

Slated to open to the public in March 2007, this Calusa archaeological site and its interpretative trail demonstrate how the natives used lightning whelk shells to terrace the land. Interpretative signs inform along a mulch pathway.

PALM COTTAGE

239-261-8164
www.napleshistoricalsociety.org
137 12th Ave. S., Naples 34102
Open: 1–4 Tues.–Sat.; Wed. and Sat. only in summer
Admission: Donation of $8 for garden and cottage tour; $5 for children under age 12

Land was selling for $10 a lot in 1895 when Naples founder Walter N. Haldeman built a winter home for fellow worker Henry Watterson. Haldeman, publisher of the *Louisville Courier Journal,* had discovered the exotic beaches and jungles of Naples in 1887 and proceeded to buy up land and sing its praises. His enthusiasm persuaded winter escapees from Kentucky and Ohio, including Watterson, his star editor, to visit. The cottage Haldeman built for his friend was made of Florida pine, tidewater cypress, and a certain type of tabby mortar made by burning seashells over a buttonwood fire. It was one of the first buildings in southwest Florida to be constructed of local materials and is Naples' oldest house. Before reaching its present museum status, the cottage—rather spartan by modern standards—knew many lives. If the walls could talk at Palm Cottage, as it eventually came to be known, they would tell of wild parties with the likes of Gary Cooper and Hedy Lamarr in attendance. The renovated cottage is now the head- quarters of the Collier County Historical Society, which conducts guided tours. In 2007, the society opened a historic garden in the adjacent lot, where visitors can find vegetation early settlers used and planted. Wednesday, 90-minute, bimonthly walking tours of Naples' historic district depart from Palm Cottage from November through April; the cost is $15 per person. From May through October the walking tours take place the first Wednesday of the month only.

SMALLWOOD STORE
239-695-2989
360 Mamie St., Chokoloskee Island 34138
South of Everglades City
Open: 10–5 daily, Dec.–May; 11–5 daily, May–Nov.
Admission: $3 adults, $2.50 seniors, children under age 12 free

A historic throwback to frontier days in the 'Glades, this museum preserves a Native American trading post of the early 1900s. Splintery shelves hold ointment containers, FlyDed insect killer, livestock spray, a sausage-making machine, and hordes of memorabilia. Rooms recall life in the pioneer days and look pretty much the same as they did at that time. One of the best features is the view from the back porch. This was the site of a Jesse James–era murder immortalized in Peter Matthiessen's novel *Killing Mr. Watson.*

Kid's Stuff
NAPLES ZOO AT CARIBBEAN GARDENS
239-262-5409
www.napleszoo.com
1590 Goodlette-Frank Rd., Naples 34102
Open: 9:30–5:30 daily (last ticket sold at 4:30)
Admission: $15.95 adults, $9.95 children ages 4–15 (plus tax)

Big cats and primates are specialties of this small, neighborhood zoo. Panther Glade, the newest exhibit, teaches awareness of the plight of the endangered Florida panther. Coming in 2007: Leopard Rock. "Meet the Keeper" programs and multimedia *Planet Predator and Serpents: Fangs & Fiction* shows further educate and advance a conservation mission. A boat ride takes a close-up look at the zoo's monkey and lemur population, which is sequestered on nine islands. Play areas amuse toddlers. Shaded, meandering, chirp-orchestrated paths take you past other fenced animals. The 52-acre grounds are attractively maintained with the lush vegetation of the zoo's once-called Caribbean Gardens (see "Gardens" in this section).

Museums
✪ COLLIER COUNTY MUSEUM
239-774-8476
www.colliermuseum.com
3301 Tamiami Trail E., Naples 34112
Open: 9–5 Mon.-Fri. (Open weekends during special winter exhibits.)
Admission: $2 donations suggested

The unique aspects at this village of history include typical Seminole chikee huts, a vintage swamp buggy that kids can climb into, the skeleton of an Ice Age giant ground sloth, a working archaeological lab, a replicated Seminole war fort, and a 1910 steam locomotive from the county's cypress-logging era. State-of-the-art exhibits of prehistoric fossils, vignettes, and artifacts up to the 1960s include a video of a Gary Cooper movie filmed in the area. New to the grounds: the original circa-1935 *Kokomis* ferry, now under restoration, once used at the old offshore Keewaydin Island Club.

HOLOCAUST MUSEUM OF SOUTHWEST FLORIDA

239-63-9200
www.swflhm.org
4760 Tamiami Trail N., Ste. 7, Naples 34103
Open: 1–4 Tues.–Fri. and Sun.
Admission: Free

This museum began as a student project, and today its photos, written materials, and artifacts take visitors chronologically through the Jewish experience from pre–World War II through post-Nazi liberation.

KEY MARCO MUSEUM

239-389-6447
Marco Island Realtors Office, 140 Waterway Dr., Marco Island 34145, at Bald Eagle Dr.
Also: Shops at Old Marco, 100 Palm Dr., P.O. Box 2282, Naples 34146
Open: 9–4 Mon.–Fri.
Admission: Free

Through photographs, artifacts, replicas, and memorabilia, this fledgling museum (for the time being in two commercial locations) depicts the past of Key Marco, as it was once known. The one at Old Marco has more stuff and is easier to find. It concentrates on the island's rich Calusa Indian culture, displaying a life-size diorama, shell tools, masks, wood carvings, and other artifacts unearthed in the 1895 archeological expedition that established Marco as an important center of the Calusa kingdom. The dig's most important find, the Calusa Cat, has become an island icon and is replicated at both locations. The original resides at the Smithsonian Institution. Plans are underway for Collier County Museum to build its fifth branch on the island and replace the two smaller museums.

Kids can play in a re-created Seminole War fort at Collier County Museum.

MUSEUM OF THE EVERGLADES

239-695-0008
www.colliermuseum.com
105 W. Broadway, P.O. Box 8, Everglades City 34139
Hours: 10–4 Tues.–Sat.
Admission: $2 suggested donation

The museum takes over a renovated historic laundry started by developer Barron Collier to serve the community of road builders during the construction of the

Tamiami Trail in the 1920s. The museum concentrates on the tremendous feat of blazing a trail through the swampy, buggy Everglades and on the region's Calusa Indian and fishing heritage.

NAPLES DEPOT MUSEUM & LIONEL TRAIN MUSEUM
239-262-1776
1051 Fifth Ave. S., Naples 34102
Corner Tamiami Trail and 10th St. S.
Hours: 9–5 Mon.-Fri., 9–4 Sat.
Admission: Free for Depot Museum; $5 for adults, $3 for children for Lionel

Gary Cooper, Hedy Lamarr, and other illuminati of yore once arrived at this circa-1927 depot. Recently, Collier County initiated a new museum here, devoted to the history of the railroad and transportation in the region. Three authentic rail cars sit alongside the depot. Future exhibits will expand to general history. Lionel has set up an elaborate display of eight operating model trains and a small railroad outside for kiddie rides on Saturdays from 10 AM to 2 PM.

Music and Nightlife

Big House Coffee (239-695-3633; www.chokoloskee-island.com; 238 Mamie St., Chokoloskee 34138) Local musicians play live acoustic music every Friday from 2 to 4 PM.

✪ **Bimini's Beach Club** (239-394-7111; 657 S. Collier Blvd., Marco Island 34145) A lively resort-scene, indoor/outdoor venue for live dance music—pop, jazz, reggae, and Motown—nightly. Serves a full food menu until midnight.

Little Bar (239-394-5663; 205 Harbor Dr., Goodland 34140) Hosts live music on Friday and Saturday nights. Site of the annual Spammy Jammy in July, where participants in pajamas bring their crazy SPAM sculptures.

✪ **McCabe's Irish Pub** (239-403-8777; 699 Fifth Ave. S., Naples 34102) Authentic Irish music and rowdy camaraderie in a Dublin-built pub.

Naples Concert Band (239-263-9521; www.naplesconcertband.org; Naples) For more than 35 years its 90 volunteer musicians have been performing free Sunday concerts once a month, from October through April, at Cambier Park in Old Naples.

Off the Hook Comedy Club (239-389-6900; www.offthehookcomedy.com; 599 S. Collier Blvd., Marco Island 34145, at Captain Brien's Seafood & Raw Bar) Nationally known comedians perform Thursday through Sunday.

The Bar at the Ritz-Carlton (239-598-3300; 280 Vanderbilt Beach Rd., Naples 34108) Live contemporary music every night.

Snook Inn (239-394-3313; 1215 Bald Eagle Dr., Marco Island 34145) Live local bands, contemporary and island music.

Tommy Bahama's Tropical Café (239-643-6889; 1220 Third St. S., Naples 34102) Lively island music in the evenings, with outdoor seating.

Zoe's (239-261-1221; 720 Fifth Ave. S., Naples 34102) One of Fifth Avenue's liveliest spots, it hosts live jazz on select evenings during the season.

Theater

Marco Players (239-642-7270; 1083 N. Collier Blvd., Marco Island, 34145, at Marco Town Center Mall) Nonprofit community theater that produces comedies and musicals from November through April.

✪ **Philharmonic Center for the Arts** (239-597-1900, 800-597-1900; www.thephil.org; 5833 Pelican Bay Blvd., Naples 34108) "The Phil," as locals call it, is home to the 85-piece Naples Philharmonic and the Miami City Ballet. It hosts audiences of up to 1,425 for Broadway shows, touring orchestras, opera, comedians, modern dance, and more than 400 other events yearly.

Stage 88 Theatre (239-513-8600; www.stage88.com; Community Hall, 27381 Old U.S. 41, Bonita Springs 34134) A new community performance group for Bonita Springs.

Sugden Community Theatre (239-263-7990; 701 Fifth Ave. S., Naples 34102) The home of the **Naples Players** (www.naplesplayers.org), a community theater troupe that has been entertaining from October through May for 50 years. The complex features a main stage, plus a more experimental black-box theater, and plays host to the Naples Jazz Society, ballet, opera, and other performances art. Every Sunday, Monday, and Tuesday at 6 PM, a local band gathers outside for a 20-minute "Naples Patriotic Moment," featuring the national anthem and "Taps" in honor of those serving in the military.

Visual Art Centers & Resources

Like its Italian namesake, Naples serves as the region's aesthetic pacesetter. Gallery-lined streets host artists of local, national, and international stature. The following entries introduce you to opportunities for experiencing art as either a viewer or a practicing artist. A listing for commercial galleries is included in the "Shopping" section.

Thrill to "the Phil"—Naples' premiere showplace.

Art League of Bonita Springs Center for the Arts (239-495-8989; www.artcenter-bonita.org; 26100 Old 41 Rd., Bonita Springs 34135) Classes, children's programs, exhibitions, and national art festivals in January and March (see "Calendar of Events").

Art League of Marco Island (239-394-4221; www.marcoislandart.com; 1010 Winterberry Dr., Marco Island 34145) Workshops, lectures, two galleries with monthly changing exhibits, and gift shop. It also sponsors an annual arts and crafts festival in January and other cultural events.

✪ **Naples Museum of Art** (239-597-1900, 800-597-1900; www.thephil.org; Philharmonic Center for the Arts, 5833 Pelican Bay Blvd., Naples 34108) Opened in 2000, Naples's latest cultural showpiece is as stunning as you'd expect. Permanent exhibits include a collection of modern American masters from between 1900 and

A Dale Chihuly chandelier makes an impressive welcome to Naples Museum of Art.

1955, including Alexander Calder, Jackson Pollock, and Stuart Davis. The museum also holds the Pollak Collection of Modern Art and a miniatures exhibit. World-renowned glass sculptor Dale Chihuly created one of his famous ceilings and two magnificent chandeliers for the museum: one that hangs from its dome glass conservatory and another suspended in the three-story stairwell. The museum's 15 galleries elegantly showcase world-class traveling exhibitions. From November through April, the museum is open Tuesday through Saturday from 10 to 5 and Sunday from noon to 5; from May through October, it closes at 4 PM, and it is closed August through Labor Day. Complimentary guided tours are available at 11 AM and 3 PM, from October through May. Admission: $6 adults, $3 students, free for children under age 5.

Philharmonic Galleries (239-597-1111; www.thephil.org; Philharmonic Center for the Arts, 5833 Pelican Bay Blvd., Naples 34108) Its signature stage-set miniatures collection includes stunning works from a 1906 production of *Carmen* to a 2005 staging of *Annie*. Admission is free with a ticket from Naples Museum of Art, which lies just across the courtyard from it. It also is open one hour before Philharmonic Center performances, post-performance, and during intermission for audience patrons only.

United Arts Council (239-263-8242; www.uaccollier.com; 2335 Tamiami Trail N., Ste. 504, Naples 34103) A central clearinghouse for culture, music, dance, theater, and visual arts in the Naples area.

✪ **The von Liebig Art Center** (239-262-6517; www.naplesartcenter.org; 585 Park St., Naples 34102) Home of the Naples Art Association, the art center holds classes, workshops, and showings for children and its members and presents other special exhibitions. The skylit library contains arts information.

RECREATION

The Ten Thousand Islands are the meat of the South Coast's recreational banquet. Here, the old-fashioned sports—fishing, canoeing, hiking—are most in style. The beaches of Naples and Marco Island serve up the newer, exhilarating side dishes, everything from parasailing to jet skiing.

Beaches

In 2003, a poll conducted by Yahoo! Travel Web site and *National Geographic Traveler* magazine ranked Naples as number 10 for "Top Sands" in the nation.

Parking fees are levied at most beaches; county residents can purchase stickers that allow them to park free. For information on county beaches, contact Department of Collier County Parks & Recreation (239-353-0404; www.colliergov.net; 15000 Livingston Rd., Naples 34109).

CLAM PASS RECREATION AREA

239-353-0404
At Naples Grande Resort & Club, off Seagate Dr., 410 Seagate Dr., Naples 34103
Facilities: Restrooms, showers, food and beach concessions
Parking: $6 per day

This beach, used by guests of Naples Grande Resort & Club but open to the public, is reached by a tram that follows a nearly 1-mile boardwalk over a tidal bay and through mangroves. Boat and cabana rentals are available at this county facility. The sand is fine and fluffy and, once past the resort crowd, leads to preserve lands. You can kayak or sail into the sea or canoe along a trail among the mangroves, which are frequented by ospreys, hawks, and a variety of other feathered creatures.

DELNOR-WIGGINS PASS STATE PARK

239-597-6196
www.floridastateparks.org/delnor-wiggins
11100 Gulf Shore Dr. N., Naples 34108
At Route 846, Vanderbilt Beach
Facilities: Picnic areas, grills, pavilion, restrooms, showers, boat ramp, volleyball, lifeguard
Admission: $5 per car, up to 8 passengers; $1 pedestrians, cyclists, or extra passengers.

This highly natural, low-key beach, named among America's 40 Certified Healthy Beaches, extends for 1 mile south from the mouth of the Cocohatchee River. The lush white sands are protected during loggerhead turtle nesting season (summer) and support stands of natural maritime vegetation, such as cactus, sea grape, nickerbean, and yucca. A nature trail leads to an observation tower at the beach's north end. This is a popular park, but you can usually find parking in one of the many lots. Restrict your swimming to south of the pass's fast-moving waters, which are a boon to fishermen.

✪ LOWDERMILK PARK

239-263-6078
257 Banyan Blvd. at Gulf Shore Blvd., Naples
Facilities: Picnic area, restrooms, showers, volleyball, playground, concessions, special
handicap access, and wheeled surf chairs
Parking: 25¢ per 15 minutes

Beach headquarters for the South Coast: There are lots of special activities at this gulfside
party spot and its 1,000 feet of sandy beach. Across the street, a deli and restaurant fuel
your beach day.

NAPLES MUNICIPAL BEACHES

239-213-3062
Gulf Shore Blvd. south of Doctors Pass, Naples
Facilities: Restrooms, shower, concessions, fishing pier
Parking: Metered and pay booth, 25¢ per 15 minutes

The historic pier on 12th Avenue South, where facilities and a parking lot are located,
anchors stretches of natural beach.

SOUTH MARCO BEACH

S. Collier Blvd. at Swallow Ave., south end
of Marco Island
Parking: $6 per vehicle

Parking is on the other side of Collier
Blvd., a half block away. A paved brick path
beneath palm trees leads to this patch of
public beach between giant high-rises. No
facilities, but there's a restaurant next
door.

SUGDEN REGIONAL PARK

239-254-4000
4284 Avalon Dr., Naples
Parking: Free

On the east side of town, it is most famous
for the water-skiing shows it hosts
Saturdays or Sundays (check www.gulf-
coastskimmers.com for schedule) on its
freshwater lake. A sand beach edges it on
the side opposite from the bleacher
stands, and here you can rent a canoe or
kayak or swim in a guarded, roped-off
area. A bike path loops the lake, plus there
are cool playgrounds, picnic areas, and a
fishing pier.

*Delnor-Wiggins State Park: a haven for birds,
beachers, shellers, sea turtles, and fishermen alike*

TIGERTAIL BEACH
Hernando Dr., north end of Marco Island
Facilities: Picnic area, restrooms, showers, water-sports rentals, restaurant, playground
volleyball
Parking: $6 per vehicle

This county-owned beach is a good place for shelling and sunning. In season, arrive early
to find a parking spot. Wooden ramps cross dunes to 31 acres of wide, marvelous beach.
The south end fronts high-rises, but the north end stretches into wilderness. The fun
playground is divided for two different age groups. Tidal pools separate the main beach
and a fronting sandbar known as Sand Dollar Island, which attracts shellers and feeding
and nesting birds.

VANDERBILT BEACH
239-353-0404
280 Vanderbilt Dr., Vanderbilt Beach, north of Naples
Facilities: Restrooms, showers, food; water-sports rentals available at nearby resorts.
Parking: $6 per vehicle at nearby parking ramp on Vanderbilt Dr.; metered on the street

This recently refurbished stretch of sand runs alongside resorts and is well suited to those
who like sharing the beach with a lot of people, as well as bar- and restaurant-hopping
along the beach.

Bicycling
City and country biking paths are available to those who prefer this slow, intimate mode of
exploration. Sidewalks, bike paths (marked with white diamonds), and roadsides accommodate cyclists. By state law, cyclists must conduct themselves as pedestrians when using
sidewalks. Avoid cycling on crowded downtown walks. Where they share the road with
other vehicles, cyclists must follow all the rules of the road. Children under age 16 must
wear helmets.

BEST BIKING
Naples has laid out a sporadic system of metropolitan bike paths. A favorite route of local
cyclists loops through 10 miles of pathway in the north-end Pelican Bay development.
Within it, a 580-acre nature preserve provides a change of scenery from upscale
suburbia.

A bike path runs the length of **Bonita Beach**, nearly 3 miles long. At its south end it
connects to another, which leads to **Vanderbilt Beach**.

Naples Bicycle Tours (239-455-4611) conducts half- and full-day excursions, with
transportation, in Naples and to the Everglades.

Bike paths traverse **Everglades City** and cross the causeway to **Chokoloskee Island**.
Back-road bikers take to the 12-mile (one-way) ✪ **W. J. Janes Memorial Scenic Drive**
through Fakahatchee Strand Preserve State Park, off Highway 29 north of Everglades City.
Royal palms, cypress trees, and air plants provide pristine scenery and bird habitat (10
miles in you'll find a popular bird feeding pond). Morning or sunset riders may spot wild
turkeys, alligators, raccoons, snakes, otters, bobcats, and deer. A 3.5-mile mountain bike
trail at ✪ **Collier-Seminole State Park** travels through cabbage palm hammock.

RENTALS/SALES
Many resorts rent bikes or provide bike use to guests.

Bonita Bike & Baby (239-947-6377; 4749 Jackfish St., Bonita Springs 34134) It delivers a variety of bikes, including kids' bikes, trailers for kids, and beach and jogging strollers.

Naples Cyclery (239-566-0600; www.naplescyclery.com; 813 Vanderbilt Beach Rd., Naples 34108, at Pavilion Shopping Center; and 239-949-0026; 27820 S. Tamiami Trail, Bonita Springs 34134) Rents a wide variety of speed bikes, recumbent bikes, surreys, and equipment for kids.

Scootertown (239-394-8400; www.islandbikeshops.com; 845 Bald Eagle Dr., Marco Island 34145) Rents scooters and bikes in various sizes and styles; also skates and strollers. Rates by the day, week, and month. Delivery available.

Boats & Boating
Naples, Marco Island, and Everglades City are lousy with marinas. These are headquarters for boat rentals, tours, and charters to serve every interest, from shelling and fishing to gaping at mansions.

CANOEING & KAYAKING
The ultimate paddling experience, Everglades National Park has marked a ✪ 99-mile **Wilderness Waterway** trail that extends from Everglades City to Flamingo, the park's main eastern access. Platform campsites accommodate overnighters. There are also good canoeing trails near the Oasis Visitors Center in ✪ **Big Cypress National Preserve**. Outfitters in Everglades City provide rentals, supplies, tours, and shuttle service. In addition to the outlets listed below, many resorts and parks rent canoes and kayaks.

Collier County is working on developing the ✪ **Paradise Coast Blueway** (www.paradisecoastblueway.com), a system of paddling trails throughout the county that will provide GPS-marked trail routes. Phase I is expected to launch in fall 2007 with the Ten Thousand Islands section, which will include one long trail from Everglades City to Goodland and at least six shorter day-trip trails.

Cocohatchee Nature Center (239-592-1200; www.cocohatchee.org; 12345 Tamiami Trail N., Naples 34110) Rents kayaks and canoes for self-guided or guided tours into the estuary wilderness of the Cocohatchee River, which empties into the gulf.

✪ **Collier-Seminole State Park** (239-394-3397; www.floridastateparks.org/collier-seminole; 20200 E. Tamiami Trail, Naples 34114, between Naples and Everglades City) Rents canoes for use on the park's 13.5-mile canoe trail into mangrove wilderness preserve. Guided tours available some Sundays in season by reservation.

Conservancy of Southwest Florida (239-262-0304; www.conservancy.org; 1450 Merrihue Dr., Naples 34102; and 239-775-8569; 401 Shell Island Rd., Naples 34133) Canoes are available to rent for use in the nature center's waterways.

Everglades National Park Boat Tours (239-695-2591, 800-445-7724 in Florida; www.nps.gov/ever; Everglades Ranger Station, P.O. Box 119, Everglades City 34139) Free ranger-led canoe trips in season (mid-December through Easter) every Saturday and Sunday from 10 AM to −2 PM; you must bring or rent your canoe or kayak. Rentals also available for self-guided tours.

North American Canoe Tours (239-695-4666; www.evergladesadventures.com; 107 Camellia St., P.O. Box 5038, Everglades City 34139) Rents 17-foot aluminum canoes, high-quality kayaks, and equipment with complete outfitting and shuttle service. Guided excursions into the Everglades range from one day to seven nights.

Saltwater Sports (239-394-9557; 231 Capri Blvd., Naples 34113) Rentals, free delivery to Marco (with advance notice), and nature tours.

DINING CRUISES

Marco Island Princess (239-642-5415; www.naplesprincesscruises.com; 951 Bald Eagle Dr., Marco Island 34145; at Rose Marco River Marina) Daily narrated eco-sightseeing cruises, lunch and dinner cruises, and sunset excursions.

Naples Princess (239-649-2275; www.naplesprincesscruises.com; Port-O-Call Marina, 550 Port-O-Call Way, Naples 34102, on U.S. 41 across the river from Tin City) Excursions include a buffet lunch, sunset hors d'oeuvres, and sunset buffet dinner. Full-service cash bar.

MARINE SUPPLIES

West Marine (239-774-3233; www.westmarine.com; 3360 E. Tamiami Trail, Naples 34104) All boating, yachting, and fishing needs. Discounts and emergency service available with membership.

PERSONAL WATERCRAFT RENTALS/TOURS

Marco Island Water Sports (239-642-2359; www.marcoislandwatersports.com; 400 S. Collier Blvd., Marco Island 34145, at Marco Island Marriott Beach Resort, Golf Club & Spa) Rents Waverunners and conducts Waverunner excursions into Ten Thousand Islands. Also parasailing.

POWERBOAT RENTALS

Big Hickory Fishing Nook Marina (239-992-3945; 26107 Hickory Blvd., Bonita Beach 34134) Rents skiffs, fishing boats, and pontoons by the half or full day. Also kayaks.

Cedar Bay Marina (239-642-6717, 239-906-2628; www.cedarbaymarina.com; 705 E. Elkcam Circle, Marco Island 34145) Top-of-the-line, fully equipped fishing and pleasure boats.

Port-O-Call Marina (239-774-0479; 550 Port-O-Call Way, Naples 34102, off U.S. 41 E.) Rents deck boats and powerboats 17 to 23 feet in length, to accommodate 6 to 12 people.

Walker's Coon Cay Marina (239-394-2797; 604 E. Palm Ave., Goodland 34140) 24-by-24-foot pontoons and 19-foot center consoles with VHF radios.

PUBLIC BOAT RAMPS

Caxambas Park (239-642-0004; www.co.collier.fl.us; 909 S. Collier Ct., Marco Island 34145) Restrooms, bait, fuel, and access to Roberts Bay.

Cocohatchee River Park (239-591-8596; www.co.collier.fl.us; 13531 Vanderbilt Dr., Naples 34108, at Vanderbilt Beach) Park with three ramps onto the river (which runs to the gulf), restrooms, picnic tables, and boat rentals. Parking fee.

Delnor–Wiggins Pass State Park (239-597-6196; www.floridastateparks.org/delnor-wiggins; 11100 Gulf Shore Dr. N., Naples 34108) The boat ramp allows access to the back bays, the Cocohatchee River, and the Gulf of Mexico, providing visitors with excellent fishing opportunities. Admission.

Marco Island approach (1 mile before the bridge on Route 951)

Naples Landing (239-213-1819; 1101 Ninth St. S., Naples 34102, off Ninth St. S.)

SAILBOAT CHARTERS
Sail *Kahuna* (239-642-7704; www.sail-kahuna.com; Rose Marco River Marina, 951 Bald Eagle Dr., Marco Island 34145) Shelling, beaching, luau, sunset, and dolphin-watch tours aboard the *Kahuna* 42-passenger catamaran. Rental, racing, and American Sailing Association (ASA) instruction.

Sweet Liberty (239-793-3525; www.sweetliberty.com; 880 12th Ave. S., Naples 34102, at the City Dock) Daily shelling, sightseeing, dolphin-spotting, and sunset trips aboard a 53-foot catamaran.

SIGHTSEEING & ENTERTAINMENT CRUISES
Look under "Wildlife Tours & Charters" for nature excursions.
Speedy Johnson's Airboat Tours (239-695-4448, 800-998-4448; www.florida-everglades.com/speedy; Everglades City 34139) You'll find any number of airboat tour operators in and around Everglades City. Many, contrary to good environmental practice, feed wildlife to attract it to the boat. This one is better than others for its accessibility to grasslands and its elevated seats.

Fishing
Many visiting sports folk arrive at the South Coast eager to fight the big fish and brave the deep waters of the Gulf of Mexico. They come equipped with their 50-pound test line, heavy tackle, and tall fish tales. Yet closer to home, in the back bays and shallow waters of Ten Thousand Islands, experienced fishermen find what's best about the region. Sea trout, snook, redfish, sheepshead, mangrove snapper, and pompano abound in the brackish creeks, grass flats, and channels.

Nonresidents age 16 and over must obtain a license unless fishing from a vessel or pier covered by its own license. You can buy inexpensive temporary nonresident licenses at county tax collectors' offices and most Kmarts and bait shops. Check local regulations for season, size, and catch restrictions.

FISHING CHARTERS/OUTFITTERS
Check the large marinas for fishing guides. Experienced guides can take the intimidation and guesswork out of open-water fishing.

Captain Lee Quick (239-695-0032; www.florida-southwest.com/quick/guide.htm; P.O. Box 804, Chokoloskee 34138) Fly and light-tackle fishing in Ten Thousand Islands and the Everglades.

Captain Paul (239-263-4949; 1200 Fifth Ave. S., Naples 34102; Tin City) Half-day back-country fishing trips into Ten Thousand Islands.

Chokoloskee Island Outfitters (239-695-0141 or 239-695-2286; www.cyberangler.com/guides/prickett; P.O. Box 460, Chokoloskee Island 34138) Captain Dave Prickett takes you out for half and full days.

Everglades Angler (239-262-8228, 800-57-FISHY; www.evergladesangler.com; 810 Twelfth Ave. S., Naples 34102) Half- and full-day backcountry fishing expeditions for up to three fishermen to the Everglades and Ten Thousand Islands, Marco Island, and Estero Bay for snook, redfish, and tarpon. Half- and full-day coastal and offshore charters for up to four and deep-sea excursions for up to six.

Hickory Bay Charters (239-947-3851; 26107 Hickory Blvd., Bonita Springs 34134, at Big Hickory Fishing Nook Marina) Board the *Ramble On II*, a 30-foot pontoon, for four-hour trips into the backcountry. Can combine fishing excursions with sightseeing, birding, and shelling.

Lady Brett 45 (239-263-4949; www.tincityboats.com; 1200 Fifth Ave. S., Naples 34102, at Tin City) Half-day offshore trips aboard a 45-foot powerboat with head on board.

Mangrove Outfitters (239-793-3370; www.mangrove-outfitters.com; 4111 E. Tamiami Trail, Naples 34112) Guides charters and, in season, teaches classes on fly-tying.

Peg Leg Charters (239-642-4333 or 250-0625; P.O. Box 171, Goodland 34140, at Stan's Idle Hour Restaurant) Captain Ron Kennedy takes anglers offshore for half- and full-day trips.

Sunshine Tours (239-642-5415; www.sunshinetoursmarcoisland.com; 951 Bald Eagle Dr., Marco Island 34145, at Rose Marco River Marina) Takes small parties aboard a 32-foot boat with bathroom for offshore excursions, half to full day. Also does backcountry fishing trips.

Tide Teaser Native Charter Guide (239-992-2857; Big Hickory Fishing Nook Marina, 26107 Hickory Blvd., Bonita Beach 34134) Captain Brad Hurd says, "No Fish—No Pay" on his back-bay and offshore fishing excursions. He specializes in light tackle, and his four-hour charters can carry up to six persons.

Snook: a prized catch on the Naples Pier

FISHING PIERS
⭐ **Naples Fishing Pier** (239-213-3062; 25 12th Ave. S., Naples 34102) Extends a thousand feet into the gulf and has a bait shop, snack bar, restrooms, and showers.

Golf
Naples earns its title as Golf Capital of the World with more golf holes per capita than any other statistically tracked metropolitan area.

PUBLIC GOLF COURSES
Bonita Fairways Country Club (239-947-9100; 9751 W. Terry St., Bonita Springs 34135) Play 18 holes at a reasonable price. Restaurant.

Lely Resort Flamingo Island Club (239-793-2223; www.lely-resort.net; 8004 Lely Resort Blvd., Naples 34113, off Route 951 east of Naples) Public course designed by Robert Trent Jones Sr. Offers 18 holes, par 72, and a golf school called Naples Golf Authority (239-821-0279).

The Links of Naples (239-417-1313; 16161 E. Tamiami Trail, Naples 34114) Lit 18-hole course with driving range, PGA lessons, and rentals.

Naples Beach Golf Club (239-435-2443; www.naplesbeachhotel.com; 851 Gulf Shore Blvd. N., Naples 34102) An 18-hole, par 72 resort course that hosts many pro and amateur tournaments. Restaurant and lounge.

Pelican's Nest Golf Club (239-947-4600, 800-952-6378; 4450 Pelican's Nest Dr., Bonita Springs 34134) A 36-hole course, par 72.

Tiburón Golf Club (239-594-2040; www.wcigolf.com; 2600 Tiburón Dr., Naples 34109, at the Ritz-Carlton Golf Resort) One of Naples's newest and most exclusive golfing venues; semiprivate with two 18-hole courses—the Black and the Gold—and a golf academy.

GOLF CENTERS

David Leadbetter Golf Academy (239-592-1444, 888-633-5323; www.leadbetter.com; LaPlaya Beach & Golf Resort, 333 Palm River Blvd., Naples 34110) Offers golf school at LaPlaya Golf Course. Lessons, classes, and golf retreats can last anywhere from one hour to three days.

Naples Golf Academy (239-732-9944; www.learninggolf.com; 5375 Hibiscus Dr., Naples 34113, at Hibiscus Golf Club) Half- to two-day courses, private lessons, weekly clinic.

The Rick Smith Golf Academy (239-594-2040; www.wcigolf.com; 2600 Tiburón Dr., Naples 34109, at the Ritz-Carlton Golf Resort) Features individualized instruction, computerized swing analysis, private video viewing rooms.

GOLF SHOPS

World of Golf (239-263-4999, 800-505-9998; www.worldofgolf.com; 4500 N. Tamiami Trail, Naples 34103) From tees to clubs, this shop carries all name-brand equipment and apparel.

Health & Fitness Clubs

The following offer daily or weekly rates for visitors.

Fitness Quest (239-643-7546; 6800 Golden Gate, Naples 34105) Complete fitness center, aerobics, karate, heart-healthy café, nursery.

Golden Gate Fitness Center (239-353-3636; Golden Gate Community Park, 3300 Santa Barbara Blvd., Naples 34116) Full range of Cybex and Keiser equipment, cardio machines, and free weights. Personal training and assessment available.

Gold's Gym (239-598-4455; www.goldsgym.com; 2151 Trade Center Way, Naples 34109; and 239-498-3339; 9110 Bonita Beach Rd., Bonita Springs 34135) Weight- and cardio-training equipment, fitness classes, physical therapists, child care, boxing room, climbing wall, and tanning with surround sound.

Marco Fitness Club (239-394-3705; 871 E. Elkcam Circle, Marco Island 34145) Top-of-the-line cardiovascular and weight machines, free weights, personal trainers, massage therapist.

Naples Fitness Center (239-262-1112; 1048 Castello Dr., Naples 34103, a block off of the Tamiami Trail) A modern, three-tiered workout club with racquetball courts, a heated swimming pool and Jacuzzi, fitness classes, and a smoothie bar.

Hiking

✪ **Big Cypress National Preserve** (239-695-4111, ext. 0; www.nps.gov/bicy; HCR 61, Box 110, Ochopee 33141) East of Route 29, short hiking trails lead off Route 839; longer trails begin about 15 miles away at the Oasis Visitor Center and join up with the Florida Trail, a national scenic trail that will eventually traverse the state's length. A boardwalk trail at the Oasis lets visitors look down at dozens of big alligators. Another good boardwalk for gator-gazing is at H. P. Williams Roadside Park, west of the Oasis.

✪ **Collier-Seminole State Park** (239-394-3397; www.floridastateparks.org/collier-seminole; 20200 E. Tamiami Trail, Naples 34114) A 7-mile trail winds through pine flatwoods and cypress swamp with a primitive campsite. A self-guided boardwalk leads into a salt marsh.

Conservancy of Southwest Florida (239-262-0304; www.conservancy.org; 1450 Merrihue Dr., Naples 34102) Guided and unguided nature hikes through a subtropical hammock. Also hosts day-trip safaris that involve hiking.

✪ **Fakahatchee Strand Preserve State Park** (239-695-4593; www.floridastateparks.org/fakahatcheestrand; W. J. Janes Memorial Scenic Dr. in Copeland, SR 29, north of U.S. 41) Several trails—actually, old logging tramways—traverse the strand off 12-mile (one-way) Janes Drive from the gates on either side of the road. They range in length from 1 to 2 miles. Summer flooding can make your hike a slosh. Adjacent **Picayune Strand State Forest** (at the end of Janes Drive) introduces access to 3.2-mile Sabal Palm Hiking Trail, which winds through cypress forest, habitat for a variety of birds.

Hunting

The Everglades provides some of Florida's best shots at hunting. You must obtain a state license and a Wildlife Management Area stamp. Permits are required for early-season hunting and special types of hunting. For information on seasons and bag limits, request a copy of the *Hunting Regulations Handbook* and *Florida Hunting Seasons* when you buy your license. (You can also download the publications at www.myfwc.com/hunting.) Skeet shooting is available at **Port of the Islands Gun Club** (239-642-8999; www.poigun club.com; 12425 Union Rd., Naples 34114) between Naples and Everglades City.

Kids' Stuff

Bonita Springs B3 Skate Park (239-992-2556; at Bonita Springs Recreation Center) New, small facility.

Coral Cay Adventure Golf (239-793-4999; www.funspotrentals.com; 2205 E. Tamiami Trail, Naples 34112) Two 18-hole miniature golf courses with a tropical island theme. Admission.

Tubular fun at Naples' latest county park, Sun-n Fun

Edge Skate Park (239-213-2037; http://cs.naplesgov.com/parks/fleischmann; 1600 Fleischmann Blvd., Naples 34102) Newly renovated, it welcomes skaters and BMX bikers.

Golden Gate Aquatic Complex (239-353-7128; Golden Gate Community Park, 3300 Santa Barbara Blvd., Naples 34116) Swimming fun for all ages, with water slides, wading pool and fountain, and competition pool with low and high dives. Admission.

Golf Safari (239-947-1377; 3775 Bonita Beach Rd., Bonita Springs 34134) Jungle-themed miniature golf.

King Richard's Family Fun Park (239-598-1666; www.kingrichardspark.net; 6780 N. Airport Rd., Naples 34109) Merlin's Moat interactive water attraction (bring your swimsuit), kiddie rides, bumper boats, batting cages, a castle full of video games, laser tag, go-carts, a rock climbing wall, and an 18-hole miniature golf course. You can buy tickets per attraction or for unlimited rides. Age restrictions apply for some of the rides.

✪ **Sun-n-Fun Lagoon** (239-254-2000; http://www.colliergov.net/Index.aspx?page=358; 15000 Livingston Rd., Naples 34119, at North Collier Regional Park) Naples' newest recreational addition, it has slides, a lazy river, and sandy beaches. In late 2008, watch for a state-of-the-art children's museum to open at the same park.

Velocity Skate Park (239-793-4414; www.colliergov.net; 3500 Thomasson Dr., Naples 34112) Formerly East Naples Skate Park, it contains a full array of pipes, drops, ramps, and rails for skaters and BMX bikers.

Racquet Sports
Tennis Center at Cambier Park (239-213-3060; www.cambiertennis.com; between Eighth and Park Streets, Naples) Twelve lit tennis courts. Fee.

Collier County Racquet Center (239-394-5454; 1275 San Marco Rd., Marco Island 34145)

County facility with two deco-turf and six Har-Tru courts, two racquetball courts, pro shop, and lessons.

Fleischmann Park (239-213-3020; 1600 Fleischmann Blvd., Naples 33940) Four lit racquetball courts.

Golden Gate Community Park (239-353-0404; 3300 Santa Barbara Blvd., Naples 34116) Lit tennis and racquetball courts.

Mary C. Watkins Tennis Center (239-435-4351; www.naplesbeachhotel.com; The Naples Beach Hotel & Golf Club, 851 Gulf Shore Blvd. N., Naples 34102) Its six Hydro-grid Har-Tru courts are open to the public for a fee; lessons and clinics available.

Naples Park Elementary (111th Ave. N., Naples 34108) Two lit courts.

Pelican Bay Community Park (239-353-0404; 764 Vanderbilt Rd., Naples 34108) Lit tennis and racquetball courts.

Tommie Barfield Elementary (101 Kirkwood St., Goodland, Marco Island 34140) Two lit courts.

Shelling
It is illegal to collect live shells in state and national parks. Collier County also discourages the collection of live shells.

HOT SHELLING SPOTS
Coconut Island (north of Marco Island) A destination for most Marco Island shelling expeditions.

✪ **Key Island** (south of Naples, accessible only by boat) A partly private, partly state-owned unbridged island, Key holds a great many shell prizes that are not as picked over as on beaches that are accessible by car.

Ten Thousand Islands Shell Island, Kingston Key, and Mormon Key provide lots of empty shells to collect.

SHELLING CHARTERS
Captain Paul (239-263-4949; 1200 Fifth Ave. S., Naples 34102, in Tin City) Daily trips to Keewaydin Island.

Sail Marco/Sea Excursions (239-642-7704; Rose Marco River Marina, 951 Bald Eagle Dr., Marco Island 34145; mailing address 821A Palm St., Marco Island 34145) Take a powered or sailing boat to unbridged barrier islands for shelling.

Spas
Everglades Spa (239-695-3151; www.evergladesspa.com; 201 W. Broadway, Everglades City 34129, at Everglades Spa & Lodge) Holistic treatments including colon hydrotherapy, ear candling, magnetic clay baths, intense pulse light therapy, and acupuncture in addition to more traditional massage, wraps, and skin care.

La Piel Spa (239-352-5554; www.la-piel.com; 6370 Pine Ridge Rd., Ste. 101, Naples 34119) A full-service day spa incorporated into a cosmetic-surgery practice. It offers facials, peels, body treatments, massages, manicures, and other services.

Mahalo Salon & Spa (239-947-5900; www.mahalosalonandspa.com; 27160 Bay Landing Dr., Bonita Springs 34135) An elegant spa that designs treatments and programs for relaxation, pampering, slendering, beautifying, and good health—from airbrush spray tanning and Moor mud wraps to metabolism testing and medical peels.

Naples Beach Hotel & Golf Club (239-261-2222, 800-237-7600; www.naplesbeachhotel .com/resort/spa/spa.htm; 851 Gulf Shore Blvd. N., Naples 34102) This vital component to a landmark Naples hotel brings full-service spa facilities, from extensive massage services (including aromatherapy, Reiki, shiatsu, neuromuscular massages) to body treatments (wraps, scrubs) and facials. A hair salon and fitness center enhance the wellness experience here.

The Ritz-Carlton Spa (239-514-6100; www.ritzcarlton.com; 280 Vanderbilt Beach Rd., Naples 34108) A divine respite from the world, it offers a full menu of massages and body treatments, hydrotherapies, and wellness evaluations and training. Signature treatments include bamboo massage and the Mimosa Extravaganza orange-flavored scrub and wrap. H2O+ Café sells yummy smoothies and healthy snacks and lunches seasonally.

SeaSide Day Spa (239-393-2288, 888-393-4SPA; www.seasidedayspa.com; 651 S. Collier Blvd., Marco Island 34145) This spa administers a full line of massage, body, and skin treatments, with a focus on facials and face treatments.

Spa 41 (239-263-1664; www.spa41.net; 4910 Tamiami Trail N., Ste. 200, Naples 34103, at Tanglewood Marketplace) Offers therapeutic massage and other spa treatments, plus tanning beds and spray tanning.

Spa on Fifth (239-280-2777; www.spaonfifth.com; Inn on Fifth, 699 Fifth Ave. S., Naples 34102) Full line of facials, massages, and body scrubs and wraps.

Viva La Difference Day Spa (239-948-1733; 9122 Bonita Beach Rd., in Sunshine Plaza at U.S. 41) Facials come in yummy flavors such as mint julep and pumpkin chiffon. Besides facials, its specialty, it offers massage, wraps, waxing, and nail services.

Spectator Sports
GREYHOUND RACING
Naples-Fort Myers Greyhound Track (239-992-2411; www.naplesfortmyersdogs.com; 10601 Bonita Beach Rd. SE, Bonita Springs 34134) Matinees, night races, simulcasting, and trackside dining. Admission.

WATERSKIING
Gulf Coast Skimmers (239-732-0570; www.gulfcoastskimmers.com; mailing address: 4002 Cindy Ave., Naples 34112; Lake Avalon at Sugden Regional Park, Outer Drive, Naples) This group stages live shows every Sunday at 3 PM, October through April and Saturday at 6:30 PM May through November.

Water Sports
PARASAILING & WATERSKIING
Florida Water Sports (239-825-4866; www.floridaparasail.com) Serving Naples and Marco Island.

Marco Island Water Sports (239-642-2359; www.marcoislandwatersports.com; 400 S. Collier Blvd., Marco Island 34145, at Marco Island Marriot Beach Resort, Golf Club & Spa) Parasailing; Waverunner and other water-sport rentals.

SNORKELING & SCUBA
Murky waters here send most divers to Florida's east coast and the Keys, although some charters take you out into deep local waters.

SCUBAdventures (239-434-7477; www.scubadventureslc.com, 971 Creech Rd., Naples 34103) Supplies, instruction, and diving arrangements.

Wilderness Camping
✪ **Big Cypress National Preserve** (239-695-4111; www.nps.gov/bicy; HCR 61, Box 110, Ochopee 33141) Four primitive campgrounds and one with facilities (cold showers) lie along the Tamiami Trail and Loop Road, about 18 miles east of Route 29. Some are closed in summer.

Big Cypress Trail Lakes Campground (239-695-2275; 40904 U.S. 41 E., Ochopee 34141, U.S. 41, 5 miles east of Route 29) Tent or RV camping in Big Cypress National Preserve, a 729,000-acre sanctuary adjacent to Everglades National Park.

✪ **Collier-Seminole State Park** (239-394-3397; www.floridastateparks.org/collier -seminole; 20200 E. Tamiami Trail, Naples 34114, 17 miles south of Naples) This 6,470-acre park straddles Big Cypress Swamp and Ten Thousand Islands Mangrove Wilderness and provides the least primitive camping in Everglades Country. There are RV hookups and tent sites; the first loop is more conducive to tenters, while the second has sites close together, a laundry, dump station, and recreational facilities for RVers. The park is full of possibilities for exploring nature and history, but no swimming is allowed.

✪ **Everglades National Park** (239-695-2591; www.nps.gov/ever) Backcountry camping along the Everglades canoe trails requires a permit, available from the Everglades City Ranger Station on Route 29. Most sites provide shelters on pilings with chemical toilets. Take mosquito repellent—gallons in summer.

Wildlife Spotting
The Florida Everglades, Big Cypress National Preserve, Ten Thousand Islands, and Florida Panther National Wildlife Refuge are home to the reclusive golden Florida panther, along with bobcats, manatees, wood storks, brown pelicans, black skimmers, roseate spoonbills, and ibises. Some creatures, such as the panther and bobcat, are rarely seen out of captivity. Others, especially the brown pelican, live side by side with residents. I've driven along Route 29 between the interstate and Tamiami Trail and spotted flocks of ibises and herds of white-tailed deer. Deep in the 'Glades birds flock like a blizzard. Optimum wildlife viewing is December through March, when birds migrate and dry weather concentrates them in diminished ponds and other waterways.

ALLIGATORS
The Everglades is the New York City of Florida's alligator population. They thrive in the freshwater ponds and brackish creeks of the River of Grass. When the sun is shining along

Alligator Alley (Interstate 75) and the Tamiami Trail, you can see hundreds of these prehistoric reptiles on the banks, sunning themselves. Crocodiles also live in the 'Glades, but they are rare on this side.

BIRDS

The South Coast is a bird-watcher's haven—especially in winter, when migrating species add to the vast variety of the coast's residential avifauna. Rare visitors and locals include roseate spoonbills, black skimmers, yellow-crowned night herons, wood storks, white pelicans, limpkins, and bald eagles. More commonly seen are frigates, ospreys, Louisiana herons, great blue herons, ibises, snowy egrets, brown pelicans, anhingas, cormorants, terns, seagulls, plovers, oystercatchers, pileated woodpeckers, owls, and hawks.

In its October 2002 issue, *Birder's World* magazine named two of the South Coast's sanctuaries among its Top 15 Birding Hot Spots. For the best bird-watching, try ✪ **Everglades National Park** (rated #4); Naples's ✪ **Corkscrew Swamp Sanctuary** (rated #5), home to the largest nesting colony of wood storks in the U.S.; ✪ **Rookery Bay National Estuarine Reserve** near Marco Island; and Ten Thousand Islands, a haven for birds of all sorts. Marco Island is a proclaimed sanctuary for bald eagles. Barfield Bay in Goodland is one of their favorite locales. At the beach, the threatened piping plover gets support and protection from local environmentalists.

The **South Florida Birding Trail**, the last leg of the Great Florida Birding Trail, completed in 2005, maps the region's best spotting venues. Corkscrew Swamp Sanctuary serves as the trail's regional gateway. For a map and more information, visit www.floridabirdingtrail.com.

NATURE PRESERVES & ECO-ATTRACTIONS

✪ BIG CYPRESS NATIONAL PRESERVE

239-695-2000
www.nps.gov/bicy
HCR 61, Box 110, Ochopee 34141
Adjacent to Everglades National Park.
Oasis Visitor Center about 20 miles east of
SR 29 on U.S. 41. Open: Oasis Visitor
Center open daily 9–4:30
Admission: Free

This 729,000-acre preserve abuts
Everglades National Park to the north and
Fakahatchee Strand Preserve State Park to
the east. From the Oasis Visitor Center you
can depart on wilderness hikes to sample
its Everglades environment. In summer
the trails—which connect to the Florida
National Scenic Trail—can be very wet.
You'll see the grasslands and bald cypress
stands for which Big Cypress is known, as

A supersized ibis pokes for food beneath the re-created sands of a Rookery Bay education center exhibit.

The boardwalk through Corkscrew Swamp Sanctuary explores a variety of ecosystems.

well as profuse birds and an alligator nursery. The preserve boasts the state's major population of the reclusive, endangered Florida panther. A small museum at the visitors center contains Indian artifacts and wildlife exhibits. Rangers lead swamp walks, bike and canoe trips, and campfire programs in season. A 26-mile scenic loop road is open to vehicles when road conditions allow. Closer to Everglades City, Birdon Road (Route 841) takes a 17-mile trip through sawgrass prairie habitat. It connects to Route 837 and then Route 839, which leads to two 2.5-mile hiking trails, one to the north and the other to the south of the intersection.

✪ COLLIER-SEMINOLE STATE PARK

239-394-3397
www.floridastateparks.org/collier-seminole
20200 E. Tamiami Trail, Naples 34114
Open: Daily, dawn to dusk; visitors center open 8–5

Admission: $4 per car, up to 8 passengers; $2 per car, single occupant; $1 cyclists or pedestrians

Here, Naples meets the Everglades. One of the region's prettiest state parks, it encompasses manicured lawns in contrast to jungle wilderness. Besides its historic attractions—a garden memorial to developer Barron Collier, the only remaining dredge used to build the Tamiami Trail across the Everglades, and a replicated Civil War blockhouse—it harbors the wealth of birds, otters, cats, manatees, and other critters who seek shelter in the outlying Everglades. Learn about them at the little visitors center in the blockhouse, then take to the nature, bike, and canoe trails. Ranger activities will provide biological background. Camping available.

✪ CONSERVANCY NATURE CENTER

239-262-0304
www.conservancy.org
1450 Merrihue Dr., Naples 34102
One block east of Goodlette Rd.
Open: 9–4:30 Mon.–Sat., also 12–4 Sun., Nov.–Apr.
Admission: Nature Center, $7.50 adults and $2 children ages 3–12. Nature trails and wildlife rehabilitation facility are free.

This tucked-away nature complex on the Gordon River was built by the Conservancy of Southwest Florida to educate the public about the environment. Within its 20 acres, it encompasses a nature store; trail walks; boat tours of the river (free with paid admission);

a rehabilitation center for birds, deer, turtles, and other injured animals; and a nature discovery center with live Florida snakes, an offshore tank (where you'll often find a loggerhead turtle swimming), fascinating touch tables, interactive games, and habitat vignettes (where you can see and hear local fauna). Friendly and chattily informative guides conduct special programs throughout the day as they feed their live critters. The Conservancy also hosts interpretative nature field trips. Canoes and kayak rentals are available for use on the Gordon River; the Conservancy also hosts guided paddle trips in Rookery Bay and at Clam Pass.

✪ CORKSCREW SWAMP SANCTUARY

239-348-9151
www.audubon.org/local/sanctuary/corkscrew
375 Sanctuary Rd., Naples 34120
Off Naples-Immokalee Rd., 21 miles east of N. Tamiami Trail
Open: Daily 7–7:30, mid-April–Sept., 7–5:30 mid-Oct.–mid-Apr.
Admission: $10 adults, $6 college students, $4 children ages 6–18.

This 11,000-acre sanctuary, operated by the National Audubon Society, protects one of the largest stands of mature bald cypress trees in the country. Some of the towering specimens date back nearly 500 years. The threatened wood stork once came to nest here in great numbers. Diminished populations still do, at which time the nesting area is roped off to protect them. A 2.25-mile-long boardwalk takes you over swampland inhabited by rich plant and marine life. You can usually spot an alligator or two. The state-of-the-art Blair Audubon Center, a national prototype, occupies a "stealth" building that blends with the pristine environment. Its Swamp Theater dramatically recreates seasons and times of day on the boardwalk, plus there are hands-on opportunities for kids.

DELNOR-WIGGINS PASS STATE PARK

239-597-6196
www.floridastateparks.org/delnor-wiggins
11100 Gulf Shore Dr. N., Naples 34108
At Vanderbilt Beach
Open: Sunrise to sunset
Admission: $5 per car, up to 8 passengers; $3 per car, single occupant; $1 cyclists or pedestrians

Prehistoric loggerhead turtles lumber ashore to lay and bury their eggs every summer, away from the lights and crowds of other area beaches. Fifty-six days later the baby turtles emerge and scurry to the sea—hopefully before birds can snatch them up. Beach turtle talks are available during the loggerhead season. Year-round, fishing, beaching, and climbing the observation tower are popular activities.

✪ EVERGLADES NATIONAL PARK/GULF COAST VISITOR CENTER

239-695-3311
www.nps.gov/ever
P.O. Box 120, Everglades City 34139
Tamiami Trail south of Naples; ranger station and visitors center on SR 29, before the Chokoloskee Causeway in Everglades City

Open: Visitor center hours are mid-Nov.–mid-Apr., daily 8–4:30; mid-Apr.–mid-Nov., daily 9–4:30
Admission: Free

This massive wetland—home to the endangered Florida panther and other rare animals—covers 2,200 square miles and shelters more than 600 types of fish and 347 bird species. It stretches from here to the Florida Keys on the east coast. Along with Ten Thousand Islands, it also contains the largest mangrove forest in the world. So what's the best way to see this seemingly overwhelming expanse of wildlife? Take your pick. From this end, you really can't drive through it, but you can from the eastern access, two hours away. U.S. Highway 41 skirts the edge of the park and Big Cypress National Preserve, which is part of the same ecosystem. Closest access to Naples is Route 29 and Everglades City. Canoe trips from 8 to 99 miles long put you in closer range of birds, manatees, dolphins, and alligators. There's also a variety of other options. The park offers boat tours, and other private sightseeing cruises exist. During the winter, ranger programs and canoe tours from the Gulf Coast Visitor Center teach about the unique environment. You can rent a pontoon boat or hire a charter captain in Everglades City for sightseeing and fishing. Get advice at the welcome center or visitors center, or see "Wildlife Tours & Charters," below. The visitors center holds a few wildlife and hands-on exhibits. Tables and a chikee hut accommodate picnickers.

FAKAHATCHEE STRAND PRESERVE STATE PARK
239-695-4593
www.floridastateparks.org/fakahatcheestrand
P.O. Box 548, Copeland 34137
W. J. Janes Memorial Scenic Dr. (SR 29) in Copeland, north of U.S. 41
Open: Preserve administration office open 9–4 weekdays
Admission: Free; donations accepted

Rangers lead swamp walks the third Saturday of the month from November through February. You can also hike on your own. Park at the gates on either side of the road and follow the short pathways into the strand. In summer the trails are often muddy and submerged. You can also access the strand (a linear swamp forest that snakes along ancient sloughs) via the 2,000-foot Big Cypress Bend boardwalk, west of Everglades City on U.S. Highway 41. The ecosystem is known for its orchids, including 31 varieties of threatened and endangered species, 14 native varieties of bromeliads, and stately stands of native royal palm. Florida panthers, black bears, mangrove fox squirrels, and Everglades minks have all been documented along the 20-mile-long strand. You're more likely to spot alligators, white-tailed deer, ospreys, ibises, and egrets. A ranger office on W. J. Janes Memorial Scenic Drive, past the old fire tower, has displays and information on the preserve. Next to the boardwalk you'll find an Indian village with a gift shop.

THE NAPLES PRESERVE
239-261-4290
1690 Tamiami Trail N., Naples 34102
Open: Daily, dawn to dusk; eco-center Tues., Thurs, Sat. 10–4
Admission: Free

Newly developing, this 9.5-acre patch of ancient ecology along the highway was recently cleaned up and fitted with a 0.4-mile boardwalk that crosses scrub oak, grassy meadow, and pine-flatwoods communities. Gopher tortoises, deer, bobcat, and birds occupy the habitat. An eco-center houses a diorama plus rotating exhibits depicting the preserve's fauna and flora.

✪ ROOKERY BAY ENVIRONMENTAL LEARNING CENTER

239-417-6310
www.rookerybay.org
300 Tower Rd., Naples 34113
Off Route 951 (Collier Blvd.) toward Marco Island
Open: 9–4 Mon.–Sat.
Closed: Sun. and, in summer, Sat.
Admission: $5 for adults, $3 for children ages 6–12

The Gulf Coast's largest and most pristine wildlife sanctuary occupies more than 110,000 acres at the gateway to Ten Thousand Islands. It's "Ding" Darling without the crowds (or accessibility) and a favorite for fishermen and bird-watchers. Rare creatures such as the American crocodile, manatee, Atlantic green and Ridley sea turtles, bald eagle, and roseate spoonbill inhabit its backwaters. For an introduction to this vast, largely inaccessible land, stop at this Department of Environmental Protection laboratory and education facility, opened in March 2004. The mangrove estuary is the star of high-tech, interactive exhibits. The centerpiece, a 2,000-gallon aquarium, has a 15-foot tall mangrove "growing" out of it and spaces into which kids can crawl and get to know the crucial habitat. Forming a back-drop to the aquarium, a curved wall holds various habitat dioramas, three-dimensional tactile displays of local creatures, local wildlife-artist murals, Crab Condo, a touch tank, Mosquito Landing, and other fun and original learning tools. An audio self-tour is avail-able for a nominal fee. The unusual polka dot batfish is the center's mascot and has been replicated in huge proportion. Kids can play with puppets and read books in the mangrove forest play area. The second floor holds exhibits exploring the area's and reserve's time-line, a replica of an Old Florida homestead, and recorded stories from the different eras. In time the center will encompass nature trails, a footbridge and boardwalk, kayaking in the canals out back, and educational programs.

Wildlife Tours & Charters

Cocohatchee Nature Center (239-592-1200; www.cocohatchee.org; 12345 Tamiami Trail N., Naples 34110) Nature and sunset boat tours dip into the pristine, bird-rich waters of the Cocohatchee River and onto the gulf, where passengers often spot dolphins.

Conservancy of Southwest Florida (239-262-0304; www.conservancy.org; 1450 Merrihue Dr., Naples 34102, one block east of Goodlette Rd.) Boat tours of the mangrove waterway are included in admission. It also hosts wildlife cruises of Rookery Bay National Estuarine Research Reserve aboard the pontoon boat *Good Fortune.*

Double Sunshine (239-263-4949; www.tincityboats.com; 1200 Fifth Ave. S., Naples 34102, at Tin City on U.S. 41) Departs five times daily for 1.5-hour narrated nature, sunset, and dolphin-sighting cruises.

Stealing a Peek at Orchids

Susan Orlean's true account of orchid lust, *The Orchid Thief*, inspired the outlandish 2003 movie *Adaptation* starring Nicholas Cage, Chris Cooper, and Meryl Streep. The setting: Florida's steamy corners—specifically, Fakahatchee Strand Preserve State Park.

Here, Orlean sloshed through the swamps with her unlikely hero searching for the coveted ghost orchid. You can, too, through ranger slough walk programs held in season. The Strand—approximately 20 miles long and 3 to 5 miles wide—has enjoyed a surge in popularity since the book and movie. As the orchid capital of the U.S., it harbors 31 species of native wild orchids listed as threatened or endangered, among them the ghost orchid. In fact, biologist Mike Owen reports spotting six specimens on a recent winter trip.

That's the good news. The bad news is, you have to get wet to see them, and the best time to view the most species a-bloom are the buggiest, hottest months, particularly September and October.

Everglades National Park Boat Tours (239-695-2591, 800-445-7724; www.nps.gov/ever/visit/tours.htm; Gulf Coast Visitor Center, P.O. Box 119, Everglades City 34139) Naturalist-narrated tours wind through the maze of Ten Thousand Islands and its teeming bird and water life; other tours take you up the mangrove-lined Turner River.

Manatees Sightseeing Adventure (239-642-8818, 800-379-7440; www.see-manatees .com; 25000 Tamiami Trail E., Naples 34114) Captains Barry and Carol take up to six passengers on a 90-minute sightseeing charter into manatee sanctuary by appointment. If you don't see a manatee, you don't pay. The boat departs from Port of the Islands development.

Shopping

Custom-designed jewelry, exclusive top-designer fashion lines, original masterpiece art, and the world's first street concierge make the experience of browsing, buying, and window-yearning in Naples entirely unique. Naples ranks with Palm Beach's Worth Avenue and Sarasota's St. Armands Circle among Florida's most chic arenas for spending. Downtown's renaissance concentrates the shopping frenzy in the Old Naples districts of Fifth Avenue South and Third Street Plaza, but a number of other fashionable shopping centers are found throughout town. Downtown shops are known for their individually owned and one-of-a-kind galleries and for designer outlets.

Shopping Centers & Malls

Coastland Center (239-262-2323; www.coastlandcenter.com; Tamiami Trail N. and Golden Gate Pkwy., Naples) Naples's largest and only enclosed, climate-controlled shopping center has 150 stores and 16 eateries, including a full array of shopping options, from major department stores to small specialty shops. Chain names include Macy's, Sears, Old Navy, Victoria's Secret, Bath & Body Works, and Ruth's Chris Steak House.

✪ **Fifth Avenue South** (www.fifthavenuesouth.com; Naples) Once upon a time, members of the Seminole Indian tribe sold their crafts from a stand on Fifth Avenue. Today it's one of Naples's most fashionable addresses. In 1996 a movement started to update the historic

Art and greenery make window-shopping along Naples' Third Street South a multidimensional experience.

district, which had begun to look run down. Famed Florida planner Andre Duany was hired to breathe new life into the district. Besides making cosmetic improvements, he brought a new bustle to the street. Tony hotels, new shops, and 20-plus restaurants and sidewalk cafés attract Naples' new "café society." Live entertainment and special events are regularly scheduled.

Marco Town Center Mall (www.marcotowncentermall.com; Collier Blvd. and Bald Eagle Dr., Marco Island) A popular cluster of more than 10 distinctive eateries and 40 shops. During season there's live entertainment Tuesday evenings from 6 to 8.

The Promenade (239-261-6100; www.promenadeshops.com, at Bonita Bay on U.S. 41) This fashionable plaza takes cues from neighbor Naples and includes Mediterranean-style

Welcome to Tin City—nautical kitsch at its best.

fine restaurants, galleries, and name shops. From January through June, the center hosts Friday Jazz Jams the last Friday of the month.

Shops of Marco (San Marco Rd. and Barfield Dr., Marco Island) One-of-a-kind clothing and gift shops.

Third Street South Plaza and the Avenues (239-434-6533; www.thirdstreetsouth.com; Naples) Visit this upscale shopping quarter in Old Naples, the heart of the arts scene, and view fine outdoor sculptures on loan from local galleries. This is window-shopping (on my budget, anyway) at its best—exquisite clothes, art, jewelry, and home decorations and furnishings. The third Thursday of the month brings live entertainment to the evening. Saturdays in season, a farmers' market convenes in the main parking lot.

Tin City (239-262-4200; www.tin-city.com; 1200 Fifth Ave. S., Naples 34102; U.S. 41 at Goodlette Rd.) I love the structure of this mall, which resurrected old tin-roofed docks. Comprising two buildings, it has 30 shops that tend to be touristy, selling mainly nautical gifts and resort wear. But it also offers enjoyable waterfront restaurants, and it's a good place to catch a fishing or sightseeing tour.

✪ **The Village on Venetian Bay** (239-261-6100; www.venetianvillage.com; 4200 Gulf Shore Blvd., Naples 34103, at Park Shore Dr.) Upscale, Mediterranean-style domain of fashion, jewelry, and art. Located on the waterfront.

Waterside Shops at Pelican Bay (239-598-1605; www.watersideshops.com; 5415 Tamiami Trail #320, Naples 34108, at Seagate Dr. and Tamiami Trail N., Pelican Bay) This shopping enclave features Saks Fifth Avenue, Victoria's Secret, Williams-Sonoma, Ann Taylor, some one-of-a-kind shops, and some fun dining options—all located in a newly renovated setting of contemporary stainless steel, cascading waters, and lush foliage.

Antiques & Collectibles

Ashley Adams Arts & Antiques (239-435-7273; www.ashadams.com; 795 Fifth Ave. S., Naples 34102) Literally packed with large European, Oriental, and American bronze, silver, and porcelain sculptures, plus clocks, furniture, and more, both new and old.

The Englishman (239-649-8088; www.theenglishmanusa.com; 1170 Third St. S., Naples 34102, at The Plaza on Third Street) For top-shelf European furniture, oil paintings, and sculpture from the 19th and 20th centuries, browse the fine treasures here.

Shirley Street Antique Mall (239-592-9882; 38 and 68 Goodlette Rd., Naples 34112) One of Naples' largest antiques malls, containing 40 sellers and antiques of every kind.

Books

Mina Hemingway's Florida Bookstore (239-598-2220; 857 Vanderbilt Beach Rd., Naples 34108, at Tamiami Trail N.) Recently taken over by a member of the Hemingway family, it carries new regional and used mainstream books.

Sunshine Book Sellers (239-393-0353; 677 S. Collier Blvd.; and 239-394-5342; 1000 N. Collier Blvd., Marco Island 34145) Large, modern stores with a complete line of books—and coffee always brewing.

Clothing

Casablanca (239-394-2511; 400 S. Collier Blvd., Marco Island 34145, at Marco Island Marriott Beach Resort, Golf Club & Spa) Fashionable and colorful women's resort apparel, such as Jam's World and Tommy Bahama.

Cottontails (239-403-3901, 474 Fifth Ave. S., Naples 34102) A wide variety of children's clothing in a large range of sizes.

Fancy Nancy's (239-261-4050; 1193 Third St. S., Naples 34102) Fun duds (dressy to casual), shoes, and accessories for women.

Freckles (239-394 6600; 188 Royal Palm Dr., Marco Island 34145, at Shops of Old Marco) Feathers, beads, sequins—the clothing and accessories here are anything but dull.

Giggles & Glitz (239-436-3793; 1170 Third St. S., Naples 34102) Fun and breezy shoes, jewelry, and other ladies' accessories.

Island Woman (239-642-6116; www.islandwoman.com; 1 Harbor Pl., Goodland 34146) Hand-painted silk fashions, gemstone jewelry, T-shirts, sarongs, tropical art, crafts, wild wigs, and other crazy stuff.

Kirsten's Boutique (239-598-3233; www.kirstensboutique.com; 5535 Tamiami Trail N., Naples 34108, at Waterside Shops) This unique shop sells African-inspired clothes, jewelry, and art.

Lear's (239-642-2372; 1089 N. Collier Blvd. #417, Marco Island 34145, at Marco Town Center) Unusual styles with flair and daring for women young and old.

Marco Island Clothing Co. (239-642-7277; 117 S. Barfield Dr., Marco Island 34145, at Shops of Marco) Stylish name-brand women's swimsuits, shoes, tropical resort fashions, and accessories.

Marissa Collections (239-263-4333; www.marissacollections.com; 1167 Third St. S., Naples 34102) Carries prestige designer labels such as Versace, Jil Sander, and Oscar de la Renta.

McFarland's of Marco (239-394-6464; 117 S. Barfield Dr., Marco Island 34145, at Shops of Marco) Specializing in tropically appropriate menswear: casual, golf, suits, and resort wear.

Mondo Uomo (239-434-9484; 4200 Gulf Shore Blvd., Naples 34103, at the Village on Venetian Bay) Fine, tasteful fashion and European styles for men: tropical wool, German cotton, sweaters, and distinctive casual and dress wear for Gulf Coast climes.

Outback T's (239-261-7869; 1200 Fifth Ave. S., Naples 34102; Tin City, at U.S. 41 E. and Goodlette Rd.) The best in souvenir T-shirts, with wildlife and local themes.

Simply Natural (239-643-5571; 4330 Gulf Shore Blvd. N., Ste. 302, Naples 34103, at the Village on Venetian Bay) High-end youthful women's fashions in lace, denim, and other contemporary fabrics and styles.

Weekends (239-949-4163; 26841 South Bay Dr., Bonita Springs 34134, at the Promenade) Sporty casual threads for Florida men and women.

Wildflower (239-643-6776; 4222 Gulf Shore Blvd. N., Naples 34103, at the Village on Venetian Bay) Distinctive fun and formal women's wear with Florida flair and style.

Zazou (239-436-3927; www.zazounaples.com; 1170 Third St. S., Naples 34102; also 239-261-2882; 2950 Ninth St. N., Naples 34103, at Hibiscus Center) Expressive women's clothing and home accessorizing products.

Consignment
Naples is a secondhand shopper's paradise. In many of the clothing consignment shops you can find designer fashions with the price tags still attached. Oh, the joys of hunting down the castoffs of the well-to-do!

Act II (239-495-6647; 8951 Bonita Beach Rd. #605, Bonita Springs 34135, at Springs Plaza, U.S. 41) Women's clothing and accessories, including "grand" sizes.

Encore Shop (239-775-0032; 3105 Davis Blvd., Naples 34104) Designer furniture, paintings, decorative items, and collectibles.

New to You Consignments (239-262-6869; 933 Creech Rd., Naples 34103, at U.S. 41) Women's designer clothing, furniture, and decorative items.

Factory Outlet Centers
Naples Prime Outlets (239-775-8083, 888-545-7196; www.primeoutlets.com; 1920 Isle of Capri Rd., mail: 6060 Collier Blvd. #121, Naples 34114; on Route 951 toward Marco

Island) Factory outlet discounts of up to 65 percent off for Harry and David gourmet foods; Mikasa crystal; and Liz Claiborne, Geoffrey Beene, and Izod clothing, among other name brands.

Flea Markets & Bazaars

Flamingo Island Flea Market (239-948-7799; www.flamingoisland.com; 11902 Bonita Beach Rd., Bonita Springs 34135) Open Friday through Sunday, 8–4, with up to 600 vendors.

Naples Drive-In Flea Market (239-774-2900; Immokalee Rd and 39th Ave., Naples 34104) Open Saturday and Sunday.

Galleries

Naples has earned a reputation as a mecca for fine art. **Gallery Row** (239-513-3888), along Broad Avenue South at Third Street South, is a good place to begin your art quest. Galleries line the street and sell a wide spectrum of art. Several more lie in the immediate vicinity. Fifth Avenue South is another arena, although the galleries there are more spread out.

The Blue Mangrove Gallery (239-293 2405; www.bluemangrovegallery.net; 1089 N. Collier Blvd. #437, Marco Island 34145, at Marco Town Center) Exhibits the paintings, glass, jewelry, and photography of local artists, including Clyde Butcher, and national artists.

Connie's Art Workshop & Gallery (239-389-2500; 953 N. Collier Blvd., Marco Island 34145) Artist Connie Zabkar sells her landscapes, still-life oils, and portraits and holds painting workshops.

The Darvish Collection (239-261-7581; www.artnet.com/darvish.html; 1199 Third St. S., Naples 34102) Features the work of North American and European masters within its seven wood-lined, clublike galleries. Most works in the four- to six-figure range.

Gallery Matisse (239-649-7114; www.gallerymatisse.com; 1170 Third St. S., Ste. C106, Naples 34102) Picasso and Chagall pieces, fine oils, art jewelry, and a bit of whimsy.

Gallery One (239-263-0835; www.galleronenaples.com; 1301 Third St. S., Naples 34102) My favorite Naples gallery, it has a large showroom that exhibits mostly three-dimensional art, including a preponderance of glass. Paintings include the work of popular local artist Paul Arsenault.

Guess-Fisher Gallery, Etc. (239-659-2787; 824 Fifth Ave. S., Naples 34102) Delightful works by namesake artists Natalie Guess and Phil Fisher, plus other locals.

Native Visions Gallery (239-643-3785; www.callofafrica.com; 737 Fifth Ave. S., Naples 34102) Remarkable works themed around Africa, the sea, and the environment.

New River Fine Art (239-435-4515; www.newriverfineart.com; 604 Fifth Ave. S., Naples 34102) Truly fine art, pieces here range from contemporary paintings to the etchings of Salvador Dalí and exquisite glass sculptures by Frederick Hart.

Riverside Park (Old 41 Rd. and Pennsylvania, Bonita Springs, downtown) When the park renovated in 2005, city officials saved a row of historic fish shacks from demolition by renovating them and turning them into a string of six art galleries. You'll find the most activity on weekends, when the artists plan on hosting special events.

Silver Eagle (239-403-3033; www.silvereaglegallery.com; 651 Fifth Ave. S., Naples 34102) Decorative Native American drums, blankets, and candles; paintings and beautiful silver and turquoise jewelry.

Sweet Art (239-597-2110; 2054 Trade Center Way, Naples 34109) Affordable tropical decorative art and home accessories.

Gifts

Some of Naples' best souvenirs are found in the gift shops at the town's visitors' attractions.

Gumbo Limbo Gallery at Big House Coffee (239-695-3633; www.chokoloskee-island .com; 238 Mamie St., Chokoloskee 34138) Selection of Florida art, books, charts, jewelry, and other lore.

Holiday House Gifts (239-642-7113; 133 S. Barfield Dr., Marco Island 34145, at Shops of Marco) Candles, country- and tropical-style items, Christmas ornaments and decorations.

Karisma (239-389-0955; www.karismagalleries.com; 599 S. Collier Blvd. #315, Marco Island 34145) Colorful and whimsical island-style furnishings, art, and decorations at high prices.

Regatta (239-262-3929; 760 Fifth Ave. S., Naples 34102) Its subtitle describes it best: "fun things for fun people." Clothes, toys, and things for the home, all in a fine and whimsical tone.

Thirsty Mouse (239-261-4148; 1200 Fifth Ave. S., Naples 34102, at Tin City, U.S. 41 E. and Goodlette Rd.) Florida food (such as smoked alligator) and gifts, sea-themed tableware, and other inexpensive decorative items.

Jewelry

Cleopatra's Barge (239-261-7952, 800-678-7934; www.cleopatrasbarge.com; 1197 Third St. S., Naples 34102) Home of "Naples Medallion" jewelry and other fine and estate pieces. Certified jewelers and diamond setters.

DuFrane Jewelers (239-495-9005, 888-DUFRANE; www.dufranejewelers.com; 26841 South Bay Dr. #152; Bonita Springs 34134, at the Promenade) Besides gorgeous jewelry and watches, this large outlet sells fine china and crystal and other elegant table- and barware.

✪ **Port Royal Jewelers** (239-263-3071; 623 Fifth Ave. S., Naples 34102) This place is like a museum: It includes 18th-century royal jewels and antique pieces in Art Deco, Edwardian, Georgian, and Victorian styles, as well as custom-designed and estate jewelry. It's so exclusive you have to ring a doorbell to get in, and there's a special vault containing the real treasures.

Schilling Jewelers (239-642-3001; 1845 San Marco Dr., Marco 34145, at Shops of Marco) Custom design and manufacturing; cloisonné turtles and fish jewelry; extraordinary sea-themed pieces.

Thalheimers Fine Jewelers (239-261-8422, 800-998-8423; www.thalheimers.com; 3200 Tamiami Trail N. #100, Naples 34103) The most respected name in jewelers, carrying quality watches, diamond jewelry, gems, crystal, and porcelain. Watchmaker, designer, and appraiser on premises.

✪ **Wm. Phelps, Custom Jeweler** (239-434-2233; www.phelpsjewelers.com; 4380 Gulf Shore Blvd., Naples 34103, at the Village on Venetian Bay) Fine-crafted pendants, rings, earrings, and pins on display, plus colored stones and diamonds for customizing.

Yamron Jewelers (239-592-7707; 5415 Tamiami Trail N., Naples 34108, at Waterside Shops) A select stock of exquisite jewelry and Swiss watches.

Kitchenware & Home Decor

El Condor Imports (239-732-5855; www.elcondornaplesfl.com; 6060 Collier Blvd. #123, Naples 34114, at Prime Outlets) Rustic pine furniture, pottery, and decorative crafts from Mexico.

Fabec-Young & Company (239-649-5501; 4360 Gulf Shore Blvd., Ste. 604, Naples 34103, at the Village on Venetian Bay) Unusual table settings, including napkins, candles, glassware, silver, and ceramics.

Gattle's (239-262-4791, 800-344-4552; 1250 Third St. S., Naples 34102) Linens for bed, bath, and table; fine home accessories and art.

The Good Life (239-262-4355, 800-846-2540; 1170 Third St. S., Ste. A101, Naples 34102) Gourmet cookware, tabletops, serving pieces, imported and colorful beach-theme tableware, quality implements, unusual gadgets, and gourmet food products.

A Horse of a Different Color (239-261-1252; 4200 Gulf Shore Blvd., Naples 34103, at the Village on Venetian Bay) Pricey one-of-a-kind, highly contemporary gifts, lamps, clocks, and other home accents.

Jennings (239-430-4321, 866-857-8152; www.jenningsofnaples.com; 449 Bayfront Place, Naples 34102; and 800-562-6616; 3652 9th St. N., Naples 34103) Fine china, crystal, silver, and other ultraelegant home accessories.

Tribal Findings' import wares

Lady from Haiti (239-649-8607; www.theladyfromhaiti.com; 476 Fifth Ave. S., Naples 34102) Steel-drum sculptures, hand-painted wooden items, fine Haitian art. Enjoy the sand on the floor and Caribbean music while you shop.

Tribal Findings and the Pot Factory (239-593-5811; www.tribalfindings.com; 5974 Taylor Rd. #2, Naples 34109) At Naples' Trade Center, this shop sells an intriguing collection of masks, carvings, pottery, ceramics, and other folk art and decorative items from West Africa, Mexico, and Haiti at reasonable prices.

Shell Shops
Blue Mussel (239-262-4814; www.bluemussel.com; 478 Fifth Ave. S., Naples 34102) Specimen and decorative shells, jewelry, and other gifts since 1962.

Marco Craft & Shell Company (239-394-7020; 1089 N. Collier Blvd., Marco Island 34145, at Marco Town Center Mall) Craft and specimen shells, locally handcrafted gifts, craft classes.

Shells by Emily (239-394-5575; www.shellsbyemily.com; 651 S. Collier Blvd. 2C, Marco Island 34145) Walk or take the elevator to the second floor to find this award-winning shell crafter, who sells specimen shells and crafting supplies.

Sporting Goods
Note: For supplies and equipment for specific sports, please refer to "Recreation" in this chapter.

Sports Authority (239-598-5054; www.sportsauthority.com; 2505 Pine Ridge Rd., Naples 34109) Complete line of sports and outdoor equipment and clothing.

CALENDAR OF EVENTS

January
Bonita Springs National Art Festival (239-495-8989; www.artinusa.com/Bonita; the Promenade, Bonita Springs) A top-rated two-day show midmonth, featuring fine artists from around the world. Also in March.

Green Flash
The sun is setting, melting, golden, into the sea like a round pat of butter balanced on its edge in a sauté pan. Just as the final crescent of light disappears, it sends up a green farewell flare on the horizon.

What you've just witnessed is a tropical phenomenon called a green flash. It occurs infrequently, and most people miss it—or only realize what they've seen after the fact.

Skeptics will tell you that green flashes are just a good excuse to sit on the beach at sunset, perhaps with a celebratory glass of champagne or rum punch. The drinking part of the sunset ritual, they further theorize, may be more responsible for green flash sightings than reality.

Physics, however, backs up the notion that the sun emits a split-second green explosion as it winks below the sea's surface. It all has to do with spectrum, wavelengths, refraction, and other terms you may remember from school science experiments. In short, it takes conditions such as those we enjoy on the Gulf Coast—sunsets over the sea and near-tropical climes—to make the green flash happen. Cloudless evening skies, which occur more regularly during the cool months, are also required.

Patience and persistence are crucial. Once you've seen a green flash, some say, your now-trained eye is apt to spot more—with or without rum.

Marco National Fine Arts & Fine Crafts Festival (239-394-4221; www.marcoisland art.com; 1010 Winterberry Dr., Marco Island 34145, at the Art League of Marco Island grounds) Two days midmonth for an outdoor art fling.

Mullet Festival (239-394-3041, 877-387-2582; www.stansidlehour.com, Stan's Idle Hour restaurant, Goodland) Celebrating Goodland's fishing heritage and an extravaganza of music and tomfoolery. Three days midmonth.

Swamp Buggy Races (239-774-2701, 800-897-2701; www.swampbuggy.com; Florida Sports Park, Route 951, east Naples) Nationally televised event; the Everglades equivalent of tractor pulls or monster truck racing.

February

Collier County Fair (239-455-1444; www.colliercountyfair.com; Collier County Fair-grounds, Immokalee Rd., Naples) A good old-fashioned fair with rides and exhibits. Early February for 11 days.

✪ **Everglades Seafood Festival** (239-695-4100; www.evergladesseafoodfestival.com; Everglades City) Three days of music, arts and crafts, and fresh seafood. Early in the month.

Grecian Festival (239 591-3430; St. Katherine's Greek Orthodox Church, Airport-Pulling Rd., Naples) Greek food specialties, music, costumed dancers, and exhibits. First weekend.

Naples National Art Festival (239-262-6517; www.naplesartcenter.org/nnartfestival.htm; Cambier Park, downtown Naples) This prime art festival event takes place over two days late in the month.

Native American and Pioneer Festival (239-394-3397; Collier-Seminole State Park) Honoring local heritage with a Seminole War battle reenactment, crafts, and bluegrass music. Third weekend of the month.

March

Bonita Springs National Art Festival (239-495-8989; www.artinusa.com/Bonita; the Promenade, Bonita Springs) Two days midmonth, featuring fine artists from around the world. Also in January.

Country Jam (239-254-4000; www.countryjamnaples.com; Vineyards Community Park, Naples) Top national country entertainers, local country acts, carnival rides and carnival games, a petting zoo, pony rides, a rock wall, a mechanical bull, and plenty of food. One weekend midmonth.

Dig the Arts Festival (239-263-8242; Lowdermilk Park, Naples) Art meets the beach in true Naples style. United Arts Council hosts a day of free music, art, sand sculpture, and kids' games. One day late in the month.

Old Florida Festival (239-774-8476; www.colliermuseum.com; Collier County Museum, Naples) Living history from the Stone Age to World War II, with food, crafts, games, and demonstrations. Last weekend of the month.

Swamp Buggy Races (239-774-2701, 800-897-2701; www.swampbuggy.com; Florida Sports Park, Route 951, east Naples) See above, under January.

May

A Taste of Collier (239-272-1907; www.tasteofcollier.com; Fifth Ave. S., Naples) Naples's renowned restaurants serve samples of their culinary specialties. Live music. One weekend day early in the month.

Great Dock Canoe Race (239-261-4191; www.greatdockcanoerace.com; The Dock at Crayton Cove restaurant, 12th Ave. S., Naples) More than 200 teams, many in festive costumes, paddle across Naples Bay in good-spirited competition that kicks of with a parade. One Saturday.

SummerJazz (239-261-2222; Naples Beach Hotel & Golf Club, Naples) A series of sunset concerts under the stars on the third Saturday of every month, May through September.

June

South Florida PGA Open (239-261-2222; Naples Beach Hotel & Golf Club, 851 Gulf Shore Blvd. N., Naples) Golf enthusiasts can qualify to play side by side with PGA pros in the four-day competition.

October

Swamp Buggy Races See above, under January. The October races kick off the season with a parade.

December

Christmas Walk and Avenue of Lights (239-435-3742; Fifth Avenue South, Naples) Holiday street- and tree-lighting festivities, open houses at shops and other merchants. Early December. Mid-December brings "A Tuba Christmas" with Christmas songs and competition for a best-dressed tuba award.

New Year's Eve Art Festival (239-435-3742; Fifth Ave. S., Naples) Fine artisans fill the street the weekend after Christmas.

7

INFORMATION

Practical Matters

We hope that you never need a hospital or a police officer, but in case you should, we offer that information here, as well as information on other topics:

Heed this warning sign at Pine Island's "World's Fishingest Bridge."

AMBULANCE/FIRE/POLICE

All five southwest coast counties have adopted the 911 emergency phone number system. Dial it for ambulance, fire, sheriff, and police. Listed below are nonemergency numbers for individual communities.

TOWN	AMBULANCE	FIRE	POLICE/SHERIFF
FOR EMERGENCY	911	911	911
Anywhere in the region		Florida Highway Patrol	800-483-5912
CHARLOTTE COUNTY			
Boca Grande		941-964-2908	
Punta Gorda		941-575-5529	941-639-4111
Charlotte County	941-743-1367	941-639-2101	941-474-3233
Florida Highway Patrol (Venice)			941-483-5911
COLLIER COUNTY			
Everglades City		239-695-2902	239-695-2301
Isles of Capri		239-394-8770	
Naples			239-213-4844

Collier County Sheriff 239-793-9300
Florida Highway Patrol (Naples) 239-354-2377

TOWN	AMBULANCE	FIRE	POLICE/SHERIFF
LEE COUNTY			
Bonita Springs	239-992-3320		
Cape Coral	239-574-0501	239-574-3223	
Captiva	239-472-9494		
Fort Myers	239-338-2000	239-334-6222	239-338-2111
Fort Myers Beach	239-463-6163	239-765-2300	
Pine Island (Matlacha)	239-283-0030		
Sanibel	239-472-5525	239-472-3111	
Lee County Sheriff			239-477-1200
Florida Highway Patrol (Fort Myers)			239-278-7100
SARASOTA/BRADENTON COUNTIES			
Anna Maria	941-741-3900	941-778-4711	
Bradenton		941-747-1161	941-746-4111
Bradenton Beach	941-741-3900	941-778-6311	
Holmes Beach	941-741-3900	941-778-7875	
Longboat	941-316-1944	941-316-1977	
Sarasota	941-951-4211	941-316-1199	
Venice	941-488-6711		
Manatee County	941-747-3011		
Sarasota County	941-951-4211	941-951-5800	
Florida Highway Patrol (Bradenton)			941-751-7647

AREA CODES/TOWN GOVERNMENT

Area Codes
The area code for the Sarasota Bay area and the Charlotte Harbor Coast is 941. The 239 code covers the entire Island Coast and South Coast.

Town Government
All incorporated cities within the region are self-governing and have councilpersons, commissioners, mayors, and city managers in various roles. The unincorporated towns and communities are county ruled.

The incorporated cities of the Sarasota Bay coast include Bradenton, Anna Maria, Holmes Beach, Bradenton Beach, Sarasota, Longboat Key, North Port, and Venice. Bradenton is the county seat for Manatee County; Sarasota is county seat for Sarasota County. On the Charlotte Harbor coast, Punta Gorda (county seat) is incorporated. Bonita Springs, Cape Coral, Fort Myers (county seat), Fort Myers Beach, and Sanibel make up Lee County's incorporated cities. Naples is Collier County's seat; Naples, Marco Island, and Everglades City are incorporated.

Banks
Several old and established banks have branches located throughout Florida's Gulf Coast. Some are listed below with toll-free information numbers.

BANK	NUMBER
AmSouth	800-267-6884
Bank of America	800 299-2265
SunTrust	800-732-9487
Wachovia	800-922-4684

CLIMATE, SEASONS, AND WHAT TO WEAR

The tropics brush the Mangrove Coast but do not overwhelm it.

—*Karl Bickel,* The Mangrove Coast, *1942*

Florida's nickname, the Sunshine State, was once as fresh as it was apt. Although overuse has tended to cloud the once-perfect image, Florida still remains the ultimate state of sunshine through the sheer power of statistics. The sun beams down on the Gulf Coast for nearly 75 percent of all daylight hours and constitutes the one asset on which locals can bank.

To residents, the sun's smile can seem more like a sneer as they await fall's begrudging permission to turn off air conditioners and open windows. They suffer their own brand of cabin fever during the summer months, which often seem to linger as long as a Canadian winter. Although visitors revel in the warmth and sunlight, they often wonder how residents endure the monotony of seasonal sameness.

The seasons *do* change along the southern Gulf Coast, although more subtly than "up north." Weather patterns vary within the region. The Sarasota Bay and Charlotte Harbor areas often get more rain. However, weather can be very localized—it may rain on the southern end of 12-mile-long Sanibel Island while the north end remains dry. Islands

Punta Gorda's historic city hall

generally stay cooler than the mainland in summer and warmer in winter, thanks to their insulating jacket of gulf water. This is especially true where Charlotte Harbor runs wide and deep, creating a small pocket of tropical climate.

Winter is everyone's favorite time of year weatherwise. Temperatures along the coast reach generally into the 70s during the day and drop into the low 50s at night. Visitors find green, balmy relief from snow blindness and frostbite. Floridians enjoy the relative coolness that brings with it a reprieve from sweltering days, steamy nights, and bloodthirsty insects. The fragrance of oranges, grapefruits, and key limes fills the air. It's a time for activity; one can safely schedule a tee time past noon. Resort areas fill up, and migratory houseguests from the north arrive.

Spring comes on tiptoe to the coast. No thaw-and-puddle barometer alerts us; the sense of spring giddiness affects only longtime residents. Floridians emerge from hibernation raring to leap and frolic—and perhaps do a little mischief. Gardenias, Hong Kong orchids, and jasmine bloom, and everything that already looks green and alive bursts forth with an extra reserve of color. It's a time to celebrate the end of another season and to greedily enjoy the domain that's been shared with visitors during the winter months.

Summers used to be reserved for die-hard Floridians. All but the most devoted residents boarded up their homes and businesses and headed somewhere—*anywhere*—cooler. Now there's a summer trade, composed of Floridians, Europeans, and northern families— enough to keep the resort communities alive through temperatures that inch up to 100 degrees. Although technically classified as subtropical, the region, starting in June, feels the bristles of a tropical brush. The pace of life slows, and late-afternoon rains suddenly and unpredictably revolt against the sun's constancy. Mangoes and guavas blush sweet temptation. Moonlit nights bring magic to the cereus vine and its white starburst blooms the size of Frisbees.

Fall appears in October as a sharpening of vision after a blur of humidity. Residents don't exactly go out and buy wool plaids, but they do break out sweatshirts. Many build fires in hearths that have held dried floral arrangements for eight months. The leathery leaves of the sea grape tree turn as red as the northern oak, and the gumbo-limbo coaxes out rakes. The best part about a Gulf Coast fall, for those residents who once endured northern winters, is that it doesn't foretell snow-proof boots and long underwear.

Winter temperatures dip, albeit rarely, into the freezing range, so be prepared for just about any weather between December and February. Fortunately swimsuits take up little room, so pack more than one. (Florida's high humidity often prevents anything from ever really drying out.) Loose-fitting togs and cotton work best in any season. Long sleeves are welcome in the evenings during winter. Summer showers require rain gear, especially if you plan on boating or playing outdoors.

Don't worry about dress codes in most restaurants. Ties and pantyhose are strictly for the office and (possibly) the theater. Worry more about comfort, particularly if your skin burns easily. Pack hats and lots of sunscreen. Bring insect repellent, too, especially if you plan on venturing into the jungle—or simply watching an island sunset, for that matter. Counties do spray for mosquitoes, but spraying has little effect on the tiny but prolific no-see-um (sand flea). The best protection against both pests is sitting under a ceiling fan— practically standard equipment in homes and hotels.

On the cloudier side, Florida weather includes a high incidence of lightning, summer squalls, tornadoes, waterspouts, and the dreaded H-word. Hurricane season begins in June, but activity concentrates toward season's end in November. Watches and warnings alert you in plenty of time to head inland or north; to be safest, do so at first mention, especially if you are staying on an island.

Florida's celebrated sunshine is at its best on the Gulf Coast. Ol' Sol visits practically every day, and it's also where he slips into bed. Gulf Coast Florida boasts the most spectacular sunsets in the continental United States. (OK, so I'm a little biased.)

Average Gulf Coast Air Temperatures

MONTH	AVG. MAX.	AVG. MIN.
Jan.	72.8°	52.8°
Feb.	73.8°	53.8°
Mar.	78.3°	57.8°
Apr.	82.5°	61.6°
May	87.7°	67.1°
June	89.7°	72.1°
July	90.5°	73.7°
Aug.	90.9°	73.8°
Sept.	89.1°	72.7°
Oct.	84.9°	66.8°
Nov.	77.9°	59.4°
Dec.	74.1°	53.8°

Gulf Coast Water Temperatures

Annual average	77.5°
Fall/winter average	70.8°
Spring/summer average	84.1°
Winter low	66.0°
Summer high	87.0°

HOSPITALS & CLINICS

Charlotte Harbor Coast

ENGLEWOOD
Columbia Fawcett Memorial Hospital (941-629-1181; www.fawcetthospital.com; 21298 Olean Blvd., Port Charlotte 33952) Emergency room open 24 hours.

Englewood Community Hospital (941-475-6571; www.englewoodcommhospital.com; 700 Medical Blvd., Englewood 34223) Emergency room open 24 hours. For 24-hour Consult-a-Nurse line, call 473-3919 or toll free 888-685-1598.

Peace River Regional Medical Center (941-766-4122; www.peaceriverregional.com; 2500 Harbor Blvd., Port Charlotte 33952) Emergency room open 24 hours.

PUNTA GORDA
Charlotte Regional Medical Center (941-639-3131; www.charlotteregional.com; 809 E. Marion Ave., Punta Gorda 33950) Emergency room open 24 hours.

Island Coast

CAPE CORAL

Cape Coral Hospital (239-574-2323; www.leememorial.org; 636 Del Prado Blvd, Cape Coral 33990) Emergency room open 24 hours.

FORT MYERS

Gulf Coast Hospital (239-768-5000; www.gulfcoasthospital.com; 13681 Doctor's Way, Fort Myers 33912)

HealthPark Medical Center (239-433-7799; www.leememorial.org; 9981 HealthPark Circle, Fort Myers 33908) Home of Children's Hospital of Southwest Florida. Emergency room open 24 hours. Twenty-four-hour medical information via HealthLine, 800-936-5321.

Lee Memorial Hospital (239-332-1111; www.leememorial.org; 2776 Cleveland Ave., Fort Myers 33901) Emergency room open 24 hours.

Southwest Florida Regional Medical Center (239-939-1147; www.leememorial.org; 2727 Winkler Ave., Fort Myers 33901) Acute care and outpatient surgery. Emergency room open 24 hours. For 24-hour Consult-a-Nurse Healthcare Referral, call 800-257-0944.

Sarasota Bay Coast

BRADENTON

HCA L.W. Blake Medical Center (941-792-6611; www.blakemedicalcenter.com; 2020 59th St. W., Bradenton 34209) Emergency room open 24 hours.

Lakewood Ranch Medical Center (941-782-2100; www.lakewoodranchmedicalcenter .com; 8330 Lakewood Ranch Blvd., Bradenton 34202) Emergency room open 24 hours.

Manatee Memorial Hospital (941-746-5111 or 941-745-7466 for emergencies; www .manateememorial.com; 206 Second St. E., Bradenton 34208) Emergency room open 24 hours.

SARASOTA

Doctors Hospital of Sarasota (941-342-1100; www.doctorsofsarasota.com; 5731 Bee Ridge Rd., Sarasota 34233) Emergency room open 24 hours.

Sarasota Memorial Hospital (941-917-9000 or 800-864-8255; www.smh.com; 1700 S. Tamiami Trail, Sarasota 34239) Emergency room open 24 hours.

VENICE

Venice Regional Hospital (941-485-7711; www.veniceregional.com; 540 The Rialto, Venice 34292) Emergency room open 24 hours.

South Coast

MARCO ISLAND

Marco Healthcare Center (239-394-8234; www.nchhcs.org; 40 Heathwood Dr., Marco Island 34145) Medical care and rehab on an outpatient basis.

NAPLES

Naples Downtown Hospital (239-436-5000; www.nchhcs.org; 350 Seventh St. N., Naples 34102) Heart and cancer institutes; emergency room open 24 hours.

North Naples Hospital (239-552-7000; www.nchhcs.org; 11190 Healthpark Blvd., Naples 34110, off Immokalee Rd.) Emergency room open 24 hours.

LATE-NIGHT FOOD AND FUEL

Certain categories of Florida liquor licensing require bars to serve food, which provides a good source for late-night eating. Many chain restaurants located along major thoroughfares—such as Grandma's Kitchen, Denny's, and Perkins—stay open late or all night.

Chain convenience stores, gas stations, and fuel/food marts also are open around the clock. These include 7-Eleven, Starvin' Marvin, Mobil Mart, and Circle K.

MEDIA

Media flood the Gulf Coast like high tide. Many publications are directed toward tourists, and some are only as permanent as the shoreline during a tidal surge. Magazines come and go, and radio stations often shift formats.

Four daily newspapers stand out for their endurance and dependability: the *Bradenton Herald,* the *Sarasota Herald-Tribune,* the *Fort Myers News-Press,* and the *Naples Daily News.* Weeklies are also firmly established in their respective communities, primarily because many are owned collectively by one corporation. Specialty tabloids address seniors, shoppers, fishermen, women, and other groups.

Magazines show the most fluctuation. Traditionally they were created to appeal to the region's upscale, mature population, which is concentrated in Sarasota and Naples. *Sarasota Magazine, Times of the Islands, Naples Illustrated,* and *Gulfshore Life* have been the stalwarts of regional lifestyle glossies, but even they shift focus to address changing populations and economic trends.

Fort Myers carries the majority of the region's broadcast media, which reach to the Charlotte Harbor and the South Coast. Much of the Sarasota Bay coast's TV comes from Tampa.

Charlotte Harbor Coast
NEWSPAPERS

Boca Beacon (941-964-2995, 800-749-2995; www.bocabeacon.com; P.O. Box 313, Boca Grande 33921) Weekly.

Charlotte Sun-Herald (941-206-1000; 877-818-6204; www.sun-herald.com; 23170 Harborview Rd., Charlotte Harbor 33980) Daily.

Englewood Sun-Herald (941-681-3000; www.sun-herald.com; 167 W. Dearborn St., Englewood 34223) Daily.

Gasparilla Gazette (941-964-2728; www.gasparillagazette.com; P.O. Box 929, Boca Grande 33921) Weekly.

Island Coast
NEWSPAPERS

Cape Coral Breeze (239-574-1110; www.breezenewspapers.com; 2510 Del Prado Blvd., Cape Coral 33904) Daily.

Fort Myers Beach Bulletin (239-463-4421; www.breezenewspapers.com; 19260 San Carlos Blvd., Fort Myers Beach 33931) Weekly.

Island Reporter (239-472-1587; www.breezenewspapers.com; P.O. Box 809, 2340 Periwinkle Way, Sanibel Island 33957) Weekly.

News-Press (239-335-0200; www.news-press.com; P.O. Box 10, 2442 Dr. Martin Luther King Jr. Blvd., Fort Myers 33901) The 10th-largest newspaper in the state in terms of circulation, it publishes editions for Charlotte County and Bonita Springs.

Observer Papers (239-765-0400; www.flguide.com; 17274 San Carlos Blvd., Fort Myers Beach 33931) Publishes weekly editions for Fort Myers Beach and other neighborhoods.

Pine Island Eagle (239-283-2022; www.breezenewspapers.com; 10700 Stringfellow Rd., Ste. 60, Bokeelia 33922) Weekly.

Sanibel-Captiva Islander (239-472-5185; www.breezenewspapers.com; P.O. Box 56, 395 Tarpon Bay Rd. #13, Sanibel Island 33957) Weekly; free subscription.

MAGAZINES

Times of the Islands (239-472-0205; www.toti.com; P.O. Box 1227, Sanibel Island 33957) Covers the local arts, business, cuisine, nature, and travel scenes.

TELEVISION

WBBH-TV	Fort Myers	NBC
WFTX-TV	Cape Coral	Fox
WINK-TV	Fort Myers	CBS
WZVN-TV	Fort Myers	ABC

Sarasota Bay Coast
NEWSPAPERS

Bradenton Herald (941-748-0411; www.bradenton.com; 102 Manatee Ave. W., Bradenton 34205) Daily.

Creative Loafing (941-365-6776; www.sarasota.creativeloafing.com; 1383 Fifth St., Sarasota 34236) Giveaway entertainment weekly with a youthful, irreverent voice.

Longboat Observer (941-383-5509; www.yourobserver.com; 5570 Gulf of Mexico Dr., Longboat Key 34228) Weekly.

Pelican Press (941-349-4949; www.pelicanpress.org; 5011 Ocean Blvd., Sarasota 34242) Weekly covering Siesta Key and Sarasota.

Sarasota Herald-Tribune (941-361-4880; www.newscoast.com; 1741 Main St., Sarasota 34236) Florida's eighth largest daily in terms of circulation.

Venice Gondolier (941-207-1000; www.venicegondolier.com; 200 E. Venice Ave., Venice 34285) Published three times weekly.

MAGAZINES

Sarasota Magazine (941-366-8225, 800-881-2394; www.sarasotamagazine.com; 330 S. Pineapple Ave., Ste. 205, Sarasota 34236) Lifestyle for upscale Sarasotans.

Sarasota Scene (941-487-1100; www.scenesarasota.com; 2015 S. Tuttle Ave., P.O. Box 1418, Sarasota 34230) Weekly covering the Sarasota-Bradenton area.

SRQ (941-365-7702; 337 S. Pineapple Ave., Sarasota 34236) SRQ is Sarasota-Bradenton International Airport's code; this slick magazine covers the dining, political, and shopping scene.

West Coast Woman (941-954-3300; www.westcoastwoman.com; P.O. Box 819, Sarasota 34230) Monthly free publication.

TELEVISION

BLAB-TV	Sarasota	
SNN-TV	Sarasota News Now	
WWSB-TV	Sarasota	ABC

South Coast

NEWSPAPERS

Bonita Daily News (239-213-6060; www.bonitanews.com; 9102 Bonita Beach Rd., Bonita Springs 34135)

Marco Island Sun Times (239-394-3050; www.marcoislandflorida.com; 317 N. Collier Blvd. Ste. 202, Marco Island 34145) Free distribution paper. Weekly

Naples Daily News (239-262-3161; www.naplesnews.com; 1075 Central Ave., Naples 34102) Daily; publisher of the two newspapers listed above.

MAGAZINES

Gulfshore Business (239-594-9980, 800-220-4853; www.gulfshorebusiness.com; 9051 N. Tamiami Trail, Ste. 202, Naples 34108)

Gulfshore Life (239-449-4111, 800-220-4853; www.gulfshorelife.com; 9051 N. Tamiami Trail, Ste. 202, Naples 34108) Longtime slick lifestyle and news guide to the southwest coast.

N, The Magazine of Naples (239-594-9404; www.nmagazine.com; 4500 Executive Dr., Ste. 320, Naples 34119) Fashion and society oriented.

Naples Illustrated (239-434-6966; www.naplesillustrated.com; 3066 Tamiami Trail N., Ste. 102, Naples 34103) Haute lifestyles glossy.

TELEVISION

WTVK-TV	Bonita Springs	CW

REAL ESTATE

Real estate prices run the gamut from reasonable to ultraexpensive. In parts of Bradenton, Sarasota, and Fort Myers, planned communities cater to young families. Exclusive areas such as Longboat Key, Casey Key, Manasota Key, Sanibel Island, Captiva Island, and Naples are known for their pricey waterfront homes and golfing developments. The most reasonable real estate, naturally, lies inland, away from the water, but prices escalate even in those areas these days. Florida's $25,000 homestead exemption gives residents a tax break on primary home purchases.

Real estate publications can be found on the newsstands, or check local newspapers. Otherwise, contact the agencies listed below.

Florida Association of Realtors (407-438-1400; www.floridarealtors.org; 7025 Augusta National Dr., Orlando 32822)

Naples Area Board of Realtors (239-597-1666; www.naplesarea.com; 1455 Pine Ridge Rd., Naples 34109)

Realtors Association of Greater Fort Myers and Fort Myers Beach (239-936-3537; www.swflrealtors.com; 2840 Winkler Ave., Fort Myers 33916)

Sanibel & Captiva Islands Association of Realtors (239-472-9353; www.sanibelrealtors .com; 1648 Periwinkle Way, Ste. F, Sanibel Island 33957)

Sarasota Association of Realtors (941-923-2315; www.sarasotarealtors.com; 3590 Tuttle Ave. S., Sarasota 34239)

REGIONAL READING

Books about the region are available in bookstores and online outlets.

Biography & Reminiscence

Brown, Loren G. *Totch: A Life in the Everglades*. Gainesville: University Press of Florida, 1993. A folksy, firsthand adventure tour of Ten Thousand Islands through the words of a former native.

Lindbergh, Anne Morrow. *Gift from the Sea*. New York: Pantheon/Village Books, 1955. A small book packed with sea-inspired wisdom from Charles Lindbergh's wife, who died in 2001. Strong evidence points to Captiva as the book's inspiration.

Newton, James. *Uncommon Friends*. New York: Harcourt, Brace, Jovanovich, 1987. Local man's memories of his friendships with Fort Myers' illustrious winterers: Thomas Edison, Henry Ford, Harvey Firestone, and Charles Lindbergh.

Orlean, Susan. *The Orchid Thief: A True Story of Beauty and Obsession*. New York: Random House, 1998. Set in Fakahatchee Strand Preserve State Park, Naples, and other local venues, Orlean tells a bizarre nonfiction tale about the elusive ghost orchid and the people who sought it.

St. Claire, Dana. *Cracker: The Cracker Culture in Florida History*. Daytona Beach: The Museum of Arts and Sciences, 1998.

Weeks, David C. *Ringling: The Florida Years, 1911–1936*. Gainesville: University Press of Florida, 1993.

James Newton's autobiography Uncommon Friends *inspired this downtown Fort Myers sculpture, which portrays camping trips that Henry Ford, Harvey Firestone, and Thomas Edison shared during their visits to the area.*

Cookbooks

Junior League of Fort Myers. *Gulfshore Delights*. Fort Myers: n.p., 1984.

——. *Tropical Settings*. Fort Myers, Fla.: n.p., 1995.

Reynolds, Doris. *When Peacocks Were Roasted and Mullet Was Fried*. Naples: Enterprise Publishing, 1993. Naples history flavored with recipes.

Fiction

Dever, Sean Michael. *Blind Pass*. Kearney, Neb.: Morris Publishing, 1996. Mystery set in Sanibel and Captiva.

Hiaasen, Carl. *Nature Girl*. New York: Alfred A. Knopf, 2006. Florida's favorite mystery man sets his 13th novel in Everglades City.

Hudler, Ad. *All This Belongs To Me*. New York: Ballantine Publishing, 2006. Set in Fort Myers, its plot revolves around the Edison Estates.

MacDonald, John D. Many of his Travis McGee and other mysteries take place in a Sarasota Bay coast setting, where he had a home.

Matthiessen, Peter. *Bone by Bone*. New York: Random House: 1999. The parents of this award-winning author live on Sanibel Island. This is the final book in a historical trilogy about the posse killing of a murderer who hid out in the frontier of Ten Thousand Islands.

——. *Killing Mr. Watson*. New York: Random House, 1990. First book in the trilogy.

——. *Lost Man's River*. New York: Random House, 1997. Second book in the trilogy.

Smith, Patrick D. *A Land Remembered*. Sarasota: Pineapple Press, 1984. This definitive historical novel about Florida's Cracker and cow-hunting eras features many scenes set in the Fort Myers and Everglades areas.

White, Randy Wayne. *Sanibel Flats*. New York: St. Martin's Press, 1990. Mystery by a local fishing guide/journalist in local setting. Several books in his Doc Ford series take place mostly along the Gulf Coast.

History

Anholt, Betty. *Sanibel's Story: Voices & Images from Calusa to Incorporation*. Virginia Beach, Va.: Donning, 1998. Written by a longtime island resident and historian.

Beater, Jack. *Pirates & Buried Treasure*. St. Petersburg: Great Outdoors Publishing, 1959. Somewhat factual, ever-colorful account of José Gaspar and his cohorts, by the area's foremost legendaire.

Board, Prudy Taylor, and Esther B. Colcord. *Historic Fort Myers*. Virginia Beach, Va.: Donning, 1992. Largely photographic treatment, written by two of the area's leading historians today.

——. *Pages from the Past*. Virginia Beach, Va.: Donning, 1990. Largely photographic treatment of Fort Myers' history.

Dormer, Elinore M. *The Sea Shell Islands: A History of Sanibel and Captiva*. Tallahassee: Rose Printing, 1987. The definitive work on island and regional history.

Jordan, Elaine Blohm. *Pine Island, the Forgotten Island*. Pine Island: n.p., 1982.

——. *Tales of Pine Island*. Ellijay, Ga.: Jordan Ink Publishing, 1985.

Matthews, Janet Snyder. *Edge of Wilderness: A Settlement History of Manatee River and Sarasota Bay*. Sarasota: Coastal Press, 1983.

——. *Journey to Centennial Sarasota*. Sarasota: Pine Level Press, 1989.

——. *Venice: Journey to Horse and Chaise*. Sarasota: Pine Level Press, 1989.

Zeiss, Betsy. *The Other Side of the River: Historical Cape Coral*. Cape Coral: n.p., 1986.

Natural History

Douglas, Marjory Stoneman. *The Everglades: River of Grass*. St. Simons, Ga.: Mockingbird Books, 1947. The book that focused the nation's attention on the developing plight of the pristine Everglades.

Ripple, Jeff. *Southwest Florida's Wetland Wilderness: Big Cypress Swamp and the Ten Thousand Islands*. Gainesville: University Press of Florida, 1992. This book celebrates the natural history of one of the most diverse, endangered, and beautiful ecosystems in the world. Stunning black-and-white photography by Clyde Butcher.

Toops, Connie. *The Florida Everglades*. Stillwater, Minn.: Voyageur Press, 1998. Written by a former national park ranger.

Pictorial

Butcher, Clyde. *Clyde Butcher: Portfolio I*. Fort Myers: Shade Tree Press, 1994. The master of natural landscape photography collects his haunting black-and-white large-format images in a coffee-table edition.

Capes, Richard. *Richard Capes' Drawings Capture Siesta Key*. Sarasota: Capes Studio of Florida, 1992. An artistic tour of the island in pen and ink, with handwritten descriptions.

Stone, Lynn. *Sanibel Island*. Stillwater, Minn.: Voyageur Press, 1991. Sanibel's natural treasures in words and striking pictures.

Travel

MacPerry, I. *Indian Mounds You Can Visit*. St. Petersburg: Great Outdoors Publishing, 1993. Covers the entire west coast of Florida, arranged by county.

Walton, Chelle Koster. *Adventure Guide to Tampa Bay and Florida's West Coast*. 3rd ed. Edison, N.J.: Hunter Publishing, 2004. Covers Tampa to the western Everglades.

Check It Out

Out-of-print books you can find in local libraries when you're visiting.

Bickel, Karl A. *The Mangrove Coast: The Story of the West Coast of Florida*. 4th ed. New York: Coward-McCann, 1989. Vintage regional history of the area from Tampa Bay to Ten Thousand Islands, from the time of Ponce de León to 1885, spiced with romantic embellishments.

Briggs, Mildred. *Pioneers of Bonita Springs (Facts and Folklore)*. Bonita Springs, 1976. Pirates, Indian healers, outlaws, and more.

Campbell, George R. *The Nature of Things on Sanibel*. Fort Myers: Press Printing, 1978. Factual yet entertaining background on native fauna and flora.

Fritz, Florence. *Unknown Florida*. Coral Gables: University of Miami Press, 1963. 213 pp., photos, index. Focuses on the southernmost Gulf Coast.

Gonzales, Thomas A. *The Caloosahatchee: History of the Caloosahatchee River and the City of Fort Myers, Florida*. Fort Myers Beach: Island Press, 1982. Memories of a native son, descendant of city's first settler.

Grismer, Karl H. *The Story of Fort Myers*. Fort Myers Beach: Island Press, 1982.

———. *The Story of Sarasota*. Tampa: The Florida G Press, 1946.

Hann, John H., ed. *Missions to the Calusa*. Gainesville: University of Florida Press, 1991.

Marth, Del. *Yesterday's Sarasota*. Miami: E. A. Seemann Publishing, 1977. Primarily pictorial history.

Matthews, Kenneth, and Robert McDevitt. *The Unlikely Legacy*. Sarasota: Aaron Publishers, 1980. The story of John Ringling, the circus, and Sarasota.

Peeples, Vernon. *Punta Gorda and the Charlotte Harbor Area*. Virginia Beach, Va.: Donning, 1986. Pictorial history authored by a local politician.

Romans, Bernard. *A Concise Natural History of East and West Florida*. Gainesville: University of Florida Press, 1962. A facsimile reproduction of the 1775 edition.

Schell, Rolfe F. *De Soto Didn't Land at Tampa*. Fort Myers Beach: Island Press, 1966.

———. *History of Fort Myers Beach*. Fort Myers Beach: Island Press, 1980.

Tebeau, Charlton W. *Florida's Last Frontier: The History of Collier County*. Coral Gables: University of Miami Press, 1966.

Widmer, Randolph J. *The Evolution of the Calusa*. Tuscaloosa: University of Alabama Press, 1988. Very technical discussion of the "nonagricultural chiefdom on the Southwest Florida Coast."

ROAD SERVICE

AAA Auto Club

Information on AAA can be found at www.aaa.com. Each of the following offices provides 24-hour emergency road service.

941-798-2211; 6210 Manatee Ave. W., Bradenton

941-929-2299; 3844 Bee Ridge Rd., Sarasota

941-362-2500; 258 Ringling Shopping Center, Sarasota
239-939-6500; 2516 Colonial Blvd., Fort Myers
239-594-5006; 5410 Airport Pulling Rd. N., Naples

Services for the Physically Impaired

Regulations concerning disabled access vary, depending on locale. In general, most restaurants, parks, attractions, and resorts provide physically impaired visitors with special ramps, bathroom stalls, and hotel rooms. Some beaches, particularly in the Naples area, provide fat-wheeled beach chairs for the physically challenged.

Tourist Information

Visit Florida (888-7FLA-USA; www.visitflorida.com; 661 E. Jefferson St., Ste. 300, Tallahassee 32301)

Charlotte Harbor Coast

Boca Grande Area Chamber of Commerce (941-964-0568; www.bocagrandechamber .com; 5800 Gasparilla Rd., Ste. A1; P.O. Box 704, Boca Grande 33921) Information center located in Courtyard Plaza at the island's north end.

Charlotte County Chamber of Commerce (941-627-2222; www.charlottecountychamber .org; 2702 Tamiami Trail, Port Charlotte 33952; and 941-639-2222; 311 W. Retta Esplanade, Punta Gorda 33950)

Charlotte County Visitor's Bureau (941-743-1900; www.charlotteharbortravel.com; 18501 Murdock Circle, Ste. 502, Port Charlotte 33948)

Englewood–Cape Haze Area Chamber of Commerce (941-474-5511, 800-603-7198; www.englewoodchamber.com; 601 S. Indiana Ave., Englewood 34223)

Island Coast

Cape Coral Chamber of Commerce (239-549-6900, 800-226-9609; www.capecoral chamber .com; P.O. Box 100747, Cape Coral 33910) Information center at 2051 Cape Coral Pkwy. E.

Estero Chamber of Commerce (239-948-7990; www.esterochamber.org; P.O. Box 588; Estero 33928)

Greater Fort Myers Beach Chamber of Commerce (239-454-7500, 800-782-9283; www.fmbchamber.com; 17200 San Carlos Blvd., Fort Myers Beach 33931)

Greater Fort Myers Chamber of Commerce (239-332-3624, 800-366-3622; www.fort myers.org; 2310 Edwards Dr., Fort Myers 33902) Welcome center located downtown.

Greater Pine Island Chamber of Commerce (239-283-0888; www.pineislandchamber .org; P.O. Box 525, Matlacha 33993) Information center located before the bridge to Matlacha at 3640 Pine Island Rd.

Lee County Visitor & Convention Bureau (239-338-3500, 800-237-6444; www.fort myers-sanibel.com; 2180 W. First St., Ste. 100, Fort Myers 33901)

North Fort Myers Chamber of Commerce (239-997-9111; www.northfortmyerschamber
.org; 3323 N. Key Dr., Ste. 1, North Fort Myers 33903)

Sanibel-Captiva Islands Chamber of Commerce (239-472-1080; www.sanibel-captiva
.org; 1159 Causeway Rd., Sanibel Island 33957) Information center located shortly after the
causeway approach to Sanibel.

Southwest Florida Hispanic Chamber of Commerce (239-418-1441; 10051 McGregor
Blvd., Ste. 204, Fort Myers 33919)

Sarasota Bay Coast

Anna Maria Island Chamber of Commerce (941-778-1541; www.amichamber.org; 5313
Gulf Dr., Holmes Beach 34217)

Bradenton Area Convention & Visitors Bureau (941-729-9177, 800-4-MANATEE; www
.flagulfislands.com; P.O. Box 1000, Bradenton 34206)

Downtown Partnership of Sarasota (941-951-2656; www.downtownsarasota.com; 1365
Fruitville Rd., Sarasota 34236)

Longboat Key Chamber of Commerce (941-387-9519; www.longboatkeychamber.com;
Whitney Beach Plaza, 6854 Gulf of Mexico Dr., Longboat Key 34228)

Manatee Chamber of Commerce (941-748-4842; www.manateechamber.com; P.O. Box
321, Bradenton 34206 or 222 Tenth St. W., Bradenton 34205)

Sarasota Convention & Visitors Bureau (941-957-1877, 800-522-9799; www.sarasotafl
.org; 70 N. Tamiami Trail, Sarasota 34236)

Siesta Key Chamber of Commerce (941-349-3800, 866-831-7778; www.siestakey
chamber.com; 5118 Ocean Blvd., Siesta Key 34242)

Venice Area Chamber of Commerce (941-488-2236; www.venicechamber.com; 597 S.
Tamiami Trail, Venice 34285)

South Coast

Bonita Springs Area Chamber of Commerce (239-992-2943, 800-226-2943; www
.bonitaspringschamber.com; 25071 Chamber of Commerce Dr., Bonita Springs 34135)

Everglades Area Chamber of Commerce (239-695-3172, 800-914-6355; www.florida
-everglades.com/chamber; 32016 E. Tamiami Trail, P.O. Box 130, Everglades City 34139)
Welcome center corner of U.S. 41 and Rte. 29.

Greater Naples Marco Everglades Convention & Visitors Bureau (239-403-2379, 800-
688-3600; www.paradisecoast.com; 3050 N. Horseshoe Blvd. #218, Naples 34104)

Marco Island Area Chamber of Commerce (239-394-7549, 800-788-MARCO; www
.marcoislandchamber.org; 1102 North Collier Blvd., P.O. Box 913, Marco Island 34145)

Naples Chamber of Commerce (239-262-6141; www.napleschamber.org; 2390 Tamiami
Trail N., Naples 34103)

If Time Is Short

Not enough time to do it all on this trip to southwest Florida? Here are some highlights that I suggest to weekenders and short-term vacationers who wonder how they can best spend their precious time. Beach time, of course, is a high priority for those with only a few days to spend in the sun. I list must-see beaches as well as other attractions, adventures, restaurants, and lodgings you should not miss.

Sarasota Bay Coast

✪ **Siesta Key County Beach** (941-861-2150; Midnight Pass Rd. at Beach Way Dr., Siesta Key), despite its weekend and high-season crowds, is the area's ultimate beach. Its sands are whiter and fluffier than a down quilt. Have dinner at **The Lobster Pot** (941-349-2323; 5157 Ocean Blvd., Siesta Key 34242), a seafoody marriage of Maine and Florida.

✪ **Downtown Sarasota** is a happening place. Take in a play and circle the galleries of the Theatre and Arts District. Don't miss the shops of **Palm Avenue** and the galleries of ✪ **Towles Court Artist Colony** (www.towlescourt.com; 1943 Morrill St., Sarasota 34239).

✪ **The John and Mable Ringling Museum of Art**, the **Ringling Estate**, and its various circus and Gilded Age attractions (941-355-5101; www.ringling.org; 5401 Bay Shore Rd., Sarasota 34243) crown in glory Sarasota's famed cultural scene. ✪ **Longboat Key** provides a drive on the coast's wealthy side. Depending on your budget, dine in high style at **Euphemia Haye** (941-383-3633; www.euphemiahaye.com; 5540 Gulf of Mexico Dr., Longboat Key 34228) or in the spirit of maritime fun at ✪ **Mar-Vista Dockside Restaurant & Pub** (941-383-2391; 760 Broadway St., Longboat Key 34228).

Stop at ✪ **Mote Marine Aquarium** (941-388-2451, 800-691-MOTE; www.mote.org; 1600 Ken Thompson Pkwy., Sarasota 34236) to check out the new interactive immersion theater and other fishy stuff.

Charlotte Harbor Coast

The best of Charlotte Harbor lies in its hidden-from-the-spotlight barrier islands. **Manasota Key** and **Englewood Beach** boast sunny beaches flecked with sharks' teeth. For a unique and nature-intensive lodging experience, book at ✪ **Manasota Beach Club** (941-474-2614; www.manasotabeachclub.com; 7660 Manasota Key Rd., Englewood 34223), a longstanding beach resort with accommodations from rustic to lavish.

On Gasparilla Island, **Boca Grande** supplies a full day of beaching, shopping, and dining. Have lunch or dinner at ✪ **PJ's Seagrille** (239-964-0806; 312 Park Ave., Boca Grande 33921) and savor something from the sea, inventive and well crafted. For a different flavor of island life, take a room at the old, gracious **Gasparilla Inn** (239-964-2201; 5th St. and Palm St., P.O. Box 1088, Boca Grande 33921), as the Vanderbilts and Du Ponts have since 1912.

Explore the extensive aquatic preserves of Charlotte Harbor aboard a catamaran or kayak with ✪ **Grande Tours** (239-697-8825; www.grandetours.com; 12575 Placida Rd., P.O. Box 281, Placida 33946). For an island wilderness adventure that returns you to the days of Florida cow-hunting, ride the bouncy swamp buggy through a modern-day cattle and alligator ranch at ✪ **Babcock Wilderness Adventures** (941-637-0551, 800-500-5583; www.babcockwilderness.com; 800 Rte. 31, Punta Gorda 33950).

Island Coast

Fort Myers's finest attraction, the ✪ **Edison & Ford Winter Estates** (239-334-7419; www.efwefla.org; 2350–2400 McGregor Blvd., Fort Myers 33902), peeks into the times and genius of America's greatest inventors, who lived side by side in winter months. Dine Victorian in the two historic homes that make up ✪ **The Veranda** (239-332-2065; 2122 Second St., Fort Myers 33902), which specializes in Southern charm and fine cuisine.

Much of what's special about the Island Coast has to do with what's wild. Half of Sanibel Island is devoted to the ✪ **J. N. "Ding" Darling National Wildlife Refuge** (239-472-1100; www.fws.gov/dingdarling; 1 Wildlife Dr., Sanibel Island 33957, off Sanibel-Captiva Rd.), home to alligators, roseate spoonbills, manatees, river otters, and bobcats. The best way to see it is by tram or kayak tour from **Tarpon Bay Explorers** (239-472-8900; www.tarpon bayexplorers.com; 900 Tarpon Bay Rd., Sanibel Island 33957).

Sanibel's beaches are renowned for their bountiful shells and minimal impact on nature's birthright beauty. Most natural and secluded is ✪ **Bowman's Beach** (Bowman's Beach Rd., off Sanibel-Captiva Rd.). To find the utmost in remote beaches, rent a boat or hop a charter to unbridged **Cayo Costa Island** and **Upper Captiva Island**, where state parks preserve slices of Old Florida.

For lively beaching, follow Route 865 through Estero Island's **Fort Myers Beach** and down along lovely, undeveloped Lovers Key en route to ✪ **Bonita Beach**. On the way you'll pass bustling resort scenes and quiet island vistas.

South Coast

To explore the highbrow face of Naples and its environs, stop for afternoon tea at the ✪ **Ritz-Carlton Naples** (239-598-3300; 800-241-3333; www.ritzcarlton.com/resorts/ naples; 280 Vanderbilt Beach Rd., Naples 34108) and take in a concert and art stroll at the **Naples Philharmonic** (239-597-1900, 800-597-1900; www.thephil.org; 5833 Pelican Bay Blvd., Naples 34104) and the new ✪ **Naples Museum of Art** next door (239-597-1900; www.thephil.org; 5833 Pelican Bay Blvd., Naples 34104). Downtown's ✪ **Fifth Avenue South** has evolved into a fashionable shopping and sidewalk-dining district. Try **Bistro 821** (239-261-5821; www.bistro821.com; 821 Fifth Ave. S, Naples 34102) for an example of the latest in Naples's cutting-edge chic.

To really have experienced Naples, you must do sunset at the ✪ **Naples Fishing Pier** (12th Ave. S.). It's a nightly ritual for fishermen, strollers, lovers, and pelicans. By day the pier is the center of activity along a beach that stretches for miles.

My favorite part of Marco Island is ✪ **Goodland**. A little fishing village "on pause," it serves fresh seafood and country fun in its restaurants and introduces the unruly flavor of Ten Thousand Islands and the Florida Everglades.

✪ **Everglades City** is headquarters for tours that explore this labyrinthine land down under. ✪ **Everglades National Park** (239-695-2591, 800-445-7724 (in Florida); www .nps.gov/ever; Everglades Ranger Station, Everglades City) has a base here, conducts boat tours, and rents canoes for launching into the 98-mile **Wilderness Trail**.

CHELLE'S HIGH FIVES

Here, I give a "high five" to my top picks in a number of offbeat categories. These are the crème de la crème of Southwest Florida, whether you're looking for the best martini or the swankiest jewelry store. Within the chapters, look for starred entries to indicate the High Fivers.

BEACHY KEEN RESORTS

1. Palm Island Resort, Cape Haze
2. Manasota Beach Club, Manasota Key
3. Colony Beach and Tennis Resort, Longboat Key
4. Marco Island Marriott Beach Resort, Golf Club & Spa, Marco Island
5. LaPlaya Beach & Golf Resort, Vanderbilt Beach

FAMILY-LOVING RESORTS

1. Sundial Beach Resort, Sanibel Island
2. Colony Beach and Tennis Resort, Longboat Key
3. Sanibel Harbour Resort & Spa, Fort Myers
4. Palm Island Resort, Cape Haze
5. Marco Island Marriott Beach Resort, Golf Club & Spa, Marco Island

CITY-SMART HOTELS

1. The Ritz-Carlton Sarasota
2. Bellasera Hotel, Naples

Kids love the shell-shaped slide at Sundial Beach Resort's pool.

3. Trianon Bonita Bay, Bonita Springs
4. Hotel Indigo, Sarasota
5. Holiday Inn Riverfront, Bradenton

INNS & B&BS
1. Harrington House B&B, Sarasota
2. Collier Inn & Cottages, Useppa Island
3. Gasparilla Inn, Boca Grande
4. The Cypress, Sarasota
5. Island Inn, Sanibel Island

COTTAGE BY THE SEA
1. Rolling Waves Cottages, Longboat Key
2. Cabbage Key Inn, Cabbage Key
3. Jensen's Twin Palm Cottages & Marina, Captiva Island
4. Gulf Breeze Cottages and Motel, Sanibel Island
5. Collier Inn & Cottages, Useppa Island

SPLURGE ACCOMMODATIONS
1. The Ritz-Carlton Naples
2. Sanibel Harbour Resort & Spa, Fort Myers
3. Naples Grande Resort & Club
4. Marco Beach Ocean Resort, Marco Island
5. Hyatt Regency Coconut Point Resort & Spa, Bonita Springs

MARTINI MECCAS
1. Blu Sushi, Fort Myers
2. Dolce Vita, Sanibel Island
3. Monkey Room, Colony Beach and Tennis Resort, Longboat Key
4. Cà d'Zan Lounge, the Ritz-Carlton Sarasota
5. Blue Water Bistro, Estero

TABLES WITH A WATER VIEW
1. Sale e Pepe, Marco Island
2. Old Salty Dog, Lido Key
3. Mar Vista Dockside Restaurant & Pub, Longboat Key
4. The Crow's Nest, Venice
5. The Dock at Crayton Cove, Naples

SEAFOOD NOSHING
1. PJ's Seagrille, Boca Grande
2. Captain Brian's Seafood Market Restaurant, Sarasota
3. Star Fish Company, Cortez
4. Captain Eddie's Seafood Restaurant, Nokomis
5. Casey Key Fish House, Casey Key

ROMANTIC RESTAURANTS

1. Beach Bistro, Holmes Beach
2. Sale e Pepe, Marco Island
3. The Veranda, Fort Myers
4. Café L'Europe, Sarasota
5. Portofino Waterfront Dining, Port Charlotte

CREATIVE CUISINE

1. The Perfect Caper, Punta Gorda
2. Derek's Culinary Casual, Sarasota
3. Chops City Grill, Bonita Springs
4. Michael's on East, Sarasota
5. Handsome Harry's Third Street Bistro, Naples

ETHNIC EATS

1. Bha! Bha!, Naples
2. Blu Sushi, Fort Myers
3. Selva Grill, Sarasota
4. Alvarez Mexican Food, Palmetto
5. Siam Hut, Cape Coral

OLD FLORIDA FUNK

1. Cabbage Key Inn, Cabbage Key
2. Dixie Moon Café, Bonita Springs
3. New Pass Grill & Bait Shop, Lido Key
4. Old Marco Lodge Crab House, Goodland
5. Snook Haven, Venice

BREAKFAST

1. The Broken Egg, Siesta Key
2. Skillets Café, Naples
3. Amy's Over Easy Café, Sanibel Island
4. Manna From Heaven, Naples
5. Gulf Drive Café, Bradenton Beach

DELI/FOOD MARKETS

1. Sarasota Olive Oil Company
2. Morton's Market, Sarasota
3. Evoo Market, Naples
4. Sandy Butler Gourmet Market, Fort Myers Beach
5. Mario's Italian Meat Market & Deli, Fort Myers

ARCHITECTURAL GEMS

1. Cà d'Zan, Ringling Estates, Sarasota
2. Gamble Plantation Mansion, Bradenton
3. Sarasota Opera House
4. Gasparilla Inn, Boca Grande
5. Van Wezel Performing Arts Hall, Sarasota

HISTORY ALIVE
1. Historic Spanish Point, Osprey
2. Edison & Ford Winter Estates, Fort Myers
3. De Soto National Memorial, Bradenton
4. Koreshan State Historic Site, Estero
5. Collier County Museum, Naples

KID COOL
1. G.WIZ, Sarasota
2. Imaginarium, Fort Myers
3. Sun-n-Fun Lagoon, Naples
4. Greenwell's Bat-A-Ball and Family Fun Park, Cape Coral
5. Sun Splash Family Waterpark, Cape Coral

QUIRKY MUSEUMS
1. Gasparilla Island Maritime Museum, Boca Grande
2. Ringling Circus Museum & Tibbals Learning Center, Sarasota
3. Sarasota Classic Car Museum, Sarasota
4. Anna Maria Island Historical Museum
5. Bailey-Matthews Shell Museum, Sanibel Island

ON STAGE
1. Van Wezel Performing Arts Hall, Sarasota
2. Asolo Center for the Performing Arts, Sarasota
3. Philharmonic Center for the Arts, Naples
4. Barbara B. Mann Performing Arts Hall, Fort Myers
5. Circus Sarasota

NIGHT PROWLING
1. Beach Club, Siesta Key
2. The Gator Club, Sarasota
3. Crow's Nest Lounge, 'Tween Waters Inn, Captiva Island
4. Bimini's Beach Club, Marco Island
5. McCabe's Irish Pub, Naples

BOATING ADVENTURES
1. Florida Sailing & Cruising School, North Fort Myers
2. Offshore Sailing School, Captiva Island
3. Grande Tours, Placida
4. Captiva Cruises, Captiva Island
5. King Fisher Cruise Lines, Punta Gorda

NATURE PRESERVED
1. Everglades National Park
2. J. N. "Ding" Darling National Wildlife Refuge, Sanibel Island
3. Rookery Bay National Estuarine Research Reserve, Naples
4. Corkscrew Swamp Sanctuary, Naples
5. Collier-Seminole State Park, Naples

ECO-ATTRACTIONS
1. Mote Marine Aquarium, Sarasota
2. Babcock Wilderness Adventures, Punta Gorda
3. Rookery Bay Environmental Learning Center, Naples
4. Manatee Park, Fort Myers
5. Conservancy Nature Center, Naples

BIKEWAYS
1. W. J. Janes Memorial Scenic Drive, Fakahatchee Strand Preserve State Park, Naples
2. Sanibel Island
3. Longboat Key
4. Cape Haze Pioneer Trail, Cape Haze
5. Historical Manatee Riverwalk, Bradenton

PADDLE HAPPY
1. Wilderness Waterway, Everglades National Park
2. Great Calusa Blueway, Greater Fort Myers
3. Paradise Coast Blueway, Greater Naples
4. Tarpon Bay/J. N. "Ding" Darling National Wildlife Refuge, Sanibel Island
5. Matlacha Aquatic Preserve, Pine Island

TAKE A HIKE
1. Fakahatchee Strand Preserve State Park, Naples
2. Big Cypress National Preserve, Everglades City
3. Collier-Seminole State Park, Naples
4. Oscar Scherer State Park, Osprey
5. J. N. "Ding" Darling National Wildlife Refuge, Sanibel Island

SHELL-SHOCKED BEACHES
1. Bowman's Beach, Sanibel Island
2. Cayo Costa State Park/Johnson Shoals
3. Bonita Beach
4. Key Island, Naples
5. Venice Beach

SECLUDED BEACHES
1. Cayo Costa State Park, Boca Grande
2. Key Island, Naples
3. Stump Pass Beach State Park, Englewood Beach
4. Don Pedro Island State Park, Boca Grande
5. Palmer Point Beach, Siesta Key

PLAYFUL BEACHES
1. Siesta Key County Beach, Siesta Key
2. Lynn Hall Memorial Park, Fort Myers Beach
3. Manatee County Park, Holmes Beach
4. Coquina Beach, Bradenton Beach
5. Lowdermilk Park, Naples

FISHY PLACES
1. Boca Grande Pass, Boca Grande
2. Nokomis Beach's North Jetty, Casey Key
3. Venice Fishing Pier,
4. Naples Fishing Pier
5. Fort Myers Beach Pier

SHOPPING ARENAS
1. St. Armands Circle, Sarasota
2. Fifth Avenue South, Naples
3. Downtown Sarasota
4. The Village at Venetian Bay, Naples
5. Olde Englewood Village

ART APPRECIATION
1. The John and Mable Ringling Museum of Art, Sarasota
2. Naples Museum of Art
3. Towles Court Artist Colony, Sarasota
4. Village of the Arts, Bradenton
5. The von Liebig Art Center, Naples

Naples Museum of Art upholds the town's reputation for fine culture.

BLING!

1. Port Royal Jewelers, Naples
2. Joan Michlin Galleries, Sarasota
3. Al Morgan, Punta Gorda
4. Congress Jewelers, Sanibel Island
5. Wm. Phelps, Custom Jeweler, Naples

BOOKWORM HOLES

1. Main Bookshop, Sarasota
2. Sarasota News & Books
3. MacIntosh Books & Papers, Sanibel Island
4. Ruhama's Books in the Sand, Boca Grande
5. Charlie's Café, Books, and Hops, Holmes Beach

FESTIVALS

1. Edison Festival of Light, February, Fort Myers
2. Ringling Medieval Fair, February, Sarasota
3. Everglades Seafood Festival, February, Everglades City
4. MangoMania Tropical Fruit Fair, July, Pine Island/Cape Coral
5. Sharks' Tooth & Seafood Festival, April, Venice

HOMEY HOMETOWNS

1. Goodland
2. Punta Gorda
3. Englewood
4. Everglades City
5. Matlacha

General Index

T

Lodging by Price Code

Inexpensive	Up to $75
Moderate	$75 to $150
Expensive	$150 to $200
Very Expensive	$200 and up

Charlotte Harbor Coast

Inexpensive to Moderate
Banana Bay on Charlotte Harbor, 137–38

Inexpensive to Expensive
Weston's Resort, 135

Moderate
Harbor Pointe Resort, 138

Moderate to Expensive
Fishermen's Village Villas, 138
The Innlet, 135

Expensive to Very Expensive
Palm Island Resort, 135

Very Expensive
Gasparilla Inn, 133
Island House Inn, 134
Manasota Beach Club, 135

Naples and the South Coast

Inexpensive to Moderate
Rod & Gun Club, 257

Inexpensive to Expensive
The Ivey House, 257

Moderate to Expensive
The Boat House, 258
Cove Inn, 259
Lemon Tree Inn, 260
Marco Island Lakeside Inn, 258

Moderate to Very Expensive
Hyatt Regency Coconut Point Resort & Spa, 256
Trianon Bonita Bay, 257
Vanderbilt Beach Resort, 263

Expensive to Very Expensive
Bellasera Hotel, 259–63
The Edgewater Beach Hotel, 260
Naples Beach Hotel & Golf Club, 260
Park Shore Resort, 261

Very Expensive
LaPlaya Beach & Golf Resort, 263
Marco Beach Ocean Resort, 258
Marco Island Marriott Resort, Golf Club & Spa, 259
Naples Grande Resort & Club, 261
The Ritz-Carlton Golf Resort, 262
The Ritz-Carlton Naples, 262

Sarasota Bay Coast

Moderate to Expensive
Banyan House, 58
A Beach Retreat, 55
Cedar Cove Resort & Cottages, 52
Historic Gulf Beach Resort Motel, 53
Holiday Inn Riverfront, 51
Rod & Reel Motel, 51

Moderate to Very Expensive
Bridgewalk, 51
Inn at the Beach, 59
Lido Beach Resort, 53
Rolling Waves Cottages, 55
Seaside Inn & Resort, 52
Siesta Key Bungalows, 57

Expensive to Very Expensive
The Cypress, 55
Harrington House B&B, 52
The Resort at Longboat Key Club, 54
The Ritz-Carlton Sarasota, 56

Very Expensive
Colony Beach and Tennis Resort, 53
Hotel Indigo, 56
Turtle Beach Resort, 57

Sanibel Island and the Fort Myers Coast

Inexpensive to Moderate
Casa Loma Motel, 173

Moderate
Ambassador Riverfront Hotel, 174

Moderate to Expensive
Bridge Water Inn, 177
Cabbage Key Inn, 172
Island Inn, 178
Silver Sands Villas, 177
Moderate to Very Expensive
Collier Inn & Cottages, 180
Gulf Breeze Cottages and Motel, 177

Jensen's Twin Palm Cottages & Marina, 173
The Outrigger Beach Resort, 176
Pink Shell Beach Resort & Spa, 176
'Tween Waters Inn, 174

Expensive to Very Expensive
Crowne Plaza Fort Myers, 175
Sanibel Harbour Resort & Spa, 175
Sanibel's Seaside Inn, 179
Sundial Beach Resort, 179

Very Expensive
South Seas Island Resort, 173
West Wind Inn, 179

Dining by Price Code

Inexpensive   Up to $15
Moderate $15 to $25
Expensive $25 to $35
Very Expensive $35 or more

Charlotte Harbor Coast

Inexpensive
The Celtic Ray Public House, 142

Inexpensive to Moderate
Placida, 141

Inexpensive to Expensive
Gulfview Grill, 140

Moderate
Zydeco Grille, 140

Moderate to Expensive
Amimoto Japanese Restaurant, 142
PJ's Sea Grille, 139
Portofino Waterfront Dining, 141

Expensive to Very Expensive
The Perfect Caper, 143

Very Expensive
Boca Bistro, 139

Naples and the South Coast

Inexpensive
Dixie Moon Café, 266
Doc's Beach House, 265

Inexpensive to Moderate
Bricktops, 271
Cilantro Tamales, 272
Old Marco Lodge Crab House, 268

Inexpensive to Expensive
Big Hickory Seafood Grille, 264

Moderate
The Dock at Crayton Cove, 272
Wyld's Café, 267

Moderate to Expensive
Bha! Bha!, 269

Bistro 821, 270
Escargot 41, 270
Naples Tomato, 273
Rod & Gun Club, 267
Tropical Reef Seafood Restaurant, 275

Moderate to Very Expensive
Baleen, 275
Handsome Harry's Third Street Bistro, 273
Ridgeway Bar & Grill, 274

Expensive
Tarpon Bay Restaurant, 266

Expensive to Very Expensive
Chops City Grill, 265
Sale e Pepe, 269

Sarasota Bay Coast

Inexpensive
Alvarez Mexican Food, 61
Island Crêperie, 62
New Pass Grill & Bait Shop, 64
Old Salty Dog, 64
The Soda Fountain, 74
Yoder's, 72

Inexpensive to Moderate
Captain Brian's Seafood Market Restaurant, 68
Captain Eddies Seafood Restaurant, 66
Casey Key Fish House, 63
Lynches Pub & Grub, 67
Mar-Vista Dockside Restaurant & Pub, 65
Rotten Ralph's, 60
Snook Haven, 73
Snook River Grill, 61
Sun House Restaurant & Bar, 62

Inexpensive to Expensive
The Crow's Nest, 73
Phillippi Creek Village Oyster Bar, 70

Dining by Cuisine

Sanibel Island and the Fort Myers Coast